Limited Classical Reprint Library

THE MINOR PROPHETS

by

Frederick A. Tatford

Volume III

Foreword by
Dr. Cyril J. Barber

Klock & Klock Christian Publishers, Inc.
2527 Girard Avenue North
Minneapolis, Minnesota 55411

PROPHET OF
ROYAL BLOOD

An exposition of the Prophecy of Zephaniah

By

FREDK. A. TATFORD

Originally published by
Prophetic Witness Publishing House
Sussex, 1973

ISBN: 0-86524-135-X

Printed by Klock & Klock in the U.S.A.
1982 Reprint

CONTENTS

FOR the student of Biblical prophecy, one of the most important features of eschatology is the Day of the Lord —a subject referred to in the Old and New Testaments nearly a hundred times. The descriptions given of that period portray it as one of clouds and thick darkness; of cosmic and celestial disturbances, of unparalleled tribulation for man, and of the outpouring of the unmitigated judgments of God.

The prophet Zephaniah, however, takes a somewhat different viewpoint from that of his predecessors. "To the earlier prophets," writes Sir George Adam Smith (*The Book of the Twelve Prophets,* vol. II, pp. 49-50), "the Day of the Lord, the crisis of the world, is a definite point in history: full of terrible, divine events, yet 'natural' ones—battle, siege, famine, massacre and captivity. After it, history is still to flow on, common days come back and Israel pursue their way as a nation. But to Zephaniah, the Day of the Lord begins to assume what we call the 'supernatural'. The grim colours are still woven of war and siege, but mixed with vague and solemn terrors from another sphere, by which history appears to be swallowed up, and it is only with an effort that the prophet thinks of a rally of Israel beyond. In short, with Zephaniah the Day of the Lord tends to become the Last Day. His book is the first tinging of prophecy with apocalypse. . . . Nevertheless, though the first of the apocalyptic writers, Zephaniah does not allow himself the licence of apocalypse. As he refuses to imagine great glory for the righteous, so he does not dwell on the terrors of the wicked. He is sober and restrained, a matter-of-fact man, yet with power of imagination, who, amidst the vague horrors he summons, delights in giving a sharp, realistic impression. 'The Day of the Lord,' he says, 'what is it?'. 'A strong man—there!—crying bitterly' (Zeph. 1: 14 b)".

He lived in a day of reformation, but the elements seemed to be loose, and the prophet was more concerned with the impending visitation of Divine wrath upon a guilty people than with the effects of the royal reforms.

Yet he closed his prophecy with the remarkable picture of the Eternal resting silent in His love.

All the Minor Prophets seem to have their message for the present day, but even a casual reading of Zephaniah will probably lead to the conclusion that his book is of more than average pertinence to our own day.

FREDK. A. TATFORD.

CHAPTER 1

The Fruitless Reformation

OF all the Old Testament prophetical books, that of
Zephaniah is probably the widest in outlook and the
most comprehensive in content. In his commentary of 1528,
Bucer, for example, said, "If anyone wishes all the secret
oracles of the prophets to be given in a brief compendium,
let him read through this brief Zephaniah", and Keil declared
(*The Twelve Minor Prophets,* vol. II, pp. 123, 124) that Zephaniah reproduced "in a compendious form the fundamental
thoughts of judgment and salvation which are common to all
the prophets." Whilst his matter was original, the prophet
did not ignore the writings of his predecessors, but freely
borrowed words and expressions from Isaiah, Joel and Habakkuk, at the same time using many similar terms in relation
to some subjects as those used by his contemporary, Jeremiah.

The primary subject of his book was the universal judgment of the day of Jehovah (in fact he quoted the term more
frequently than any other Old Testament writer), although
he apparently saw the Divine judgment, not only as a future
eschatological event, but also as an immediate visitation upon
a sinful people.

He lived in an atmosphere of unbelief: paganism and
idolatry were prevalent, and the prophet's scathing denuncia-
tions and his threats of punishment were pertinent and justified
by the conditions. A popular syncretism approved the
association of the worship of Jehovah with that of false

deities, and a tolerant eclecticism produced a grave unconcern for justice and a strong inclination to materialism. Resolute condemnation of the people's attitude and an urgent call to repentance were demanded by the circumstances of the day.

The book is not quoted or alluded to in the New Testament, although its message and contents virtually find their full confirmation in the Apocalypse.

AUTHOR

The prophet described himself as Zephaniah—a name used of others in 1 Chron, 6: 36; Jer. 21: 1; 29: 25, 29; Zech. 6: 10, 14, and meaning "he whom Jehovah hides". It has been claimed by some writers that he was a member of the tribe of Simeon and came from the mountainous area of Sarabatha, but there is no evidence to substantiate this. D. L. Williams identifies him with a priest of the same name, who was slain by the King of Babylon at Riblab (2 Kings 25: 18-21; Jer. 21: 1; 29: 25, 29; 37: 3; 52: 24-27), but this theory is equally without factual support, although this priest was obviously contemporaneous with the prophet.

Zephaniah specifically claimed to be a descendant of Hezekiah. The only pre-exilic individual named Hezekiah of whom there is any record is King Hezekiah (2 Kings 20), and most commentators have accepted the conclusion of Aben Ezra that this king was the prophet's ancestor and that he was consequently of royal blood. Although there were only two generations (Manasseh and Amon) between Hezekiah and Josiah (during whose reign Zephaniah prophesied), Manasseh reigned for 55 years (2 Kings 21: 1) and there was, therefore, time for the four generations mentioned in Zeph. 1: 1.

On the basis of Zeph. 1: 4, 10, 11, it is usually considered that Zephaniah was resident at Jerusalem (as might perhaps be expected of a member—however remote—of the royal family), but there is no definite confirmation of this.

No serious question has been raised regarding the canonicity of the book, although some critics have argued that more than one hand took a part in its compilation.

It is explicitly stated in the opening verse of the book that Zephaniah prophesied during the reign of Josiah, i.e. during the period 641 to 609 B.C., and he was consequently—as already indicated—a contemporary of Jeremiah (see Jer. 1: 2). There is, however, no conclusive indication of the precise dates of the prophet's ministry.

Josiah had been preceded by two evil kings, Manasseh and Amon, whose idolatry, witchcraft and spiritism undid most of the good done earlier by Hezekiah (2 Chron. 32,33). The worship of the Baalim, the host of heaven (the sun, moon and stars) and Molech had corrupted the land. In the eighth year of his reign, however, the heart of young king Josiah turned to Jehovah and he began to remove the altars of the false gods and the images of those deities, and to restore the worship of Jehovah (2 Chron. 34: 3-7). Ten years later a copy of the book of Deuteronomy was found in the temple and, at the king's instigation, a reformation commenced in Judah. Kleinert (*Zephaniah*, p. 4) points out that the principal royal reforms were all crowded into Josiah's eighteenth year, viz. "the appointment of the temple repairs (2 Chron. 34: 8 ff) and the events which followed the discovery of the law on this occasion (2 Chron. 34: 15 ff; c.f. 2 Kings 22: 8 ff); the consultation of the prophetess Huldah (2 Chron. 34: 20 ff), the convocation of the people (29 ff), and the feast of the passover (2 Chron. 35 : 1 ff)".

It is argued by some expositors that Zephaniah's messages must have been uttered prior to the king's reformation, because he did not allude to these events and because he specifically referred to the false cults which were current in the days of Manasseh and Amon.

Per contra, there is the reference in Zeph. 1: 4 to "the remnant of Baal", implying that, however large the remnant, the majority of Baal-worshippers had been destroyed and that the worship of Baal had very largely been checked. Moreover, the prophet frequently quoted the book of Deuteronomy, inferring thereby that the book had, by this

13

time, been discovered in the temple and that its contents were known to the people through the public reading mentioned in 2 Kings 23: 1 ff. Furthermore, the prophet's description of current conditions is parallel to the description given by Jeremiah, who began to prophesy in the thirteenth year of Josiah, so that Zephaniah presumably prophesied at approximately the same time.

It is evident from Zeph 2: 13 that the fall of Assyria and the destruction of Nineveh, which occurred in 612 B.C., had not yet taken peace. Zephaniah's prophecy must, therefore, have antedated them. The most common view is that his messages were uttered after the period of reformation (630-624 B.C.), but before 612 B.C.

It has been suggested that the prophecy was originally inspired by predatory attacks made upon Judah by the Moabites and Ammonites in 597 B.C. (Jer. 49: 1-6; Ezek. 25: 1-11), but these apparently occurred some time after Zephaniah. Eakin (*Boardman Bible Commentary*, vol. 7, p. 270) maintains that the prophecy sprang from an attack by the Scythians on Palestine. Whilst it is probable that an invasion of some kind did precipitate the outburst of Zephaniah, he gave no information regarding it which would enable us to identify the invader or to determine the date of the prophecy thereby.

Taking all the relevant factors into consideration, it seems reasonably certain that the prophecy should be dated within the period 624 to 609 B.C.

BACKGROUND

The reformation carried out by Josiah and his advisers was neither complete nor fully successful when the prophet commenced his ministry. Despite the attempts to put a stop to the worship of Baal, a remnant of Baal-worshippers (probably of appreciable numbers) was still firmly entrenched in the land. The astral deities, whose shrines had been removed from the temple of Jehovah, were still openly worshipped: in the evenings men blatantly bowed down to them and to

14

the queen of heaven on their flat housetops. Children were still being sacrificed to the god Molech. Priests of the false gods served the idols unashamedly and without concealment. Idolatry continued to be woven into the warp and woof of life: indeed, commerce was partly dependent upon the acknowledgment of the gods of the nations. The disregard for the claims of Jehovah may not have been as widespread as in the days of Manasseh, but it was still characteristic of the upper classes. Even if the king was not personally involved, his closest relations were.

The nobility had adopted foreign fashions as well as foreign gods. Materialism had displaced spirituality and, in their pursuit of riches, the wealthy indulged in cruelty and oppression. Justice was prevented and corruption prevailed. The sceptics cynically concluded that God was so little interested in this conduct that He would do neither good nor evil. The tide continued to flow against the king's efforts to effect a spiritual reformation in the nation.

At the same time, the storm clouds were once more gathering in the north, "black and pregnant with destruction." The threat this time was not from Assyria, but from another frightening power. "From the hidden world beyond" Assyria, writes Smith (*ibid.* p. 15), "from the regions over Caucasus, vast nameless hordes of men arose and, sweeping past her unchecked, poured upon Palestine. This was the great Scythian invasion recorded by Herodotus. . . . Living in the saddle, and with no infantry nor chariot to delay them, these centaurs swept on with a speed of invasion hitherto un-known. In 630 they had crossed the Caucasus, by 626 they were on the borders of Egypt. Psamtik I succeeded in pur-chasing their retreat, and they swept back again as swiftly as they came. . . . But they shook the whole of Palestine into consternation. Though Judah among her hills escaped them, as she escaped the earlier campaigns of Assyria, they showed her the penal resources of her offended God. Once again the dark, sacred north was seen to be full of the possibilities of gloom". There are not wanting those, however, who see in

15

the threatened judgment, not the Scythian invasion, but the Babylonian, and there is something to be said for this view.

These were the circumstances in which Zephaniah lifted up his voice to his people.

ANALYSIS

The book may be analysed as shown below.
1. The superscription (1 : 1).
2. Judgment upon nature (1 : 2, 3).
3. Judgment upon Judah (1 : 4 — 2 : 3).
   (a) cause and extent (1 : 4-13).
   (b) imminence (1 : 14-18).
   (c) call to repentance (2 : 1-3).
4. Judgment of the Gentiles (2 : 4-15).
   (a) Philistia (2 : 4-7).
   (b) Moab and Ammon (2 : 8-11).
   (c) Ethiopia (2 : 12).
   (d) Assyria (2 : 13-15).
5. Further warning to Judah (3 : 1-7).
6. Divine grace in restoration and salvation (3 : 8-20).
   (a) Jehovah's wrath (3 : 8).
   (b) Restoration (3 : 9-13).
   (c) Ultimate future (3 : 14-20).

APOCRYPHAL ADDITIONS

Clement of Alexandria (*Strom.* v. 11, § 77) quotes an apocryphal prophecy attributed to Zephaniah. It runs: "And the spirit took me and carried me up into the fifth heaven, and I saw angels called lords, and their diadem placed upon them by the Holy Spirit, and the throne of each of them was seven times brighter than the light of the rising sun, dwelling in temples of salvation, and hymning the unspeakable God Most High." There are also other fragments, for which his authorship has been claimed, which have been preserved in a Coptic version.

16

CHAPTER 2

The Warning to Judah

DESPITE the superficial revival under Josiah, the moral and spiritual condition of the nation of Judah rendered judgment inevitable. Opinion differs regarding the instrument used by God to inflict the judgment, but C. I. Scofield and others consider that the Babylonian invasion was in view and that the Babylonian captivity was the impending punishment to which Zephaniah referred. His message may have received greater emphasis because of the character and status of the messenger.

THE SUPERSCRIPTION

The word of Jehovah, which came to Zephaniah, the son of Cushi, the son of Gedaliah, the son of Amariah, the son of Hezekiah, in the days of Josiah, the son of Amon, king of Judah (Zeph. 1: 1).

The introductory formula to the book is identical with that found in other prophetical books (e.g. Hos. 1: 1; Joel 1: 1; Mic. 1: 1) and is a claim that the words which follow are of Divine authority and inspiration.

Zephaniah is unique in tracing his genealogy to the fourth generation. Pusey (*The Minor Prophets*, vol 2, p. 235) provides an i n t e r p r e t a t i o n of the names mentioned: "Zephaniah, 'whom the Lord hid'; Gedaliah, 'whom the Lord made great'; Amariah, 'whom the Lord promised'; Hezekiah, 'whom the Lord strengthened'." It is certainly interesting to note that there is a reference to Jehovah in each of the names. If the Hezekiah referred to was the king of that name, Zephaniah was evidently his great-grandson.

The messages of the book were uttered, according to this opening verse, in the days of Josiah, king of Judah. **Wm. Kelly** (*Lectures Introductory to the Study of the Minor Prophets*, p. 348) says, "there was but a short space indeed that separated Josiah's bright burst of pious effort for God's glory from the awful evils which succeeded and brought an insupportable judgment from God on the guilty people. Zephaniah was one of those who spoke in Jehovah's name during those promising times." But the period was probably not quite so bright as Kelly implies: the first flush of enthusiastic repentance seems to have vanished.

Having announced himself, his authority and his status, the prophet proceeded immediately to a declaration of the Divine message to the guilty nation.

UNIVERSAL JUDGMENT
I will sweep away everything from the face of the earth, says Jehovah. I will sweep away man and beast; I will sweep away the fowls of the heaven and the fish of the sea and the ruins with the wicked. I will cut off mankind from the face of the earth, says Jehovah (*Zeph.* 1: 2, 3).

When the message came, it must have shattered the complacency and self-sufficiency of Josiah's subjects, for Jehovah announced a universal judgment. Every living thing was to be affected. Although, as one writer remarks, "the cosmological upheaval usually associated with apocalyptic is not present," the intention was evident. The ultimate day of Jehovah will be cataclysmic, but what was now predicted was such a complete destruction as to be an apt symbol of what still lies in the future.

God declared that the earth was to be swept clean of every living thing; man and beast would be destroyed ("I will cut off man", *adam*, "from the fact of the earth", *adamah*—the land man had defiled). The heavens would be denuded of bird life and the sea of aquatic life. The destruction would

18

be more effective and more extensive than even the Noahic deluge. The opportunity to repent, which had been afforded by the royal reformation, had been despised: the opportunity had only increased the responsibility of the people, and punishment for the hardened impenitent and sceptic was inevitable.

The term "stumbling blocks", used in the A.V., is better rendered "ruins" (c.f. Isa. 3: 6). The reference is possibly to "the objects and rites of their idolatrous worship" (c.f. Ezek. 14: 3, 4, 7). The Septuagint renders the last two clauses of verse 3, "As for the wicked, they shall be without strength; and I will remove transgressions from the face of the land". Man had rebelled against the rule of God and against his ordinances; in consequence, every moral, social and political institution ultimately fell into ruins. The ruins would be swept away with the sinners who were virtually the cause of the desolation.

There is no doubt that what is envisioned is the final collapse at the end of time, as described, for example, in Rev. 15 et seq. The immediate judgment was intended as a warning of what was yet to come—the dread day of Jehovah, which still lies in the future. If the impending troubles were terrifying, they were but a pale reflection of that ultimate judgment day. The adumbration was, however, certainly one to cause fear and to awaken men to the need to turn to God in repentance.

Judgment always commences with the house of God, and the prophet turned from the general picture to portray the hand of discipline falling upon the degenerate theocracy of Judah.

THE CHASTISEMENT OF JUDAH

I will also stretch out my hand against Judah and against all the inhabitants of Jerusalem. And I will cut off from this place the remnant of Baal, and the name of the Chemarims with the priests, and those who, on the roofs, bow down to the host of the heavens, and those who bow down and swear by Jehovah and yet swear by Malcham; and those who have turned back from Jehovah, and those who have not sought Jehovah, nor enquired of him (Zeph. 1 : 4-6).

The storm clouds of Divine wrath were gathering and the whole earth was threatened, but the lightning struck first on the nation of Judah and the capital city of Jerusalem. If the hostility of the Gentile nations demanded judicial action in retribution, how much more richly deserved was the punishment of God's own people. Blessed above all other nations, their base ingratitude to and despite of the One who had covenanted with them were all the more reprehensible. They boasted arrogantly of their relationship with Jehovah and yet turned their backs upon Him, but now He would stretch out His hand against them. He had seen their disloyalty to Him and their association of other deities with His worship, and the day of reckoning had now come.

His stretching out of His hand against them symbolised His preparation for punitive action. He saw the towers of the city of Jerusalem, He discerned the idolatrous practices of the citizens, and announced His intention of dealing with them all. Each class of offender was to feel the weight of His hand.

"I will cut off from this place the remnant of Baal." It seems almost incredible that in the metropolis itself in spite of all the efforts of the king to put an end to idolatry and to restore the true worship of God there were still some who paid their homage to Baal. Originally a personification of the sun, Baal was also a fertility god. Literally the word means "lord" or owner, and he was regarded as supreme in the Canaanite pantheon. The name was often attached to deities of varying characteristics, and even sometimes to Jehovah Himself (e.g. in 1 Chron. 12: 5 the name Bealiah means "Jehovah is Baal", i.e. lord). Tablets discovered at Ugarit in northern Syria show that Baal was regarded, not only as the god of fertility, but as the lord of clouds, rain and storm. He was frequently confused with other gods, and the Old Testament often refers to a Baal of a certain district as well as to the plural Baalim (i.e. lords or gods of various locales).

20

Baal's consort was his own sister Anat, a warrior-goddess, who was not infrequently confused with Astarte (or the plural Ashtaroth). Their cult involved the utmost licentiousness, usually carried out on the summits of hills and mountains or in the woods ("under every green tree").

Baalism was apparently first introduced into Israel by Jezebel, the wife of Ahab (1 Kings 16: 31, 32) although it was in evidence in much earlier days (Jud. 2: 13). It was anathematised by true followers of Jehovah, who usually replaced the name of Baal by *Bosheth* (shame). The worship of Baal certainly continued up to the time of the exile and it was obviously in existence in Judah in Josiah's day. The king's reformation had not completely ousted this false religion, with all its attendant dangers to morality, and Jehovah now declared that he would cut off the remaining worshippers of Baal.

The name of the Chemarim and the priests was also to be wiped out. The Chemarim were idolatrous priests, who officiated in the heathen cults, offering sacrifices on the high places or mountain-tops. Feinberg says that the Hebrew root means "black" and that they were so termed because of the black garments they wore, or that it also has the significance of "zealous", referring to their fanatical enthusiasm in their idolatrous services. The implication of the Divine judgment upon these deceivers was that their posterity would be blotted out.

Judgment was also to fall upon the men and women who were to be seen at the point of sunset on their flat roofs, paying homage to "the host of heaven". From early days of human history, the sun, moon and stars have been worshipped. In Egyptian, Sumerian and Akkadian religion, the sun has been regarded as a deity, and there were certainly sun worshippers in Babylonia and Assyria. Sabaism (the worship of the stars) was also practised widely among the Semitic peoples. Manasseh not only introduced astral worship into Jerusalem, but set up altars to the astral deities in the temple of Jehovah, which Josiah subsequently destroyed (2 Kings

21

21: 3-5; 23: 4, 5). Jeremiah implies that this worship was almost universal in Jerusalem (Jer. 19: 13).

The worship of Baal and of the host of heaven was one of the sins leading to the collapse of the northern kingdom of Israel (2 Kings 17: 16). Yet the people of Judah were foolishly following the same course, despite the action taken by the king. The time had come for judgment to fall upon them.

There were others who bowed down to Jehovah and simultaneously to Malcham. The latter was a reference to Milcom or Molech (or Moloch). The word has sometimes been interpreted as "their king", but it is reasonably clear that it was the god Molech wtho was intended. There are repeated references to Molech or Milcom in the Old Testament, from Lev. 18: 21 onwards, and his worship was common in Israel. He was the principal god of the Ammonites, and his service demanded human sacrifice (e.g. 2 Kings 16: 3). This was an abomination to God, but children of His people were often sacrificed to Molech by their parents.

The condemnation of Zephaniah is that this evil system was being combined with the worship of Jehovah—a syncretism even more objectionable than some of the other practices condemned. Any attempt to associate others with God is intolerable to Him: He claims sole and absolute loyalty.

Finally there were two other classes: first, those who had known the truth but had apostasised from God. Whether or not they followed false religions is not stated but it is not really relevant. They had turned their backs upon Jehovah after tasting His grace and favour. The second class were those who did not seek Jehovah or enquire of Him. They were not openly opposed to Him, nor did they adopt the policy of the syncretist: they had not turned to idolatry, but they were completely indifferent to Jehovah. They had dispensed with Him and lived their lives independently of Him. Upon those also the hand of judgment was to fall .

Zephaniah lived and prophesied in a day over 25 centuries ago, but the picture he painted still retains its relevance today. The world of the twentieth century seeks other lords and is prepared to be tolerant of all beliefs and principles. Sincerity is all that matters. It is often said that a study of comparative religion indicates the common origin of all religion and that every attempt should, therefore, be made to draw the various faiths together again.

If we do not worship the pagan deities of the nations, we bow at the feet of power or mammon. Those who have deliberately turned their backs upon the true to follow their own inclinations are not restricted to the occupants of the pew, but often tragically include deniers of the faith in the pulpit. And who shall say that the majority do not completely ignore the claims of God and view religion with apathetic indifference? The prophet's picture is a mirror reflecting not only conditions of a past age but the attitudes of our own day.

The warning, however, is clear. The God, who has shown amazing grace and mercy and who has withheld the merited punishment for so long, will not always delay and the indications today are that judgment cannot much longer be postponed. The clarion note of warning should be sounded loud and clear.

CHAPTER 3

Terror Strikes

IT was patent that nothing had escaped the eye of Jehovah. The idolatrous practices of His people and their complete disregard of His claims upon their allegiance and loyalty had reached a stage where punishment was inevitable. His purpose had been announced but, before the blow fell, He called for a pause to give the nation the opportunity of realising what was about to happen.

JEHOVAH'S SACRIFICE

Be silent at the presence of Adonai Jehovah: for the day of Jehovah is at hand. For Jehovah has prepared a sacrifice: he has hallowed his guests. And it shall come to pass on the day of Jehovah's sacrifice that I will punish the chiefs and the king's sons and all who clothe themselves with foreign apparel. On that day also, I will punish everyone who leaps over the threshold and those who fill their masters' houses with violence and fraud (Zeph. 1: 7-9).

The announcement of the impending judgment had been made by the prophet. Now, in the guise of the herald who enjoins silence on the approach of his ruler, he commands the people to be silent before the coming of the Sovereign Lord, Adonai Jehovah. There is ample reason for quietness: the day of Jehovah was at hand. The awfulness of that day seems to have seized the prophet himself. He was aware of the description given by other prophets of that day. Now the dreaded moment approached.

25

Like many another Biblical prophecy there has been more than one fulfilment of the predicted day of trouble and the ultimate and complete fulfilment is still delayed. But the experiences confronting Judah were so dire that they were aptly deemed a reflection of the final day of judgment. Under Divine inspiration, Zephaniah was adopting the same pattern as his predecessors.

The day of Jehovah will be the culmination of all judgment and is consistently depicted as a period of unparalleled trouble, starting suddenly and unexpectedly, coming "as a thief in the night" (1 Thess. 5: 1, 2). The character of that period is indicated in Isaiah's words, where he enjoined the people to "Enter into the rock and hide in the dust, for fear of Jehovah and for the glory of his majesty . . . and they shall go into the holes of the rocks and into the caves of the earth, for fear of Jehovah and for the glory of his majesty, when he arises to shake terribly the earth" (Isa. 2: 10-19; Joel 1: 15; 2: 1, 2, 31; 3: 16; Amos 5: 18; Isa. 34: 1-8; 2 Pet 3: 10, etc.).

In 2 Thess. 2: 2-4 the apostle Paul stated that the day of the Lord will not come until the appearance of the man of sin. Our Lord's words in Mark 13: 14-19, coupled with Daniel's in Dan. 9: 27, revealed that that would occur halfway through the seven years referred to in the latter verse. It will apparently conclude with the dissolution of the earth and the heavens (2 Pet. 3: 10). During that long period Divine wrath will be poured out upon earth, but the dark clouds of trouble will be dispersed for a thousand years during the reign of Christ upon earth, only to regather at the end of the millennium and to break in a final outburst at the end of time.

If that awful period was near, a silence might well fall upon the people. Zephaniah declared that Divine preparations had been made for the outpouring of wrath upon the guilty. But he described judgment, not as a slaughter, but as a sacrifice. In the words of one writer, what was to happen assumed the character of a holy sacrificial act. The symbolism was, of course, taken from the Levitical offerings and the

26

term employed had its application primarily to the peace offering. The animal to be sacrificed as a peace offering was brought to the priest, and the offerer identified himself with the animal by laying his hands upon its head. If the animal was accepted, he was accepted in it; if it was rejected, he was rejected also. Part of the sacrifice was consumed upon the altar as the food of Jehovah, part became the portion of the officiating priest, and the remainder was eaten by the offerer and his family (Lev. 3: 1-17; 7: 11-21). The sacrificed animal had to be consumed within two days, any part left after that period being destroyed (Lev. 7: 15-18).

Jehovah used this type of sacrifice as a symbol of the destruction He was about to inflict upon the guilty (Isa. 34: 6; Jer. 46: 10; Ezek. 39: 17-21). He regarded Judah as no better than her Gentile neighbours, and she would accordingly be destroyed at the same time.

The worshipper under the Levitical economy invited guests to share the meal with him. So God declared that He had bidden, or hallowed, or consecrated guests to feast upon His sacrifice (c.f. Isa. 13: 3). Kleinert (ibid. p. 14) maintains that the guests will be the heathen nations whom Israel was about to destroy, but most commentators take the view that Israel (or Judah) and the nations are themselves the sacrifice and that the identity of the guests is deliberately left vague— that the feature is introduced merely to complete the picture.

Jehovah specifically stated that, on the day of His sacrifice, He would punish five classes of people in Judah. The first were the civil leaders, the "princes" or "chiefs", who were officers of the royal court and advisers of the king. They were the magistrates and dispensers of justice, but they had, in fact, become the principal oppressors of the poor (1 Kings 4: 2; 9: 23; 20: 14; Jer. 24: 1; 36: 12). The Divine sentence upon them was executed in due course (2 Kings 24: 12-14).

King Josiah was not himself named. His heart beat true to God and the Divine hand did not fall upon him (2 Kings 22: 19, 20). But "the king's sons" were to suffer, since they had evidently declined to walk in the ways of their pious father. Some difficulty arises over the interpretation of this class. In the 18th year of Josiah, his son, Jehoiakim was only 12, Jehoahaz was 10, and Zedekiah had not yet been born. At that early age they could scarcely have exhibited the impious character that merited destruction. The prophecy may have anticipated a later period when they also would be punished for their sins, or it may have referred to other members of the royal household who are not named. Whoever they were, it is made clear that Jehovah was perfectly well aware of their manner of life and of their sinfulness in His sight.

The third class to come under sentence were those who arrayed themselves in foreign apparel. Certain regulations had been laid down for the people's costume (Num. 15: 38; Deut. 22: 11, 12), but full details of God's requirements were never given. Some of the people, who had adopted the idols of the heathen, also adopted the dress of their neighbours. Assyrian fashions, in particular, were being aped. These people were making themselves like the world around them, whereas it had always been God's purpose that they should be separate from the nations of the earth.

"The strange apparel shows the estranged heart," writes Kleinert (*ibid.*, p. 15). "The infringement of the popular manners and the contempt of the natural costume evince the decay of the nation's spirit." It is possible that the change of dress was partly due to the desirability of getting on with neighbours, and that a spirit of compromise gradually developed. As clothes are to the body, so are habits to the real man, and the judgment of these people probably has a significance for this day as well as for Zephaniah's.

The fourth class singled out for particular mention were described as those who leap over the threshold.. Eakin (*ibid.*, p. 279) writes, "The threshold was judged in antiquity to be the abode of a demon (or demons), thus a place of particular danger. In Roman times this belief found expression in the protective carrying of a bride across the threshold". One

28

version renders the clause, "who ascends the pedestal", i.e. the pedestal upon which stood a pagan altar. This would merely be a further description of idolatry. The ward translated "threshold", however, is used also in 1 Sam. 5: 4, 5; Ezek. 9: 3; 10: 4; 46: 2; 47: 1; and in every instance (as well as in non-Biblical literature) has reference to the threshold of a temple or a sacred building; it was never used of the threshold of a private house or of any other building.

The significance must, therefore, be related to the incident described in 1 Sam. 5. The Philistines had captured the ark of God and had placed it in the temple of Dagon at Ashdod. The following morning the image of Dagon had fallen down before the ark. The next day they found the image across the threshold of the temple, decapitated and minus its hands. From that time, no one entering the temple stepped on the threshold (v. 5), and it became a cultic practice to leap over the threshold. In time, the reason for the practice was doubtless forgotten, but the practice continued. Jehovah condemned those who adopted this heathen rite in their religious observances. He had judged Dagon by destroying his image on the threshold of his temple. Those who followed the pagan mode of access by jumping over the threshold were virtually aligning themselves with paganism against the true God.

Some expositors link the fifth class with the fourth and conclude that the servants of the wealthy, in their zeal to despoil others of their goods, would leap over the threshold of their master's house, to rush out to the scene of robbery and violence. This is untenable for the reason already stated. Others have suggested that the servants were those of the temple and that their purpose was to enrich the house of their master, the false god, and, in leaving the temple, they would follow their normal custom of leaping over the threshold. But the word used for "master" is the common one, *adonim*, and not the word *baalim*, which would be used of the gods.

Those described were evidently dishonourable servants of unscrupulous masters, who used violence and cruelty to extort treasures from the poor and unprotected. By their oppression and fraud, they filled their masters' houses with ill-gotten gains. But their actions did not escape the eye of omniscience and Jehovah announced His intention of calling them to account.

The day of Jehovah would be a day of reckoning for all who had offended Him, and as the hour of that day burst upon the consciousness of the people, lamentations would arise from every quarter.

WIDESPREAD GRIEF

And it shall come to pass on that day, says Jehovah, that there will be the noise of crying from the fish gate, and a wailing from the second quarter, and a great crashing from the hills. Howl, inhabitants of Mortar, for all the traders are cut down; all who weigh out silver are destroyed (Zeph. 1: 10, 11).

The realisation of what was involved in the punitive justice of the day of Jehovah will produce universal consternation, according to the picture painted by Zephaniah. The victorious shouts of the invaders in their ruthless onslaught of plunder and rapine, will scarcely be heard because of the shrieking and howling of the besieged. The wailing and lamentation will resound through the streets of the city, echoing from the fish gate through the lower part of Jerusalem to re-echo in the hills as the crashing of falling houses and palaces reverberates through the valleys.

The fish gate was the nearest of the city gates to the road to Jaffa and the coast (Neh. 3: 3; 12: 39; 2 Chron. 33: 14), although one writer insists that it obtained its name from its proximity to the fish market where fish, caught in the lake of Tiberias or in the River Jordan, were brought for sale. Although some place this gate in the western wall and others in the north, Keil confidently asserts that it was in the eastern wall. Unfortunately, he provides no evidence to support his theory. It has also been identified with the present Damascus Gate, but the evidence for this is slight.

The "second quarter", or the lower city, was located to

the north and west of the temple area. It was here that the wealthy lived in their luxurious dwellings. It was here also that the prophetess Huldah lived (2 Kings 22: 14; 2 Chron. 34: 22).

When attacked, the people usually fled to the hills, but the sound of crashing was to echo from the hills. Destruction was to sweep through the city. Feinberg (*ibid.*, p. 48) says that verse 10 "indicates the progress of the enemy until they occupy the prominent positions in the city". This would certainly be appropriate if the thesis is accepted that the prophet is referring throughout to the impending Babylonian invasion, as a type of the ultimate day of Jehovah.

The wailing extended to the inhabitants of Maktesh, or Mortar, the lower, basin-like section of the city. This name was applied to the Tyropoeon Valley. It was in this area that the Phoenician and Jewish merchants engaged in their occupations, whom the prophet termed "Canaanites", i.e. traffickers, a term expressive of contempt. "Hammackhtesh, the mortar (Prov. 27: 22), which is the name given in Jud. 15: 19 to a hollow place in a rock, is used here to describe a locality in Jerusalem", writes Keil (*ibid.*, p. 133), and perhaps as an indication of the unscrupulous trading and usury of these merchants. Both the traders and the money changers (as there was no standard coinage, silver was used for transactions and it was weighed out by the money-changer or the banker) were to be destroyed. There was no need for them in the day of Jehovah.

JUDGMENT OF THE IRRELIGIOUS

And it shall come to pass at that time, that I will search Jerusalem with lamps, and punish the men who are settled on their lees, who say in their heart, Jehovah will not do good, neither will he do evil. Therefore, their goods shall be plundered, and their houses laid waste. They will build houses, but shall not inhabit them. They will plant vineyards, but they shall not drink wine from them (Zeph. 1: 12, 13).

There were others who also merited judgment and who

31

could not be allowed to escape, and Jehovah declared that He would search Jerusalem with lamps to discover them, i.e. the most diligent and minute search (c.f. Luke 15: 8). His penetrative glance would discover the guilty, wherever they might take refuge. To quote Laetsch (*The Minor Prophets,* p. 361), "There is no possibility of hiding from Him; not even the huge natural and artificial caves and tunnels, which honeycombed the hill on which Zion was built, will safeguard them from His avenging wrath (c.f. Psa. 139: 7 ff; Amos 9: 1 ff)". Jerome says that "princes and priests and mighty men were dragged even out of sewers and caves and pits and tombs, in which they had hidden themselves for fear of death".

The prophet picturesquely described these as men who had settled on their lees. The figure was, of course, drawn from that of new, fermenting wine, which was left on the "lees", the solid matter and the impurities which had settled at the bottom, only long enough for it to acquire sufficient strength, colour and flavour. It was then strained off, being poured from one vessel to another to free it from sediment and any further impurities (Isa. 25: 6; Jer. 48: 11). If allowed to remain longer, the liquid became thick and syrupy and soon became unpalatable. The expression used by Zephaniah was a stronger term than "settled" and meant "thickened" or "hardened"—possibly a reference to the hard crust which forms on the surface of fermented wine if it is left undisturbed for a long time.

"The characters stigmatised by Zephaniah are obvious," writes Smith (*ibid.*, pp. 52, 53). "They were a precipitate from the ferment of fifteen years back. Through the cruel days of Manasseh and Amon, hope had been stirred and strained, emptied from vessel to vessel, and so had sprung sparkling and keen into the new days of Josiah. But no miracle came, only ten years of waiting for the king's majority and five more of small, tentative reforms. . . . Of course, disappointment ensued—disappointment and listlessness. The new security of life became a temptation; persecution ceased, and religious men lived again at ease. So numbers of eager

and sparkling souls, who had been in the front of the movement fell away into a selfish and idle obscurity."

Left undisturbed, these people had become "thickened"
or callous and unresponsive to the claims of God. They had
become hardened in iniquity and religious indifference. So
flagrantly did they dishonour Jehovah that they concluded
that He was of no different character from the idols of the
pagans, with neither the interest nor the ability to intervene in
the affairs of men. They denied Divine providence in the
universe and declared that Jehovah produced neither blessing
nor calamity.

There could be only one reply to such impious impertinence. Hence Jehovah announced that He would search
them out to bring them to account. But is the attitude of
God's people very different today? The apathetic indifference
to His claims, the unresponsiveness to the challenge of
spiritual need, the general inertia on the part of Christians, all
suggest another period in which people have "settled on their
lees". Another writer refers to the "pubescence of respectability" and says that "respectability may be the precipitate
of unbelief". Certainly we are more concerned with our
respectability than the claims of Christ. Zephaniah's thunder-
ous tones warned that the day of Jehovah was at hand, but
with equal fervour and force the Holy Spirit today warns that
"the coming of the Lord draws nigh". When the Lord Jesus
Christ returns for His church, the Christian will be manifested
at His *bema*, to give account of life and deeds on earth. That
moment is imminent. It is time for the complacent and
slothful, who are settled on their lees, to awake and realise
the seriousness of their attitude. The eye of the Eternal still
searches the heart.

The morons of Zephaniah's day foolishly ruled out the
possibility of Divine interest in human affairs. Everything in
life, they argued, happened in accordance with natural laws.
There was virtually no place for the supernatural. It was a
tacit denial of the authority and immanence of God. Yet there
are Christian leaders today who adopt a similar doctrine, and

declare that the One, who redeems a soul, leaves the individual to guide his own life and choose his own course and never intervenes to encourage or to check. This is not the character of the God of the Bible.

Condign punishment was to fall swiftly and unexpectedly upon these irreligious characters of Judah. Their possessions would be plundered by the invader and their wealth would become the spoil of their enemies. Their houses would be laid low. There would be ample evidence now that there was a God in the heavens who had not surrendered His rule to any other. The punishments specified for those who despised His name would be meted out (Lev. 26, 32, 33; Deut. 28, 30, 39; Amos 5: 11; Mic. 6: 15). Life would be completely disrupted. They might build houses, but they would never be allowed to inhabit them. They might plant vineyards, but they would never drink of the wine therefrom. Those who despised Jehovah would pay the penalty for their insensate folly.

CHAPTER 4

The Character of the Day

L EST there should be any dubiety about the nature of the
forthcoming judgment, Zephaniah vividly described some
of the features of the day of Jehovah. All sense of security
must have dissolved at his words. There was no place now
for complacency. But it was too late to avert the storm: the
rumblings of thunder could already be heard in the distance.
The armies of the enemy were on the march.

IMMINENCE

*The great day of Jehovah is near. It is near and
hastening fast. The sound of the day of Jehovah is bitter:
the mighty man cries bitterly there (Zeph. 1: 14).*

Possibly still with the intention of arousing the slothful
and lethargic, of disturbing the self-complacent, and of
shaking the irreligious out of their condition, the prophet
warned that the day of trouble was near and was speeding
fast to fulfilment. Nothing could now stop its course. The
sounds could be heard with ever-increasing distinctness.
Zephaniah continued to describe the approaching judgment as
the day of Jehovah, although it was but a prefiguring of that
calamitous period. It was, however, so terrible that even its
sound would strike fear into the heart. Even the experienced
warrior, who had passed through battle and strife, would be
so awed by its character that he would shriek out in abject
terror at the sight. This will certainly be true when the actual
period commences and the unprecedented sufferings of the

great tribulation are experienced by earth. Indeed, our Lord Himself declared that, so dreadful would that period be that, unless it was shortened, no one would be saved (Matt. 24: 21, 22).

The Septuagint renders the last clause of verse 14 as "dreadful things are ordained", but it is difficult to see the origin of this.

Zephaniah's note needs to be struck again in our twentieth century. The coming of Christ is near and it is now speeding on to the day of fulfilment. The opportunities of the present will soon be gone and the potentialities of life will be for ever behind our backs. With all the urgency of which we are capable, we should proclaim the fact that that day is coming. "It is near and hastening fast."

THE NATURE OF THE DAY

That day is a day of wrath, a day of tribulation and distress, a day of ruin and devastation, a day of darkness and gloom, a day of clouds and gross darkness, a day of trumpet blast and battle cry against the fortified cities and against the high battlements (Zeph. 1: 15, 16).

The day of Jehovah is pre-eminently one of wrath and Zephaniah made this clear at the outset. The hymn on judgment, written by Thomas of Celano in 1250, entitled *Dies irae, dies illa* ("That day is a day of wrath") was based on verse 15.

The advent of that period of judgment would mean the complete devastation of everything for man: he would be utterly helpless, suffocated by the overwhelming flood which submerged him. The universal distress would be increased by the darkness and gloom, the clouds and thick darkness (Joel 2: 31; Matt. 24: 29). These are the features described by all the prophets who refer to that day. The light and glory of Divine favour will be hidden in the outpouring of His judgments upon a guilty world.

The prophet went on to use the metaphor of an attacking army. The sound of the trumpet was to be heard on every side. The war cry of the enemy was to ring out as the fortified

36

cities were besieged. The hordes of foes sweeping into the land threatened every inhabited town. The corners and battlements of the fortified walls would re-echo the trumpet blast, as the signal for the destruction which was about to commence. The immediate instruments of the Divine wrath may have been the ruthless, terrifying Scythians, or the prophet may have anticipated the later Chaldean invasion. God was not limited for instruments (see Note at end of chapter).

DISTRESS FOR ALL

And I will bring distress upon mankind, that they shall walk like blind men, because they have sinned against Jehovah; and their blood shall be poured out like dust and their flesh like dung. Neither their silver nor their gold shall be able to deliver them in the day of Jehovah's wrath. But the whole earth shall be consumed by the fire of his jealous wrath; for he shall make a full, even a sudden end of all the inhabitants of the earth (Zeph. 1: 17, 18).

The Divine visitation in that day will be universal. All mankind is to suffer and the affliction will obviously be sore. Because of their sin, men would walk as those deprived of sight, declared the prophet. This was precisely what was foretold in the law as part of the punishment of the dis-obedient— they would be smitten with blindness (Deut. 28: 28, 29). Just retribution was, therefore, predicted. There would be no escape: they would stagger about hopelessly like blind men, exactly in accord with the provisions of the law. All attempts to seek a way out of their trouble and distress would be unavailing; all sense of direction would be lost.

Man's life is in the blood (Lev. 17: 11), but so worthless would be the blood of those men that it would be poured out like dust (c.f. 2 Kings 23: 7; Isa. 49: 23), and their bodies would be regarded as of no more value than offal. They had discounted Divine providence and had insulted God by declaring, not only that He had no interest in mankind, but that He was virtually unable to affect the course of life. Now

37

the full penalty would be exacted by One who estimated them as worthless.

In the past they had purchased immunity from punishment by heavy payments of silver and gold to venal judges. They had even possibly bought off potential invaders of their country. They would soon be faced by invaders who could not be bought off and, in the ultimate, they would face the Eternal, whose dread judgments could not be warded off by effort or by payment (c.f. Ezek. 7: 19). There will be no salvation in the day of Jehovah's wrath.

The whole earth will be consumed by the fire of God's wrath. In perfect justice that fire will sweep over a guilty world and all mankind will be speedily destroyed. Zephaniah looked far beyond the immediate to the ultimate, and his words related, not merely to the terrible period of the great tribulation but, in all probability to the final outpouring of the wrath of God, when the fire of heaven will destroy the rebels of earth and the world itself be dissolved (Rev. 20: 9, 11; 2 Pet. 3: 10-12).

CALL TO REPENTANCE

Gather together, yes, gather together, O shameless nation, before the decree is implemented, before the day sweeps you away like drifting chaff, before the fierce anger of Jehovah come upon you, before the day of Jehovah's anger come upon you. Seek Jehovah, all you humble of the land, who do His commands: seek righteousness, seek humility. It may be that you will be hidden in the day of Jehovah's anger (Zeph. 2: 1-3).

The judgment of the whole earth had been predicted, and Judah, in particular, had been warned of the imminence of the impending tribulation. But, almost unexpectedly, there came a call to the nation to repent. They were called to gather together. Feinberg (*ibid.*, p. 53) says, "The word translated 'gather together' ordinarily means to gather together stubble as fuel for burning. . . . The nation is addressed in a derogatory manner because of their sin."

38

These people were summoned to assemble like slaves bending down to gather the stubble for the fire, in recognition of their worthlessness and sinfulness.

Judah was even called upon as a *nation*—a Hebrew word used for a Gentile nation whom God did not recognise as related to Him. So low had Judah sunk that she was regarded as no better than her pagan neighbours. If there was to be any reconciliation to Jehovah, there must be penitence and an acknowledgment of guilt and shame. The Authorised Version describes her as a "nation not desired", but the real significance is a "nation without shame". Sin had so hardened their sensibilities that they were dead to shame.

Yet the opportunity was given to them to repent. Let them seek Jehovah before His decree, or sentence of punishment, was put into execution—before it was too late. If they failed to do so, the storm of Divine wrath would sweep them away like chaff, and the fury of Jehovah's anger would be meted out upon them. In the immediate context, there was, of course, no repentance. Nor will there be when the great tribulation breaks upon God's ancient people. The pleas of the age will continue to fall upon deaf ears.

If the people had striven to carry out the commandments of God and to fulfil His ordinances, if they had made it their earnest desire to seek righteousness and humility, there would have been a complete transformation in their prospects. They would have been sheltered from the storm in the day of trouble. In a still future day, the same facts are appropriate. Repentance and contrition for sin, a determination to walk aright and humbly in the fear of God, would still protect them from the outpoured wrath of the great tribulation. But there is no sign of penitence or of humbling before Him, and the judgment must inevitably fall.

The conclusion is a tragic one. Unrepentant to the end, unaffected by the warnings of the prophet or his predecessors, blind to the claims of the Eternal, the people faced the inevitable and inescapable chastening of God—and still do!

Note.

It is usually contended that the events of the day of Jehovah, described by Zephaniah, were practically fulfilled in the Babylonian invasions and the subsequent captivity of the people of Judah. On the other hand, there are many who consider that the fulfilment was through the medium of the Scythians. This is doubtful because the Scythians did not overrun Judah and they left Jerusalem untouched at their invasion of Palestine.

The Scythians were a very ancient race, who claimed descent from Targetaus, the son of Zeus. They were a nomadic race, extremely backward in civilisation, and seem to have originated in the highlands of Asia. As Scoloti, they settled in the area to the north of the Black Sea and the Caspian Sea.

They invaded Persia but were checked by Sargon II. They attacked the Medes and Cimmerians, and later swept through Palestine to invade Egypt about the time when Zephaniah was prophesying. Psammetichus, king of Egypt, a contemporary of Josiah of Judah, bought them off and saved his country from the cruelties and sufferings which these fierce and ruthless barbarians would have inflicted.

Some later settled at Bethshean (which acquired the name of Scythopolis), but they played little part in Judah. The New Testament refers to them in Col. 3 : 11.

CHAPTER 5

The Gentiles Under Review

THE judgment predicted by Zephaniah was not a local one, restricted to the relatively small country of Judah. It was a universal one, covering all the Gentile nations. All, however, were not specifically detailed by name. Four countries which bordered on Judah were selected as illustrative of the whole.

PHILISTINE CAPITALS

For Gaza shall be deserted, and Ashkelon shall become a waste. They shall drive out Ashdod at noonday, and Ekron shall be rooted up (Zeph. 2: 4).

Four of the five cities which constituted the Philistine league (Josh. 13: 3) were named for judgment. The fifth, Gath, had ceased to exist at this time. These old foes of Judah were to be dealt with by Jehovah. Pusey pertinently points out (*ibid.*, p. 254) that the names of these cities "expressed boastfulness and so, in the Divine judgment, carried their own sentence with them, and this sentence is pronounced by a slight change in the word. Thus *Azzah* (Gaza), *strong*, shall be *Azoobah, desolated; Ekron, deep-rooting,* shall be *Teaker, uprooted;* the *Cherethites, cutters off,* shall become *Cheroth*, diggings; *Chebel,* the *land* of the sea-coast, shall be in another sense *Chebel, an inheritance,* divided by line to the remnant of Judah; and *Ashdod, the waster,* shall be taken in their might, not by craft, nor in the

41

way of robbers, but *driven forth* violently and openly in the *noonday*."

Gaza was one of the most ancient cities of the world and it existed before the times of Abraham. It marked the southern limit of Canaan (Gen. 10: 19). Originally inhabited by the Avims, it was conquered by the Philistine tribe, the Caphtorims (Josh 13 : 2; 3). It stood on the main road from Egypt to Mesopotamia and an important trade route. It was captured by Judah, but changed hands many times, Philistines, Assyrians, Egyptians and Greeks capturing it. It was captured and held for some time by the Maccabees and later fell into the hands of the Romans. It was, of course, the scene of Samson's greatest exploit (Jud. 16: 21-31). Under the hand of Jehovah, Gaza was to be deserted. The proud city, with its centuries of history, was to become an abandoned site. The present city is, in fact, on a new site.

Ashkelon, 12 miles north of Gaza, was occupied from Neolithic times. It was captured by Judah (Jud. 1:18), but was later taken by the Philistines and subsequently by the Assyrians, Babylonians, Persians, Greeks and Maccabees and ultimately by the Romans. It was set on fire by the Jews in Roman times. It was the birthplace of Herod the Great. Philo said in 40 A.D., "The Ascalonites have an implacable and irreconcilable enmity to the Jews, their neighbours." Their recompense had come. The city's doom was pronounced by Jeremiah about the same time as Zephaniah (Jer. 47: 5-7). The latter declared that it would become a waste, a prediction fulfilled centuries ago.

Ashdod, 18 miles north-east of Gaza, was one of the principal ports of Philistia. It contained the chief temple of Dagon (1 Sam. 5: 1-6). Like other Philistine cities, it passed through the hands of most of the great powers. Originally a city of considerable importance, it evidently wasted away (Jer. 25: 20). Zephaniah declared that the Ashdodites would be driven out at noon—the hottest time of the day and the most unlikely time for any military action.

Ekron was captured first by Dan at the conquest of

Canaan, and then by Judah, but was retaken by the Philistines, falling later into the hands of greater powers. It was the centre of worship of Baal-Zebub. The prophet declared that Ekron would be rooted up. So completely has this been fulfilled that today there is not a trace of the city.

The hatred of these Philistine cities for the Jews continued in terrible atrocities committed later against Christians. The judgment which fell upon them was well-merited.

THE COAST LANDS

Woe to the inhabitants of the sea coast, the nation of the Cherethites! The word of Jehovah is against you, O Canaan, the land of the Philistines; I will even destroy you till no inhabitant is left. And the sea coast shall become pasture land, caves for shepherds and folds for flocks. And the sea coast shall become the possession of the remnant of the house of Judah. They shall feed therefrom. In the houses of Ashkelon they shall lie down in the evening. For Jehovah their God will be mindful of them and turn away their captivity (Zeph. 2: 5-7).

As long ago as the time of Abraham, Philistines had settled along the Mediterranean coast (Gen. 21 : 32, etc). A Hamitic nation, they had apparently originated in Caphtor (Amos 9: 7) or Crete. Zephaniah referred to them as the nation of the Cherethites (see also 1 Sam 30: 14; Ezek. 25: 16), a name which is assumed to have been derived from Cretans: indeed, the Septuagint uses the latter word. They were associated with the Pelethites as David's guard (2 Sam. 8: 18; 20: 23) and T. C. Mitchell maintains that the Cherethites were Cretans and that the Pelethites were Philistines, but there is no evidence to confirm this. The Cherethites evidently settled in southern Palestine along the sea-coast.

A woe was pronounced upon these people and the prophet stated that the word of Jehovah was against them. The storm which was to sweep the rest of the country was to

43

affect them also. The land itself was described as "Canaan, the land of the Philistines". Pusey (*ibid.*, p. 259) says, "in that name lay the original source of their destruction. They inherited the sins of Canaan and with them his curse." They were to be completely blotted out. The curse laid by Noah upon his grandson was to be fulfilled in his descendants (Gen. 9: 25). Not a single inhabitant of the region was to be left.

The depopulated coastlands would then become pasture lands, in which the nomadic shepherds would provide themselves shelters, either in caves or in huts dug out of the ground as a refuge from the sun, and where folds would be constructed for their flocks. The area which had once teemed with life and bustling activity was to revert to the quiet of pastoral life—a prediction which has been completely fulfilled. The hordes of Scythians wiped out the inhabitants and left the land bare.

According to Zephaniah, the coastlands were to become a possession of the remnant of the house of Judah. Philistia, for her sins, had forfeited all entitlement to it, but the mass of Judah were in no better spiritual state. The land was, therefore, to become the possession, not of the nation as a whole, but of the restored remnant. An area, once covered with cities and the scene of trade and commerce, was to provide food for Judah from its fertile soil.

If Ashkelon had become a desolation, the remnant was to find shelter for the night in the empty houses of the city. There they would be able to lie down in quiet security, fearing no ferocious beast or evil intruder. For the prophet's vision rises above the storm-clouds of the present to the Divine mercy of the future. Jehovah would once more be mindful of His people and He would restore them again. The immediate and the distant future seem inextricably entangled, but the prophet unquestionably saw not merely the return of Judah from the Babylonian captivity (which had not then commenced), but doubtless the ultimate restoration to the land and the peace and blessing of the millennial age.

MOAB AND AMMON

I have heard the taunting of Moab and the revilings of the Ammonites, wherewith they have taunted my people and have boasted against their territory. Therefore, as I live, says Jehovah of hosts, the God of Israel, surely Moab shall be like Sodom, and the Ammonites like Gomorrah, a possession of nettles and salt-pits, and a permanent desolation. The remnant of my people shall pillage them, and the remnant of my nation shall possess them. This shall they have for their arrogance, because they have reviled and vaunted themselves against the people of Jehovah of hosts (Zeph. 2: 8-10).

The Philistines were located to the west of Israel and Judah, but the Moabites and Ammonites were on the east. These two nations had, of course, descended from the sons born of an incestuous relationship of Lot with his daughters (Gen. 19: 36-38). They were consistently opposed to God's people and were frequently denounced by the prophets as the inveterate foes of Israel and Judah (Jer. 48: 1—49: 6; Ezek. 25: 1-11, etc.). They were notorious for their pride and haughtiness (Isa. 16: 6), their idolatry (1 Kings 11: 7) and their inhumanity (2 Kings 3: 27).

The Moabites claimed that their land had been bestowed upon them by their principal god, Chemosh (see Appendix), and described themselves as the people of Chemosh (Num. 21: 29). The Ammonites similarly claimed that their land was the gift of their god, Molech (1 Kings 11: 7). The two deities have often been identified with each other, but there seems no doubt that they were separate. Both demanded human sacrifice (Jer. 7: 31) and were, therefore, abhorred by Israel and Judah.

Not only were they bitterly opposed to God's people, but they rejoiced at every calamity suffered by them. They displayed their enmity on every possible occasion and reviled and reproached the nation of Judah. The day of reckoning was to come, however. Those who attack God's people are virtually opponents of Him. He declared that He had heard their taunts and had observed their boastful arrogance and

45

the way in which they had vaunted themselves against His people.

Moab and Ammon had come into existence in consequence of Lot's escape from the judgment which had fallen on Sodom and Gomorrah. But now Jehovah would make them like Sodom and Gomorrah. Their insults would boomerang. Their punishment would be permanent and irrevocable, being confirmed by the Almighty's solemn oath— "as I live, says Jehovah of hosts, the God of Israel." Sodom and Gomorrah had once flourished in wealth and glory, only to be destroyed. Now Ammon and Moab were to share their fate. The two countries were located in the vicinity of the Dead Sea and it seemed appropriate that the fate of the ancient cities of that area should become theirs also.

Their fertile land was to become a mournful waste. The nettles (Job 30: 7), which grew lavishly and in abundance in waste places, would overrun the land of Moab and Ammon. The southern shore of the Dead Sea provides an almost inexhaustible supply of rock salt. The land would be covered with salt pits, declared the prophet: the symbol was one of utter ruin and sterility. Pusey (*ibid.*, p. 271) says, "The soil continues, as of old, of exuberant fertility; yet in part, from the utter neglect and insecurity of agriculture, it is abandoned to a rank and encumbering vegetation; elsewhere, from the neglect of the former artificial system of irrigation, it is wholly barren. At the present day it seems irretrievably lost, but this is precisely what Zephaniah foretold: the land was to become a permanent desolation with no hope of recovery."

They had despised Judah, but God declared that the remnant of His people would plunder the Ammonites and Moabites and possess them personally (by implication, as slaves). So complete would be the ruin and humiliation of these arrogant nations. There is a God in the heavens with whom men have to do and although, as Longfellow wrote, "the mills of God grind slowly, yet they grind exceeding small; though with patience He stands waiting, with exactness grinds He all". (*Retribution*). It is a lesson which men still

46

need to learn. We cannot please ourselves how we live and what we do. Nor can we escape the consequences of our actions to others.

The fate of the two nations was well-deserved. They had scoffed at and condemned Jehovah's nation. Their pride was now to be recompensed. What He had threatened would be their lot in return for their arrogance and haughtiness and their vaunting of themselves against His people. The higher the boaster exalts himself, the greater is his fall.

THE FALSE GODS

Jehovah will be terrible against them: for he will make all the gods of the earth waste away. And men shall bow down to him, each in his place, even all the lands of the nations (Zeph. 2: 11).

The nations of the earth have their gods, whom the Bible regards as nonentities. In His wrath against the nations, Jehovah would also deal with the idols they worshipped. In the language of the prophet, He would famish them or make them lean; He would so deprive them of strength and sustenance that they would waste away. Without the worship and support of their adherents the idols would exercise no influence or power. It was the Divine intention to destroy them and leave men and nations again with the choice of submission or not to Himself.

Deprived of their false deities, men from every land will, in the day envisioned by the prophet, bow down to Jehovah, each in his own place. Submission to the true God may not be universal, but from every tribe and nation praises will ascend to Him. In a glimpse into the golden age of the millennium, Zephaniah saw the widespread recognition of the Eternal of which other prophets speak. Elliott (*ibid.*, p. 28) says that one of the "objects of these judgments upon the nations is that Israel may come thereby to the knowledge of the glory and power of his God, and learn to stand in fear of His severity and bow to His goodness." But the prophecy reaches beyond Israel to the Gentile nations of earth and to

47

the destruction of their false objects of worship that the only true God may be exalted.

The A.V. uses the term "the isles of the heathen" or nations, an expression taken from the islands and coastlands to symbolise the whole of the world (Isa. 41: 1).

ETHIOPIA'S SUFFERING

You Ethiopians also, you shall be slain by my sword (*Zeph.* 2: 12).

The prophet's glance swung away from the west and east to focus on the south, where the Cushites had made their home in the south and southwest of Egypt.

The Ethiopians, or Cushites, were descendants of Cush, the son of Ham (Gen. 10: 6). They ruled Egypt from 720 to 654 B.C. and some commentators consider that it is Egypt that Zephaniah has in view in this verse. The invasions of Esarhaddon and Ashurbanipal reduced Ethiopia and Egypt to mere tributary states. They had little connection with Israel, although they did attack Asa and were soundly defeated (2 Chron. 14: 9-13). Their judgment at God's hands was not, therefore, as in other cases, related to their attitude to the chosen people.

No reason for their trials is given. They may have been included as an indication of the universality of the judgment. Their sentence, however, was to be executed by the sword. In other words, their country would be ravaged by war and the people would perish at the hands of whatever invaders Jehovah employed as His instrument.

ASSYRIA CALLED TO ACCOUNT

And he shall stretch out his hand against the north and destroy Assyria; and will make Nineveh a desolation and a dry waste like the desert. Herds shall lie down in the midst of her, all the beasts of the nations. Both the pelican and the hedgehog shall lodge in her capitals; a voice shall sing in the windows; rubbish shall be on the thresholds; he shall lay bare the cedar work. This is the exulting city which dwelt in security, which said to herself, I am and there is none beside me. What a desolation she has become, a place for wild beasts to lie down in. Everyone who passes by her shall hiss and wag his hand (Zeph. 2: 13-15).

From the south the prophet now swept to the north, the direction from which trouble so often emanated for Israel. Assyria was actually situated to the northeast of Israel, but her armies always invaded Israel from the north and the prophetical books always refer to her as the power in the north.

The great Assyrian empire dominated the ancient world from the 9th to the 7th centuries B.C. By the time of Zephaniah's prophecy the great colossus had begun to totter but it had not yet fallen. The prophet now declared that Jehovah was about to stretch out His hand to destroy Assyria. This could not have been foreseen at the time, but very shortly afterwards the joint armies of Media and Babylonia attacked the empire and completely broke her power. As instruments in God's hands, they were employed to bring about a speedy fulfilment of the prophecy. "The ruins with which for nigh three centuries she had strewn Western Asia," says another, "to these were to be reduced her own impregnable and ancient glory. It was the end of an epoch."

The proud capital of the empire had a long and glorious history. It was built by Asshur in the earliest days of human history (Gen. 10: 11) and became the centre of government and the residence of the emperor. A centre of learning and with a very large library, it was yet renowned for its cruelty. Indeed, Nahum describes her as "the bloody city" (Nah. 3: 1).

This great city, according to Zephaniah, was to become a complete desolation and a dry barren waste, inhabited only by desert animals. When the Medes, Babylonians and Scythians besieged the city, a sudden rise of the River Tigris swept away a great part of the city's wall of sun-dried bricks and rendered her defenceless. Her devastation was complete.

49

The description given of the forsaken city was a lamentable one. Every detail spoke of its ruin.

Herds of beasts of every conceivable kind would lie down in the middle of the city. Pusey pertinently remarks (*ibid.*, p. 275), "No desolation is like that of decayed luxury. It preaches the nothingness of man, the fruitlessness of his toils, the fleetingness of his hopes and enjoyments, and their baffling when at their height. Grass in a court or on a once beaten road, much more, in a town, speaks of the passing away of what has been. . . . It leaves the feeling of void and forsakenness. But in Nineveh not a few tufts of grass here and there shall betoken desolation, it shall be one wild rank pasture, where flocks shall not only feed, but *lie down*, as in their fold and continual resting-place, not in the outskirts only or suburbs, but in the very centre of her life and throng and busy activity."

The pelican, an unclean bird (Lev. 11 : 18) which inhabits isolated places, is pictured as finding a home in the deserted city. The R.S.V. translates as "vulture" and the Septuagint as "chameleon", but the "pelican" is probably what was intended. The A.V. "cormorant" can hardly be accepted. The Asiatic hedgehog (rather than "bittern") usually dwells in waste lands. But the pelican and the hedgehog were described as lodging in the carved capitals of the massive pillars, which had evidently crashed to the ground.

The moaning of the wind through the open windows of the city must have sounded like a funeral dirge, so that the prophet declared that a voice would sing through the windows. The R.S.V., without much justification, translates this as "the owl shall hoot through the window", and the Septuagint as "wild beasts shall utter their cries in its vaults", but the explanation suggested above seems more appropriate.

In the destruction of the city it would be logical to expect rubbish on the thresholds of palaces, temples and mansions, precisely as the prophet indicates. Both the R.S.V. and the LXX consider that the reference is to the croaking of the raven on the thresholds or in the gates, but this interpretation is doubtful.

The whole picture is one of tragic destruction, such as actually occurred in 612 B.C.—probably soon after the prophecy. The description of a dry barren waste, in place of the prosperous, bustling city, is remarkably apt in view of its complete disappearance from history. It is only in the last few decades that much has been discovered of it.

The destruction of the palaces and temples left exposed the elaborately carved cedar wood of the ceilings and the panelling of the walls: this valuable work was left to decay in the vicissitudes of weather and circumstances. Nineveh had reached her end.

The glory and majesty of the Assyrian empire were universally acknowledged. Her power had been felt worldwide and Judah and Israel had suffered with others. The imperial victories and triumphs had been boisterously celebrated in Nineveh. In her self-sufficiency, the city deemed herself completely invincible. In her pride she proclaimed that she had no equal and there was none to disturb her serenity. In 401 B.C., however, Xenophon could find few traces of the great city and concluded that it had been destroyed because Zeus had deprived the people of their wits— a conclusion for which there was some justification.

Zephaniah declared that the exulting city would become a desolation, a place where wild beasts might make their lairs. Because of her attitude in the past, she would become an object of scorn and derision. The passer-by would maliciously hiss at her and shake his fist. For centuries the very site of the city was forgotten. The words of God proved true. A well-merited fate was meted out to her.

CHAPTER 6

The Condition of Jerusalem

ZEPHANIAH turned once more to his own people and to the capital city of Jerusalem in what was tacitly a final appeal to repentance and a warning of the dangers attendant upon a refusal to repent. Yet the very condition of the city would have dispelled any hope and he pronounced a woe on her.

THE IMPENITENT CITY

Woe to her that is rebellious and unclean, the city of oppression. She hearkened not to the voice; she accepted not correction. She trusted not in Jehovah: she drew not near to her God (Zeph. 3: 1, 2).

Jerusalem was no better than her pagan neighbours whose doom had been announced. So low had she sunk in the spiritual scale that the prophet ignored her proper name, which meant "city of peace", and described her instead as the "city of oppression". She had been far more highly privileged than the Gentile nations; the revelation of God had been made to her; she had received the oracles of God; a Divinely appointed ritual and form of worship had been prescribed for her; messengers had been sent repeatedly with the message of Jehovah. Yet she had rejected every means of grace and had obstinately turned her back upon her God.

Not only was she refractory but also unclean—an active rebel against the Divine will and defiled by the sin in which she delighted. Above all others, she might have been expected to render loyal obedience to Jehovah and to conduct herself in conformity with His revealed will. Her superficial orthodoxy and her external observance of the Levitical ceremonial could not compensate for her heart rejection of God and her long continuance in wrongdoing. Hence the only message the prophet could bring was one of denunciation.

Faithfulness would have induced a consideration for the poor, a practical sympathy for the widow and orphan, a protection of the rights of the under-privileged. Instead, Jerusalem was a city of oppression: the rights of others were completely ignored, the help for others which should have been in evidence was conspicuous by its absence, and the compassion to be expected from a city so favoured was displaced by a vindictive cruelty.

Sin must meet with correction, but Jehovah had dealt leniently with His erring people: admonition and rebuke and even specific punishment had been employed to win them back to His ways. Yet this city refused to listen to the witness of the law or to the warnings of the prophets; she declined to accept discipline, and the lessons intended to be learned, through the chastisements inflicted, were ignored. Her faith should have been reposed in God, but she turned her back upon Him to serve the idols of the pagans. She should have drawn near to Jehovah, in penitence and contrition, to re-dedicate herself to Him, but she showed no inclination for communion with Him. He was deemed unworthy of her trust and confidence.

It is a deplorable picture, but of how many believers today the same expressions would be applicable. Every spiritual blessing has been bestowed upon the Christian, but the love and devotion to Christ, which ought to be in evidence, are often gravely lacking; the duty to friends and neighbours is grievously ignored; the ways of the world are reflected in the church; the power of the Holy Spirit is completely missing; and the radiant glory of the Christ is not to be seen. Woe to the city, declaimed the prophet. Woe to such a believer too!

54

Her officials within her are roaring lions. Her judges are evening wolves which leave nothing for the morning. Her prophets are vainglorious and faithless persons. Her priests have profaned the sanctuary; they have done violence to the law (Zeph. 3: 3, 4).

Zephaniah proceeded to denounce the leaders in every sphere, and his words patently referred to the country as a whole and not merely to the metropolis. A nation takes its character, at least partially, from its rulers. A church reflects, to some extent, the nature of its leaders and ministers. Every community is inevitably affected in attitude and outlook by those who stand in the forefront: this is inescapable. Hence the appropriateness of the prophet's words. If a cancer affected the whole body, its roots were to be found in the head. He dealt with all four categories of leaders.

The princes or civil officials were described as roaring lions. Instead of respect, they inculcated fear. They should have been guides and monitors to the people: instead they sought to devour. They fed upon power and were not con-concerned for those for whose condition and safety they were responsible. They were like roaring lions, constantly seeking a prey instead of caring for the flock.

The magistrates were the ministers of justice. In the administration of the law, their work was to protect the innocent and to punish the guilty. But Zephaniah implied that they utterly ignored their responsibilities and were concerned only with their own well-being. He painted them as the evening wolves from the Arabian desert who, in insatiable greed, issued forth ravenously at sunset, to seize the prey. Like the wolves they gluttonously devoured what they caught and even gnawed the bones lest something should be left till the morning. In their rapacious greed they devoured all. "Under the pretence of law and justice", says one writer, "they mercilessly fleece their victims and are never satisfied, always hungry for more gain (Amos 2 : 6-8; Matt. 23 :

14, 25)". Our Lord used similar expressions in respect of the teachers of the law of His day.

The prophets were even more seriously reprehensible perhaps. Called of God to warn the people of evil practices and to reveal to them the mind and will of the Eternal, they practised the very sins which they should have condemned. They were wanton or vainglorious, utterly frivolous and irresponsible, empty boasters claiming to be the messengers of God. They were treacherous or faithless, deceiving those whom they should have enlightened. It was a serious indictment.

The priests were virtually the mediators between the nation and Jehovah. The whole sacrificial system was, in effect, dependent upon them. It was through them that communion with God was established and maintained. Yet the prophet declared that they had profaned the temple. They had made the sacred common. Jeremiah, at roughly the same time, exposed their shameful wickedness (Jer. 7: 9-11). The prescribed ritual mattered little to them; the spiritual needs of the worshippers were discounted; they did violence to the law which had been entrusted to them to implement. Laetsch (*ibid.*, p. 375) says scathingly, "They manipulated the law of God chiefly for the purpose of filling their purses and paunches". The whole religious system was being distorted.

When the leaders were so culpable, it is little wonder that the nation was corrupt. "Like master, like man", wrote George Farquhar nearly three centuries ago, and he was quite right. The character of the leaders is inevitably reflected in those who are led.

A RIGHTEOUS GOD

Jehovah, in the midst of her, is righteous: He does no wrong. Morning by morning He brings His justice to light without fail. Yet the unjust knows no shame (Zeph. 3: 5).

Despite the perversity of His people, Jehovah remained in their midst. In view of their shameless conduct, His grace was amazing. Yet He made it clear that He was the righteous

56

One with Whom there was no iniquity. By inference, the very presence of the One, who was infinitely holy and perfectly just, was a condemnation of the guilty city and nation.

In the east, the early morning is the most suitable time for conducting business and it was formerly the hour for the administering of justice. Appropriately, therefore, Zephaniah declared that Jehovah unfailingly brought His justice to light each morning. "God's justice," says Kleinert (*ibid*., p. 27) "is neither His teaching nor His righteous administration, but the announcement of the judgment which it was right for Him and obligatory upon Him to bring those mad practices." By whatever method He might speak (and it could conceivably be in the circumstances of life), the significance ought to have been born home to the sinner.

"Yet the unjust knows no shame," said Zephaniah. Lifting up his voice at approximately the same time, Jeremiah said, "Were they ashamed when they had committed abomination? Nay, they were not at all ashamed, neither could they blush" (Jer. 6: 15). Not only was there no sign of contrition: there was not the slightest indication of shame. The people were oblivious to the holiness of God and the shamefulness of their iniquity. They could not even blush. When there is a consciousness of guilt and a sense of shame that evil practices had been tolerated or engaged in, there is some hope. But when all sense of shame at doing wrong has disappeared, the probability of a change of attitude is negligible.

JUDGMENT EXEMPLIFIED
I have cut off the nations: their battlements are in ruins. I made their streets waste, that no one walks in them. Their cities are desolate, so that there is no man, there is no inhabitant. I said, Surely she will fear me, she will receive correction, so that their dwellings should not be cut off. However I punished them, but they rose early and corrupted all their doings (Zeph. 3: 6, 7).

God condescended to provide examples to His people of

57

the character of His judgments by reference to His dealings with other nations, who were not identified. It was only necessary for Judah to recall the facts of recent history, or to gaze upon the ruined fortifications on the hill-tops surrounding them, to realise that the hand of God had been laid upon the nations which had perished. The empty streets of the devastated cities were a silent reminder of the Divine visitation upon the guilty nations. The decimated populations of their neighbours was a fact which could not be ignored. Yet they were insensitive to the message and unheeding of the Divine voice.

With these examples before them, surely Judah and Jerusalem would heed the lesson and, if only to avert the judgment which must otherwise fall upon their own dwellings, would listen to admonition and turn in filial fear to the One through whom these judgments came. The warning was clear. The enemy was almost within the gate, but grace still lingered to provide the opportunity for repentance. After God's strenuous efforts to make clear their danger, surely they would flee to Him for shelter from the oncoming wrath.

They did not. In blind and insolent obstinacy, they pursued their evil occupations with unabated—if not increased —vigour. Pusey (*ibid., p.* 282) writes, "There are as many aggravations of their sin as there are words. The four Hebrew words bespeak eagerness, wilfulness, completeness, enormity, in sin. *They rose early,* themselves deliberately *corrupted,* of their own mind made offensive *all* their *doings,* not slight acts, but *deeds,* great works done with a high hand." There was not a sign of repentance: they were eager to do wrong, to engage in what was offensive to God. How could long-suffering continue?

The conditions are not entirely dissimilar to those of the present day. The grace of God has been revealed in an incomparable way at Calvary. His judicial acts have been seen in the fall and suffering of the nations. His message has rung out clearly in the happenings of life. But men refuse to listen to the warning. They are eager to pursue what they

58

know to be evil. The sense of shame has gone. No more can they blush. But a holy God will not permanently delay His judgment. His longsuffering has postponed the hour for long, but the lightning seems now about to strike.

CHAPTER 7

The Golden Age

BEFORE the blessings of the future burst upon his vision, Zephaniah brought a final message regarding the judgment of the nations and the outpouring of the Divine wrath, leading on quite naturally from the preceding section.

JEHOVAH'S WRATH

Therefore, wait for me, says Jehovah, for the day when I rise up to the prey. For my fixed purpose is to gather together nations, to assemble kingdoms, to pour out upon them my indignation, the full fury of my anger; for in the fire of my jealousy shall all the earth be consumed (Zeph. 3: 8).

This verse is the only one in the Old Testament in which all the letters of the Hebrew alphabet are included.

The evidence of the justice of Jehovah was now to be demonstrated. He had, in longsuffering, permitted men to follow their own course, and even His own people had deliberately indulged in wrongdoing in defiance of Him. Now He called upon the nation to wait for the day when He would rise up to the prey or, according to Sir George Adam Smith, the R.S.V. and other versions, when He would rise up as a witness or to testify. It matters little which translation is taken; the intention is clear. God was about to arise as His own witness, to testify of His perfect justice, and to demonstrate it as, like a hunter, He seized the prey.

Nations and kingdoms would be gathered together in

61

order that His indignation might be poured out upon them, His intolerance of sin would be evidenced by the unmitigated punishment resulting from His wrath. The whole earth would be consumed by the fire of His zeal. There would be no doubt as to His attitude to sin and to the unrepentant sinner. The day of mercy would be past: Divine vengeance would exact the full penalty from the inhabitants of the earth.

The language employed clearly anticipates the final judgment of earth, although earlier partial fulfilments (even including the outpouring of wrath preparatory to the introduction of the millennium) are plainly visualised. God's ways in judgment are made clear in the pages of history and will continue to be until the final day of reckoning comes. The thinking man must recognise that a Supreme Ruler sits upon the throne and that His authority has been delegated to no other. Consequently, sin against Him must meet with His condemnation, and His sentence must inescapably be executed.

A NEW SPEECH

At that time, I will change the language of the people to a pure language, that they may all call on the name of Jehovah, and serve him with one accord (Zeph. 3: 9).

Prima facie, the first promise in connection with the restoration of Israel was a reversal of the judgment at Babel when language was confused (Gen. 11: 7-9). The word used, however, means "lip" rather than "language". The lip was regarded as the organ of speech. The lips express the inward thoughts, and the character of the thoughts of the heart was figuratively imputed to the lips. Those who invoked the names of idols were deemed to have unclean lips, defiled by the names of the false gods (Hos. 2: 19; Psa. 16: 4). Those, whose hearts had been purified, called upon Jehovah with clean lips because their thoughts were clean (c.f. Jer. 32: 39). Implicitly, Jehovah promised a cleansed heart and thereby a cleansed lip, which would enable the individual of whatever nation to call upon Jehovah.

Such would serve Him "with one shoulder", i.e. in perfect accord and unanimity. The metaphor was derived from the practice of two men bearing a burden between them, possibly suspended from a yoke on their shoulders. The regenerated people of all nations in the future millennial age will be one in the worship and service of Jehovah.

ISRAEL'S RESTORATION

From beyond the rivers of Ethiopia, will they bring my worshippers, the daughter of my dispersed ones, as my offering. On that day you shall not be put to shame because of your doings whereby you have transgressed against me. For then will I take away from the midst of you those who exult in your pride, and you shall no longer be haughty on my holy mountain. I will leave in the midst of you a humble and poor people, and they shall trust in the name of Jehovah. The remnant of Israel shall not work unrighteousness, nor speak falsehood, nor shall a deceitful tongue be found in their mouth. For they shall feed and lie down, and none shall make them afraid (Zeph. 3: 10-13).

Zephaniah once more looked far beyond the immediate future to the ultimate restoration of Israel to her own land. The prophetical books repeatedly predicted that day when God would gather out of all countries those whom, centuries ago, He dispersed as a penalty for their wrongdoing. In this particular instance, the regathering was to be from beyond the rivers of Cush or Ethiopia (c.f. Isa. 18: 1). The rivers of Ethiopia were the Blue Nile, White Nile, Atbara and Astasobas, and it was from the hinterland that the exiles were to be gathered. The Falashas of western Abyssinia, for example, claim Jewish descent and have a knowledge of Judaism and may consequently be among those to be gathered one day.

From these areas the nations were to bring to Jehovah, as an offering, worshippers who were no other than the descendants of His dispersed people. The word used for "offering" was *minchah*, "meal offering" (see Lev. 2). This

63

particular offering is usually considered to be an apt figure of the perfect life of our Lord Jesus Christ. It was composed of fine flour, symbolising the purity and perfect evenness of His character; olive oil, signifying the sanctifying influence of the Holy Spirit in His life; frankincense, indicative of the fragrance of His moral and personal glories; salt, the type of the preserving potency of the Word of God which sustained Him. If Israel is to be such an offering to God, there is a clear implication of a regeneration of such a character and extent that the life will be a reflection of that of the Perfect Man.

The comprehensive cleansing of God's people is confirmed in verse 11. The shame of the past is to be removed: the remorse for the sins and transgressions of earlier days will give place to a quiet satisfaction in Jehovah. Pride and self-exaltation were once characteristic of Israel—and still are to some extent—but that will all disappear in the Messianic era of which the prophet spoke. There will be no room for personal or national arrogance or haughtiness in the temple mount (Isa. 11 : 9).

Those who return to the land in that future day of blessing will be a humble and lowly people, exhibiting none of the characteristics of the past. The stamp of true piety will be seen in their attitude: they will seek refuge in the name of Jehovah; their trust and confidence will be solely in Him.

The picture presented by Zephaniah is stark and austere. Other prophets tell of the glory and blessing of the millennial age, but he is concerned with practical living. To quote Smith (ibid., pp. 70, 71), "A thorough purgation, the removal of the wicked, the sparing of the honest and the meek; insistence only upon the rudiments of morality and religion; faith in its simplest form of trust in a righteous God, and character in its basal elements of meekness and truth— these and these alone survive the judgment".

The restored remnant of Israel, the prophet declared, would not commit iniquity or practise deceit or falsehood. Like sheep they would feed in the lush pastures and lie down in peace, with no fear of being disturbed. The reference is quite clearly, not to the returned exiles from Babylon but to those gathered back by the Messiah at His Second Advent. The words will never be true until then.

ISRAEL'S JUBILATION

Sing, O daughter of Zion; shout aloud, O Israel; rejoice and be jubilant with all the heart, O daughter of Jerusalem. Jehovah has taken away the judgments against you. He has cast out your enemy. The king of Israel, even Jehovah, is in your midst. You shall not see evil any more (Zeph. 3: 14, 15).

In the light of the glorious age to come, the people were bidden to give expression to their jubilation in song and shout. Nothing was to hinder their joy. With a full heart they were to exult in the presence of Jehovah.

"Sing, it is the inarticulate yet louder swell of joy, a trumpet-blast; and then too, deep within, *be glad,* the calm even joy of the inward soul; *exult,* the triumph of the soul which cannot contain itself for joy; and this, *with the whole heart,* no corner of it not pervaded with joy. The ground of this is the complete removal of every evil, and the full presence of God" (Pusey, *ibid.,* p. 288).

The causes for praise and jubilation were many. In the first place, Jehovah had removed the judgments against His people. Not only had the judicial charges and sentence been cancelled, but the chastisements, which had been inflicted upon them to teach them the discipline of God, had been lifted. Every burden had gone. Their transgressions had been forgiven. Never would they experience trouble again, for the King of Israel, Jehovah Himself, was in their midst.

The King of Israel was in the midst. "Although it is incorrect to see eschatological ideas monolithically," writes Eakin (*ibid.,* p. 288), "at least one idea associated with the *eschaton* was that the absolute rule of Yahweh would be re-established. This was the event to which Zephaniah points." The kingship of God is a constantly recurring theme in the Old Testament. Jehovah's throne is said to be established in the heavens and His kingdom to be eternal and universal (Exod. 15: 18; Psa. 103: 19). With the election of Israel, the kingdom of God was closely identified with that nation. "With the decline and fall of the Davidic dynasty," says Prof. F. F. Bruce, "the expectation of a future and more permanent manifestation of the kingship of God emerged with increasing clarity and can be traced from the Old Testament prophets right on into our Lord's lifetime."

When our Lord was born into this world, there was no doubt regarding His status as king. Even prior to His birth, in the annunciation to Mary, Gabriel declared, "He shall be great and shall be called the Son of the Most High: and the Lord God shall give unto Him the throne of His father David: and He shall rule over the house of Jacob for ever; and of His kingdom there shall be no end" (Luke 1: 32, 33). When the wise men came to see Him, they were aware of the royal status of the One they sought, for they asked, "Where is he who is born King of the Jews?" (Matt. 2: 2).

It is sometimes argued that the purpose of the incarnation was no more than the atonement and the outcalling of the church, and that it had no reference to the Old Testament prophecies of a literal earthly kingdom and that the Lord Jesus Christ never offered such a kingdom to Israel during His earthly life. This is patently fallacious. "Repent," enjoined John the Baptist, "for the kingdom of heaven is at hand" (Matt. 3: 2). As every Jew who listened must have concluded, his reference was to the promised theocratic kingdom described in Dan. 2: 44; 7: 14, etc. Our Lord, after the temptation, used the same words (Matt. 4: 17) and, in all the synagogues of Galilee, He preached the gospel of the kingdom (Matt. 4: 23). There could, of course, be no kingdom without the king; but the King was now present and the kingdom was available in Him. Acceptance of Him was essential if the kingdom was to be introduced.

After Peter's confession at Caesarea Philippi, the Master charged "His disciples that they should tell no man that He was Jesus the Messiah" (i.e. the One by whom the kingdom would be introduced), and *"from that time"* told them of His impending crucifixion (Matt. 16: 20, 21). When He rode into Jerusalem on Palm Sunday, He specifically stated that it was done to fulfil the prophecy of Zech. 9: 9, "Behold your king comes to you" (Matt. 21: 5). The crowds who gathered cried, "Blessed be the King who comes in the name of the Lord" (Luke 19: 38). Our Lord did not rebuke them for any misconception (v. 40). They were familiar with their own prophets and fully realised the implication of Christ's words: He had come as King and the kingdom was at hand. His claims were clear, e.g. "if I with the finger of God cast out demons, no doubt the kingdom of God is come upon you" (Luke 11: 20). "The law and the prophets were until John: since that time the kingdom of God is preached" (Luke 16: 16). He told the Pharisees, "the kingdom of God is among you" (Luke 17: 21), and the people later concluded, in view of His preaching, "that the kingdom of God should immediately appear" (Luke 19: 11).

The nation had the opportunity of accepting Him and the long-promised kingdom and, referring to His rejection, He said, "The kingdom of God shall be taken from you and given to a nation bringing forth the fruits thereof" (Matt. 21: 43). When Pilate challenged Him, "Art thou the King of the Jews?" He replied in affirmation, "Thou sayest" (Luke 23: 3). Even the dying thief cried, "Lord, remember me when Thou comest into Thy kingdom" (Luke 23: 42).

His disciples plainly anticipated the establishment of the kingdom during His lifetime and, even after His resurrection, they asked Him, "Wilt Thou at this time restore again the kingdom to Israel?" (Acts 1: 6). Words have no meaning if our Lord did not come as King and did not imply that the kingdom was available to Israel by acceptance of the King. We have spent some time on this point in view of the contrary teaching prevalent in some quarters. God has not given up His people and one day Israel will be seen plainly as a kingdom with a king. The abundance of Old Testament predictions will reach their fulfilment. Jehovah is King in the midst

67

of His earthly people. Consequently trials and troubles will then dissolve. The people will "not see evil any more".

THE LOVE OF GOD

On that day it shall be said to Jerusalem, Fear not: and to Zion, Let not your hands grow weak. Jehovah your God in your midst is mighty. He will save. He will rejoice over you with gladness. He will be silent in His love. He will exult over you with loud singing (Zeph. 3: 16, 17).

There will be no need for paralysing fear for God's people. The despondency, which would weaken them and cause their hands to fall listlessly to their sides, has no place now, for Jehovah their God, like a mighty warrior will be in their midst to deliver. There should be no abatement in their service for Him: their hands should be strong.

Jehovah Himself would rejoice in His people. The Eternal expressed His pleasure and gladness in this restored nation of the future—a nation which had done despite to Him and had deserted His ways. In a daring anthropomorphism, the prophet declared that He would be silent in His love, "an expression used to denote love deeply felt, which is absorbed in its object with thoughtfulness and admiration" (Keil, *ibid.*, p. 161). He will quietly rest in His love. Eakin (*ibid.*, p. 289) says that the word used is not *chesed* (covenant love) but *ahabah*. According to Snaith, "*'Ahabah* is the cause of the covenant; *chesed* is the means of its continuance. Thus *'ahabah* is God's election-love, whilst *chesed* is His covenant-love".

At the same time Zephaniah declared that God would exult over His people with loud singing. His superabundant joy in His own redeemed and restored nation would be evident in the songs of the celestial heights.

If this is to be true of Israel in a future day, is it not true in the experience of the church today? Of our Lord Jesus Christ, it was specifically said that He loved His own to the end (John 13: 1) and He prayed that His loved ones might be with Him to behold His glory (John 17: 24). His

68

joy is in them (John 15 : 11). In a coming day, He will sing praise to God in the midst of the church (Heb. 2: 12).

THE FINAL REGATHERING

I will gather those who are sorrowing for the set feast, those of you to whom the shame of it was a burden. Behold, at that time, I will deal with all who maltreat you. And I will save the lame and gather her who was driven out. And I will make them a praise and a name in every land where they were put to shame. At that time I will bring you again, at the time when I gather you. For I will make you renowned and praised among all the peoples of the earth, when I turn again your captivity before your eyes, says Jehovah (Zeph. 8: 18-20).

During their exile, Israel had been unable to make the annual pilgrimages to Jerusalem for the set feasts (i.e. all of them and not merely the feast of tabernacles), and sorrow had filled their hearts. Their mourning over their banishment and consequent separation from these religious observances and the shame they felt were a burden to be borne. Zephaniah now promised that Jehovah would gather them back to their own land and dismiss their shame. Moreover, He would then deal with their oppressors: those who had maltreated them would suffer for their actions.

The lame and the dispersed would be regathered. The prophet echoes the promises made through his predecessors. God fully intends to restore Israel to her own land and will bring them back from the four corners of the earth. When that has been accomplished, Jehovah "will make them a praise and a name in every land where they" suffered shame at the hands of their oppressors. Kleinert (*ibid.*, p. 34) says that "praise and name" is a "hendiadys for a celebrated name, which is praised, so that the original promise (Gen. 12) is fulfilled, and all nations long to be invested with the citizenship of the new community (Psa. 87; c.f. also Zech. 8: 23; Isa. 4: 1)."

The promise of regathering and of the gift of a celebrated

69

name was repeated in the closing verse of the prophecy and Jehovah declared that their restoration would be undertaken before their own eyes. This restoration was promised by law and prophet long before (Deut. 30: 3-5; Isa. 11: 11, 12; Jer. 23: 3-8; Ezek. 37: 21-25). His words implied the exaltation of Israel above the nations of the earth. The promises to the fathers must inevitably be fulfilled. Sir George Adam Smith (*ibid.*, p. 49) does less than justice to Zephaniah when he says that, in the book, "there is no prospect of a redeemed and faithful land, but only of a group of battered and hardly saved characters; a few meek and righteous are hidden from the fire and creep forth when it is over. Israel is left a poor and humble folk. No prophet is more true to the doctrine of the remnant, or more resolutely refuses to modify it." Zephaniah's prophecy, however, concludes with Jehovah's regathering of His people and His exaltation of them above all others, their name renowned and other nations prepared to acknowledge them. All this is to be fulfilled in a coming day.

APPENDIX

The Moabite Stone

A BLOCK of black basalt, 3′ 10″ high and 2′ wide, and allegedly dating back to the 9th or 10th century B.C., was found in Moab in 1868 by a German missionary named F. Klein. Both the Germans and the French endeavoured to purchase it but, on the intervention of Turkish officials, the Arab owners broke it in pieces in the hope of securing a higher price. The pieces were eventually acquired in 1873 for the Louvre. It is the only writing of any length surviving from Moab. Some of the wording of the stele is not entirely complete, but it is clear that it was made by Mesha, king of Moab, and supplements the account of 1 Kings 16: 23-28 and 2 Kings 3: 4-27. It is also clear that Chemosh was the national god of the Moabites.

The account runs as follows:

"I Mesha, son of Chemosh-Melech, king of Moab, the Dibonite. My father reigned over Moab thirty years, and I reigned after my father; and I made this monument to Chemosh in Khorkah, a monument of deliverance, because he saved me from all invaders and because he let me look upon all who hate me. Omri was king of Israel; and he afflicted Moab many days, for Chemosh was angry with his land. And his son succeeded him, and he also said, I will afflict Moab. In my days Chemosh said I will see my desire upon him and upon his house, and Israel perished with an everlasting destruction. And Omri took possession of the land of Medeba and Israel dwelt in it, in his days and in the days of his son,

71

altogether forty years. But Chemosh dwelt in it in my days. And I built Baal-Meon and I made ditches in it and I built Kiriathaim. And the men of God dwelt in the land of Ataroth from time immemorial, and the king of Israel built for him Ataroth. And I warred against the city; and I took it and I slew all the mighty men of the city, for the well-pleasing of Chemosh and Moab; I captured there the Arel of Doda and dragged him before Chemosh in Kerioth; and I made to dwell in it the men of Siran, and the men of Macharath. And Chemosh said to me, Go, take Nebo from Israel. And I went by night and I fought against it from the break of dawn till noon, and I took it, and I slew all, seven thousand men, boys, women, girls and maid-servants; for I had devoted them to destruction for Ashtar Chemosh. And I took from thence the vessels of Jehovah and I dragged them before Chemosh. And the king of Israel built Jahaz and dwelt in it, while he warred with me. And Chemosh drove him out before me and I took from Moab 200 men, all chiefs, and I took them against Jahaz and took it to add to Dibon. I built Khorkah, the wall of the forests and the wall of the citadel; I built the gates thereof, and I built the king's house, and I made prisons for the guilty in the midst of the city. And there was no cistern within the city, in Khorkah, and I said to all the people, Make for yourselves every man a cistern in his house. And I dug the canals for Khorkah by means of the prisoners of Israel. I built Arnon and I made the high road in the province of the Arnon. I built Beth-Barmoth, for it was destroyed. I built Bergen, for it was in ruins. And all the chiefs of Dibon were fifty; for all Dibon was subject, and I placed a hundred chiefs in the towns which I added to the land. And I built Beth-Medeba and Beth-Diblelathain and Beth-Bad-Meon, and I transported thereto the shepherds and the pastors of the flocks of the land. And at Horonain there dwelt . . . . And Chemosh said to me, Go, fight against Honorain and I went and fought against it. And Chemosh dwelt in it during my days. I went up from thence . . . . And I . . . ."

PROPHET OF
THE RESTORATION

An exposition of the Prophecy of Haggai

By

FREDK. A. TATFORD

Originally published by
Prophetic Witness Publishing House
Sussex, 1972

ISBN: 0-86524-135-X

Printed by Klock & Klock in the U.S.A.
1982 Reprint

CONTENTS

PREFACE

THE Minor Prophets were so named because their writings were so much smaller in bulk than the Major Prophets of Isaiah, Jeremiah and Ezekiel. In the Hebrew Bible, they were bound together as the Book of the Twelve; according to a rabbinical tradition quoted by Kimchi, this was "lest one or other of them should be lost on account of its size, if they were all kept separate". The writings were penned over a period ranging from the 9th to the 5th centuries B.C. Keil declares that, when taken "with the writings of the greater prophets, they comprehend all the essentials of that prophetic word, through which the Lord equipped His people for the coming times of conflict with the nations of the world, endowing them thus with the light and power of His Spirit, and causing His servants to foretell, as a warning to the ungodly, the destruction of the two sinful kingdoms, and the dispersion of the rebellious people among the heathen and, as a consolation to believers, the deliverance and preservation of a holy seed, and the eventual triumph of His kingdom over every hostile power".

These prophets lived at a critical period of history and their messages naturally had a particular pertinence to that period. But there can be no question that the messages uttered so many centuries ago have also a special significance for our twentieth century. This is more evident in the case of some of them than of others. It is worth considering current conditions in the light of the end times of which most of the Old Testament prophets spoke.

The problems of today are of greater magnitude and more difficult of solution than those of any previous period. One which is constantly on the lips today is the population explosion. By 2000 A.D. the population of the world will be 7,000 million, but in another 50 years it will be 30,000 million. China, with a population of 800 million, is increasing by a million a month. In 1850, four cities in the world had a population of a million; a century later the figure had risen to

141; by 1980 it will be over 300. The greatest increases are in the poorer and undeveloped countries, and a resentment is building up against countries like America which are better off.

A second major problem is the ecological one. Air, land and water are being polluted as never before in history. Rivers and seas are being poisoned by household and industrial waste: in consequence, fish, and the marine plant life on which they feed, are being destroyed. A valuable food supply is thereby being reduced.

Problems of this kind (and these are but two of many) are serious and, in some respects, frightening. But they are only symptomatic of a more basic malaise. *The world is in revolt.* This is true in every sphere.

We live in a permissive society. From pulpit and press, we are told that what matters is not what we do, but the motive that prompts it. Joseph Fletcher, in *Situation Ethics*, blesses all our actions, provided they hurt no one else. Infidelity is no longer scandalous, but commonplace. In Sweden, 10 per cent of children born are illegitimate. In America, the figure is 300,000 a year and a million abortions. In the U.K. 20 per cent of brides are no longer virgins at the date of marriage. Pornography has reached an all-time low. Biblical standards and moral conventions have gone. *The world is in revolt.*

In the biological realm, the first step in the revolt against accepted conventions was taken in artificial insemination. An unknown donor can father dozens of children by women he has never seen. By 1980 it will be possible to determine the sex of an unborn child. But by 1985 it will be possible for a woman to purchase a tiny frozen embryo, choosing the sex, colour of hair and eyes, and probable I.Q. If she does not want it implanted in her own body, she will be able to raise it in an artificial uterus.

Scientists now know a good deal about the basic building blocks of life—the D.N.A. molecules—and are beginning to crack the code for building them. In 1968 there was assembled the first totally synthetic gene: the way is opening now for the manipulation of human biology. We will soon be able to

8

plan the type of men we need, and it is estimated that by the end of the century we will be in complete control of human genetics. Given the nucleus of an adult cell, it will be possible to produce a new organism with the same genetic characteristics as the donor. Dr. W. H. Thorp of Cambridge has well said, "The ethical problems . . . raised by genetics and neurophysiology . . . are at least as great as those arising from atomic energy and the H bomb".

Physiologists suggest that there should be a greater control of the cerebral functions of men and foresee the monitoring of the mind by electrical stimulation of the brain and by the planting of electrodes in the brain to secure the desired response or behaviour. *A revolt is taking place* almost unnoticed.

There is a widespread revolt by young people against discipline and authority. The incompetence of the older generation and the mess they have made of the world has cost the respect of youth, and the latter discount completely the standards and conventions, the advice and authority of their elders. The problem is accentuated by the rapid increase in knowledge. The flow is too great for many young people and they either become rebels or drop-outs. *Youth is in revolt.*

Another alarming field of revolt is that of racialism. What happened in the Congo is likely to happen elsewhere. Any repression inevitably produces a reaction. In the U.S.A. the coloured people no longer want equality, but power. Two-thirds of the population of Washington, the capital, is coloured. The blacks are overwhelmingly outnumbered in the country as a whole, but already thinking people are visualising the possibility of civil war within ten years. The apartheid policy of other countries can only result ultimately in an explosion. *A revolt is afoot.*

On a scale unequalled in history, people have turned from Christianity to the occult. Astrology is taking a serious hold in Britain, but there are other features. There are now 30,000 practising witches in the U.K. and half a million people who are interested in black magic. The widespread use of ouija boards by young children is bringing youthful minds under the control of unseen forces, and the effect upon the nervous and emotional system is serious.

Spiritism is spreading alarmingly and, with it, the actual worship of Satan. The church of Satan in San Francisco has adherents in Britain and many other countries. We are unleashing forces of evil which we will never be able to control. *Men are in revolt* against Biblical prohibitions and conventions.

There is a revolt in the professing church against the authority of God and the Scriptures. Theologians evacuate the Bible of the miraculous. New versions eliminate the prophecies of Christ. We are told that certain statements are unreliable and were only the opinion of the writers. The deity of Christ, His virgin birth, His atonement, His second advent are denied from pulpit and platform.

Canon Montefiore publicly stated that Christ was probably a homosexual. Instead of criticism or discipline, he was made a bishop. Another minister declared that our Lord was the illegitimate son of a soldier: but no one seems concerned. At the National Assembly of the Baptist Union in 1971 the Principal of the Northern Baptist College said, "God was active in Jesus, but it will not quite do to say categorically that Jesus was God". When his lecture was reviewed subsequently, the Baptist Union Council refused to repudiate the statement and left him to continue training young men for the ministry. In another circle we are told plainly in one publication that, if Jesus was ignorant of one thing, He may have been ignorant of others. The rot in the church is spreading. *There is a revolt*, which is gaining ground.

Alvin Toffler says in *Future Shock*, "It has become a cliché to say that what we are now living through is a second industrial revolution". It is, of course, something far greater, and he rightly says that it "represents nothing less than the second great divide in human history, comparable in magnitude to the 'shift from barbarism to civilisation'". The boundaries of knowledge have burst in our lifetime. C. P. Snow justifiably declares that, until this century, change was so slow that it passed almost unnoticed, but now "the rate of change has increased so much that our imagination cannot keep up".

We are in the midst of a scientific and technological revolution. Ninety per cent of the world's leading scientists of all time are alive today. In 1825 the first steam locomotive travelled at the frightening speed of 13 miles an hour! Men now orbit the earth at 20,000 miles an hour. Four centuries ago we knew eleven chemical elements. We now know ten times as many. Four centuries ago Europe produced 1,000 new books a year. She now produces 1,000 a day. Science is moving a hundred times faster than a century ago. Events speed past us. Ideas come and go at a fantastic rate. Life is made up of countless experiences. We have to decide upon our rôle when the experiences confront us—to determine how to act or what to say. But now the experiences rush upon us so quickly that the entire structure of life is complicated. We cannot adapt ourselves quickly enough, we cannot reach decisions in time, and consequently we either become quite ineffectual or else we opt out and let the events pass us by. If the changes are too fundamental, we cannot cope and we either panic or refuse to recognise them. Values alter with change, and the strain of seeking to adjust may lead to neurosis. Stability goes and some people take to drugs, magic, spiritism or immorality.

A young man finds that in 20 years the amount of knowledge he must acquire is four times that at the date of his birth. But when he reaches 50, the amount is 32 times as much. Dr. Ralph Lapp says, "No one . . . not even the most brilliant scientist today, really knows where science is taking us. We are aboard a train which is gathering speed, racing down a track, on which there are an unknown number of switches, leading to unknown destinations". *The revolution is out of control.*

This is a gloomy picture of an exciting period in human history, but it is a true one, even if it has been only faintly and sketchily drawn. Clearly we are reaching a crisis in world affairs—not merely in economics and international relations, but in every field. On every side it is being said that it is now imperative for a strong hand to take control. The need is vital and today it is urgent.

Whenever in history a man of a certain character or with certain abilities has been needed, the circumstances have thrust up the type of man who was needed. The Bible indicates that one day a superman will arise, who will demonstrate his power to control, and that the nations of the world will willingly accept and bestow their authority upon him. Yet it reveals that the revolt of today will be concentrated in the same person and, far from saving the world, he will send it crashing to its doom.

But the Bible also discloses that the God against whom men are in revolt is still behind the scenes and that ultimately He will once more break into human affairs and establish His authority upon earth through the Man whom he has appointed, His Son, Jesus Christ. Patently that time cannot long be postponed, but before it occurs, the New Testament tells us that the Saviour will break through the sky to summon His people to meet Him in the air. That event must obviously be close. To that, the Old Testament prophets make no reference. Their allusions are solely to the period of judgment which must ensue thereafter and to the establishment of the long-awaited theocratic kingdom upon earth, but what they have to say in relation to events which are to follow the removal of the church from this scene, is necessarily of extreme interest to the one who is observing the times. And the counsel they give for the last days is of great significance to those who are living on the verge of that period. Hence the value of studying these books.

FREDK. A. TATFORD.

CHAPTER 1

THE EXILES' RETURN

IN fulfilment of the warning given to Hezekiah long before (Isa. 39: 6, 7) and in consequence of the sin of the people of Judah, the forces of Nebuchadnezzar swept the land, deporting most of the people to Babylonia, burning the temple and spoiling it of its treasures (2 Kings 24, 25). Repeated admonitions had been ignored and the blow eventually fell. Judah's rebellion against Jehovah was to be punished by a servitude of seventy years (Jer. 25:11). But the period had now expired and the hand of God had fallen upon Babylon, precisely as the prophet had foretold. The Persians had first annexed the kingdom of the Medes and had then proceeded to conquer Babylon.

One of the first actions of the Persian ruler, Cyrus, after the capture of Babylon, was, as predicted by Isaiah (Isa. 44:28), to issue a decree, authorising the exiled Jews to return to their own land and to rebuild the temple. The vessels stolen by Nebuchadnezzar were restored and funds were provided to assist in the rehabilitation of the building (2 Chron. 36:22, 23; Ezra 1:1-4, 7; 3:7). While Cyrus's own monotheism would naturally dispose him to look favourably upon the Jews, other exiles were, at the same time, permitted to return to their homelands with their gods. Not all the Jewish exiles took advantage of the provisions of the edict: only a proportion of the priests and Levites returned and 42,360 men (probably the equivalent of 200,000 men, women and children) and 7,337 slaves formed the caravan of 536 B.C. Stanley vividly describes the return in his *Jewish Church*, "when the day at last arrived, which was to see their expectations fulfilled, the burst of joy was such as has no parallel in the sacred volume: it is indeed the Revival, the Second Birth, the Second Exodus of the nation. There was now 'a new song', of which the burden was that the Eternal again reigned over the earth, and that the gigantic idolatries which surrounded them had received a deadly shock: that the waters of oppression had rolled back, in which they had been struggling like drowning men: that the snare was broken, in which they had been entangled like a caged bird. It was like a dream, too good to be true".

They had a journey of nearly four months before them, but, in the joy of the Lord, they evidently regarded it as nothing. Danger and difficulty were of no account: they were going home. The desert which they had to cross, Stanley describes as "a hard gravel plain, from the moment they left the banks of the Euphrates till they reached the northern extremity of Syria; with no solace except the occasional wells and walled stations: or, if their passage was in the spring, the natural herbage and flowers which clothed the arid soil. Ferocious hordes of Bedouin robbers then, as now, swept the whole tract." They returned home and, after having made a tour of their desolate cities, they assembled once more at Jerusalem to commence the rebuilding of the temple. It was disfigured by fire and was little more than a mass of blackened stones and débris—a complete ruin.

On the first day of the seventh month, they cleared away sufficient of the rubble to leave a space in the court in front of the former building, and here they erected the altar upon its bases (Ezra, 3:3). It is recorded that they celebrated the feast of tabernacles, a seven-day festival which commenced on the fifteenth day of the seventh month, so that presumably they also observed the feast of trumpets, which was celebrated on the first day of that month (Lev. 23:23–25). If so, it coincided in this instance with the setting up of the altar.

14

The feast of trumpets marked the commencement of the civil year and was a day of rest. Whilst the *shofar* or ram's horn is blown today, the silver trumpets of the temple were originally used, although they may not, of course, have been available on this particular occasion. The blast of the shofar is said to recall "the promise of redemption, the time when the prophet Elijah will appear to announce the arrival of the Messiah, and from the top of the mountains will sound the mighty shofar of freedom and equality of mankind". This interpretation, while significant, has no apparent Biblical basis. The Jews, in general, regarded the sound of the trumpet on this day as a summons to assemble to God in a spirit of penitence and self-analysis. Lange declares that it was "a feast of joyous sounds to awaken a national festal disposition by means of a festival blowing".

It was appropriate that the altar should have been set up on this day, for specified sacrifices—burnt, meal and sin offerings (Num. 29:1-5)—were to be presented to God on the altar on that day. The temple might be a ruin, but the altar now stood in front of the house for sacrifices to be presented and prayer to be offered.

The building of an altar may at first appear a strange way to start rebuilding a temple, but a second's thought will show how logical it was. There was no basis for the temple and no ground for the temple worship until the altar had first been erected. It was virtually the centre of the Jews' religious system. Approach to God could only be by way of the altar and its sacrifice. The altar was a confession of human need and an acknowledgment of the need for appeasement of and reconciliation to Jehovah. The sacrifices offered on the altar were an implicit recognition of the need for atonement by blood—by the death of another. The erection of the altar was an essential prerequisite to the building of the temple.

The application to the Christian is obvious. There can be no acceptable service for God until first the altar has been built; in other words, until the individual has first been in

15

spirit to Calvary and viewed the supreme sacrifice there and experienced practically the efficacy of that atoning blood. The unbeliever has no part in the service of God: it is only the blood-washed believer who can engage in that ministry. Even after conversion, there must still be the altar before there can be acceptable service for Christ. As the apostle Paul so plainly indicates, there must be the presentation of the body to God as a living sacrifice—symbolically a whole burnt offering (Rom. 12:1). Only in that complete self-immolation is to be found the surrendered and submissive life which God can use.

Again, in every act of service, it is essential to commence at the altar. Before the evangelist goes forth to preach the gospel, before the pastor sets out to visit the sick, before the shepherd goes to seek the erring one, in fact before any act of service is commenced, it is vital first to get a fresh glimpse of Calvary and to appreciate once again the wealth of love, mercy and compassion demonstrated there. Then, with the heart stirred in responsive love to the Saviour, it is possible to go forth to engage in work for Him.

Immediately after the erection of the altar, the people entered into negotiations with the Zidonians and Tyrians for the supply of timber for the reconstruction of the temple and, seven months later they laid the foundation of the temple (Ezra, 3:7, 10). Led by the priests and Levites, with the accompaniment of trumpets and cymbals, the people burst forth into songs of joy and thanksgiving. Their rejoicing was nevertheless not completely unalloyed, for the sound of loud lamentations and unrestrained weeping mingled with it to such an extent that the inspired record declares that it was impossible to distinguish "the noise of the shout of joy from the noise of the weeping" (Ezra 3:12, 13). Tears were not flowing for sheer happiness, nor in contrition for the sins of the past and the apostasy which had caused the destruction of the first temple. They were the expression of the grief of the old men, who remembered the glory and splendour of the earlier temple, and who were mortified at the conditions in which

16

they now found themselves. They were not concerned with the fact that Jehovah was greater than the temple: they looked only at the outward appearance and felt humiliated by the absence of the externals in which they had previously taken pride.

There are not lacking in our own day those who selfishly dampen the ardour and enthusiasm of the more zealous by their constant harping on the lost glory of the past and the tragic imperfections of the present. We do well to be concerned at the moral declension so plainly evidenced on every side, but this is a challenge to be up and doing, rather than to indulge in lachrymose lamentation. Zeal and enthusiasm may as easily be dissipated today as in that earlier era by the foolishness of misplaced grief. The Master is still supreme and His work goes on.

It was not long before other problems presented themselves. When the ten tribes of the northern kingdom of Israel had been deported by the Assyrians, Esarhaddon had repopulated the deserted cities with conquered peoples of other nations, and these Samaritans had adopted an adulterated form of worship of the true God (2 Kings 17:24–33). Seeing the progress made by the Jews, the Samaritans sent a deputaton to Zerubbabel, offering assistance in the work, on the ground that they worshipped the same God and sacrificed to Him. The Jews, however, disclaimed any affinity with them and peremptorily rejected their offer of help (Ezra 4:1–3). These men were "aliens from the commonwealth of Israel and strangers from the covenants of promise" (Eph. 2:12): how could they have fellowship in the work of God? Moreover, they had had no part in the building of the altar and had no experience of redemption. Only those, who had participated in the sacrifice and knew something of the significance of the shed blood, could engage in the work. The same principle applies today: only God's people may engage in His service. The unbeliever is frequently ready to offer his help by gift or practical assistance, but this work is reserved for those who have appreciated the value of Calvary's blood.

17

The rejection of their overtures converted the Samaritans into the bitterest of adversaries, and they did their utmost to hinder the work. In addition to the withholding of supplies and to active local obstruction, they hired counsellors to lodge accusations and misrepresentations with the Persian monarch, and eventually Cyrus's successor, Cambyses (the Ahasuerus of Ezra 4:6), apparently ordered a suspension of the building operations. Their intrigues finally proved completely successful for, on the ascension of Pseudo-Smerdis (the Artaxerxes of Ezra 4: 7–23) to the throne, they secured from the usurper an edict specifically prohibiting the prosecution of the work.

Faced with the royal decree, the Jews were compelled to decide between continuing in faith upon God or obedience to the prohibition of the earthly ruler. With broken spirits they took the latter course. But it is pertinent that the rescript of Artaxerxes was not issued until 13 to 14 years after the laying of the foundation of the temple—a plain indication of their lethargy and lack of enthusiasm, for in that time the building could have been far more advanced than it evidently was. Their early ardour and zeal were dead, and for fifteen years the work lay neglected. The lukewarmness and indifference, which had patently characterised their attitude, may have been due to other causes than the local difficulties and opposition. As Keil remarks (*The Twelve Minor Prophets*, p. 171), "there were no doubt a considerable number of men among those who had returned, who had been actuated to return less by living faith in the Lord and His Word, than by earthly hopes of prosperity and comfort in the land of their fathers. As soon as they found themselves disappointed in their expectations, they became idle and indifferent with regard to the house of the Lord."

Artaxerxes was succeeded by Darius Hystaspes after a year. The former's decree ceased to be effective at his death, but the Jews apparently made no effort to get it rescinded or to recommence the work, until the prophet Haggai arose to stir them to action. Their own interests had taken priority and it was not until the voice of God was heard through His messenger that they became conscious of their failure and neglect.

NOTE A

THE TEMPLE

1. *Solomon's Temple.* When David was settled on his throne, he conceived the desire of building a permanent dwelling-place for God in place of the temporary abode of the tabernacle. It was revealed to him, however, that this work was reserved for his son, Solomon, and David consequently devoted himself to amassing vast quantities of materials for the purpose. In the fourth year of Solomon's reign, the work was commenced and it took $7\frac{1}{2}$ years to complete. The building was erected on Mount Moriah, on the site of the threshing-floor of Araunah the Jebusite, and it proved to be a magnificent temple (2 Chron. 2 to 5). Because of the sin of the people of Judah, however, they were delivered into the hands of the Babylonians in 586 B.C. The temple was plundered and partially destroyed, its treasures being carried away to Babylon (2 Kings 24 and 25).

2. *Zerubbabel's Temple.* The decree of Cyrus permitted the exiled Jews to return to their own land and authorised the rebuilding of the temple, the temple vessels removed by Nebuchadnezzar's forces being restored (Ezra 1:1–4). It is with the construction of this temple that Haggai was concerned. Although it was started in 538 B.C., it was not until 515 B.C. that it was completed. This second temple was naturally inferior in riches and splendour to the original one of Solomon's day, and no ark of the covenant occupied the inner shrine and no shekinah glory was seen there.

20

3. *Herod's Temple.* The Idumean king, Herod the **Great,** decided to built a more magnificent structure, partly in the hope of attracting the loyalty of the Jews to himself. This third temple took a total of 46 years to build and, according to Josephus, it was a dazzling sight (see also Matt. 24:1, 2). But it was completely destroyed by the Roman army in 70 A.D., precisely as our Lord had predicted, not a stone being left standing on another.

4. *Spiritual Temple.* There is, of course, no temple in Jerusalem today, and the site of the earlier ones is occupied by the Dome of the Rock, or the Mosque of Omar. In its place, this era knows only the spiritual temple of the church, built for a habitation of God through the Spirit (Eph. 2:21, 22). That temple will, of course, be removed at the coming of Christ for His church.

5. *Antichrist's Temple.* The New Testament makes it clear that a fourth physical temple will one day be erected in Jerusalem. Our Lord, for example, referred to the abomination of desolation standing there in a future day (Matt. 24:15), and the apostle Paul indicated that "the man of sin" would sit in that temple, claiming to be worshipped as divine (2 Thess. 2:4). Presumably this temple will be destroyed at the Second Advent of Christ to earth, but no details of its destruction are given in the Scriptures.

6. *Millennial Temple.* Ezekiel discloses that, in the millennium, there will be a fifth physical temple, which will be the centre of worship for Israel and all the Gentile nations, and into which the God of Israel will enter (Ezek. 44:2). The glory of God, which occupied Solomon's temple, will reappear in that day and will fill the millennial temple with its wonder.

CHAPTER 2

THE PRINCIPAL CHARACTERS

THE exiles had been led from Babylon to Jerusalem by the high priest, Joshua, and by Zerubbabel, who became their civil governor. Joshua (Jeshua in Ezra 2:2) is described as the son of Josedech (Jehozadak in 1 Chron. 6:15), who was one of the deportees to Babylon. It is commonly thought that Joshua was born in Babylon. His father, to whom the high priesthood pertained, apparently died in exile and Joshua, therefore, became the legitimate successor to the office of high priest (see *Prophet of the Myrtle Grove*, p. 39). He is referred to in the Prophecy of Haggai, not merely as the high priest, but as McCurdy (*Haggai*, p. 9) points out, "also, to a certain extent, as ruling the people jointly with the civil governor. Such authority was gradually more and more assumed by the high priests after the dissolution of the kingdom until the tendency culminated in the Maccabean princes, who formally united the two functions in one person."

Zerubbabel, who is also described in Ezra as Sheshbazzar, was referred to in the first verse of Haggai as the son of Shealtiel, but the chronicler referred to him as the son of Pedaiah, who was a brother of Shealtiel (1 Chron. 3:18, 19). The New Testament record adds a further complication in describing him as the son of Salathiel (i.e. Shealtiel) and the grandson of Neri (Luke 3:27). The explanation furnished by Keil (*ibid.*, pp. 175–6) is worth quoting *in extenso*. He says that the various accounts can be reconciled "if we bear in mind

23

the prophecy of Jeremiah (Jer. 22:30) that Jeconiah would be childless, and not be blessed with having one of his seed sitting upon the throne of David and ruling over Judah. Since this prophecy of Jeremiah was fulfilled, according to the genealogical table given by Luke, inasmuch as Shealtiel's father there is not Assir or Jeconiah, a descendant of David in the line of Solomon, but Neri, a descendant of David's son Nathan, it follows that neither of the sons of Jeconiah mentioned in 1 Chron. 3:17, 18 (Zedekiah and Assir) had a son, but that the latter had only a daughter, who married a man of the family of her father's tribe, according to the law of the heiresses (Num. 27:8; 36:8, 9), namely Neri, who belonged to the tribe of Judah and the family of David. From this marriage sprang Shealtiel, Malkiram, Pedaiah, and others. The eldest of these took possession of the property of his maternal grandfather, and was regarded in law as his (legitimate) son. Hence he is described in 1 Chron. 3:17 as the son of Assir, the son of Jeconiah, whereas in Luke he is described, according to his lineal descent, as the son of Neri. But Shealtiel also appears to have died without posterity, and simply to have left a widow, which necessitated a Levirate marriage on the part of one of the brothers (Deut. 25:5–10; Matt. 22: 24–28), Shealtiel's second brother, Pedaiah, appears to have performed his duty, and to have begotten Zerubbabel and Shimei by this sister-in-law (1 Chron. 3:19), the former of whom, Zerubbabel, was entered in the family register of the deceased under Shealtiel, passing as his (lawful) son and heir, and continuing his family." Zerubbabel's alternative name of Sheshbazzar was a Chaldean cognomen and implies that he held an appointment under the Persian king. Indeed, he was appointed *pechah* or Persian governor over Judah.

It was to these two men, Joshua and Zerubbabel, that Haggai's first words were addressed.

Of Haggai himself, we know extremely little. His name means "festive" and is sometimes thought to have been merely a pseudonym. No information is given of his genealogy or of the tribe to which he belonged. Tradition declares

24

that he was born in Babylon during the exile, but the more general view is that he was among those carried away captive by Nebuchadnezzar and was one of the few survivors who returned to the land. In support of this, Ewald argues from Hag. 2:3 that the prophet must have seen the first temple over 70 years earlier, but there is no support for this theory. He is said to have been a member of the Great Synagogue and an eminent scholar, who took part in the settling of the canon of the Old Testament. Ezra 3:2 to 6:22 (except 4:6–23 and 6:14) are said to have been written by him and edited later by Ezra. The authorship of certain of the Psalms is also attributed to him. Epiphanius states that he was buried at Jerusalem among the priests.

The prophet's style has been criticised as tame and prosaic. "The mantle of prophecy had fallen upon him, it is said, from the earlier prophets", writes Perowne (*Haggai and Zechariah*, p. 20), "but it had fallen upon him in 'shreds and tatters'." Although his style is certainly simple and severe, the criticism is hardly justified when one sees the effect of his brief messages upon his people. They were galvanised into activity by what he said in the power of the Holy Spirit.

The Hebrew prophet was not, of course, merely a predicter of future events. Haggai certainly did foretell what still lay (and yet lies) in the future, but his primary purpose was to awaken the people from their spiritual torpor, to convict them of their failure and to stir them to action.

No question arises regarding the date of his book, for he repeatedly dates his utterances in a way that leaves no room for dubiety. It was the custom for Jewish writers to date their messages from the reigns of their own kings. They had now no sovereign of their own, and the prophecy accordingly used the chronological notation of the Medo-Persian power. At the same time the months quoted were those of the Jewish calendar.

The canonicity of Haggai has never been in doubt. Here were messages from the Eternal and the book was accepted into the Old Testament canon as a part of "The Book of the Twelve".

Haggai's book is extremely brief and may be analysed as follows:

1. Superscription. 1:1.
2. Remonstrance with the people for their neglect of the temple. 1:2–11.
3. Result of the appeal. 1:12–15.
4. Future glory of the temple. 2:1–9.
5. Uncleanness and rejected sacrifices. 2:10–19.
6. Ultimate convulsion of the universe. 2:20–23.

Although the people had accepted the prohibition imposed by Artaxerxes, troubles and distress still came upon them. When eventually, Haggai and Zechariah succeeded in arousing them, as recorded in the prophecy, fresh opposition faced them. Haggai does not refer to this, but according to Ezra 5, their actions were queried by Tatnai, the satrap of Syria, and other officials to whose authority they were subject. The Jews quoted the decree of Cyrus in their defence and Tatnai submitted the matter to the Persian ruler, Darius Hystaspes. No trace could be found of Cyrus's decree at Babylon, but it was discovered, after careful search, at Achmetha (Ecbatana) in Media. There could be no question regarding its terms or of the illegality of Artaxerxes' rescript, and Darius accordingly authorised the rebuilding of the temple and the provision of materials for the sacrifices (Ezra 6:1–10).

From this point in time the work went forward until it was completed. Within five years the temple had been finished and was rededicated with rejoicing. The priests and Levites resumed their ministry. True, there was no ark of the covenant and no golden mercy seat in the holy of holies of this building, but it was still God's house and provided a way of access to Him.

NOTE B

CHRONOLOGY

The Jewish year was originally a lunisolar one, alternate months consisting of 29 days and 30 days. The year was consequently eleven days short of the true solar year. Periodically, therefore, a thirteenth month, called Ve-Adar, was intercalated to rectify this. The necessity became apparent because the year was linked with the seasons and it was evident when the time for adjustment had arrived.

The following chronological table is borrowed from *The Cambridge Bible for Schools and Colleges* and may give a fairly clear idea of the relevant dates.

B.C.

536   The proclamation of Cyrus for the return of the captives.

        7th month (October). The altar built. Sacrifices resumed. The feast of tabernacles kept.

535   2nd month. Foundation of the temple laid.

535–520 Rebuilding of the temple stopped through the intrigues of the Samaritans.

520   The work resumed through the prophecies of Haggai and Zechariah and the subsequent decree of Darius.

        (September) Haggai's first prophecy, ch. 1 : 1–11.

(October) Haggai's second prophecy, ch. 2:1–9.
(November) Zechariah's first prophecy, ch. 1:1–6.
(December) Haggai's third and fourth prophecies, ch. 2:10–19; 20–23.

519   (January) Zechariah's second prophecy, ch. 1:7–6:15.

518   (November) Zechariah's third prophecy, ch. 7:1–8:23.

515   (March) The temple completed.

CHAPTER 3

JUDAH'S NEGLECT

FOR fifteen years the house of God lay desolate. If the people paid homage to Him at all, it must have been amidst the rubbish and ruins among which the altar stood facing the temple. Whether or not they continued to offer their sacrifices is not indicated. They had, in any case, turned away from the work of God to follow their own selfish pursuits. Discouraged and apathetic, they seemed to have lost their interest in spiritual things. The gross idolatry of pre-exilic days had gone, but its place had been taken by an attitude which, in some respects, was more grieving to the Almighty.

One of the biggest tragedies of the present day is the Christian who has become "weary of well-doing". What a heartache there must have been behind the words of the apostle Paul to the Galatians, "You did run well; who did hinder you?" (Gal. 5:7). This spiritual torpescence was the characteristic of the Jews of Haggai's day, and the whole ministry of the prophet was directed against this growing evil of inertia. His public ministry lasted for less than four months and comprised but five short utterances, but the dynamic power of those brief messages stirred the people to the depths of their being and utterly revolutionised the national conditions and outlook.

29

SUPERSCRIPTION

In the second year of Darius the king, in the sixth month, on the first day of the month, the word of Jehovah came by Haggai the prophet to Zerubbabel the son of Shealtiel, governor of Judah, and to Joshua the son of Josedech, the high priest (1:1).

Although Haggai dated his message by reference to the Medo-Persian ruler instead of by reference to a Jewish king, since the latter no longer existed, he still used the month of the Jewish calendar instead of the month of the king's reign. It was the sixth month, i.e. Elul, which overlaps August and September. The prophet claimed that the message of Jehovah came by him on the first day of the month. This was, of course, the day of the new moon, when special offerings were presented and religious meetings were held (Num. 28:11-15). "On this day," says one writer, "Haggai might expect some susceptibility on the part of the people for his admonition." He declared that the word of Jehovah came, not *to* him, but *by* (or through) him. In other words, he was only the medium or instrument to convey the Divine message to those to whom it was sent.

The message was sent to the civil governor and the religious leader, clearly emphasising their responsibility for the conditions existing.

THE FALSE EXCUSE

Thus says Jehovah of hosts, This people say the time has not come, the time that Jehovah's house should be built (1:2).

The title of God employed by the prophet was Jehovah Sabaoth, the Lord of hosts. It is common to the last three prophetic books of the Old Testament—Haggai, Zechariah and Malachi—being used over 80 times in these books. The concept of the hosts of heaven had primary reference to the stars and these were worshipped by many heathen nations. Haggai, by implication, refused to recognise these as deities and inferred that they were the possession of Jehovah: He was the supreme One and universal dominion belonged solely to Him. The origin and significance of the title are lucidly explained by Archdeacon Perowne (*ibid.*, pp. 151, 152). He says, "Its introduction is contemporaneous with the rise of the Jewish monarchy . . . One of the early acts of Saul's reign was the formation of a nucleus of a standing army (1 Sam. 13:2). This was developed and organised by David, who was pre-eminently a warlike king. It was only necessary that this newly developed military idea should be engrafted, as it could not fail to be, upon the theocratic idea which was the ruling principle of the Jewish nation, to suggest and render popular the phrase, 'the Lord of hosts', as an appellation of the God of Israel."

In lieu of "This people say" in verse 2, T. V. Moore renders the clause, "This people! They say . . ." As he remarks (*Haggai and Malachi*, p. 56), "There is something contemptuous in the abrupt expression, 'This people!' It is a most emphatic exordium to the indignant reproof that was about to follow." Whether or not this rendering is accepted, the nation's attitude had been indefensible. Artaxerxes' prohibition had related specifically to the rebuilding of the city and had made no reference to the reconstruction of the temple (Ezra 4:21): the withdrawal from the latter work had, therefore, been without real justification. In any case, the edict ceased to be effective at Artaxerxes' death, yet no attempt had been made to resume the work. And now they pleaded that it was not time to rebuild the temple.

The argument may have been that the work was so great and of such importance that it was beyond the people's present resources and that it ought consequently to wait until greater preparation had been made. A possible rendering of the clause is "It is not time for us to come in, the time to rebuild Jehovah's house". They were occupied in the fields with labour for their own benefit; the crops might suffer and they might be the losers if they came in from the fields to the city and engaged in the heavy and unremunerative work

31

of rebuilding the sanctuary. The true reason for their attitude was their apathetic indifference to the claims of God. The temple was His dwelling-place. Here, as the covenant God, He abode in the midst of His people. The shekinah cloud of glory, which was the symbol of His presence, had filled the earlier temple. The altar might imply a periodical visit by Jehovah to accept the sacrifices offered thereon, but a temple inferred that He permanently dwelt among His people.

Their plea that the time had not yet come was a disingenuous one and merely a cover for what was really culpable procrastination. Wm. Kelly (*Lectures Introductory to the Minor Prophets*, p. 389) says, "As long as they looked to Jehovah, they found blessing and security; but directly Jehovah ceased to fill their eyes, then not merely the adversaries were seen, but plausible reasons for settling themselves down began to be felt. The altar was an admirable testimony to their faith . . . They allowed it to be a substitute . . . for the temple." As he points out (p. 391), "It was not unnatural that the Jews should be afraid of their watchful enemies; but they should have looked to Jehovah. Where there is simplicity of confidence in the Lord, it is astonishing how the tables are turned, and the adversaries stand in dread of the feeblest folk who have faith in the living God."

But the same attitude is found today. The young student will maintain that his studies claim first priority and that he is unable to engage in the Lord's service until he has graduated and then found a job. The business man will argue that the stress and strain of business life are such that he is unable to afford time and energy for the Lord's work. One day they will detach themselves from the present obsessions and fulfil their responsibilities to the Master, but the time has not yet come. The paltry pleas are, of course, totally unworthy of the true Christian. The obligations face us *today*; souls are perishing *today*; others are in need of a helping hand *today*. To wave aside the responsibilities and to speak glibly of *tomorrow* does not really justify our sloth and neglect. One day we must give account of life at the judgment seat of

Christ. It will be too late then to plead that the time has not yet come.

THE REMONSTRANCE

Then came the word of Jehovah by Haggai the prophet, Is it time for you, yourselves, to dwell in your panelled houses, while this house lies desolate? (1:3, 4).

The prophet had addressed his initial remarks to Zerubbabel and Joshua, the civil and religious leaders of Judah, who might have been expected to have taken immediate action to arouse the people and to inspire them to recommence the work of God. But nothing had happened: the leaders had been quite unresponsive. The word of Jehovah now came, therefore, to the people themselves.

It was sixteen years since the foundation of the temple had been laid and the people were now arguing that the time for building had not yet come. Jehovah challenged their inconsistency. His house lay desolate under the plea that the time to reconstruct it had not yet arrived. Yet the people found time to build their own luxurious homes. If they had not the resources to build His house, they could still expend their resources upon their own dwellings. Not only that, but the modest stone buildings, with which they might reasonably have been content, were regarded as inadequate. They must have wainscotted walls and ceilings. Stone was available in abundance at low cost; timber was scarce and expensive, but nothing would satisfy them but the best. Their homes must be both comfortable and elegant.

This was more than a supine neglect. They were robbing God of His due. They had neither money or effort to render to Him, but they could devote both to their own ends. "For all look after their own interests, not those of Jesus Christ", wrote the apostle Paul to the Philippians (Phil. 2:21). It is a characteristic of the present day, but the One, who reads the hearts, is aware of the selfish hypocrisy and the callous neglect of His work, and He still asks, "Is it time for you to dwell in your panelled houses, and this house lie desolate?".

33

PAUSE AND CONSIDER

Now, therefore, thus says Jehovah of hosts, Consider your ways. You have sown much and have harvested little; you eat but you have not enough; you drink but you are not filled with drink; you clothe yourselves but no one is warm; and he who earns wages earns wages to put it into a bag with holes. Thus says Jehovah of hosts, Consider your ways (1:5-7).

Four times in his book, Haggai uses the injunction, "Consider your ways" (1:5, 7; 2:15, 18). The exhortation is to ponder, earnestly and with all one's heart, one's ways and actions, and the conditions resulting therefrom. J. H. Michaelis suggests that it means to give serious thought "to your designs and actions and their consequences". The prophet's purpose in this instance, however, was to direct their attention to their practical experiences and to induce them to give some thought to the causes thereof. As Moore says (*ibid.*, p. 66), "The events of life are the hieroglyphics in which God records His feelings for us".

Judah had not relieved themselves of troubles and trials by yielding to the command of a usurper like Pseudo-Smerdis or Artaxerxes. Distress and tribulation had multiplied. The opposition of the Samaritans had been replaced by drought and famine and the attendant difficulties. They had fully proved the truth of one writer's words, "No man ever gains anything by trying to cheat God. He makes a fool's bargain, bartering a real good for a perishing bauble, and losing at last even what he has gained."

The Jews had sown plentifully, but the harvest was poor—not for one year but for several years—and the prophet later indicated the reason: the Creator had smitten them with blight, mildew and hail. The causes may have seemed natural ones, but a Divine hand was behind the inflictions. Eating and drinking did not suffice. The cold of the nights demanded warm clothing, but their threadbare garments were inadequate to keep them warm. Their wages were deposited in worn-out money-bags which were incapable of retaining the contents;

34

because of the dearth and scarcity, prices were so high that money drained away. The period of these deprivations coincided with that of their neglect of God's work, yet they had not read the signs of God's providential dealings with them. It is little wonder, therefore, that He repeated the injunction, "Consider your ways". Did they not yet understand?

"God punishes men in both ways," writes Calvin, "both by withdrawing His blessing, so that the earth is parched, and the heaven gives no rain, and also, even when there is a good supply of the fruits of the earth, by preventing their satisfying, so that there is no real enjoyment of them. It often happens that men collect what would be quite a sufficient quantity for food, but for all that, are still always hungry. This kind of curse is seen the more plainly when God deprives the bread and wine of their true virtue, so that eating and drinking fail to support the strength."

It is a salutary thought that neglect of God's work may bring leanness of soul to the believer. Those who are occupied with their own affairs and ambitions may, in their indifference to spiritual realities, lose the true joy of life. Moreover, it is still possible that the Father who loves His children may blight the material possessions in order to win the heart back to Himself. Even in a superficial occupation with the service of Christ, we may find a barrenness which can only be the result of affections directed elsewhere. "I find no satisfaction in my ministry and no joy in my Bible teaching," confided one full-time minister. But the reason was not far to seek. His heart had strayed after the material things of life and he had found the means of (quite legitimately) increasing his income. This had become an obsession and had brought leanness to his soul. Our Lord seeks the undivided allegiance of His own—their full and ready service to Him.

CHAPTER 4

THE WAY BACK

HAGGAI'S short, trenchant message must obviously have made some impression upon his fellow-countrymen, for his second message proceeded to direct their activities. They were not to dwell upon their misfortunes, but to busy themselves once more in the work of God. His words were pertinent in view of the implicit accusation he had earlier levelled against them. They purchased timber at considerable expense for their own dwellings. Now they were to obtain it for God's house.

PROVIDING THE MATERIALS

Go up to the mountain and bring wood and build the house, and I will take pleasure in it and I will be glorified, says Jehovah (1:8).

Cedar from Lebanon had been acquired for the building of Solomon's temple. Materials were now required for the reconstruction of the temple. "Go up to the mountain," came the prophet's incisive message. It is unlikely that the reference was to a particular mountain in the vicinity of Jerusalem: it is more probable that what was indicated was the hill country of the centre of Palestine, where wood was to be found. Indeed this is implied by the Septuagint rendering. Although wood is appropriately mentioned, presumably other materials were sought as well: Ezra 5:8, for example, specifically refers to "great stones and timber".

It was time to act and it is evident from the latter half of the chapter that the prophet's words had their desired effect. In the revival of this remnant of two and a half millennia ago, there is surely a message for the Christian today. The deadening influence of a pusillanimous passivity has crushed the spirit and vitality of the church. The service of God is neglected for the pursuit of the temporal, mundane things of life; personal ambitions and hopes are placed before the Lord's work. The words of the prophet still have their application. Let us leave the earthly puerilities and trifles which obsess us and renew again our work for the God who called us. "Go up to the mountain and bring wood and build the house". Let us rise again into those spiritual realms of communion with God and, drawing from Him the needed supplies and strength, go forth to work and to build for Him.

If the people responded to the exhortation, God declared that He would take pleasure in the building, that is, that He would accept it as an offering (cf. Mal. 1:10, 13, where the word is translated "accept"). Moreover, He would obtain honour or glory to Himself in the work. Not only would the people's efforts bring glory to Him, but He would glorify Himself therein. It is still difficult to appreciate that the Eternal can find pleasure in the service of His creatures and that man should be able by his puny efforts to bring glory to His name.

THE HAND OF GOD

You looked for much, and lo, it came to little; and when you brought it home, I blew on it. Why? says Jehovah of hosts. Because of My house that is desolate, while you run every man to his own house. Therefore the heaven above you withheld the dew, and the earth withheld its fruit. And I called for a drought on the land and on the hills, and on the corn, and on the new wine, and on the oil, and on that which the ground brings forth, and on men, and on cattle, and on all the labour of the hands (1: 9–11).

The prophet now disclosed that the disasters and calamities

experienced by the people were no mere natural coincidences, but were the hand of God laid in discipline upon His people for their neglect of His work. When they had anticipated an excellent harvest, they had been disappointed by its paucity and, when they had gathered it in, Jehovah declared, in vivid figure, that He had blown it away. The implication may be that the offerings presented to Him (including the meal offering) were unacceptable because of the people's disloyalty. "God was no longer maintaining His throne in Israel," says one writer, "but He did not for all that relax His moral government".

He specifically stated that the judgment which had fallen upon them was because of their neglect of His work. Yet, when the temple lay desolate, no one troubled to bestir himself to show any interest in it, although, at the same time, they moved quickly enough where their own houses were concerned.

Barnes points out that the word translated "says" in verse 9 is the special term, *neum*, which is used to introduce a message conceived of as coming directly from God.

"The dews of the Syrian nights are excessive," says Sir George Adam Smith (*Historical Geography of the Holy Land*, p. 65); "on many mornings it looks as if there had been heavy rain, and this is the sole slackening of the drought which the land feels from May to October". The Scriptures frequently refer to the blessing of the dew. But the Creator had withheld the copious dew from their fields and, in consequence, the fields were depicted as withholding their produce. The fertility of the soil depended upon the dew. Its absence was a further indication of the Divine displeasure.

In fact, at His command, the land had suffered drought. Grain, vines, olives and crops had all suffered. Both men and cattle had experienced hardship, and labour had been useless. The Septuagint not irrelevantly substitutes "sword" (*hereb*) for "drought" (*horeb*), on the assumption that the judgments referred to were virtually the wielding of Jehovah's sword. There may also be a play on words in verses 9 and 11. The

39

temple was desolate or waste (*chareb*) because of the people's neglect. Consequently their punishment was a drought (*choreb*).

Jehovah made it clear that He had not abdicated and that He was still concerned with His people's conduct. Moore (*ibid.*, pp. 66, 67) writes, "God has not abandoned the universe to the sightless action of general laws, but is so related to that universe as to be able to direct its laws to the fulfilment of His purposes, whether in rewarding the good, punishing the evil, or answering prayer, without deranging or destroying the normal action of those laws themselves". It is important to realise that the throne is still occupied and that the doings of men are all under the eye of the Omniscient.

AN AROUSED PEOPLE

Then Zerubbabel the son of Shealtiel, and Joshua the son of Josedech, the high priest, with all the remnant of the people, obeyed the voice of Jehovah their God, and the words of Haggai the prophet, as Jehovah their God had sent him; and the people feared before Jehovah (1:12).

The effect of Haggai's remonstrations now became evident. The whole of the people—governor, high priest and ordinary people—obeyed the message and a spirit of godly fear was created in their hearts. The Bible frequently associates the service of God with the fear of God. This fear is not, of course, a dread of God's wrath, but rather the profound, reverential awe and supreme respect we feel when we realise the greatness of the Almighty. Faith in God removes the burden of unworthy fears and dreads and substitutes for them the supreme fear—one which creates no terror but, on the contrary, inspires the intense desire never to be separated from God or to bring dishonour on His name (*Life Isn't All Honey*, by Tatford, p. 34). Obedience and fear are naturally linked together.

Not only the rulers, but "all the remnant of the people" obeyed the prophet's message. The term "remnant" has assumed a semi-technical sense in the Scriptures in relation to

40

the nation of Israel and that part of the nation which is regarded as the true Israel. In verse 12, the reference, of course, is merely to that portion of the nation which had returned from exile.

THE DIVINE PRESENCE

Then spoke Haggai, Jehovah's messenger, in Jehovah's message to the people, I am with you, says Jehovah (1:13).

The building had evidently been resumed with zest and vigour, when the prophet was sent with a further message to them. He is described as Jehovah's messenger in Jehovah's message. (It is the only time such a description is given of any of the prophets.) The word came, not at his impulse or by his reasoning: he spoke with the full authority of Jehovah.

"I am with you, says Jehovah", came the message. It was only a short sentence, but those few words were the assurance of strength and power. The work was Jehovah's and the necessary supplies and equipment were provided by Him; His presence denoted all-sufficiency. Throughout the ages, that presence has been the stay and strength of His people. "Certainly I will be with you", came the words to Moses out of the burning bush (Exod. 3:12). "I will be with you", was the divine promise to Joshua when he assumed the leadership in succession to Moses (Josh. 1:5). "I am with you", declared Jehovah in Isaiah's day (Isa. 41:10). And from the risen and exalted Christ today comes the same message to His followers, "Lo, I am with you always, even to the end of the age" (Matt. 28:20). In our day, as much as in Haggai's, the work is not ours but God's, the power is God's, and the supplies are God's, and we have the assurance of His presence with us to the end of the road. In the consciousness of His presence, difficulties vanish and obstacles melt away.

In the power of the prophet's message, the spirits of the people were stirred up and, heartened and invigorated, they toiled in the rebuilding.

41

STIRRED SPIRITS

And Jehovah stirred up the spirit of Zerubbabel the son of Shealtiel, governor of Judah, and the spirit of Joshua the son of Josedech, the high priest, and the spirit of all the remnant of the people; and they came and performed work in the house of Jehovah of hosts, their God, on the twenty-fourth day of the sixth month, in the second year of Darius the king (1 : 14, 15).

No longer was there hesitation. The voice of God had rung clearly in the ears of the Jews and their hearts had been touched. They abandoned their other occupations and now assembled at the temple site and exerted all their energies to complete the building.

Their spirits were stirred up. Barnes (*ibid.*, p. 10) says that the spirit "is that part of human nature which God gave (Eccles. 12:7) and upon which He exercises unseen influence; thus according to Deut. 2 : 30 Jehovah 'hardened' the spirit of Sihon to resist Israel, and according to Ezra 1 : 1 He 'stirred up' the spirit of Cyrus to issue an edict in favour of the temple". (See Note C at the end of the chapter.)

Barnes suggests that the date in verse 15 is erroneous and that the ninth month should be substituted for the sixth month, in view of chap. 2:10, but there is no other evidence for not accepting the date given.

NOTE C

MAN'S NATURE

While all theologians are agreed that man is more than a corporeal being, opinions are divided regarding his actual constitution. Broadly speaking, there are two views. The first maintains that the human being is a dichotomy of soul and body, the body being formed of the dust of the earth, and the soul being the principle of life (Gen. 2:7). To quote one writer, "The soul is the principle of the whole life of . . . man or beast. It is the principle of all life, physical, intellectual, moral, religious. There is not one substance, the soul, which feels and remembers, and another substance, the spirit, that has conscience and the knowledge of God." According to this theory, "The soul of man is the same in kind with that of the brute, but it differs in being of a higher order".

The other view—which seems more logical—is that man is a trichotomy of body, soul and spirit, and the apostle Paul specifically defines these as the component parts of man (1 Thess. 5:23). It has been said that the tripartite nature of man is a reflection of the Holy Trinity. Gen. 1:26 certainly records that "God said, Let Us make man in Our image, after Our likeness", and it has been suggested that a parallel may possibly be seen between human soul, body and spirit, and the relationships of Father, Son and Holy Spirit in the God-head. It is probably unwise, however, to press this comparison too far.

The body is the material part of man's constitution. Through its medium he enters into communication with his

43

fellow-creatures. The body was derived from the dust of earth and, at death, it decomposes and returns to dust. The soul has been described as "the principle of animal life: man possesses it in common with the brutes: to it belong understanding, emotion, and sensibility." The spirit, according to Prof. J. D. Davis, "is the mind, the principle of man's rational and immortal life, the possession of reason, will and conscience".

Through the body, man expresses himself to others; through the soul he comprehends himself; through the spirit he can approach his Creator. Dr. C. I. Scofield says, "The spirit is that part of man which knows (1 Cor. 2 : 11), his mind; the soul is the seat of his affections, desires, and so of the emotions and of the active will, the self . . . Because man is 'spirit', he is capable of God-consciousness and of communication with God; because he is 'soul', he has self-consciousness; because he is 'body' he has, through his senses, world-consciousness." Prof. Schöberlein writes, "The body is rooted with all the fibres of its being in the soul. Nay, the soul, on its nature-side, bears already within itself the essence, the potentiality, of a body".

The three components of man's nature, while integral parts of the individual, are separable from each other. At death, for instance, the soul and the spirit depart, leaving the empty shell of the body to be consigned to the grave. Again, the soul and the spirit are evidently distinguishable from each other, for the writer to the Hebrews declares that the Word of God is able to pierce, "even to the dividing asunder of soul and spirit" (Heb. 4 : 12).

The body is the outward expression of man and the form by which he is known. During the natural life the body is accommodated to the needs of the animal nature and it appears from 1 Cor. 15 : 44 that it is dominated by the soul, for the apostle states that, when it dies, it is sown a natural (i.e. soulual or psychical) body. The resurrection body, however, will be adjusted to a spiritual existence and will apparently be under the domination of the spirit, for in the same verse it is said to be raised a spiritual body. That the body is an essential part of man is clear from the fact that it is identified with him in resurrection. Indeed, the spirit which is absent from the body is described as unclothed (2 Cor. 5:1–4). The future life is to be enjoyed, not as bodiless spirits, but as corporeal saints.

The identity of the soul is obvious from the fact that man has a self-conscious existence, but the nature of the soul is not easy to explain. Indeed the Scriptures seem frequently to use the terms 'soul' and 'spirit' almost interchangeably. Delitzsch declares that "The soul is the *doxa* of the spirit, immaterial, but similarly formed to the body, which the spirit through it ensouls. It is, as the outside of the spirit, so the inside of the body which, in every change of its material condition, maintains it in identity with itself." This is perhaps an over-simplification though. The soul is evidently the real ego, and it is so closely identified with the individual that, throughout the Bible, the word is frequently used to denote the individual.

Job declares that "there is a spirit in man" (Job 32:8), and the apostle Paul asks, "What man knows the things of a man, save the spirit of man which is in him?" (1 Cor. 2:11). The spirit of man seems to be his inmost being—the higher consciousness and the means by which he can in some measure understand spiritual things and Divine realities. It is the medium of his approach to God and his capacity to comprehend the supernatural.

CHAPTER 5

DISPARAGEMENT AND ENCOURAGEMENT

A S the revival of interest demonstrated itself in willing labours on the temple site, the Jews became painfully conscious of the pronounced inferiority of the temple to the magnificent building erected by Solomon. Their relative poverty precluded them from ever attaining the incomparable splendour of that earlier sanctuary, and the realisation of this fact discouraged and disheartened them. Again, therefore, Haggai was sent to them with a message from Jehovah.

THE COMPARISON
In the seventh month, on the twenty-first day of the month, came the word of Jehovah by the prophet Haggai, Speak now to Zerubbabel the son of Shealtiel, governor of Judah, and to Joshua the son of Josedech, the high priest, and to all the remnant of the people, saying, Who is left among you that saw this house in its former glory? And how do you see it now? Is it not in your eyes in comparison of it as nothing? (2:1-3).

When the foundation of the temple was laid, the joyful shouting of the younger men at the first signs of the restoration of the sanctuary was almost overwhelmed by the loud lamentations of the older men at the recollection of the splendours of the past. The contrast between the two buildings was now becoming even more apparent, and disparaging remarks were evidently being made by the older folk as they watched the efforts of their juniors.

47

It was the last day of the feast of tabernacles (Lev. 23 : 33–43), when the nation should have been rejoicing after the seven days of rest and happiness and of religious gatherings. But the deprecatory comments must have continued with their depressing and discouraging effect. The rites of the festive season brought no relief from the dejection caused by the critical comparisons. On that very day, the last day of the feast, Haggai, addressing the governor, the high priest and the people, called upon the ancients, who could recall the temple of Solomon, to express their views on the present building. They could remember the glory and splendour of the earlier sanctuary. Was not this one worthless by comparison? The minority to whom he spoke must have been very small in number. Solomon's temple was destroyed in 586 B.C. and it was now 520 B.C. Those who had seen it were few and it is possible that some of the criticisms were being uttered by others who had not been alive at the date of the destruction.

That there was an inferiority could scarcely be questioned. Pusey says, "Besides the richness of the sculptures in the former temple, everything which admitted of it was overlaid with gold. Solomon overlaid the whole house with gold, until he had finished all the house, the whole altar by the oracle, the two cherubims, the floor of the house, the doors of the holy of holies and the ornaments of it, the cherubims thereon, and the palm trees he covered with gold fitted upon the carved work; the altar of gold and the table of gold, whereupon the shewbread was, the ten candlesticks of pure gold, with the flowers and the lamps and the tongs of gold, the bowls, the snuffers and the basons and the spoons and the censers of pure gold, and hinges of pure gold for all the doors of the temple. The porch that was in the front of the house, twenty cubits broad and a hundred and twenty cubits high, was overlaid with pure gold; the house glistened with precious stones; and the gold (it is added) was gold of Pawaim, a land distant of course and unknown to us. Six hundred talents of gold (about £4,320,000) were employed in overlaying the holy of holies. The upper chambers were also of gold; the weight

48

of the nails was fifty shekels of gold."

It is little wonder that the present building seemed paltry by comparison. In addition, Moore (*ibid.*, p. 69) points out, "The Jews were accustomed to say that there were five things in the first temple that were wanting in the second: (1) the sacred fire; (2) the shekinah; (3) the ark and cherubim; (4) the urim and thummim; (5) the spirit of prophecy"

WORDS OF ENCOURAGEMENT

Yet now be strong, O Zerubbabel, says Jehovah; and be strong, O Joshua son of Josedech, the high priest; and be strong, all you people of the land, says Jehovah, and work; for I am with you, says Jehovah, according to the word that I covenanted with you when you came out of Egypt. So my spirit abides among you: fear not (2:4, 5).

To the depressed and discouraged toilers came a message of inspiration from the prophet. "Be strong", or "Take courage" came the threefold injunction. It was not for them to sit down despondently and to deplore the lost glory of the past. They had been given a work to do in their own day. The past was irretrievable: it had gone beyond control. Let them occupy themselves in the work of God today and listen no longer to the mawkish maundering of the ancients whose own days were nearly over.

At the exodus from Egypt, Jehovah had been with them in the pillar of fire by night and in the cloud by day. His presence had been proved and He had never deserted them to their foes. The covenant He had made with them had never been repealed. There could be no revocation. His Spirit abode with them and nothing should, therefore, depress or discourage them. It was His work upon which they were engaged and nothing mattered but His purpose.

By comparison with the extraordinary times of blessing in apostolic days, or even in the times of some of the great warriors of the past, the service of God's children today may appear decidedly inferior, and the consciousness of the inferiority frequently produces discouragement and despon-

49

dency. Many speak regretfully (and not altogether wisely) of "the good old days" and contrast the feeble efforts of the present day. But we are not called to live in the past. Our lot was cast in the present, with all its abounding and unprecedented opportunities—with possibilities perhaps far greater than have ever been seen in history.

Is our service, in fact, absolutely valueless? Is it the Divine will that we should sit down in deplorable inactivity, and mourn the past and decry the present? Perish the thought! Such an attitude is a virtual recognition, not merely of human failure, but, by implication, of Divine failure. The implication is that God's ear is now heavy that He cannot hear, that His arm has become shortened that He cannot save, that His power has become limited and that He is unable to work through His people as in days of yore. What footling nonsense! Our service may appear poor and feeble to us, but it is performed in association and partnership with our blessed Lord. "Who has despised the day of small things?" asked the Lord of the prophet Zechariah (Zech. 4:10). Let us not despise the present or dwell upon past glories, but rather strive with every power and ability to do His service now in anticipation of the day when He will assess our labours at their true value. His power is with us. Let us go on.

JEHOVAH'S INTERVENTION
For thus says Jehovah of hosts, Yet once, it is a little while, I will shake the heavens and the earth and the sea and the dry land; and I will shake all nations, and the desire of all nations shall come, and I will fill this house with glory, says Jehovah of hosts. The silver is mine and the gold is mine, says Jehovah of hosts. The latter glory of this house shall be greater than the former, says Jehovah of hosts; and in this place will I give peace, says Jehovah of hosts (2:6-9).

Suddenly—and almost irrelevantly—Jehovah declared that, once again, in a little while, everything would be convulsed by His power. The use of the words "once again", as Heb. 12: 26 makes clear, had an implied reference to the scene at Sinai

50

at the giving of the law, when "the whole mount quaked greatly" (Ex. 19:18; Psa. 68:8). Similar convulsions were prophesied by Isaiah and other prophets of the future day of judgment (Isa. 2:19, 21; 13:13; Hab. 3:6) and it is clear from the Apocalypse that a tremendous cosmic convulsion will take place when the Eternal sits to judge (Rev. 20:11).

To what event did Haggai's prophecy refer? Many commentators lay stress on the phrase "it is a little while" and maintain that the fulfilment of the prediction must have occurred at an early date after the announcement. Hengstenberg, for example, says that "whosoever speaks to men, must speak of things according to a human method of thinking; or if he does not, he must make it clear that this is the case. The prophet lays stress on the brevity of the time, for the purpose of comforting. And only what is short in the eyes of men is fitted for this". This argument, of course, ignores the possibility of more than one fulfilment of a prediction. But the fact remains that no event comparable with the earthquake and Divine revelation of Sinai took place in the near future after Haggai's utterance of the prophecy.

Some writers interpret the prophecy as relating to the imminent destruction of the Medo-Persian empire by Greece and as possibly also anticipating the conflicts of the Ptolemies and the Seleucids and the ultimate government of the world by the Romans. Calvin and others, however, see the universal convulsion as symbolic of the spiritual effect of the preaching of the gospel on the nations of the world. Neither of these alternatives is really a satisfactory explanation, and the only possible conclusion is that the reference is to the events described in the New Testament, following the great tribulation. Our Lord declared that, immediately after that period, "shall the sun be darkened, and the moon shall not give her light, and the stars shall fall from heaven, and the powers of the heavens shall be shaken" before the coming of the Son of man in the clouds of heaven (Matt. 24:29, 30). The descriptions given in the various relevant passages imply physical and natural convulsions as well as social and political dis-

51

turbances. The intervention of Christ in the affairs of men on the next occasion will have cataclysmic effects. Keil (*ibid.*, p. 192) says, "if the shaking of heaven and earth effects a violent breaking up of the existing condition of the universe, the shaking of all nations can only be by one by which an end is put to the existing condition of the world of nations, by means of great political convulsions, and indeed, according to the explanation given in verse 22, by the Lord's overthrowing the throne of kingdoms, annihilating their power, and destroying their materials of war, so that one falls by the sword of the other, that is to say, by wars and revolutions, by which the might of the heathen world is broken and annihilated"

The shaking of all nations was to be followed by the coming of "the desire of all nations". This phrase has been interpreted in a variety of ways. The noun "desire" is a feminine singular substantive, but the verb "come" is a plural masculine one. The Septuagint renders the phrase, "the choice things of all the nations shall come", and the R.S.V. translates it as "so that the treasures of all nations shall come in". A common interpretation is that the shaking of the nations results in their bringing their treasures of gold and silver to the temple to adorn the building (cf. Isa. 60:5), but Barnes insists that "the desire" refers to nations whom God has chosen to worship in the new temple. Isaiah and Micah both refer to the nations flowing to the mountain of God's house.

If the event referred to is consequent upon the shaking of nature and nations, however, it is more logical to regard "the desire of all nations" as having a Messianic significance. In other words, as one commentator puts it, the reference is to "the glorification of the temple through the appearance of Jesus in it" (cf. Ex. 40:34, 35; 1 Kings 8:10, 11; 2 Chron. 5:13, 14).

The coming of "the desire of all nations" is immediately associated in verse 7 with the filling of the temple with glory. The Jews were unable to adorn the building with gold and silver and some undoubtedly must have deplored the lack of resources which rendered them unable. But Jehovah declared that the silver and the gold were His. The people's inability was irrelevant. The One, to whom the treasures belonged, had accepted the responsibility of glorifying the building.

Moreover, viewing all the temples as one, He declared that the latter glory would be greater even than the former glory. The splendid magnificence of Solomon's temple will pale into insignificance by comparison with the glory of a future day. Presumably the prophet was anticipating the flooding of the millennial temple with the glory of Jehovah (Ezek. 44: 4), or even the ultimate fulfilment in the eternal state, when the Lord God Almighty and the Lamb are the only temple needed and the glory of God illumines the whole city (Rev. 21 : 22, 23).

It is not for us to be concerned with the adornment of the work. The apparently trivial and humdrum service we perform in the name of our Lord may seem unexciting and almost worthless. But, in a coming day, the Master's hand will touch the threads we have woven together and out of the drab, dull pattern the light will glow in superlative glory. And, from an even broader point of view, the latter glory may be greater even than the former. Was there blessing in the early days of the church? Were souls swept into the kingdom by revivals of more recent days? And is the present day one of comparative powerlessness and infertility? The cry still rings out, "The latter glory shall be greater than the former".

As a final blessing, Jehovah added that, in this temple, He would give peace. Kelly (*ibid.*, p. 426) comments that Christ "*made* peace at His first coming, He will *give* peace at His second". The prophet again was doubtless looking on to the day when, in a later temple, Messiah will speak peace to all who seek Him. His second advent to the earth will bring judgment, but He will also come to establish peace on earth, a peace to be enjoyed as never before (Isa. 60: 18). The Septuagint adds at the end of verse 9, "and peace of soul for a possession to everyone who founds and raises up this temple anew", but the justification for the addition is doubtful.

Thus God replied to the doubts and fears of a feeble

53

remnant. The future was far more glorious than the past and surpassed every concept they had harboured in their thoughts.

CHAPTER 6

UNFAITHFULNESS EXPOSED

HAGGAI'S penultimate message was of a totally different character, although an integral part of his book. In their neglect of the temple, the people had evidently concluded that their attendance at the altar and the periodical presentation of their sacrifices and gifts were a recognition cf the claims of God and that equity demanded that they should consequently be accepted by Him. In his next message the prophet tore away their moth-eaten robe of hypocrisy and displayed their true character to the nation.

THE PRINCIPLE OF DEFILEMENT

On the twenty-fourth day of the ninth month, in the second year of Darius, came the word of Jehovah by Haggai the prophet, Thus says Jehovah of hosts: Ask now the priests concerning the law, saying, If one carries holy flesh in the skirt of his garment, and touches with his skirt bread, or pottage, or wine, or oil, or any meat, does it become holy? And the priests answered and said, No. Then said Haggai, If one, who is unclean by contact with a dead body, touches any of these, does it become unclean? And the priests answered and said, It does become unclean. Then answered Haggai and said, So is this people and so is this nation before me, says Jehovah; and so is every work of their hands; and what they offer there is unclean (2:10–14).

The prophet's exposure of the nature of the people was made through illustration and figure. The priests were the exponents of the law and it was their responsibility to teach the people, but they had been concerned only with the superficial detail and not with the basic principles. The people had brought sacrifices as required by the law. They had satisfied the literal requirements, and the priests had evidently presented the offerings which had been brought under the apprehension that, because they conformed to the legal requirements, they must be acceptable to God. Both priest and offerer had blindly ignored the neglect of God's work which left the temple unbuilt. How could offerings brought by such worshippers be acceptable? There was no inherent efficacy to be ascribed to the offerings. God first looked at the heart. These people had turned aside from His house to build their own luxurious dwellings, and then thought to appease Him by the presentation of a lamb or a goat at His altar. The sacrifice did not sanctify the unsanctified.

The worshipper stood before the altar in clean garments. Part of the flesh of the victim in some cases (e.g. the peace offerings) became the food of the worshipper and his family, and he might well wrap it up in a corner of his garment to carry it home. It was holy flesh, but its holiness could not possibly extend to anything it touched.

Per contra, a man who had become defiled could convey his pollution to other things. If contact with holy flesh did not sanctify, contact with what was defiled did defile. Uncleanness might be contracted in many ways, but contact with a dead body was a common one (Num. 19:11) and communion with God was impossible until the contamination had been ceremonially removed.

By his questioning of the priests, Haggai taught the lesson that, through their neglect of Jehovah and His temple, the people themselves, their offerings, and all the works of their hands had become unclean in His sight. Because they were personally unclean, their offerings to God were unacceptable. "That which is holy," wrote J. N. Darby, "cannot sanctify unclean things; but an unclean thing defiles that which is holy; for holiness is exclusive with respect to evil."

It was a salutary lesson. Neglect of God's work was regarded as sin. The offerings presented had been ineffective in atoning for their guilt or in reconciling them to God. Their sin remained upon them. Even the very offerings were deemed to be unclean. And what was true of Judah is true of believers today. We cannot pacify God or persuade Him to ignore our negligence and sloth by the gift of money or by indulging in pious phraseology. Neglect of His work is sin and the individual is defiled in His sight. His offerings are worthless: they too are unclean.

DIVINE RETRIBUTION

And now, I pray you, consider from this day and backward, from before a stone was laid upon a stone in the temple of Jehovah. From the times when one came to a heap of twenty measures, there were but ten: when one came to the winevat to draw fifty vessels out of the vat, there were but twenty. I smote you with blight and mildew and hail in all the work of your hands. Yet you did not return to me, says Jehovah (2:15-17).

The prophet now drew attention to their experiences. He called upon them to recall what had happened from the time when they were about to commence the building of the temple. Everything seemed to have been cursed. Where they had anticipated a full store of grain, they found only half: instead of twenty measures, there were only ten. When they visited the winevat, they found far less in the lower receptacle than they had expected. Instead of filling fifty vessels, there was only enough juice to fill twenty.

Jehovah carefully explained that it was His punitive hand laid upon them in chastisement. Blight, mildew and hail were His natural instruments. Discipline is inflicted in the Divine plan, to bring the soul back to God. But it was completely ineffective in this case. They did not return to Him. The purpose had not been achieved. They had not seen His hand

57

in the happenings of life and had not been conscious of any need for repentance or change of heart.

Blight and mildew were threatened as punishments under the law (Deut. 28:22) and Amos had also referred to these inflictions in the same sense (Amos 4:9). The people had, therefore, no excuse for not recognising the Divine hand in their sufferings, but they were blind and made no attempt to return to God.

DIVINE MERCY

Consider now from this day and backward, from the twenty-fourth day of the ninth month, even from the day that the foundation of Jehovah's temple was laid, consider it. Is the seed yet in the barn? As yet the vine, and the fig tree, and the pomegranate, and the olive tree, have not brought forth. From this day I will bless you (2:18, 19).

Again the people were called upon to consider the events from the laying of the foundation of the temple up to the present day. They had known hardship and deprivation and, looking back in retrospect, they must have recalled the absence of the material prosperity and the constant failure of the crops. The reason had already been stated and they should now have conned the lesson.

The harvest had not yet been gathered in. The crop was not in the granary. The vine, fig, pomegranate and olive had not yet produced their fruit. Was the harvest to be a repetition of their experience of the past years?

Suddenly there came the gleam of hope. "From this day I will bless you." It was a critical time of the year. It was December. If the showers now fell, the wheat harvest four months later might exceed their expectations and the fruit trees might produce fruit in abundance. Jehovah declared that from that moment they should experience His blessing. After the years of neglect and spiritual failure, the people had turned to God and had recommenced their labours on His house, and the One, who had inflicted trouble upon them in order to secure that very end, now promised to transmute

58

discipline into blessing. Now that the evil had been removed, He was in a position to deal with them in grace.

The neglect at any time of God's service renders the servant unclean in His sight, and He cannot bless anything which is done until the defilement is removed. When the neglectful and slothful believer turns again to his Lord, however, the uncleanness is removed, and He is again in a position to bless.

CHAPTER 7

FINAL SECURITY

IN the last of his brief messages, Haggai reverted once more to the shaking of heaven and earth and the overthrow of kingdoms and powers. The Jews might reasonably have been disturbed by the prophecy and uncertain of their own future in the catastrophic circumstances portrayed. Jehovah accordingly imparted the assurance of their security in that day of universal upheaval.

CONVULSION OF ALL THINGS

And again the word of Jehovah came to Haggai on the twenty-fourth day of the month, Speak to Zerubbabel, governor of Judah, saying, I will shake the heavens and the earth. And I will overthrow the throne of kingdoms, and I will destroy the strength of the kingdoms of the nations; and I will overthrow the chariots and their riders; and the horses and their riders shall come down, every one by the sword of his fellow (2:20-22).

This message was addressed throughout to Zerubbabel as representative of the people. He was the civil governor and their security and welfare depended upon him. Jehovah warned again that He was about to shake the heavens and the earth and to deal with the rulers of the nations. "The allusion is no doubt," says Barnes (*ibid.*, p. 19), "to the convulsions of the Persian empire in the earliest years of Darius, when province after province sought to establish its own indepen-

dence." But, even allowing for eastern hyperbole, it is difficult
to see how the expressions used could be restricted to such
narrow circumstances. No heavens and earth were shaken in
Zerubbabel's time. There was no serious disturbance in the
vast Persian empire (which now covered two million square
miles). As Perowne (*ibid* , p. 45) remarks, "The terms here
employed are too wide to be satisfied by any event in the life
of Zerubbabel . . . The prophecy reaches forth to the more
distant future and still awaits its full accomplishment."

Thrones were to be overthrown, the inherent power of
kingdoms was to be destroyed, military forces were to be
completely routed, and confusion created among them. The
picture painted is of some terrible event affecting the whole
world. It can only refer to the second advent of our Lord,
when He rides forth from the celestial heights in all His power
and glory to execute judgment in a guilty world. In that day,
nations will be trampled underfoot, thrones toppled down and
rulers destroyed. As many prophecies indicate, the armies of
the nations, gathered up to besiege the holy city, will be
destroyed by the Son of Man in all His glory and power. No
other event can satisfy the description given. This is a happening which is unparalleled in human history. Powers of north
and south, east and west will be destroyed at the coming of
the mighty Conqueror in that day.

Judah might well bear the judgments of that day, but the
concluding verse of the prophecy provided the assurance they
so sorely needed.

THE CHOSEN ONE

*In that day, says Jehovah of hosts, will I take you, O
Zerubbabel, my servant, the son of Shealtiel, says Jehovah,
and will make you as a signet; for I have chosen you, says
Jehovah of hosts* (2:23).

The storms were about to rage around them and the tempest
was going to engulf nations, but the people of God were
forever secure. Their value and importance to Him would
only be emphasised by the general destruction and dissolution.

In the day of unparalleled trouble, God promised that Zerubbabel, as representative of the people (and, as a prince of the house of David, as representative also of the royal line) would be made a signet, or signet ring.

The oriental constantly carried his signet with him: it was his valued possession. It was not always a ring, but was frequently an engraved stone, hung by a chain from the neck or arm (cf. S.Sol. 8:6; Jer. 22:24). Zerubbabel (and Judah as seen in him) was so dear to the heart of Jehovah that he was set as a signet in the place of Divine strength (the arm) and affection (the heart).

God declared that this was because He had chosen him. So far as Zerubbabel personally was concerned, the implication was probably that the Messianic promises had been transferred to him and his family as descendants of David. God has chosen His king and He will yet seat Him on the holy hill of Zion. That One will be a descendant of David's line—great David's greater Son.

But Jehovah has chosen the nation. In covenant mercy He has unconditionally and irrevocably committed Himself to their ultimate blessing. He must implement His pledges to His chosen people.

The day of Divine judgment is rapidly approaching, but the disciples of Christ do not fear the darkening storm. As a seal upon His heart and a signet upon His arm, they are absolutely secure. Though all else should be removed, He is the pledge of their eternal security. Before the clouds break, those whom He has chosen will be 'ranslated to be with Himself.

Thus Haggai completed his ministry. It lasted only three months and twenty-four days and during that time he uttered only five short messages. But his words aroused a lethargic nation and converted a slothful people into zealous servants of God. Unknown, without genealogy or personal history, he passed off the stage, his ministry accomplished and the Divine purpose through him achieved.

Although the opposition of the Samaritans was again aroused by the resumption of building, it was overruled in the providence of God. Within a few more months, the restoration temple was completed, and its dedication took place amidst general rejoicing (Ezra 6:15, 16). The adversary may seek to hinder and obstruct, but the omnipotent God is on our side. "Therefore, my beloved brethren, be steadfast, unmovable, always abounding in the work of the Lord, forasmuch as you know that your labour is not in vain in the Lord" (1 Cor. 15:58).

APPENDIX

HAS ISRAEL A FUTURE?

DESPITE the specific assurance given to Zerubbabel in the closing verses of Haggai's prophecy, it is claimed by some expositors that the book gives no prospect of any future to the nation of Israel and is no bar to the allegorisation of many of the Old Testament prophecies regarding that nation. It is freely said that the New Testament "chosen people" have superseded those of the Old Testament, and that the physical and material have now been succeeded by the spiritual. Even the most superficial study of the subject, however, induces doubt regarding the reliability of this interpretation. Indeed, the Scriptures seem to abound with evidences to the contrary, but it may be useful to trace the story briefly through the centuries.

"It took Europe 1,600 years after the decline of Greece to realise that her literature, science and architecture had their roots in Grecian civilisation," says Max. I. Dimont in *Jews, God and History*. "It may take another few hundred years to establish that the spiritual, moral, ethical and ideological roots of western civilisation are embedded in Judaism." The Jews have made a contribution to every culture and civilisation and have outlived each dying form to survive in its successor, and, at the same time, have preserved their ethnic identity through every alien culture. They are an amazing people. Fewer than 0.5 per cent of the population of the world, they have made an impression far beyond what could be expected from their relatively small numbers. In science, literature, music, religion, finance and philosophy, they have made their impact. They are a people who cannot be ignored.

About 4,000 years ago, Terah, his son Abram and his grandson Lot turned their backs upon the cosmopolitan city of Ur in Babylonia and, crossing the river Euphrates, became the first Ivriim, or Hebrews, i.e. "the people who crossed over", or "the people from the other side of the river". They travelled some 600 miles to the land of Haran. Here God met with the patriarch and entered into a treaty with him. Abraham was now 75 years of age and had been called out of Ur of the Chaldees in order that a new and distinct nation might be created, separated unto God, a pure theocracy (Gen. 11:31; Deut. 7:6; Num. 23:9). The nation was God's chosen people, whom He had selected in Divine sovereignty, and His love was set upon it (Deut. 7:8; Isa. 43:3, 4; Mal. 1:2).

The covenant into which the Eternal entered with Abraham was unconditional and irrevocable. It was, moreover, one of such importance that He repeated it in various forms ten times—six times to Abraham himself, and two each to Isaac and Jacob (Gen. 12:1–3; 13:14–17; 15:1–7; 17:1–18, etc.). In addition to the promises which related to Abraham personally, blessing was specifically promised to his descendants, who were likened to the stars of heaven, to the sand on the seashore and to the dust of the earth (Gen. 15:5; 22:17; 13:16). The pledges made to the nation descended from Abraham have been aptly summarised by Prof. J. F. Walvoord in *The Millennial Kingdom*, "The nation itself shall be great (Gen. 12:2) and innumerable (Gen. 13:16). The nation is promised possession of the land. Its extensive boundaries are given in detail (Gen. 15:18–21). In connection with the promise of the land, the Abrahamic covenant itself is expressly called 'everlasting' (Gen. 17:7) and the possession of the land is defined as 'an everlasting possession' (Gen. 17:8)."

The covenant was unconditional upon Abraham and was binding only upon God. No provision was made for its revocation, and it was not subject to amendment or annulment.

In Gal. 3:17 the apostle Paul argues that the Mosaic law, given 430 years later, cannot abrogate the provisions of the covenant. The promise must be fulfilled. It is sometimes argued that Israel's sin broke the covenant and, therefore, nullified its provisions, but the implementation of the covenant was not dependent upon Israel's character or conduct. In Isa. 54:10 God declared that the mountains would depart and the hills would be removed, but that His covenant with Israel would not be removed. Ezek. 37:25–28 plainly states that they will dwell in the land given to Jacob and that it will be for ever, and that God will dwell in the midst of them and sanctify His people.

The Divine purpose was, of course, that Israel should be a witness to Him among the nations surrounding them, but they failed completely. The prophet declares that, in a future day, they will be "priests of the Lord" and "ministers of our God" (Isa. 61:6). This was always the Divine purpose for them, but it has never yet been achieved.

When famine swept the country, the Hebrews turned to Egypt for food and eventually found their home there for four centuries as God had previously foretold (Gen. 15:13, 14). The Hyksos, who invited the Israelites to live in Egypt, were swept out of power by Rameses II, and Abraham's descendants, like many others, were reduced to the position of slaves. They were Divinely delivered from Egypt, however, and after their exodus, were presented with—and accepted— the Mosaic law and came under the specific rule of God. The Torah, or the law given by Moses, was not the first written code: the Sumerian code of laws dates back to 2500 B.C., but the Torah was unique in its concepts of equality and justice.

Israel soon wearied of a theocracy and demanded a monarchy like other nations (1 Sam. 8:5), and God graciously granted them their desire. When their second king was established on his throne, God entered into a covenant with him, in which He promised that his house, throne and kingdom would be established for ever (2 Sam. 7:12–16). As in the case of the

Abrahamic covenant, no conditions were imposed on the beneficiary. It was an unconditional covenant, binding only upon God. As Prof. Walvoord writes in *Israel in Prophecy*, "this covenant assured to David that his political rule as well as his physical posterity would continue for ever, even though it might be interrupted, just as the possession of the land was temporarily interrupted". It was quite irrevocable and in Psa. 89: 28, 29, 34-37, it is specifically stated that the covenant with David will not be broken and that David's seed will endure for ever and that his throne will be as permanent as the sun. Jer. 33 : 20-26 categorically declares that only if day and night cease to be, will the covenant with David be broken or his seed be disowned. Isa. 54 : 8-10 puts it equally strongly: the mountains and hills will be displaced before the Davidic covenant is disturbed. The covenant is an everlasting one (Ezek. 37 : 26).

When David's son, Solomon, died, his son Rehoboam was confronted by the leaders of the nation with a request for redress of their grievances. The new king arrogantly refused to listen, and the ten tribes of Israel crowned Jeroboam, the son of Nebat, as their king, leaving the two tribes of Judah and Benjamin to serve Rehoboam. The two kingdoms of Israel and Judah continued as separate entities for over two centuries. The throne of Israel was an uneasy one for its occupant and few of the 19 kings of Israel died of natural causes. In 721 B.C., the sin of Israel met with its punishment. Sargon II of Assyria captured Samaria and deported the entire population of Israel.

The kingdom of Judah had a chequered history but although it continued until the sixth century B.C., its power was ultimately broken and the population carried off to Babylonia by the forces of Nebuchadnezzar.

When Babylonia was conquered by the Persians, Cyrus took the logical line that, by returning the Jews to their own country, he could be reasonably certain of a desolated land being transformed into a profitable source of revenue, and he authorised the return of all who wished it (Ezra 1 : 1-3). A considerable number accordingly returned and their descendants were in the land when the Messiah came. He declared that He was sent only to "the lost sheep of the house of Israel" (Matt. 15:24) and that "salvation is of the Jews" (John 4: 22), but His message was ignored and the Messiah was rejected.

Our Lord made clear the consequences of their rejection when He declared, "the kingdom of God shall be taken from you" (Matt. 21:43). Although the mercy of God still reaches the individual Jew who puts his trust in Christ, the nation has been temporarily set aside and judicially blinded until the purposes of God for the Gentiles have been fulfilled (Rom. 11:8, 25). God has not permanently cast off His people (Rom. 11:26), but their rejection of the Messiah resulted in a severance of their national relationship with Him. Through Israel's unbelief and consequent fall, blessing has become available to others, but Divine mercy will one day restore the nation to favour again (Rom. 11:24).

In 70 A.D., after four years of bloody war, the Roman army destroyed Jerusalem and the temple. In 113 A.D. a second Jewish war broke out and for three years Trajan threw his armies against this recalcitrant nation. A final revolt came twenty years later when Simon bar Cochba, claiming to be a descendant of David and also to be the Messiah, provoked two years of Roman butchery, ending in his own death and the permanent exclusion of Jews from Jerusalem. They gradually drifted back, however, and for a while lived in relative peace among both Christians and Arabs.

In the early part of the seventh century, Mohammed, who claimed descent from Ishmael, succeeded in bringing under his control the wild tribes of Arabia, and within ten years of his death in 632 A.D. his followers had established a great Moslem empire, ruled from Damascus. In 637 A.D. the Caliph Omar took Jerusalem and a few decades later the first Dome of the Rock was built on the temple site. The Moslem empire lasted—with the exception of 90 years of Crusaders' rule and 270 years by the Mamelukes of Egypt—until 1517, when Palestine fell into the hands of the Turks and remained part of the Ottoman empire for four centuries.

Throughout the four centuries of the Turkish régime, Arabs and Jews lived side by side, both chafing under the foreign yoke and yearning for the day when they could throw off the fetters and take unhindered possession of the land again. When Turkey entered the First World War, Britain conveyed to the Arabs an offer of financial assistance if they rose against the Turks and joined the Allies. The offer was accepted, subject to a promise of recognition of the political independence of the Arab countries after the war. This was agreed.

Early in the war, Britain found it impossible to obtain an adequate supply of wood alcohol for the production of acetone, which was used in the manufacture of explosives. Prof. Chaim Weizmann, of Manchester University, was called in to produce synthetic acetone and his services proved of such outstanding value to the country that it was purposed to bestow an honour on him. The Jewish scientist declined the honour, however, and claimed, as his reward, a home in Palestine for the Jewish people. Despite objections, the request was ultimately acceded to and on the 2nd November, 1917, the then Foreign Secretary, A. J. Balfour, addressed a letter to Lord Rothschild, to the effect that Britain viewed with favour the establishment in Palestine of a national home for the Jewish people and would use its best endeavours to facilitate the achievement of that object.

When the war was over, Britain was appointed the mandatory power for Palestine and the substance of Lord Balfour's letter was incorporated in the mandate. In the succeeding years, a large number of Jews entered the country as immigrants, and the influx was greatly increased by the persecution in Central Europe in the inter-war period, until the difficulty of settling such large numbers, coupled with the increasing friction with the Arabs, resulted in a restriction on immigration.

The mandate was terminated in 1948 and, on the 14th May of that year, a Jewish State was proclaimed and Dr.

70

Weizmann became the first President of Israel. The proclamation added fuel to the fires of Arab wrath and there seemed little prospect of the new State's survival. Half a million Jews were surrounded by nearly 42 million Arabs, determined to drive the Jew into the sea. To the amazement of the world, however, the Arabs were defeated by a handful of Jews. This story was repeated in 1956 and 1967. On each occasion, it is clear that the victory was not won by Jewish military strength or strategy, but unquestionably by the intervention of God.

For 19 centuries God has been calling out a church from Jew and Gentile, but there are now indications that that work is nearly complete and that He is now turning once more to Israel. The pledges to Abraham and David are still to be implemented. The Divine promise is clear. "In a little wrath I hid my face from you," said God centuries ago, "but my kindness shall not depart from you, nor shall the covenant of my peace be removed" (Isa. 54:8–10). Jeremiah further declared that sun, moon and stars must disappear before Israel loses her national position (Jer. 31:35, 36). God declared that He would scatter Israel among the heathen, from one end of the earth to the other, that they would find no rest for the sole of their foot and that they would constantly fear for their life. Yet He would not cast them away nor destroy them completely, but would eventually have compassion on them and gather them out of the nations and restore them to their own land (Lev. 26:33–39; Deut. 28:64–67; 30:1–5).

Before that day of blessing comes, however, the land is to be deluged with blood. It is evident from Dan. 11:36–39 that the country will suffer the rule of a strong dictator, who is an apostate Jew (with no respect for Jehovah or for the promise of the Messiah) and is a servant of spirit forces. Rev. 13:12–17 indicates that this man will be in close alliance with another great political power—the great western ruler over ten nations, referred to in Dan. 7:23–25; 9:27; Rev. 13:1–8, etc. The two will apparently be linked by a seven-year treaty under which the western power will, in all probability, guarantee military assistance in the event of an invasion of Israel from the north (Dan. 9:27).

It is clear that the Gentile ruler will equally be subject to diabolical domination and that both men—Jew and Gentile—will be serving the purposes of the unseen prince of darkness. With a desire to resurrect the Caesar worship of the past, the western ruler (according to Dan. 9:27) will put a stop to all existing religious observances throughout the ten countries under his control and—with the connivance of his Jewish coadjutor—in Israel as well. In place of all other forms of religion, he will substitute the worship of himself. To this, the Jewish ruler, acting as a "false prophet", will give his complete support. Indeed, he will direct the erection of a statue to the Gentile in Jerusalem and, drawing upon the supernatural powers bestowed upon him by the forces of evil, will impart life to the inanimate statue and cause it to speak. At his command, all who behold will be compelled to worship the statue on pain of death. In addition, this infidel ruler will countenance the entry of the Gentile dictator into the temple of God at Jerusalem, to sit in the temple, blasphemously claiming to be God (Rev. 13:14, 15; 2 Thess. 2: 3, 4). When the pious in Israel see the desolating idol and the blasphemous ruler in the temple, they will flee to the mountains for shelter, for trouble will then ensue such as Israel (or indeed the world) has never known before (Mark 13:14–20). So dreadful will be this period, which our Lord Himself describes as the "great tribulation", that unless it was shortened, none would be saved.

It is evident today that, whatever attempts may be made to negotiate peace in the Middle East, it can never be better than an uneasy truce. Sooner or later a humiliated Egypt must again turn upon Israel, precisely as foretold by the prophet Daniel two and a half millennia ago. It is equally clear that Soviet Russia is becoming increasingly involved militarily in that area of the world. Despite the large reserves in Russia, the oil wells of the Middle Eastern kingdoms are a constant source of temptation. The need for warm water ports is also a relevant factor. There are many who argue today that

Russian involvement in the Middle East will inevitably lead in the end to military intervention. This again is precisely what the student of Biblical prophecy anticipates. When the attack upon Israel comes from the south, Daniel discloses that the northern forces will pour into the country to lay the land waste, and to sweep through in destruction, carnage and rapine, to take possession also of North Africa (Dan. 11: 40–43). The horrors of that period can scarcely be imagined, but current conditions suggest that they cannot be long postponed.

To fulfil the guarantee given by the western treaty, forces from that direction will evidently invade Israel in the attempt to deliver Jerusalem and to aid the Jews in their desperate conflict. But from the east as well the invaders will come to add to the tribulations of the little country (Rev. 16:12). If Israel's woes have been great in the past, those awaiting her in the future are incomparably greater. Never has a nation suffered as she is destined to suffer.

It will be futile to look for help in any direction of the compass. The hand of every man seems to be against the Jew. But, in the hour of Israel's extremity, salvation will come. God will never surrender His people to their fate and He will again intervene on their behalf. The Messiah Himself, with all the myriads of His redeemed following Him, is to ride forth from heaven in glory and might and power. He will come to war against the nations of earth and to bring deliverance to His people. His feet will stand on Mount Olivet and, at the impact, the mountain will split in two, opening up a great valley for the inrush of the waters from the sea (Rev. 19:11–15; Zech. 14: 3–5). The mighty Warrior will smite the opposing armies and cast the great western ruler and his Jewish confederate into the lake of fire (Rev. 19:17–21).

The northern forces, ravaging Egypt, will hear the tidings of His coming and return in fury to attack the One who has come to deliver Israel, but the great army will be routed— destroyed upon the mountains of Israel (Dan. 11:44, 45; Ezek. 39:4). So countless will be the number of the dead that it will take seven months to bury the skeletons, whose flesh will have been devoured by the birds of prey (Ezek. 39:12).

Salvation at last will have come to Zion. The Messiah will have come, not only to deliver His people, but also to fulfil the age-long promises of her blessing. Before the long-hoped-for kingdom is instituted, however, the nation of Israel must be dealt with. Not all Jews of that day will have put their trust in God or will have accepted the Messiah. "For they are not all Israel who are of Israel", wrote the apostle Paul (Rom. 9:6). Only those who have been regenerated by the Holy Spirit will be eligible to enter the kingdom. Ezekiel declares that the Lord will gather Israel out of the countries in which they are scattered and bring them into the wilderness (presumably on the borders of the land) to be dealt with. There He will purge out the rebels and transgressors and exclude them from the land of Israel (Ezek. 20:34–38).

The righteous dead of Israel are to be resurrected to receive rewards for their lives and work before entering into the millennium (Dan. 12:2, 3; Isa. 26:19). (The statement in Dan. 12:2 is, of course, a general one and does not indicate the gap between the resurrection of the righteous and that of the unrighteous of Israel.)

The land promised to Abraham will at last be inherited by his descendants. Its topography will be altered and a fertile plain will replace the mountainous terrain (Zech. 14:4, 8–10). An abundance of rain will water the earth (Joel 2:23, 24), and the once-barren countryside will be transformed into a fertile field (Isa. 29:17). For a thousand years the Lord Jesus Christ will be supreme (Rev. 20), but a vice-regent of David's line will sit on the throne at Jerusalem (Ezek. 34:23, 24; 37:24, 25; Jer. 30:9; 33:15–17). Righteousness and equity will characterise Christ's rule, and blessing will abound on every side.

The millennial temple will be filled with the glory of God (Ezek. 43:1–4). God will dwell in Zion, and Jerusalem will be a holy city and the political centre of His government (Joel 3:17; Mic. 4:7). Representatives of the nations will be required to attend the feast of tabernacles each year in Jerusalem (Zech. 14:16).

All the prophecies of a kingdom age of blessing and prosperity will be fulfilled, and Israel will be supreme above the nations of the earth. There is a glorious future awaiting the Jew.

Prophet
of the Reformation

An Exposition of the Prophecy of Malachi

By

FREDK. A. TATFORD

Originally published by
Prophetic Witness Publishing House
Sussex, 1972

ISBN: 0-86524-135-X

Printed by Klock & Klock in the U.S.A.
1982 Reprint

CONTENTS

PREFACE

SOME time ago one was urged by a colleague in the Prophetic Witness Movement to embark on a series of expositions of the prophetic books of the Bible and the first of these — on the Prophecy of Zechariah — has already appeared under the title, *Prophet of the Myrtle Grove.* It was presumably envisaged that each volume would constitute a contribution to the study and understanding of Biblical prophecy. But the message of the Old Testament prophets is not always predictive. As Prof. Jacques Ellul says in *The Judgment of Jonah,* "As Christians we normally allow that prophetic writings are such by relation to Jesus Christ; on the other hand the Jews could allow them to be such, not because they announced the Messiah, but because they conveyed God's judgment here and now on the elect people, because they were God's word fashioned for His people and relating to its history." Not infrequently the prophets were concerned primarily to correct current abuses or to warn the people of the consequences of their wrongdoing, rather than to forecast the future or to disclose details of remote events.

"Any healthy society," writes Dr. Henry McKeating, "needs its critics, and the prophets performed this function. In our own society the same function is fulfilled by the press, by the parliamentary opposition and by all sorts of consumer organizations and citizens' councils." This is rather too mean a view of the prophetic function, however, and he rightly goes on, "But the prophet is far more than all or any of these, He is first and foremost a man of God. He is a religious visionary. His criticisms, therefore, were felt to have a force and authority with which we should not credit the criticisms of any modern functionary, and our society, therefore, offers no real parallel to his office."

Malachi was, *par excellence*, a critic of the conditions of his day. It is true that he did look on to the coming of Messiah to His temple, but the main burden of his message was the spiritual inconsistency of the restored remnant and the gross impropriety of their murmurings against God. His book, to quote Keil, "contains one single prophecy, the character of which is condemnatory throughout. Starting with the love which the Lord has shown to His people (1 : 2-5), the prophet proves that not only do the priests profane the name of the Lord by an unholy performance of the service at the altar (1 : 6; 2 : 9), but the people also repudiate their divine calling both by heathen marriages and frivolous divorces (2 : 10-16), and by their murmuring at the delay of the judgment; whereas the Lord will soon reveal Himself as a just judge, and before His coming will send His messenger, the prophet Elijah, to warn the ungodly and lead them to repentance, and then suddenly come to His temple as the expected angel of the covenant, to refine the sons of Levi, punish the sinners who have broken the covenant, and by exterminating the wicked, as well as by blessing the godly with salvation and righteousness, make the children of Israel the people of His possession (2 : 17 — 4 : 6)."

Malachi's message is as relevant to today as it was to the particular period when it was first altered and, even if the predictive element is less in content than the admonitory, the book still has a value which cannot be discounted. The author trusts that the following pages will not blunt the edge of the prophet's rebukes nor divert attention to what may be less relevant.

FREDK. A. TATFORD

8

CHAPTER 1

INTRODUCTION

IN THE Hebrew Scriptures, in the Septuagint and in the Peshitta, the Minor Prophets formed one book, "the Book of the Twelve," which was divided into twelve parts. The position of the book itself differed in the various versions, but the prophecy of Malachi consistently occupied the last place within the book. This was appropriate because Malachi was, in fact, chronologically the last of the prophets of Israel. His inspired utterances, probably three quarters of a century after those of Haggai and Zechariah, closed the canon of the Old Testament and prepared the way for the New Testament. Nagelsbach says, "Malachi is like a late evening, which brings a long day to a close; but he is also the morning dawn, which bears a glorious day in its womb." The prophet's book denounced the sins and abuses of his day and revealed the spiritual need of his people. The New Testament, four centuries later, opened with a clear indication of the provision which had been Divinely made for that need. The Old Testament concluded with a threatened curse: the New Testament ended with the pronouncement of the grace of the Lord Jesus Christ.

The Author

Of the prophet himself we know nothing at all. The name "Malachi" simply means "messenger," and it has been suggested that the word has not the form of a proper name and that it has been taken from chapter 3 : 1 as a title for the book. The second book of Esdras, dated the second century A.D., treats the name as that of the author, but the Septuagint virtually interprets the word in the opening verse of the book as "messenger." Keil refers to a note in the Talmud that Malachi was a member of the Great Synagogue. He also quotes sources to the effect that Malachi was a Levite of the tribe of Zebulun and was born at Supha. The Aramaic Targum Jonathan, of the fourth century A.D., adds to the first verse, "whose name is called Ezra the scribe," but the evidence for Ezra's authorship is actually non-existent.

The absence of any details of the author's parentage, origin or birthplace, is not unique: Obadiah and Habakkuk gave no information about themselves, and Campbell Morgan pertinently remarks that if "we argue that it is merely a title, let it be remembered that Joel means 'the Lord Jehovah'." Caspair (*Micha*, p.8) asserts that, "All the prophets, whose writings have come down to us in the canon, have given their own names to the headings of their books, that is to say, the names which they received at their birth; and the names of the rest of the prophets of the Old Testament are also their real names." There is at least as much ground for assuming Malachi to be the name of the author as for treating it as a mere appellative adopted for the book. It must be admitted, however, that the view of most modern writers is that the authorship of the book is anonymous.

Date

There is very much greater agreement on the date of the book, although there is not complete unanimity. The prophecy was obviously post-exilic, because the Nabatean conquest of Edom had already taken place (Mal. 1 : 2-5). The reference to the civil governor (Mal. 1 : 8; cf. Hag. 1 : 1; Neh. 8 : 14) places the book, *prima facie*, in the Persian era. The rebuilding of the temple, which occurred in the days of Haggai and Zechariah, had been completed (Mal. 1 : 10) and there had been a deterioration in the conduct of the priesthood and a disregard for the payment of tithes on the part of the people (Mal. 1 : 12-14; 3 : 8-10), both of which imply a lapse of some years after the completion of the building. The prevalence of divorce and of marriage with foreign women (Mal. 2 : 14-16), which were characteristics of the days of Ezra and Nehemiah, suggests a date in the fifth century B.C., since Ezra returned from Babylon in 458 B.C. and Nehemiah's visits to Jerusalem were subsequent to this. The implication that gifts were presented to the governor (Mal. 1 : 8) is evidence that the book was written (or its messages uttered) after the period during which Nehemiah occupied the office of civil governor, for Nehemiah clearly indicates that he accepted no gifts and was not a charge upon the people during his governorship (Neh. 5 : 10, 14, 15, 18).

T. V. Moore (*Haggai and Malachi*, pp. 103, 104) argues that "Malachi prophesied about the time of the second return of Nehemiah from the court of Persia, which was somewhere between the 32nd year of Artaxerxes Longimanus, B.C. 432, and the year B.C. 424; for Artaxerxes died after a reign of 41 years and Nehemiah returned the second time to Jerusalem during his life (Neh. 13 : 6)." As Nehemiah was the last civil ruler, Moore maintains that Malachi must have prophesied before Nehemiah's death and that, all things considered, the book must be assigned a date coincident with the second reformation of Nehemiah, or about 424 B.C. The general consensus of opinion is that it was around this date.

Canonicity

No question has ever been raised regarding the canonicity of the book. It appears in all the authoritative lists of canonical books and it is repeatedly quoted in the New Testament. No doubt has been expressed that this is indeed one of the sacred writings inspired of God.

11

Style and Background

Malachi's style was unique in the Old Testament. The book was composed of a series of paragraphs cast in dialectical form. First a charge was made against the people, who at once provocatively questioned the accuracy, significance or justification of the charge, which the prophet then defended logically with detailed evidence and argument, driving home the charge with renewed force. There is nothing comparable in the pages of the Old Testament.

Before the captivity, the people had repeatedly indulged in idolatry, and other prophets had denounced their practices and called them back to the worship of Jehovah. But on their return from exile, whatever their neglect of the temple and the requirements of the law, they no longer gave themselves to the service of the false gods of their heathen neighbours. In pre-exilic days they had been primarily an agricultural and pastoral people, but those who later returned to the land had largely become a nation of traders. The messages of Haggai and Zechariah had inspired them in the building of the temple, but once the work was done, their enthusiasm apparently evaporated. Religious observances seemed unprofitable, the obligations of the law were ignored, a new scepticism was generated, and a widespread spiritual depression resulted in both civil and ecclesiastical abuses. Nehemiah's reformation corrected the former and Ezra's the latter, but it was the ministry of Malachi which really aroused the people and revived their respect for God and His law and moral and spiritual requirements. He was not merely the prophet of the reformation period but essentially one whose messages in themselves effected reformation.

Contents

A key word of the book is the repeated question, "Wherein?" and the contents may be treated as a series of paragraphs revolving around this word. Alternatively, a more appropriate analysis might be as follows:—

12

1 : 1, Superscription.

1 : 2-5, Jehovah's love for Israel.

1 : 6 to 2 : 9, Sins of Priests and People.

2 : 10-16, Marriage and Divorce.

2 : 17 to 3 : 6, Impending Judgment.

3 : 7-12, Withheld Tithes.

3 : 13 to 4 : 6, Coming of Messiah.

More than half of the book is concerned with the conditions of the people, and the predictive element is restricted
to the last two chapters. Old Testament prophecy, of course,
was not always concerned with the future. The prophet was
one who acted as the mouthpiece of God (cf. Exod. 4 : 16;
7 : 1). He was inspired to deliver a message, which might
relate to the past, present or future. He might be called upon
to interpret the experiences of the past, or to admonish the
people for their actions of the present, or to foretell events
which still lay in the future. Malachi's primary concern
under God was with the spiritual state of his people and only
secondly with the events of the future, but the latter nevertheless found an important place in his prophecy.

It has frequently been pointed out that the conditions described by Malachi are extremely similar to those of the present day and that his message of over two millennia ago is
as pertinent to the twentieth century as to the days in which it
was originally uttered. He anticipated the First Advent of our
Lord, whereas we await His Second Advent, but the parallel
is very marked. It is patently a book with a message for the
present day.

CHAPTER 2

DIVINE LOVE

THE ten tribes of the nation of Israel were carried away into exile in 721 B.C. by Sargon II of Assyria. From 598 B.C. to 587 B.C. there were also deportations to Babylon of most of the people of the two tribes of the kingdom of Judah. Since the Babylonian Empire covered a great deal of the area of the Assyrian Empire, which it had succeeded, it is highly probable that descendants of the dispersed Israelites intermingled with and possibly intermarried with members of the exiled people of Judah. When, eventually, under the decree of Cyrus, the Jews were allowed to return to their own land (Ezra 1 : 1), there is little doubt that individuals from all the twelve tribes returned. Prof. H. E. Ryle (*Ezra and Nehemiah*, p. 6) says, "there is good reason to suppose that some captives from the Northern tribes, who had preserved their lineage and their national religion, availed themselves of the opportunity which the decree of Cyrus offered them." While acknowledging the possibility of this, Dr. C. I. Scofield considers that "speaking broadly, the dispersion of the ten tribes still continues; nor can they now be positively identified. They are, however, preserved distinct from other peoples and are known to God as such."

The Superscription

The majority of the exiles who returned from the captivity were almost undoubtedly members of the kingdom of Judah, but Malachi viewed the whole nation as still one in the Divine purpose and, although in chap. 2 : 11 and 3 : 4, he addressed his words to Judah and Jerusalem, the superscription referred to Israel as the object to which the message was directed. "The burden (or oracle) of the word of Jehovah to Israel by Malachi," he said (1 : 1). The old distinctions between the two kingdoms were regarded as obliterated. Those who had returned to the land were deemed to be representative of the whole, undivided nation, and the prophet, therefore, appropriately used the name of Israel. In the eyes of God the nation was still one — as it will demonstrably be in a future day.

Esau and Jacob

"I have loved you, says Jehovah. But you say, Wherein hast Thou loved us? Was not Esau Jacob's brother? says Jehovah. Yet I have loved Jacob, and I have hated Esau, and have laid his mountains and his heritage waste for the jackals of the wilderness. Whereas Edom says, We are impoverished, but we will return and build the desolate places; thus says Jehovah of hosts, They shall build, but I will throw down; and they shall call them, The border of wickedness, and the people against whom Jehovah has indignation for ever. And your eyes shall see, and you shall say, Jehovah will be magnified from beyond the border of Israel" (1 : 2-5).

The returned exiles and their descendants might reasonably have been expected to demonstrate the utmost gratitude and loyalty. They had been restored to their own land by a pagan ruler, whose very name and decree had been Divinely foretold two centuries earlier (Isa. 44 : 28). The temple had been

16

rebuilt and the walls of the city had been reconstructed, and the nation enjoyed the temperate rule of the Persians. Even the hostility of the neighbouring nations, from whom they had initially suffered harassment and distress, had tended to diminish in consequence of Nehemiah's stand. Their circumstances should have inclined them to thanksgiving for the Divine mercies bestowed upon them and to devotion to the One who had so manifestly blessed them.

Yet there was an astonishing disregard for Jehovah and an unpardonable contempt for His requirements. "This ingratitude was," says Laetsch (*The Minor Prophets*, p. 511), "rooted in their selfishness, the prevailing sin of post-exilic Judaism, which finally led to their own rejection by the Lord." There may have been an outward — and imperfect — performance of the works of the law, but the nation's heart was not in it. Prosperity had destroyed spirituality and had fostered a self-centred attitude which was really as objectionable as the idolatry of pre-exilic days.

The basic ingratitude of the people and their disrespect for the claims of God merited unmitigated denunciation, but Jehovah addressed His wayward people in terms of affection. "I have loved you." How great was the evidence of the truth of the statement in their history! Undeserving and unstable, vacillating and sinful though they were, the Divine attitude had never changed. His mercy and compassion pierced the dark clouds of their tribulations as a ray of future hope. "I have loved you." Even their recent experiences, their restoration and revised prosperity were proof of His love.

There could be no doubt regarding the warm tenderness of their eternal Lover. Yet the people turned querulously and insolently to challenge the Divine statement. "Wherein hast Thou loved us?" The sheer impertinence of the question is astounding. True it was a rhetorical one asked by the prophet himself, but it was the expression of their inmost thoughts, even if the actual words had never been uttered. How could the creature so audaciously query the assertion of the Creator? How could the nation of Israel, of all people,

17

throw doubt upon His affirmation? God might have laboriously recounted the numberless examples of His goodness in their experience and heaped instances together to rebut the implied challenge. Instead, He chose the one outstanding example which was completely irrefutable.

"But you say, Wherein hast Thou loved us?" The inane vacuity of thought which could conceive such a retort to the declaration of Divine affection was exposed in a moment by the reply of Jehovah. "Was not Esau the brother of Jacob? . . . Yet I have loved Jacob and I have hated Esau." Was there need for any further proof? Was there room for any additional question or argument?

The primary reference was, of course, to the two races of Edom and Israel, but the words plainly alluded also to their two ancestors. Esau and Jacob were twin brothers, although Esau was, in fact, the firstborn (Gen. 25:25). To him belonged the birthright, i.e. a double portion of the inheritance (Deut. 21 : 17). Nevertheless, God set His love upon Jacob in preference to Esau. And this Divine choice operated prior to their birth. As the apostle Paul so clearly intimated centuries afterwards, "the children being not yet born, neither having done any good or evil, that the purpose of God according to election might stand, not of works, but of Him who calls, it was said unto her, The elder shall serve the younger. As it is written, Jacob have I loved, but Esau have I hated" (Rom. 9 : 11-13).

It may perhaps be argued that the revelation of Esau's character subsequently confirmed the wisdom and propriety of the Divine choice. The low estimation that he placed upon his birthright, as to be willing to sell his entitlement to his brother to satisfy his physical hunger, justified the later description of him as "immoral" or "irreligious" (Heb. 12 : 16). His tears of regret when he sought the blessing were insufficient to blot out his earlier folly. Despite the pre-natal prediction (Gen. 25 : 23), Isaac had determined to bless his favourite son, but Jacob was the recipient of the blessing (Gen. 27 : 27-41). If it be maintained that Divine foreknowledge of the character of Esau was the reason for his rejection and for the choice of his brother, one is still faced with the difficulty that Jacob was by no means a deserving individual. He was prepared to bargain with a hungry brother for the latter's birthright, to deceive his blind father, and to cheat his father-in-law. He was a supplanter and a deceiver, he was not marked by outstanding righteousness, his cupidity was evident. He was even ready to bargain with God. Yet God loved him and not Esau.

The word "hated" in the context does not imply a positive hate for an individual, but rather the complete absence of love. In verse 30 of Gen. 29 it is stated that Jacob loved Rachel more than her sister Leah, but in the following verse it is stated that the latter was hated. God had an affection for Jacob: He had none for Esau. Prof. John Murray, however, contends that there is a holy hate in God that cannot be defined merely as not loving, and that the Divine attitude to Esau was one of positive disfavour: he was the object of Divine displeasure. Floyd S. Hamilton points out (*The Epistle to the Romans*, p. 155) that, "while the election of Jacob was undeserved and the casting off of Esau was determined before his birth, the hatred on the part of God was not arbitrary, but was predicated of God *after* Esau and his descendants turned their backs upon God and worshipped idols. It was the rebellious sinner Esau who was the object of the Divine hatred and wrath."

So far as the nation of Israel was concerned, God made it perfectly clear that His love was not based upon their merits. Moses specifically informed Israel, "Jehovah did not set His love upon you or choose you because you were more in number than any people; for you were the fewest of all people; but because Jehovah loved you, and because He would keep the oath which He had sworn to your fathers, has Jehovah brought you out with a mighty hand, and redeemed you from the house of bondage, from the hand of Pharaoh, king of Egypt" (Deut. 7 : 7, 8). Again, God declared that the land He was giving to them was not bestowed

19

upon them because of their righteousness or the uprightness of their heart: they were, in fact, a stubborn and rebellious race (Deut. 9 : 5-7). His love was sovereign. He loved them because He loved them and for no other reason comprehensible to man. Divine election was not related to human conduct but, as Hodge says, "was determined by the will of Him who calls."

The mystery of Divine election is one which appears inexplicable to man. It seems clear, on the one hand, that man is a relatively free agent, capable of free volition and responsible for his actions and decisions. On the other hand, it is equally plain that the Almighty has a plan for His universe and that He so orders His government as to achieve what He has determined. This, of course, gives no support to the fatalistic view that no one is an arbiter of his own destiny but that "all events are determined by a blind necessity."

As the sovereign and inalienable owner of all things, God has a perfect right to do as He wills with His own possessions. Just as a potter does what he pleases with the clay he handles, leaving the clay with no basis for complaint, so God has a right to act as He wills in relation to His creatures, without giving reason or explanation. None can question His actions. Why did He choose to work out an amazing plan on this small planet, earth, instead of on one of the very much larger orbs available to Him? Why did He choose Abraham and call him out of Ur of the Chaldees? Why did He set His love upon Jacob instead of Esau? Why did He bring particular individuals into a relationship with Christ, while others were allowed to go their own way?

The apostle Paul disclosed that the Christian was chosen in Christ before the foundation of the world (Eph. 1 : 4) and our Lord explicitly stated that He had chosen His own out of the world (John 15 : 19). That election, the apostle Peter declared, was according to the foreknowledge of God (1 Pet. 1 : 2), but it is entirely of grace and is unrelated to the merit or the works of the individual. To quote C. I. Scofield, it is "the sovereign act of God in grace whereby certain are chosen

20

from among mankind for Himself." Rebellious man had forfeited all claim upon his Maker, but God, in a past eternity, planned the reconciliation of the rebel to Himself. From a guilty and condemned race, He called out some to Himself. Whilst the individual is responsible to exercise faith in the Saviour divinely provided, God's election is not completely contingent upon man's act of faith. Our Lord declared that "All whom the Father gives Me shall come to Me" (John 6 : 37), but He also plainly stated that "No man can come to Me except the Father who has sent Me draws him" (John 6 : 44).

The Divine choice is deliberate. At Antioch, the apostle Paul stated that "as many as were ordained to eternal life believed" (Acts 13 : 48) and he informed the Ephesian church that the choice was made even before creation (Eph. 1 : 4, 5; see also 2 Thess. 2 : 13).

Those, to whom such favour has been shown, should surely respond in gratitude and devotion. Yet how many Christians there are today, who are found questioning the Divine love as much as did the Jews of Malachi's day. Ill-health, the lack of material benefits, an unappealing environment, the unsympathetic attitude of the world, are frequently all regarded as plain evidence that no special favour has been shown to the believer as contrasted with those around him. How utterly foolish is this attitude in the face of the demonstration of the love and compassion of God! "Wherein hast Thou loved us?" In the light of Calvary, the question is almost blasphemous.

In the providence of God, Esau had become the possessor of the hill country of Seir — not barren, uncultivated land, but an area which sustained sheep and cattle and was fruitful in crops. His descendants, the Edomites, by this time had become strong and powerful. Yet, because of their attitude to Israel, an earlier prophet had foretold the desolation of their land (Jer. 49 : 17; see also Ezck. 35 : 1-9; Obad. 4-10). As proof of His love for Israel and His rejection of Esau, Jehovah declared that this had now been fulfilled. Esau's

21

hill country had been laid waste and his possessions had been given to the jackals of the wilderness. Since the feminine word was used for "jackal," the reference was presumably to the lairs in which the female jackals suckled their cubs: the animals were pictured as in secure and undisturbed possession of Esau's heritage (cf. Isa. 34 : 13; 35 : 7). The Nabatean Arabs, the descendants of Esau's own cousin, Nebaioth, had, in fact, driven the Edomites out of their land and had themselves occupied it. They were still settled in Petra (probably the Sela of 2 Kings 14 : 7), the capital city of Edom, over a century later. The predicted judgment had fallen upon Esau. Permitted, as this had been, by Jehovah Himself, it was surely an indication to Israel that His love had been set upon them and His disfavour upon Esau. "Whereas Jacob had recovered, in consequence of the love of Jehovah, from the blow which had fallen upon it (through the Chaldeans)," says Keil (*The Twelve Minor Prophets*, p. 43), "Esau's territory was still lying in ruins from the same blow, in consequence of Jehovah's hatred."

The Jews had returned to their own land and had rebuilt their cities. The Edomites, defeated and dispossessed as they had been by the Nabateans, determined similarly to return and to recover their own territory and to rebuild their cities. But God declared that, whatever they built, He would throw down. All their attempts were, in fact, unsuccessful: they never regained their land. The Nabateans established a civilisation in Edom which lasted for nearly five centuries, until the area came under the control of the Roman empire. So completely was the Divine statement fulfilled.

The Nabateans, who so completely humbled Edom, are described by N. Glueck, in *The Other Side of the Jordan* (p. 200), as "one of the most remarkable peoples that have ever crossed the stage of history. Springing swiftly out of the deserts of Arabia to a position of great power and affluence and glory, they were thrust back by the Romans even more swiftly into the limbo of history whence they came. While their turn lasted, the Nabateans wrought greatly, developing overnight, almost, into builders of magnificent cities, unique in the history of the handiwork of men. They were tradesmen and farmers and engineers and architects of great energy and skill. The ruins which they left behind them testify eloquently to the glory which was theirs."

They were evidently the instrument employed to fulfil the Divine purpose. There was no hope for Edom. The prophet declared that Edom would contemptuously be termed "the border of wickedness," i.e. a land (since "border" is used to denote the whole area enclosed by the border) which had come under judgment for its wickedness. The Edomites, moreover, would be recognised as a people upon whom Divine wrath permanently rested. Their active antagonism to Israel had been fully recompensed.

With this irrefutable evidence of God's deliverance of Israel from all possibility of invasion by their ancient enemy within the then foreseeable future, and the demonstration of His love for His people and His hatred of those who were, after all, their blood relations, the Jews must surely accept the significance of what they saw. They must acknowledge that the supreme power and authority of Jehovah had been — and would be — demonstrated beyond the boundaries of Israel. In a future day, He will be magnified throughout the whole earth, but already they could see the foreshadowing of His glory in His action against Edom.

It was but one illustration of Jehovah's affection for Israel, but it was a most significant one. Was any other proof needed to convince this self-sufficient and self-righteous race? It should have more than sufficed.

CHAPTER 3

BLEMISHED SACRIFICES

THE ALMIGHTY is not required to explain His actions or His attitude. If He does so, it is an act of gracious condescension. He had declared His love to Israel and had given an outstanding illustration of it to convince His wayward people. But it seems to have been completely ineffective and He now turned logically to strip away the veil which hid their insincerity and basic disloyalty.

A Dishonoured Name

"*A son honours his father and a servant his master. If I then am a father, where is my honour? And if I am a master, where is my reverence? says Jehovah of hosts to you, O priests, who despise my name. And you say, Wherein have we despised thy name?*" (1 : 6).

The fundamental reason for the people's attitude was their complete lack of respect for God and this affected all their actions, even to the presenting of blemished sacrifices and the withholding of the tithes required by the law. If they questioned the fact of Jehovah's love for them, it was a reflection of their lack of love for Him. They owed everything to Him and should have dedicated themselves unreservedly to Him. His honour should have been the supreme object of their life, and to do His will should have been their constant delight. Yet they were defrauding Him of His due and insulting Him by offering defective sacrifices on His altar. If they treated His claims so irreverently, it was little wonder that love and affection were lacking. Indeed, their actions were clear evidence of the absence of such feeling.

The fifth commandment in the decalogue required that honour should be paid to parents (Ex. 20 : 12). Jehovah was described as the Father of Israel in the song of Moses (Deut. 32 : 6), and the prophets similarly designated Him (Isa. 63 : 16, Jer. 31 : 9). Israel proudly claimed that this was His peculiar relationship to them. If so, the filial respect of the nation should obviously have been paid to the eternal Father. But there was no trace of honour being rendered to Him. If He was their Father, where was the respect due to Him? It was conspicuously absent.

God was their sovereign ruler: if He was their supreme master (the plural form of the word, implying royalty), then homage and reverential awe should be paid to Him. Where was the reverence due to Him? Again, there was no trace of it. The inclination of heart is demonstrated by the character of the external action and there was a complete absence of any indication of loyalty and devoted obedience.

The attitude of a people is, generally speaking, a reflection of that of their leaders or, alternatively, is the consequence of the teachings — or lack of teaching — of such leaders.

The reason for Israel's condition was to be found in the spiritual declension of the priests. It was they who were the exponents of the law and it was they who should have been inculcating in the people a sense of holy fear and an appreciation of the supreme holiness of God. It was their failure to teach the character and claims of God that was responsible for the deplorable condition of the nation, and Jehovah

26

addressed them as those who despised His name. Wm. Kelly, in his *Lectures on the Minor Prophets* (p. 512), says, "The higher the relation, the greater the danger where God is not before the soul. It is not only that sin in such is more serious, but also there is greater exposure to it. A priest has to walk not merely as becomes a man outside the sanctuary, but as one who goes into it. There was a more complete consecration in the case of a priest than with an Israelite; and familiarity with the presence of God, unless it be kept up in His fear, borders on contempt." The priests' non-recognition of the character of God was, by implication, a disrespect which embodied an embryonic despite.

The failure of the priests was more reprehensible because of the effect upon the people. Not only had they failed to inculcate reverence, but their practices had naturally led the people to conclude that no reverence was due. It was completely inconsistent with what they professed. "Why do you call Me, Lord, Lord," said the Master in a later day, "and do not the things which I say?" (Luke 6 : 46). It was an insincerity deserving of even greater condemnation because of the privileged position and professed piety of those to whom the words applied.

The Mosaic law specifically laid down that the offerings presented to God should be unblemished (e.g. Lev. 4 : 3; 9 : 2). The priests in Malachi's day, however, not only permitted, but apparently encouraged, the sacrifice of animals proscribed because of their imperfection. They showed a total disregard of the legal requirements and thereby invoked a disrespect for the law and a lack of reverence for its Author. They virtually despised God's name. Yet so blind were they to the significance of their conduct that they said, "Wherein have we despised Thy name?" Alexander Maclaren appropriately remarks in his *Expositions of Holy Scripture, Ezekiel to Malachi*, p. 324, "The name is the sum of the revealed character. . . . The pollution of the table of the Lord is the overt action by which the attitude of mind and heart, expressed in despising His name, is manifested; but the overt action is secondary and not primary — a symptom of a deeper-lying disease." 'The effect of all sin," he goes on to say (*ibid*, p. 326), "is to make us less conscious of its presence. . . . We lose our sense of the moral character of any habitual action." This was clearly the case with the priests of Malachi's day: they were completely oblivious to the obvious implications of their conduct and practice. In ignoring the clearly expressed will of God and refraining from insisting upon the conscientious observance of His requirements, they brought dishonour upon Him. Yet, tragically, they seemed unaware of the effect of their actions.

The words are not entirely irrelevant to the present day. when Biblical standards are declared obsolete and inappropriate, when the explicit statements of Scripture are brought into question and the teachings of the Son of God are ridiculed, when doubt is cast upon our Lord's deity or His virgin birth, upon His resurrection and His promised return. The theologians who so unashamedly mislead God's people, not only, by inference, despise His name themselves, but induce a lack of reverence on the part of others because of their teaching. The One Who discerned the hidden motivation of the heart in Malachi's day is still reading the hearts of men today. "You despise My name," He declares. John A. T. Robinson, whose writings are at least partially responsible for the permissive society of our 20th century, writes, "The religious sanctions are losing their strength, the moral landmarks are disappearing beneath the flood, the nation is in danger. This is the end-term of the apostasy from Christianity: the fathers rejected the doctrine, the children abandoned the morals." Are we not doing despite to His name?

A Desecrated Altar

"You offer polluted bread upon my altar: and you say, Wherein have we polluted Thee? In that you say, the table of Jehovah is contemptible. And if you offer the blind for sacrifice, it is not evil. And if you offer the lame and sick

it is not evil. Offer it now to your governor; will he be pleased with you, or accept your person? says Jehovah of hosts" (*1* : *7, 8*).

It has been a common idea, in many pagan religions, that the gods require to be fed in the same way as human beings and that food, consumed by fire on the altar devoted to the deity worshipped, would, in some mysterious way, delight the deity and satisfy his appetite. (There was also, of course, the idea that the sacrifice of another being — animal or human — appeased the god and averted his wrath from the worshipper). This concept was not given any specific sanction in the detailed regulations regarding the Levitical offerings, although Ezek. 41 : 22 and 44 : 16 refer to the altar as Jehovah's table and Lev. 21 : 6, 8, 17, 21, 22; 22 : 25, etc. describe the sacrifice as "the bread of God." Malachi's words do, however, seem to countenance the idea that the sacrifice presented on the altar was not merely to appease God (which might be applicable in the case of a sin offering, but could scarcely be so in the case of a burnt offering), but to provide an offering in which He could find delight. If, indeed, the Levitical offerings are regarded as figurative of Christ, in the various aspects of His life and work, there is justification for this view.

The priests had indignantly reacted against the charge that they had despised God's name. In what demonstrable respect could this be true? they had enquired. Patiently, as though explaining to a child, the reply came, "You offer polluted bread upon My altar." If the sacrifice on the altar was "the bread of God" and His "food" (Lev. 21 : 6; 3 : 11), it must necessarily be perfect and the law repeatedly emphasised that offerings must be unblemished and free from any. defect. Yet the priests were evidently accepting and offering sacrifices which did not satisfy the Divine requirements. A blemished offering was defiled "bread" to God. This should have been so apparent as to have convicted these guilty men of the seriousness of the crime they had committed. They had defiled the altar by their polluted sacrifices.

Yet, with no apparent sense of the impropriety or impiety of their actions, they responded in amazement to the charge, "Wherein have we polluted Thee?" It is true that the question was merely a rhetorical one on the part of the prophet, but it patently represented the attitude of those on whose lips he metaphorically placed the question. It seems almost incredible that they should have been unaware of their crass folly and disobedience. But is not this characteristic generally of those who, consistently ignoring God's claims, finally become oblivious to them and unaware that they are not fulfilling His will? Confident of the rectitude of their ways, they cannot conceive that they could possibly be unacceptable to Him. How could they defile Him?

There was, of course, a further consequence which Malachi does not mention. In accepting blemished offerings (and possibly even encouraging them), the priest condoned the sin of the offering in presenting them, and thereby became a partner in the offerer's guilt. A defiled priest committed sin in standing before God to offer at His altar. Yet such were the men who impudently enquired, "Wherein have we polluted Thee?"

The answer left no room for further argument. "In that you say, The table of Jehovah is contemptible." Their actions implied that the altar was despicable. If the Divine requirements were so lightly esteemed and if they so actively aided and abetted the breach of the law, they were treating the altar as undeserving of respect. It had virtually become despicable in their eyes. The law explicitly declared, for example, of the firstling of the flock or the herd — which was to be set apart to God — that "if there is any blemish in it, as if it is lame, or blind, or has any ill blemish, you shall not sacrifice it to Jehovah your God" (Deut. 15 : 21). Of the peace offerings and freewill offerings, it had been said earlier, that "it shall be perfect to be accepted. There shall be no blemish in it. Blind, or broken, or maimed, or having a wen, or scurvy, or scabbed, you shall not offer these to Jehovah." Nothing 'bruised, or crushed, or broken, or cut" was to be offered. In

30

fact, "whatever has a blemish you shall not offer: for it shall not be acceptable for you" (Lev. 22 : 20-24).

The prohibitions were crystal clear. No possible doubt could exist. Yet it is plain that blind, lame and sick animals were being offered, but the priests regarded this as no evil and Malachi quoted them as asserting this. The law no longer mattered: they had set themselves up as arbiters of what should be accepted, Maclaren (ibid, p. 328) takes the view that the priests "were probably dishonest as well as mean, because the worshippers would bring sound beasts, and the priests, for their own profit, slipped in a worthless animal, and kept the valuable one for themselves. They had become so habituated to this piece of economic religion, that they saw no harm in it." This is possible and, if true, could only accentuate the seriousness of the crime, but it is more likely that the example and teaching of the priests had rendered the people as degenerate as themselves, and thy were prepared to give to God only what was of no use to themselves. Campbell Morgan says, in his Studies in Malachi, p. 35, "these men have lost the sense of what worship means, in that they have retained the finest of the flock for themselves, and brought to the altar that which engenders its contempt, simply to keep up the form of sacrifice and the appearance which they so much covet." They had lost sight of the fact that God measured the value of the offering by its worth to the offerer and placed the same estimate upon the man himself. The Lord Jesus Christ made this clear in a later day, when He declared that the widow who threw two mites into the temple treasury had cast in more than all the wealthy who had given of their abundance, since she had given her all (Mark 12 : 41-44).

A tragic feature was that the priests had lost all sense of right and wrong. They saw no evil in what they were doing. They were not concerned that they were defrauding the Almighty. Ironically, the Divine speaker bade them to offer the blemished animals to the governor. Would the Persian satrap be delighted with the blind, lame and sick animals, which they dared to offer to God? (The use of the word *pehah*, which applied to governors of the Persian provinces, may be an argument for dating the book in the Persian period.) Their acceptance by the governor depended upon the acceptability of their gifts. Would he accept such gifts and, if he did not, did they think that they personally would find acceptance? Yet they offered to God what they would not dare to offer to an earthly ruler. Sacrilege, says one writer, does not necessarily involve breaking into church and stealing the collection money: it is more often found in attendance at the service and putting the smallest possible coin in the collection box. We offer God what we do not want for ourselves. The time, talent and ability, which should be devoted to His service, are employed for our own ends, and we condescendingly give Him what is left over. Yet, like the priests of Malachi's day, we see no evil in it.

Can God be Appeased?

"And now, I pray you, beseech the face of God that he will be gracious to us. This has proceeded from your hand. Will he accept any persons because of you? says Jehovah of hosts" (*1* : *9*).

The situation was serious. The sin of priests and people was of such a character as to invoke condign punishment. Was mercy still available for those who had virtually rebelled against God?

The usual interpretation of verse 9 is that, having exposed the sin of priests and people, God now challenged them to entreat His favour and, by implication, to avert the curse that would otherwise come upon them. Moore (*ibid*, p. 119) paraphrases, "Intercede for us with God, for you (priests) are the men whose office calls you to this duty; you are the professed avenues to God." Divine mercy is always ready to listen to the penitent sinner's cry and, even in the conditions of Malachi's day, it is possible that the plea was being made to the priests to intercede on behalf of their fellows. But that

32

virtually ignores their own need and assumes that their inter-cession for others would be heard.

It is more probable that the irony of the preceding verse is being continued, especially in the light of the following verse. Laetsch takes the view — for which there is some support — that the prophet is ironically urging the priests to appease God while, at the same time, they are continuing to offer their blemished sacrifices and unrepentantly to show no sign of amending their ways. This seems a more logical interpretation. The evil had proceeded from the priests: they were the instigators of the sinful practices of the people. But they were the appointed intercessors on behalf of the people and they confidently continued to follow their normal ritual on the assumption that they were thereby placating God for others. How could Jehovah accept anyone on the basis of the intercession of such men? Their sacerdotal ministry was a sheer mockery. Their insincerity would render futile any approach to God, and it would be pointless for them to intercede on behalf of either individual or nation. It is un-likely that, in those circumstances, Jehovah would enjoin them to entreat His favour.

The prayer of the impenitent, who has no intention of altering his ways, can only be ineffectual. How can the Almighty listen to his cry? If we are going to gain the ear of God, there must be a willingness to acknowledge our sin-fulness as well as our need and a determination to eschew evil in future. We cannot expect the blessing of heaven if we continue in sin.

Excluded from the Temple

Far from His appealing to obdurate sinners to seek His favour, God's intention was apparently to debar them from any approach to Him. Neither they nor their offerings were acceptable to Him. His people no longer brought Him any delight and He now implied that His desire was their exclus-ion from His presence. This is not apparent in the A.V.,

33

which gives an entirely different emphasis from what was evidently intended.

"Oh that there was one among you who would shut the doors, so that you might not kindle fire on my altar to no purpose! I have no pleasure in you, says Jehovah of hosts, neither will I accept an offering at your hand" (1 : 10).

The A.V. rendering is virtually a Divine lament that no one was prepared to perform a service for God without reward: they were not prepared to shut the temple doors or to kindle a fire upon the altar without payment for their labours. This was probably true in Malachi's day, as so often it is in our own. The willing service for Christ, which anticipates no reward but His smile, has been superseded by a cold, calculating spirit, which estimates what should be the recompense for everything that is done. Many are more concerned with getting than giving. The perfect Exemplar unhesitatingly and unreservedly gave His all for the salvation of others. The apostle Paul told the Corinthian church, "I will not be burdensome to you, for I seek not yours, but you" (2 Cor. 12 : 14).

Nevertheless, while all this is true, it is more likely that the Divine Speaker was expressing the desire that the temple should be closed against the false worship and malpractices of His people. Since He was not prepared to accept their blemished offerings and found no pleasure in their temple services, it would be far better if the whole of their empty ritual was stopped. The plain inference is that He found the whole thing objectionable and nauseating. Accordingly, He voiced the yearning that someone would close the doors and put a stop to the desecration of His altar. "Where is there among you," says Moore (*ibid,* p. 120), "some Phinehas, who will rise in holy indignation and shut the doors of my house against such desecration, and prevent the smoking of useless and polluting sacrifices upon my altar? Better withhold your beggarly apology for religion than insult me, and add to your own guilt by palming it upon your conscience as an acceptable service to God." In an earlier day, another prophet had voiced the Divine disgust with the insincere worship offered to Him, "To what purpose is the multitude of your sacrifices unto me? says Jehovah. I am full of the burnt-offerings of rams, and the fat of fed beasts; and I delight not in the blood of bullocks, or of lambs, or of he-goats" (Isa. 1 : 11).

In His infinite holiness, God cannot tolerate the hypocrisy and insincerity of service which is false. It is not only unacceptable, but repellent to Him. Dare we come into His presence with unclean hands and impure motives and hope to deceive the Omniscient? Is not our service for Christ sometimes as defiled and blemished as the offerings of Israel? Is our profession of loyalty and allegiance not belied by the inconsistency of our actions and motives? The character of God does not change and we too may deprive ourselves of communion with Him and find our service rejected if we pursue Israel's course.

A Name to be Feared

"For from the rising of the sun even to the going down of the same, my name shall be great among the Gentiles; and in every place incense and a pure offering shall be offered to my name. For my name shall be great among the Gentiles, says Jehovah of hosts. But you have profaned it, in that you say, The table of Jehovah is polluted, and the fruit of it, even his meat, is contemptible. You said also, Behold what a weariness it is! And you have snuffed at it, says Jehovah of hosts; and you have brought that which was torn, and the lame, and the sick; thus you brought an offering. Should I accept this of your hand? says Jehovah. But cursed be the deceiver, who has in his flock a male, and vows, and sacrifices to Jehovah a corrupt thing. For I am a great king, says Jehovah of hosts, and my name is feared among the Gentiles" (*1 : 11-14*).

Judah and her priests had defiled the altar, dishonoured the name of Jehovah, and had robbed Him of the glory that was His due. God now announced that He would vindicate His honour and that His name would be glorified throughout the nations of the world. The plain inference was that Israel was to be displaced and that the Gentiles would render to Jehovah what His elect people had failed to do, Isaiah had earlier declared that "the Gentiles shall come to thy light, and kings to the brightness of thy rising" (Isa. 60 : 3) and that God's glory would be declared among the Gentiles (Isa. 66 : 19). The Jew always concluded that any blessing enjoyed by the Gentiles would come through contact with the chosen people, but the clear implication of God's word through Malachi was that blessing would be bestowed direct upon the Gentiles and that the fear of God would be evidenced by the Gentiles when Israel had failed Him. The words must have come as a startling shock to those who heard.

Sir George Adam Smith's comments, in *The Twelve Prophets,* p. 359, seem to imply that the words were applicable at that time and did not relate primarily to the future. He says, "It is not the mere question of there being righteous people in every nation, well-pleasing to Jehovah because of their lives. The very sacrifices of the heathen are pure and acceptable to Him. Never have we had in prophecy, even the most far-seeing and evangelical, a statement so generous and catholic as this." The words could scarcely be true of the days in which they were uttered, however. The worship of the nations was anything but pure. The most abominable practices were associated with their idolatrous rites, and the name of Jehovah was certainly not great among the people, for every conceivable god and goddess was worshipped, and homage paid to the creature rather than the Creator.

In the glorious millennial age, the name of Jehovah will be feared in every part of the world "and His glory from the rising of the sun" (Isa. 59 : 19). During the reign of Christ the knowledge of God will be universal, and Malachi's words will be true that, from sunrise to sunset, He will be worshipped by the nations and His name will be magnified. The term "incense" in verse 11 is a frequent symbol of prayer and praise and is appropriately used in the context. Prayer and worship will ascend to God from every part of the world, for in that day, the Gentile nations will acknowledge Him.

In some respects, the description may be regarded as pertinent to the present day and the prophet's words may have had in view the present era, in which Israel no longer occupies a favoured position in the Divine purposes, but the Gentiles have been brought to a knowledge of salvation because of Israel's failure (Rom. 11 : 11). The barrier between Jew and Gentile has been swept away, but the church period is one pre-eminently of Gentile blessing. It is true today that the name of God is magnified among the Gentiles (rather than among the unrepentant members of Israel) and that prayer and worship ascend to Him from every land. The primary reference, however, seems to be to the future age when the Divine glory will again be seen on earth.

If the Gentiles are to pay honour to Jehovah's name, He declared that, by their attitude, the priests had by contrast profaned it. They had argued that the altar was polluted and the offerings contemptible. At first sight, the attitude seems incredible, but they were reaping what they had sown. Having condoned — if not encouraged — the offering by the people of the sick, defective, diseased and worn-out animals, which were valueless to the offerers, the priests found that the reward for their services at the temple and the only food which they had to eat were the same despised offerings. No wonder that, in their chagrin, they declared that the altar was defiled and the meat contemptible.

Their service in the temple brought them no joy. It should have been their supreme delight to be engaged in ministry for God and His people. Instead they found it utterly wearisome and would gladly have relieved themselves of the irksome responsibility. They "snuffed at it." But it was their own fault! They presented for sacrifices what was forbidden (Lev. 22 : 20). If a beast had suffered by being taken by violence, the culprit was obliged to make compensation to

37

the offended owner and then to bring an unblemished tres- pass offering to atone for his guilt (Lev. 6 : 2-7). But the culprit in Malachi's day outrageously brought the torn beast itself as his trespass offering. Others brought the lame or maimed, the sick and weakling. The whole procedure was an insult to God. "Should I accept this of your hand?" He asked.

The priests suffered for their own lowering of the standard. They had tolerated — and had evidently encouraged — the violation of the law and the flaunting of the Divine demands, and eventually they suffered from the inevitable repercus- sions. Their portion came from the offerings presented by the worshippers. If the sacrifices were of poor quality, the priests' recompense was correspondingly poor. Laetsch (ibid, p. 519) aptly pictures their plight: "What a weariness to stand all day long and be ready whenever someone feels like bringing his sacrifice, to slay it, and skin it, and gut it, and cut it up, a filthy bloody job, and what do we get out of it? A few pieces of tough meat, unfit for food." It could have been poor consolation to realise that the blame was their own. Had they maintained the Divine standards and taught the people that only the best should be presented to God, their own portion would have been of the best animals too.

The tolerance of lower standards — and, worse still, the active encouragement of the lowering — inevitably reacts upon the foolish proponents of such a policy. If respect for God and His Word is diminished, there will be a consequen- tial loss of respect for the ministers of His Word, who en- courage such a course. The church never benefits by con- formity with the world's outlook or by tolerance of practices which are out of accord with the Divine revelation. On the contrary, its power wanes and its authority is reduced, and ultimately its witness to a living God becomes a lifeless re- petition of formalisms.

The Psalmist declares that Jehovah "is a great king over all the earth" (Psa. 47 : 2). It was this that both priests and people had forgotten, and God reiterated the fact through the lips of Malachi. "I am a great king," He asserted, "and my name is feared among the Gentiles." While His people treated Him so disgracefully, there was a reverential worship on the part of the nations — a claim that will ultimately be realised in a future day, but which does imply that He took account of the attitude of the heathen, even in their blindness and lack of knowledge. The Septuagint not inappropriately uses the word "illustrious" in place of "feared" or the A.V.'s "dreadful."

His greatness as the supreme Sovereign made the culpability of His people even more unpardonable, and He pronounced a curse upon them for their conduct. The dissimulating cheat, who dared to offer to God a cheaper female animal in lieu of the choice male which should have been sacrificed (possibly with the plea that he had not one in the flock or was unable to procure one), was revealed for what he was and the curse of God lighted on him. The one who brought as a votive offering an animal that was blemished, in place of the faultless one required by the law, was equally guilty and came under the same curse. They had defrauded God and had foolishly attempted to deceive Him. How could they hope to act thus with impunity? The eye of omniscience rested on them and their deceit was exposed.

The significance of the Divine statement cannot be ignored. The principle is applicable in every day. The Eternal seeks the sacrifice of our all. Yet so often we insult Him by offering our second best. In the Person of His Son, God gave His all. Dare those, who have been redeemed by the blood of Calvary, withhold aught from Him? Rather should we prostrate ourselves at His feet in a sheer and utter abandonment of life, talents and possessions, to the One Who alone deserves our devotion. The life that is withheld becomes spiritually atrophied; the offering of the second-rate results in spiritual loss; the attempted deception of the Almighty rebounds upon the head of the deceiver. When Ananias and Sapphira tried to deceive God they paid the penalty for their prevarication (Acts 5 : 1-11). God is "a great king over all the earth."

39

CHAPTER 4

AN UNFAITHFUL PRIESTHOOD

THE priesthood was responsible, not only to mediate between the people and Jehovah, but also to make clear the teachings and obligations of the law. In the second respect they had miserably failed. To ingratiate themselves with the people, they had discounted the specific requirements of the law and had evidently evacuated its injunctions of force and meaning. The spiritual condition of the people had resulted, at least partially, from the conduct of a corrupt priesthood. God, therefore, arraigned the priests for their unfaithfulness.

Threatened Punishment

"And now, O you priests, this charge is for you. If you will not hear, to give honour to my name, says Jehovah of hosts, I will even sow the curse upon you, and I will curse your blessings. Yes, I have cursed them already, because you do not lay it to heart. Behold, I will corrupt your seed, and will scatter dung on your faces, even the dung of your solemn feasts, and it shall take you away with it. And you shall know that I have sent this charge to you, in respect of my covenant being with Levi, says Jehovah of hosts" (2 : 1-4).

41

The priests were virtually the representatives of the people and were, therefore, the first to be admonished. There was a special relationship between Jehovah and the tribe of Levi, but their conduct had run entirely counter to that relationship. They were accordingly warned of the consequences if there was no repentance or change of heart on their part. In effect, a final opportunity was being afforded to them to listen to God's injunction and to render to Him the honour due to His name. Hitherto they had dishonoured Him in toning down His claims upon His people: they had failed as the teachers of Israel and had been ineffective as mediators on behalf of the people. They had misrepresented God and His character, since they had persuaded the people that His demands were of little account. Would they now recognise their guilt, turn penitently to God, and henceforth teach the truth to men?

This was the issue. If the priests did not avail themselves of this opportunity, punishment would no longer be averted. The words of Moses centuries earlier had been clear and explicit. If the people failed to observe the commandments of God, then specific curses would fall upon them — field, cattle, family, health, commerce would all be affected (Deut. 28 : 15-68). Such curses were now threatened for the priests: in fact, God declared that the curse had already been pronounced since their stubbornness and refusal to listen were already apparent.

He announced that He would curse their blessings. The reference may have been to a drying up of their sources of income: since their teaching had induced a lack of respect for the law, the people might reasonably conclude that there was no point in supporting the priests by payment of the tithes required by the law. On the other hand, Keil (*ibid*, pp. 442-3) takes the view that the reference was to "the blessings pronounced by the priests upon the people by virtue of their office. These God will curse, i.e. He will make them ineffective, or turn them into the very opposite." This is not a very satisfactory explanation, since the transformation into a curse of the blessing pronounced upon the people would have been a judgment upon the people rather than upon the priests, who were under review.

A curse was also pronounced upon the field. The seed sown in the field was to be corrupted, or blasted, before it came to maturity: as another puts it, the potential blessing was converted into the elemental curse of famine. They had complained of the poor quality of the reward for their services (the torn and blemished meat from the sacrifices): now they were to suffer where they were most vulnerable. There is some difficulty about this interpretation, however. The priests were not farmers and the blasting of the crops would, *prima facie*, affect them only indirectly: it could hardly be regarded as a punishment directly appropriate to them. Keil suggests that (changing the pointing) the words, "I will corrupt your seed," would be better rendered, "I rebuke your arm." Inability to lift the arm would mean "the neutralising of the official duties performed at the altar and in the sanctuary." The common rendering has more support, however, and is perhaps more relevant in the light of the later blessing in Mal. 3 : 11. In any case, the priests would feel the effects of famine equally with the people — and perhaps to a greater extent if they were dependent upon an unfaithful people.

The offal of sacrificial victims was burned outside the camp (Ex. 29 : 14; Lev. 4 : 12; 16 : 27) in the wilderness and in the valley of Hinnom in the land. But Jehovah declared that He would scatter the offal of their sacred festivals (possibly sacrifices) upon their faces — the most ignominious indignity that could be contemplated. Their corruption was such that He rejected their sacrifices and festivals as a filthy mockery. "Their sanctimonious mien, their hypocritical piety, will be turned into an abhorrent spectacle," says Laetsch (*ibid*, p. 522). And because they were so repellent, they would be swept away like filth to the dung pits (cf. 1 Kings 14 : 10). The terms used may seem highly distasteful, but they are indicative of the abhorrence felt by the Almighty for a corrupt priesthood. It is impossible to ignore the New

43

Testament counterpart, where our Lord declared of the nauseating lukewarm church of Laodicea, "I will spue you out of my mouth" (Rev. 3 : 16). Where God's honour is impugned and His commands are brought into disrepute by those who profess to honour Him, the punishment is related to the corruptness displayed.

The relationship of the priestly tribe of Levi with God imposed certain duties and responsibilities upon them, which were clearly detailed. Their privileged service of the sanctuary, moreover, required a corresponding physical and moral purity. Jehovah referred to this relationship and the detailed demands made upon the priesthood as His covenant with Levi, and declared that it was because of this covenant that He had sent this charge (i.e. the announcement of their punishment for their wrongdoing) to them. Koehler says, "They will perceive that just as Jehovah had hitherto regulated His conduct towards Levi by the terms of His covenant, which was made with it at the time of its departure from Egypt, so will He henceforth let it be regulated by the terms of the decree of punishment which He has resolved upon now, so that this decree of punishment takes the place, as it were, of the earlier covenant."

The Covenant with Levi

"My covenant with him was of life and peace; and I gave them to him for the reverence wherewith he reverenced me, and was afraid before my name. The law of truth was in his mouth, and iniquity was not found in his lips: he walked with me in peace and equity, and turned many away from iniquity. For the priest's lips should keep knowledge, and they should seek the law at his mouth: for he is the messenger of Jehovah of hosts" (2 : 5-7).

The covenant with Levi having been given as the reason for the punishment of the erring priesthood, emphasis was laid upon the character and conduct expected from those who were subject to the covenant.

44

When Phinehas, the priest, slew the Israelite and the Midianite woman with whom he had sinned, Jehovah declared, "I give unto him my covenant of peace: and he shall have it, and his seed after him, even the covenant of an everlasting priesthood" (Num. 25 : 12, 13). He had been zealous in vindicating God's honour, and the covenant of peace was his reward. Malachi stated that the covenant with the tribe of Levi was of life and peace and that these blessings had been bestowed upon Levi because of the reverence he paid to God and the awe which he demonstrated of the Divine name. Security and quiet were guaranteed to the priestly tribe when they showed the respect due to the Eternal.

The character of the priest at an earlier day was totally different from that of the priest of Malachi's day. His decisions and his counsel of the people were not biased or partial: true justice was found in his mouth. He was not influenced by proffered bribe or by active antagonism. He stood in the fear of the Lord and discharged his calling faithfully. No prejudiced or untrue word did he utter: "iniquity was not found in his lips." He walked with God in peace and equity. Since there was nothing unrighteous in his words or ways, his path was in full fellowship with Jehovah: he was in perfect accord with Him and knew only the righteousness of His ways.

Here was no passive conformity to a set pattern though. The work of the priest entailed, *inter alia*, the guiding of the people in the right paths, the reclaiming of the backslider from his waywardness, and the recovery of the sinner from his evil ways. The priests of old had fulfilled their responsibility, and the inspired prophet declared that, because of their sacerdotal ministry, many had been turned away from unrighteousness — the sinful life, the impure walk, the defiling conduct. Of the prophets of another period, Jeremiah said that, if they stood in God's counsel and had caused His people to hear His words, they would "have turned them from their evil way and from the evil of their doings" (Jer. 23 : 22). What those prophets had neglected to do, the earlier descendants of Levi had done. Those priests had faithfully discharged their responsibility.

It was appropriate that the priest should act thus. The knowledge of God and His Word should be found with him — not merely stored up in his heart, but readily available to be proclaimed by his lips. He should guard the Word with his life, for the people would seek guidance and direction (rather than "the law") at his mouth. They should be able reasonably to anticipate that the priest would tell them the right course to follow or the proper decision to make. Moses had said long before, "You shall come to the priests, the Levites, and to the judge who shall be in those days and enquire; and they shall show you the sentence of judgment" (Deut. 17 : 9). It was proper to seek direction from the priest, declared the prophet, because he was one who ministered before Jehovah. He stood before the people, therefore, as the messenger of God to them.

Here was the crux of the matter for, far from fulfilling their responsibilities, the priests had miserably failed.

Teachers Who Had Failed

"But you are departed out of the way; you have caused many to stumble at the law; you have corrupted the covenant of Levi, says Jehovah of hosts. Therefore have I also made you contemptible and base before all the people, according as you have not kept my ways, but have been partial in the law" (2 : 8, 9).

The counsel of those who should have been the guides of the people was of no value, since they had personally departed from the way. Instead of meticulously observing the Divine will in all things, they had rendered it ineffective in their own lives. Consequently, others, who looked to them for leadership and direction, were stumbled by the priests' teaching: they had compromised and watered down the law to such an extent that the people did not concern themselves with its requirements of regulations. "By the Deuteronomic law," says

Barnes (*ibid,* pp. 9, 10), "the 'priests, the Levites' (at Jerusalem) were appointed to decide appeals on matters too hard to be settled by local tribunals (Deut. 17 : 8-13; 24 : 8). Cases of all kinds came before them, for there was no sharp line of distinction between the civil and the religious in Israel." But the priests had shown partiality, or respect of persons, in their interpretation of the law, and had thereby invoked a disrespect for the law and for the judgments they based upon it.

The laxity of the priests in the administration of the law and the partiality they had shown in its interpretation and application, which had inevitably led to a complete disregard for law and, therefore, further transgressions and illegal practices on the part of the people, had virtually vitiated the covenant with Levi. Their actions had destroyed their relationship with God (cf. Neh. 13 : 29). Retribution was inescapable. There would be, as Rabbi D. Kimkhi says, "Measure for measure. You despise me and I will make you despised" (cf. 1 Sam. 2 : 30).

They had caused God's Word to be despised by others. Consequently He declared that He would make them contemptible and base before all the people. Instead of the priesthood being respected, it would be despised. How could it be otherwise? Those who observed the disregard paid to God and His will by the priests, who were responsible to defend His honour and to teach His ways, could scarcely find respect for those who were guilty of taking such a course. The result was almost automatic. Moore (*ibid,* pp. 128-9) says, "as they had violated the conditions of the covenant, God would inflict its penalty. As they had exercised their priestly functions, judicial and otherwise, partially, respecting the persons of one class while they disregarded those of another, God would visit them with punishment." The people now regarded them as contemptible and undeserving of recognition as the ministers of God. It is a serious thing to trifle with the Word of God.

47

Foreign Marriages

*"Have we not all one father? Has not one God created us?
Why do we deal treacherously every man against his brother,
by profaning the covenant of our fathers? Judah has dealt
treacherously, and an abomination is committed in Israel and
in Jerusalem. For Judah has profaned the holiness of Jehovah,
whom he ought to love, and has married the daughter of a
strange god. Jehovah will cut off the man who does this, the
teacher and the scholar, out of the tabernacles of Jacob, and
him who offers an offering to Jehovah of hosts"* (2 : 10-12).

The Divine complaint was not only against the priests, but
against the people as a whole, and Malachi now dealt with the
outstanding sins of his day. "Immorality prevailed among all
classes," writes G. A. Smith (*ibid*, p. 343). "Adultery, perjury,
fraud, and the oppression of the poor were very rife," but the
prophet was primarily concerned with the evil practice of the
divorcing of Jewish wives and the subsequent marrying of
foreign wives.

Jehovah was the Father of Israel (Deut. 32 : 6; Jer. 31 : 9;
Hos. 11 : 1), and the members of the nation were consequently deemed to be a brotherhood, with fraternal obligations to each other. What affected one affected all, but a
crime committed by a member of the nation against any
other member affected not only the person immediately concerned, but Jehovah Himself. Yet He accused them of acting
treacherously against each other, thereby desecrating the
covenant which had brought them into relationship with God.
The covenant referred to was, of course, the Sinaitic covenant, the provisions of which were being violated by the practices in which the people were indulging.

Judah was accused of acting treacherously, but the prophecy also declared that an abomination was being committed in Israel and in Jerusalem. *Prima facie*, the occupants of
the land were regarded as representatives of the whole of the
undivided nation of Israel, and the two divisions of Judah
and Israel were mentioned to indicate that the sin was com-

mon to both. One commentator suggests that the term "Israel" implied the unlettered laymen throughout Judah, and that "Jerusalem" referred to the better instructed inhabitants of the capital and even to the priests (Ezra 10 : 18-44). But Israel was the national name and Jerusalem was the capital of the nation. Whatever interpretation is placed upon the words, the clear implication is that the offence was widespread.

The sin was one which had defiled the holiness (or "sanctuary") of God and it was described as an "abomination" (a term frequently used almost as a synonym for "idolatry"). The people had been separated from the Gentile nations and had been sanctified to God (Lev. 20 : 24). They had been forbidden to intermarry with the nations of Canaan (Deut. 7 : 3), but God now accused them of profaning His holiness by marrying those who were worshippers of false gods, who would, in due course, by inference, introduce idolatry into the land (cf. 1 Kings 11 : 1-8). This may well have arisen in the first place through the earlier intermarriage of the descendants of Jews whom Nebuchadnezzar had left in the land (2 Kings 25 : 12, 22) and the introduction of idolatry through these mixed marriages. But the practice was a violation of an explicit command (e.g. Ex. 34 : 10-16).

Keil pertinently remarks (*ibid*, p. 449), "Through the sin which it had committed, Judah, i.e. the community which had returned from exile, had profaned itself as the sanctuary of God, or neutralised itself as a holy community, chosen and beloved of God." Judah ought to have loved God. To Him was the nation's homage due, but the foreign marriages would lead inevitably to the worship of other gods (a feature not yet in evidence in the land since the return from exile).

This was intolerable to God and He threatened that He would completely destroy the male members of the household of the man who thus defiled His holiness. Those who had followed this course had virtually destroyed their relationship with God. As Hengstenberg says, "He who annuls the distinction between an Israelite and a heathen woman

49

proves by this very action that he has already annihilated the distinction between the God of Israel and the idols of the heathen, that he has no longer the theocratic consciousness of God." God would, therefore, terminate their relationship. None would be left to act as head of the household and to offer sacrifices on their behalf. No one would be left to present an offering to expiate the guilt of the sinful man. The punishment would be sweeping and complete. If the threatened judgment seems severe, the seriousness of the sin must be apciated. Jehovah's specific and stated purpose was that Israel should be a people separated to Him and detached from the Gentile nations around them. Only thus could purity of worship and of race be maintained. The defiling of the race by intermarriage and of the worship by idolatry could not be tolerated.

Divorce

"And this have you done again, covering the altar of Jehovah with tears, with weeping, and with sighing insomuch that he regards not the offering any more, nor receives it with good will at your hand. Yet you say, Wherefore? Because Jehovah has been witness between you and the wife of your youth, against whom you have dealt treacherously, though she is your companion and the wife of your covenant. And did he not make one? Yet had he the residue of the spirit. And wherefore one? That he might seek a godly seed. Therefore take heed to your spirit, and let none deal treacherously against the wife of his youth. For Jehovah, the God of Israel, says that he hates putting away: for one covers violence with his garment, says Jehovah of hosts. Therefore take heed to your spirit, that you deal not treacherously" (2 : 13-16).

The people's sin was not confined to intermarriage with foreign women who were idolators. It was coupled with the divorce of existing Jewish wives to enable marriage with the foreigners to take place. "This second thing you have done," said Jehovah. It was a further profanation of the holy relationship which should have existed between the people and Himself.

He pictured the altar as wet with tears, with the sounds of sighing and weeping ascending from those who stood there. It is suggested by a number of expositors that the picture was of the guilty husbands, pouring out their lamentations and displaying all the tokens of fasting and humiliation, "Yet it was not the sorrow of penitent sinners, bewailing their sins," says Laetsch (*ibid*, p. 527). "These outbursts of woe and anguish were the complaints of intractable children, who in stubborn self-satisfaction demanded the Father's blessings and favours, while refusing to give Him the love and obedience they owed to Him." To their mortification, however, they found that their daily offering was not accepted. God did not regard it and refused to accept it from them as well-pleasing. Alternatively, their weeping and sorrow may have been because He had rejected their sacrifices and refused to find pleasure in the offerers. Since they had no intention of amending their ways, how could He accept their sacrifices?

It would perhaps be equally legitimate to adopt (as some commentators do) the view that the tears were not those of the erring husbands but of the wronged wives. The cries of the injured women rose up to God and their tears metaphorically covered His altar, so that the offering upon the altar was not visible to Him and He could not regard it. The blind, callous question of verse 14 implies that the men failed to understand the reason for the rejection of their offerings, and may possibly give weight to the first interpretation, however.

It seems incredible that individuals should have been so oblivious to right and wrong and to the holiness of God that they could call into question His rejection of their sacrifices. "Wherefore?" they asked, and Jehovah condescended to explain in such a way that there could be no possible dubiety. He declared that He had been a witness to their marital vows. When they had been joined together in their youth, it was a union which only death could sever (Gen. 2 : 24), and it was, by inference, a covenant before Him (Prov. 2 : 17). The husband was to surround his wife with a lasting love and affection, which nothing should destroy.

If Jehovah had been a witness of the marriage vows, however, He now stood as witness between the man and his injured wife. He was fully cognisant of the wrongs she had suffered and He called the guilty husband to account for his actions. The man had arbitrarily divorced his wife in order to marry the foreigner. It was clearly the original purpose of God that marriage should be permanently binding. It is true that the law made provision for divorce in particular circumstances (Deut. 24 : 1-4), but our Lord affirmed that this was not originally intended, but was introduced because of the "hardness of heart" of the people (Gen. 2 : 24; Matt. 19 : 3-9). But the people of Malachi's day had adopted a process of easy divorce in order to satisfy their lust. God stood as judge and witness of the unfaithfulness of such men to the one who had been their life's companion and the bride of their youth.

Having stated the reason for His rejection of their offerings, Jehovah reverted to the earlier statement of verse 10, which implied the oneness of the race, or nation of Israel, "Did he not make one?" He asked. Luther and some of the older commentators interpret verse 15 as applying to Abraham (who is referred to as "one" in Ezek. 33 : 24 and Isa. 51 : 2) and to his putting away of his wife Sarah (which did not occur) to find a seed through Hagar or, alternatively, to his putting away of Hagar to find a godly seed through Sarah. This interpretation is quite out of harmony with the context, however, and cannot be accepted.

Packard suggests that the reference is to the "one flesh" of Gen. 2 : 24. God's intention being that marriage should be a permanent union, He hoped thereby to perpetuate a godly seed. This did not exhaust His creative power : in the life-giving power of the Holy Spirit, He could have created more than one pair. This explanation again is not really satisfying.

It is simpler, and more in harmony with the context, to take the view that the subject is still the oneness of Israel. The nation had one Father and there was a national homogenity in consequence. Mixed marriage destroyed this oneness and frustrated the Divine purpose. The oneness was with the intention that a godly seed might be produced, but the children of mixed marriages contaminated the line. Jehovah sought a repository of His truth — an undefiled nation which would be the constant witness to Him and His truth and which would ultimately produce the Messiah — but the adulterous unions with foreign women made Israel no different from any other nation.

The blessings He had purposed for Israel did not exhaust His power. The "residue of the Spirit" — an inexhaustible fulness of power and blessing — was still with Him. If, therefore, it was asked why He restricted Himself to one nation, it was not because the power of the Spirit was restricted, but rather that He might achieve His purpose of a seed through Israel. It is possible that the verse contains at least a hint of the Seed who was still to come at that time (Gal. 3 : 16). Barnes renders the first sentence of verse 15 as "And not one has done so who had a residue of the spirit," but there appears no support for this.

In view of the gravity of the sin and its effect upon the Divine purpose, God enjoined the guilty husbands to take heed to their spirit and not to act unfaithfully against the wife of their youth. One writer rather effectively paraphrases the injunction, "Take heed, for your breath (your life) is at stake."

Luther construes verse 16 as giving approval to divorce: "if you hate her, put her away." But this is quite inconsistent with the context, which is wholly condemnatory of divorce — or, at least, of the reasons for the divorce among these people. The plain statement by Jehovah that He hated divorce seems more in harmony with the context. The following clause, "for one covers violence with his garment," is probably related to the same subject. Covering with a garment was frequently used in reference to the conjugal relationship (Deut. 22 : 30; Ruth 3 : 9; Ezek. 16 : 8). The Divine hatred was based partly upon the violence and injustice demonstrated towards the marriage relationship. The husband's love had turned to hatred and he brutally put away his wife in order to take another in her place. The sorrow caused by the unkindness and the cruel rejection by the partner of years was something of which the Almighty took account, and again He commanded these men to take heed to their spirit that they should not deal treacherously, or unfaithfully.

In our Lord's lifetime, the school of Hillel held that Deut. 24 : 1 permitted a husband to divorce his wife for almost any reason, e.g. the burning of food, although the school of Shammai interpreted the law as implying that only adultery was a permissible ground for divorce. When the question was posed to the Master, He pointed out that the original purpose was that marriage should be an indissoluble union, and declared that the only ground for divorce was unchastity (Matt. 19 : 9). The attitude taken in our modern culture was never envisaged in the Scriptures and the easy divorce of the present day (in some cases, virtually divorce by agreement) is clearly opposed to the teaching of both Moses and Christ. The Divine purpose was that marriage should be a permanent and binding relationship: today it is treated as a contract which can be broken at will. The Master described remarriage during the lifetime of a partner, divorced for any other reason than "fornication," as adultery. Today it is entered upon quite lightly. But Divine principles are still applicable: this thing God hates.

CHAPTER 5

IMPENDING JUDGMENT

Murmuring Against God

*Y OU have wearied Jehovah with your words. Yet you say,
Wherein have we wearied him? When you say, Everyone
who does evil is good in the sight of Jehovah and he delights
in them; or, Where is the God of judgment?"* (2 : 17).

The actions of the people were indicative of their true
state of heart. They had departed from the law, they had no
real desire for spiritual things, they defrauded God of the
tithes and offerings due, and had reached the conclusion that
there was no profit in doing His will. They considered themselves poorly rewarded for their observance of their religious
duties (even though such observance was purely nominal and
cursory). They proclaimed that God was unfair and that their
godless neighbours were more prosperous than they were.
There was no justice.

"You have wearied Jehovah with your words," said the
prophet (cf. Isa. 43 : 24), but the purblind wretches retorted
indignantly, "Wherein have we wearied Him?" They could
not conceive that there had been anything improper or im-

55

pertinent about their murmurings. They had neglected their obligations to Him and had complained of His ways. Surely there was nothing unreasonable or objectionable about that? What they had said had seemed to them so completely logical. How could they possibly be accused of wearying Him?

The Almighty took up the very comments which they had undoubtedly been making. Were these not a sufficient answer? They had maintained that the evildoer was deemed good in His sight and was His delight. Ignoring their own shortcomings and their dereliction of their duties, they pointed to the prosperity of the heathen as proof of Jehovah's biased judgment. The heathen did not worship Him: they had their own idols. These Gentiles did not observe the requirements of the law and were often filthy in life and sinful in character. How could God bless them if His dealings were equitable? Their impertinent arguments were audaciously uttered as though God was both deaf and blind.

If Jehovah was really just, where was the God of justice? There seemed little justice in life for them. Why did He not intervene and restore the balance? Were the nations to escape the judgment threatened by the prophets and was Israel always to be trodden down? Would they never be rewarded for their well-doing? It is no wonder that God declared that He was wearied with their words. They had asked where judgment was. He proceeded to disclose what lay ahead for Jew and Gentile too.

The Coming Messenger

"Behold I will send my messenger, and he shall prepare the way before me: and the Lord, whom you seek, shall suddenly come to his temple, even the messenger of the covenant, whom you delight in. Behold, he shall come, says Jehovah of hosts. But who may abide the day of his coming? And who shall stand when he appears? For he is like a refiner's fire, and like fuller's soap. And he shall sit as a refiner and purifier of silver: and he shall purify the sons of Levi, and purge them as gold and silver, that they may offer to Jehovah an

offering in righteousness. Then shall the offering of Judah and Jerusalem be pleasant to Jehovah, as in the days of old and as in the former years" (3 : 1-4).

The word "messenger" in chap. 3 : 1 in Hebrew is "Malachi" and it has often been suggested that the book acquired its title from this verse. As indicated in Chapter 1, we prefer to follow the traditional line and to treat the name in Mal. 1 : 1 as a proper name.

The unbelieving people had asked sarcastically where the God of judgment was. The reply came in the opening verses of the third chapter of the prophecy. First of all, God was to send a messenger to prepare the way before Him. Long before, Isaiah had referred to the same messenger, "The voice of him who cries in the wilderness. Prepare the way of Jehovah, make straight in the desert a highway for our God" (Isa. 40 : 3). The New Testament declared that these words applied to John the Baptist (Matt. 3 : 3; John 1 : 23; see also Luke 1 : 76): indeed, Mark quoted the words of both Malachi and Isaiah and applied them to John (Mk. 1 : 2-4). Our Lord subsequently stated plainly that the prediction was fulfilled in John the Baptist (Matt. 11 : 10; Luke 7 : 27). It is sometimes questioned why Matthew and Mark specifically quoted Isaiah as the source and not Malachi, but Hengstenberg points out that the prophecy in Malachi rested on that in Isaiah and hence the original was quoted as the earlier and greater. The Minor Prophets were, of course, regarded as one book and were rarely quoted by name.

Hengstenberg argues that Malachi's prediction of the forerunner did not apply exclusively to John the Baptist, and that Isa. 40 : 3 (with which Mark connected the later prophet's statement) implied a series of individuals, John being the one in whom they all culminated. The forerunner was the footman, who ran before the king's chariot (1 Sam. 8 : 11) and who was responsible for any necessary preparation for the king's coming (Luke 9 : 52). The same description was given to the scouts who travelled in advance to prepare the way for the army which was following. The actual word (*prodromos*) is used only once in the New Testament and then as descriptive of Christ, who has preceded His people into the holy of holies within the veil (Heb. 6 : 20). Isaiah declared that the forerunner would level and straighten the road and that this "preparation of the way" was to precede the revelation of the glory of God.

The forerunner of whom Malachi spoke was to prepare the way before Jehovah. In applying the prediction to John the Baptist as His own forerunner, our Lord patently implied His own personal identification with Jehovah — as, of course, He did on more than one occasion. Israel was a self-righteous nation, but John's teaching aroused the people to repentance in the light of impending judgment. When our Lord entered upon His public ministry, it was to find that His forerunner's preaching had already created an expectant spirit and had also induced a spirit of penitence. The Baptist recognised that he was only a forerunner and he bore testimony to the fact that the One who was to follow him was infinitely superior to him (John 1 : 15). He had prepared the way for the greater One who was to come.

The people had asked where the God of judgment was, implying that He was completely oblivious to all that was going on and that consequently the wicked flourished and the pious suffered. The One whom they sought, or about whom they enquired, was described by Malachi as the Lord (*ha-Adon*, the supreme Lord, as in Isa. 1 : 24). That One, declared the prophet, would suddenly come to His temple. Were their hopes to be realised and all their expectations now to find their fulfilment? This was hardly what the statement was evidently intended to convey. Judgment always begins at the house of God (1 Pet. 4 : 17) and they might well have feared as they realised the significance of the designation given to the coming One. If His coming was to be to the temple, it must obviously be to purge it first. The time was not ripe yet for the return of the glory to the building (Ezek. 43 : 2-4). If they had hoped that His advent would mean immediate blessing for them, the prophet's words gave them little encouragement. Before our Lord's ministry commenced, John the Baptist declared that He would come to purge and to burn up (Matt. 3 : 12), and one of His last public actions was to drive out of the temple the money-changers and traders (Matt. 21 : 12). It is possible that there is still a further fulfilment to be anticipated, since judgment must precede blessing.

The coming One, whom the people so eagerly waited, the Messiah whom they expected to bring temporal benefits to them, was also described as "the messenger of the covenant, whom you delight in." The word translated "messenger" might equally well have been translated "angel" and the reference is clearly to the Angel of Jehovah, who is so often mentioned in the Old Testament. This One is always distinguished in Scripture from other angels. "Wherever he is mentioned," says one writer, "he immediately takes his place at the centre of the event." Gerhard Von Rad says in his *Old Testament Theology* (Vol. 1, p. 286), "he is a being who helps, and who everywhere acts in Israel's favour, saving and protecting her; he is Jehovah's aid to Israel personalised almost in the way of a mediating official of the covenant relationship." In some instances, the Angel of Jehovah is identified with Jehovah Himself (e.g. Gen. 21 : 17, 19; 31 : 11, 13; Ex. 3 : 2, 4; Jud. 6 : 12, 13). Prof. Joseph Packard says, "He is represented as the Mediator between the invisible God and men in all God's communications and dealings with men. To this Angel divine names, attributes, purposes and acts are ascribed. He occasionally assumed a human form . . . He went before the camp of Israel on the night of the exodus."

Malachi described Him as the messenger or Angel of the covenant. Hengstenberg writes, in *Christology of the Old Testament* (pp. 600, 601), "The divine messenger is designated as a 'covenant messenger' because he is a messenger on account of the covenant, His manifestations, as well for blessing as for punishment, a consequence of the covenant. . . . his appearing had been desired by the murmurers with an appeal to the covenant. The covenant designates not one individual act, but the covenant relation of God to Israel, enduring through all times. Violation of their covenant on the part of the people, especially the priests, was the chief theme of the preceding discourses (2 : 10, 11, 14); violation of this covenant on the part of God was the chief object of the complaints of the people. The appearing of the covenant angel was to demonstrate the injustice of these complaints, and show the reality of the covenant in the punishment of the despisers." The common idea that the reference was to the new covenant of Jer. 31 : 31 scarcely seems appropriate. What was in view was presumably — as Hengstenberg suggests — the covenant relationship generally.

The Angel of the covenant was clearly the Lord Jesus Christ. His coming was again confirmed by Jehovah, "He shall come." But that advent was to be in judgment. Our Lord's First Advent was potentially in blessing, but it is evident that Malachi was here looking on to His Second Advent in judgment. He came nineteen centuries ago in humiliation: He will come again in power and glory.

The future period of judgment, which is to be experienced by earth after the removal of the church (1 Thess. 4 : 15-17), is repeatedly referred to in the Old Testament prophets under the title of the day of the Lord, or of Jehovah. It is described as a period of unparalleled trouble, of clouds and thick darkness, of cataclysmic events and universal disturbances — a period of dread and suffering. It will culminate in the Second Advent of Christ to execute the righteous vengeance of God upon a guilty earth.

None can face that day without fear. None can stand when He appears (cf. Rev. 6 : 17). That day (possibly that One Himself), according to the prophet, will be like a refiner's fire and fuller's soap. The fire destroys the dross and impurities, and purifies the metal that passes through it. In similar fashion, the people's perversity and sinfulness, their flagrant wrongdoing and corruption will all be consumed, but Israel will experience the full suffering of that fire which our Lord aptly described as the great tribulation (Matt. 24 : 21).

Like fuller's soap, or lye, that day will purge away the uncleanness of Israel. "Soap was unknown to the ancients," says Packard, "and this was a vegetable substance, from the saltwort, which was burned and water poured on its ashes." Barnes (*in loc.* p. 15) says that it was "probably an alkali obtained from species of salsola and salicornia, abundant on salt marshes and on the shores of the Dead Sea, where the Arabs still collect these plants and burn them for potash. This potash is mixed with boiled oil and so made into soap." Presumably the practice has now ceased, since the Arabs in the area use the normally manufactured soap.

The day of judgment had been likened to a refiner's fire. The angel of the covenant was logically described as sitting as a refiner and purifier of silver. The picture painted is of the old-fashioned refiner or smelter, who sat, watching the molten metal and periodically skimming off the dross, until ultimately he could see unhinderedly his reflection in the metallic liquid. Then, when all trace of impurities had been removed, the container would be taken off the fire and the metal allowed to cool and solidify once more. The silver had been refined and purified. By implication, there was something of value in rebellious Israel, but the refining fires must have their way if all dross and impurity was to be removed by the Master's skill, and the true silver left behind. He would bring out the best through their suffering and adversity.

Judgment was to commence with the priests. The great Refiner would purify the sons of Levi and purge them as gold and silver. The fires would pass over them, consuming the dross and implicitly destroying the wicked: what was left would be pure gold and silver, from which every trace of impurity had been removed (cf. Isa. 1 : 25). This was essential if the priests were to fulfil their proper function before God on behalf of the people.

No longer would defective offerings be brought by offerers who were deliberately defrauding God. Offerings would in future be brought in righteousness: the worshipper would be in a right state of mind and heart and would present only what was proper under the law. And there would be a cleansed priesthood, fitted to offer upon the altar sacrifices which were acceptable to God. One rendering of the last clause of verse 3 makes the intention clear: "that Jehovah may have priests who bring offerings in righteousness." The ultimate purpose of judgment is not to destroy but to re-create the conditions in which God may find satisfaction in His people and their ways.

In those days, when guilt has been judged and put away, when priests and people have been cleansed from defilement, Jehovah will experience the pleasure He formerly did before sin had severed His people's communion with Him. The offering of Judah and Jerusalem would be His delight — not merely because of the intrinsic value of the sacrifice, but primarily because of the character of the people, who would now desire only to please Him and to do His will. The offering would be accepted, not only because it conformed with the requirements of the law, but because the people were accepted. It is evident that the prophecy anticipates the cleansing of the people at the coming of their Messiah in order to fit them for their future place in His millennial kingdom.

Swift Judgment

"And I will come near to you to judgment. And I will be a swift witness against the sorcerers, and against the adulterers, and against false swearers, and against them who oppress the hireling in his wages, the widow, and the fatherless, and who turn aside the stranger from his right, and fear not me, says Jehovah of hosts. For I am Jehovah: I change not. Therefore you sons of Jacob are not consumed" (3 : 5, 6).

Zechariah earlier had portrayed the law entering into the houses of the guilty to convict them of their sin and to consume houses and possessions in execution of the curse of the law (Zech. 5 : 1-4). Malachi warned that God would come near to execute judgment in a future day. The individual's accountability for his actions is inescapable and, when the day of reckoning comes, Jehovah will personally ensure that judgment is meted out on a just basis and that the guilty do not escape the penalty for their sin, He will draw near for the purpose of the judgment.

In His discourse on Mount Olivet in the last week of His earthly life, our Lord stated that, when He came back to earth in glory with all His angels, He would sit on His throne to judge the living peoples of earth. No other will execute judgment: the people will be brought before Him, and He will determine whether the individuals shall enter into His millennial kingdom or be immediately condemned to everlasting punishment (Matt. 24 : 31-46). This is essential if everything that defiles is to be excluded.

This judgment of the Gentiles, however, is not what was primarily envisioned in Mal. 3 : 5. The prophet's reference was patently to Israel in the first instance. An earlier prophet had already described the manner in which God would gather His people out of the nations and bring them into the wilderness to deal with them face to face. There He would bring them under the rod and purge out the rebels and transgressors, the idolators and those who polluted His name (Ezek. 20 : 33-44). Not only the living nations, but Israel as well will be brought to judgment in the day of Messiah's power.

The prophet makes no reference to the judgment seat of Christ (Rom. 14 : 10; 2 Cor. 5 : 10), since that relates to the assessment of Christian life, and the Christian era is not portrayed in the Old Testament. But the principle of personal accountability applies equally to the Christian. When we stand at the *bema* of Christ, we will have to give account of our life and works.

Judgment must not only be fair, but acknowledged to be such, and it is, therefore, necessary that the sinner should be aware of the nature of his transgressions and of their effect upon others. A just and holy God will consequently assume the character of a "swift witness" against the subjects of the judgment. In His omniscience He is fully cognisant of every detail and it is His intention to bring home to the guilty the realisation of their guilt before the due punishment is inflicted upon them. The final book of the New Testament, painting the awful picture of the final assize, reveals that the records of human life are to be opened to disclose all that has taken place in the history of the individual, and that judgment will be executed on the basis of those records. The individual will be made perfectly aware of the details of the record and will be without argument against the sentence to be pronounced (Rev. 20 : 12). By inference, the procedure to be adopted by the Judge in Malachi's prophecy is identical, but He will personally be the witness against the guilty: the records are open before Him.

The classes against whom He will bear witness were described as sorcerers, adulterers, false swearers and oppressors. The essential characteristics of each class were sins under the Mosaic law and must, therefore, be punished. The Jews had become particularly addicted to sorcery, or witchcraft, but this was specifically prohibited and the penalty for practising it was death (Ex. 22 : 18; Deut. 18 : 10). Adultery was forbidden by the decalogue and was punishable by death if the woman was married (Ex. 20 : 14; Deut. 22 : 22-24). Perjury or false swearing was equally a sin under the law (Lev. 5 : 4; 19 : 12), and the cruel oppression of the stranger and others was strictly forbidden (Ex. 23 : 9; Deut. 24 : 14; 27 : 19). The prophet traced the source of all these crimes to the fact that the people no longer feared Jehovah. If they had revered Him, how could they so blatantly have violated His commandments!

Although the people must suffer for the offences they have committed, Jehovah had covenanted with Jacob that his descendants should be blessed (Gen. 28 : 14). His covenant was unconditional and His purpose was not affected by the failures of those whom He had designed to bless. He named Himself as Jehovah, the eternally existent One, and declared that He was unchanging. By implication, the people's security was assured by His immutability and unalterable purpose. Because of His character, they were not consumed (cf. Lam. 3 : 22). Maclaren (*ibid*, p. 351) says, "the calm might of His eternal will acts, not in spasms of successive volitions preceded by a period of indecision and equilibrium between contending motives, but is one continuous uniform energy, never beginning, never bending, never ending." What He had purposed, that will He perform. His Divine plan is not contingent on the vacillations or variations of a wayward people.

The Jews were appropriately described as the "sons of Jacob," not only as a reminder of the unconditional covenant made with their forefather, but probably also in reference to the similarity of their character and conduct to those of their ancestor: if he was a deceiver, so were they; if he had been guilty of treachery, so had they; if his life had been selfish and self-centred, so had theirs. But the God, who had been well aware of Jacob's true nature, had determined to bless him and his descendants, and nothing would divert Him from that intention. Because of this, the "sons of Jacob" were not consumed.

A Plea For Repentance

"Even from the days of your fathers you have turned aside from my ordinances, and have not kept them. Return to me, and I will return to you, says Jehovah of hosts. But you say, Wherein shall we return?" (3 : 7).

Despite the grace and compassion shown towards them, the Jews of Malachi's day (like their descendants since) demonstrated no desire for God and no intention to implement His will. It had always been so in the history of the nation (Isa. 43 : 27; Ezek. 2 : 3; Hos. 10 : 9). Long afterwards, Stephen similarly accused them, "You stiffnecked and uncircumcised in heart and ears, you do always resist the Holy Spirit: as your fathers did, so do you" (Acts 7 : 51). It was certainly true of those now addressed.

The will of God had been revealed in ordinances and specific commands. The path they should take, in conformity with His will, was clearly indicated. Yet they had turned aside from the way and had not fulfilled the Divine commands. They had added to their deliberate transgressions the sins of omission and evasion and were doubly culpable. If ever a nation deserved to be rejected and to experience the punitive hand of God, it was this people.

Yet the superabounding grace of Jehovah reached out in a plea for their repentance. If they would turn to Him, He declared that He would turn to them. They had been punished with scarcity for their defrauding of God, but the rich blessing of Divine favour could still be theirs if they penitently changed their attitude. He still refrained from casting them off and recompensing them as they so richly deserved. "What a gracious invitation God gives them to return and repent," says Matthew Henry (*in loc.*). "Return unto me and to your duty, return to your service, return to your allegiance, return as a traveller that has lost his way, as a soldier that has run from his colours, as a treacherous wife that has gone away from her husband; return, thou backsliding Israel, return to me; and then I will return unto you, and be reconciled, will remove the judgments you are under and prevent those you fear."

Even in our own days, when the sinful condition of the world might justifiably invoke the outpouring of heaven's wrath, the mercy and longsuffering of God hold the well-merited judgment in check, since He is "not willing that any should perish, but that all should come to repentance" (2 Pet. 3 : 9). The heart of love still yearns over backslider as well as sinner, and pleads with him to return (e.g. Gal. 4 : 19).

CHAPTER 6

THE WHOLE TITHE

THE PLEA for repentance and return to God demanded more than a mental assent. These must be a genuine change of heart, and this involved an amendment of the people's ways. They had denied the claims of God and had defrauded Him of His due. This must be rectified if they were going to be reconciled to God. The prophecy accordingly dealt with this question before the revelation of the illimitable blessing which heaven was ready to pour out.

Defrauding God

"Will a man rob God? Yet you have robbed me. But you say, Wherein have we robbed thee? In tithes and offerings. You are cursed with the curse: for you have robbed me, even this whole nation" (3 : 8, 9).

On Nehemiah's return to Jerusalem by permission of Artaxerxes, he recorded that the tithes for the support of the Levites had not been given to them and that they had consequently deserted their service in the temple in order to cultivate their own fields. He took immediate action and the tithe of the corn, the new wine and the oil was brought by the people to the storehouses (Neh. 13 : 10-12). Evidently the people quickly relapsed into their old ways and Malachi reveals that the tithes and offerings had been withheld.

Was it possible that men would deliberately defraud God? The tithe was His as of absolute right. Gifts and freewill offerings were rendered voluntarily from glad hearts in addition, but the tithe was not a gift: it was God's inalienable right. The withholding of the tithe was a deliberate theft. Yet these Jews had robbed God. The tithe was holy (or sanctified) to Jehovah (Lev. 27 : 30) and yet they had dared to retain it.

The firstlings of flocks and herds were God's and, in addition, a tenth of the corn, wine and oil produced (Deut. 14 : 22, 23). This tithe was used for the maintenance of the Levites. Certain portions of the offerings presented for sacrifice were used for the maintenance of the priests (Lev. 6 : 16; 7 : 14, 32-34; Deut. 18 : 3, 4; etc.), in addition to a tithe of the Levites' revenue (Num. 18 : 26-28). Moore (*ibid*, p. 159) says, "The tithes required by the Mosaic law were, first, a tenth of all that remained after the firstfruits (which belonged to God and must be given to Him), which tenth was God's, as the original proprietor of the soil, and was paid to the Levites for their maintenance (Lev. 27 : 30-32). Secondly, from this tenth the Levites paid a tenth to the priests (Num. 18 : 26-28). Thirdly, a second tenth was paid by the people for the entertainment of the Levites and their own families at the tabernacle (Deut. 12 : 18). Fourthly, another tithe was paid every third year for the poor, widows, orphans, etc. (Deut. 14 : 28, 29)."

The reprehensible withholding of the tithes and offerings was, therefore, not only a robbery of God, but a defrauding of priests and Levites, the widows, fatherless and strangers. If blessing ensued from obedience to the law, punishment was incurred by disobedience. The curse of scarcity fell upon the people. "They withheld tithes," says Packard (*ibid*, p. 22), "notwithstanding that God had already visited them with severe punishment, which aggravated their guilt. They had

68

been cursed . . . with failure of the harvest and famine. This curse corresponded to their sin. As they had refused to give God His due by offering defective sacrifices and by withholding the tithes and offerings, so had He withheld from them the products of the field." In face of all this, they could ask, "Wherein have we robbed Thee?" Either they were completely blind to their failure or else they had insolently determined to brazen it out.

For their robbery, God declared that they had been cursed with the curse, and that the whole nation was culpable. There were no extenuating circumstances: a national attitude had been adopted. Presumably the Levites had failed in the same way as the people. Their special relationship with Jehovah was temporarily ignored. Malachi referred to the nation of Judah throughout as *goi* (the Hebrew term for the heathen), thereby refusing to recognise them as the people of God.

A similar condemnation might be passed upon the people of God today. Even so far as material possessions are concerned, there is a defrauding of God. No longer is there an exercise of heart about the tithing of income, but rather a bland assumption that the requirements of the law have been annulled and are no longer applicable — as if the giving to God under grace could conceivably be less than it was under law! And, in regard to the giving to Him of time, talent, ability, service, how few there are who could plead that they are not culpable. The Divine word remains the same: "You have robbed Me."

The Way to Blessing

"Bring all the tithes into the storehouse, that there may be meat in my house, and prove me now herewith, says Jehovah of hosts, if I will not open you the windows of heaven, and pour you out a blessing, that there shall not be room enough to receive it. And I will rebuke the devourer for your sakes, and it shall not destroy the fruits of your ground; neither shall it blight your vine in the field, says Jehovah of hosts. And all nations shall call you blessed: for you shall be a delightsome land, says Jehovah of hosts" (3 : 10-12).

Despite the evil of Judah's ways, it was not too late for repentance, and God bade them to perform the requirements of the law and to bring "the whole tithe" (rather than "all the tithes") into the storehouse. They had brought the lame, blind, torn and blemished for sacrifices and had withheld part, if not all, of the tithes specified by the law, and the plea came for a complete rectification. The words inferred more than the yielding up of the full amount of the tenth of the products of the field.

Was there perhaps an even deeper significance in the plea? The defrauding of God could only be the outcome of a heart already turned away from him. Practical delinquency followed moral apostasy. To be truly acceptable, the rendering of the whole tithe should spring from a sincere devotion to God and His will. "My son, give me your heart," came an earlier appeal, "and let your eyes observe my ways" (Prov. 23 : 26). If the heart's affections were surrendered to God, there would be no problem regarding the fulfilment of His commands. The whole tithe may well have involved the reconsecration of the whole being to God.

If the whole tithe was brought into the storehouse, there would be meat (or food) in Jehovah's house. The word *tereph*, translated "meat," implies a portion torn off and may refer either to the tithe as a portion of the whole, or to that part of the sacrifices consumed upon the altar as the food of God. Of the two alternatives, the first is the more likely. The "storehouse" related, of course, to the "chambers" or "treasuries" for the reception of the goods offered (see 2 Chron. 31 : 11, 12; Neh. 10 : 38, 39; 12 : 44; 13 : 12). Some have seen a reference to the storehouse in the "closet" of Matt. 6 : 6, but it is extremely improbable that this was intended.

Let Judah put God to the test by rendering to Him what was His due, and He would respond, said Malachi, by opening the sluice gates of heaven in blessing and this would be so copious that it would be impossible to find a capacity to contain its superabundance. The windows of heaven, says Barnes (*in loc.*) were "the 'openings' through which God

70

sends rain upon the earth (Gen. 7 : 11; 8 : 2; 2 Kings 7 : 2). In Gen. 1 : 6-8 heaven is described as a 'firmament,' a dome stretching out over the earth and separating the upper waters (the rain) from the lower waters (the sea). To enable the upper waters to descend, the *windows* of heaven must be opened." Rain is, of course, one of the greatest blessings of the Middle East and it was here promised to people who had evidently suffered from drought and famine. This did not exclude other and more spiritual blessings implicitly offered, but the welcome rain must have been foremost in Malachi's mind.

The phrase "the windows of heaven" is used only four times in the Old Testament. The earlier occurrences were first in Gen. 7 : 11, where it is said that the windows of heaven were opened to allow the outpouring of the heavy rains which contributed to the judgment of the flood of Noah's day. The second and third were in 2 Kings 7 : 2, 19, where they were employed in disbelief of the Divine prediction made through the mouth of Elisha. In Malachi's prophecy the floodgates were to be opened, not in judgment, but in richest blessing.

The people had apparently suffered a scarcity of food as a judgment upon them for their unfaithfulness to God. The judgment may have come through drought — and this is implied by the character of the blessing of rain just promised — or even possibly by a locust plague as in the days of Joel, or by storms or wild beasts. Whatever the cause, God was prepared to hold it in check if they now showed the signs of penitence. The fields had been laid waste: they were barren and desolate, but the Divine promise now was that they would no longer be rendered fruitless by the curse. The vines had been blighted and the unripe fruit had fallen and perished. This would be stopped, said Jehovah. If they turned to Him, blessing would attend the work of their hands.

With sorrow turned into joy and the curse into blessing, Judah would be deemed a happy nation by her neighbours. Adversity would have been converted into prosperity and the shadows caused by their own sin and default would have been dispersed. The prophet was doubtless anticipating the wonders of a future age and not merely the restoration of blessing in the immediate future. What occurred at that time in consequence of repentance and the renewal of the people's devotion to God, was but a foretaste of the unprecedented blessings of a future day, when Messiah would reign in peace over His people.

The land itself would become a delight to Jehovah. Others might find a pleasure in it, but this was His land and, at long last, it would bring joy and delight to Him. In its fullest sense, the words can be true only of the golden age of the millennium, when the land will be holy and there will be nothing to grieve Him (Zech. 14 : 20, 21).

The Murmurers

"Your words have been stout against me, says Jehovah of hosts. Yet you say, Wherein have we spoken so much against thee? You have said, It is vain to serve God: and what profit is it that we have kept his ordinance, and that we have walked mournfully before Jehovah of hosts? And now we call the proud happy. Yes, they who work wickedness are built up. Yes, they who tempt God are even delivered" (3 : 13-15).

Earlier in the prophecy the Jews had impertinently accused God of partiality and of disregarding what was done in His name. They still continued pertinaciously in their complaints, never seeming to realise the blasphemous character of their criticisms. Who were they to level criticism against the Almighty Sovereign? Yet they did, and finally He declared that their words against Him had been offensive language. He might justifiably have blotted them out of existence, but He condescended to discuss the matter with these rebels.

Again they displayed their utter blindness to reality. Completely ignorant of any cause of offence, they asked in what respect they were accused of having spoken so harshly and offensively against Him. Their appalling lack of appreciation of the significance of their words is amazing and virtually

72

only aggravated their fault. If they failed to see the impropriety and the lése-majesty of such slanderous statements, what hope was there of their renewal and restoration? Their attitude and conduct had been such that He had previously said that He had no pleasure in them (1 : 10) and later that their words had wearied Him (2 : 17), but there had been no change in their ways and He now found their expressions offensive (3 : 13).

Centuries earlier, Job had quoted the wicked as saying, "What is the Almighty that we should serve him? And what profit should we have if we pray to him?" (Job 21 : 15). Those were the words of sinners, but they were virtually what the people of Judah were saying in their day. They asserted that it was pointless to serve God. They had been exhorted to pay their tithes and offerings, but they saw no value in observance of the law's requirements or in the keeping of the festivals and the fast. They had lost all joy in the temple service and could see no personal benefits in the fulfilment of their legal responsibilities.

There had been no profit in keeping God's ordinance or charge. Obedience to the letter of the law had produced no reward (not that there had been undeviating obedience, in any case). These ungodly men, by implication, demanded Divine recognition and reward of an imperfect obedience and were aggrieved that their Gentile neighbours, who certainly made no endeavour to appease God, seemed more prosperous than thy were.

They had fasted and behaved as mourners, donning the garments of penitence and humbling themselves, as a mode of reparation for their transgressions. Their habit of life had been evident to all, and they deluded themselves into believing that theirs was a genuine mourning for sin and that it must, therefore, propitiate God. The spirit of Phariseeism had already been born. Despite all their efforts, God apparently paid no regard to them. It was all in vain. They had done it as unto Him, but no account had been taken of their sham piety. It was vain to serve Jehovah. Their endeavour was utterly unrewarding.

73

Their impudent wickedness reached its climax in their final conclusion that the proud could be called happy, and that the wicked would be granted prosperity, and that those who tempted God escaped with impunity. One pertinent rendering of the first clause of verse 15 is, "And from henceforth we are going to pronounce the presumptuous ones (i.e. those who defied God) to be happy." The prosperity of others was in such sharp contrast to their own adversity that the illogicality of the contrast so embittered them that they could make foolish statements of this kind. In effect, their words charged the Almighty with inequity: He paid regard to the unrighteous and ignored the righteous. In fact, He apparently rewarded the unworthy and contemned those who deserved His blessing. They even maintained that those, who tempted God and should have suffered the weight of His punitive judgment, escaped all consequences of their action. It was vain to serve God. It was a criminal folly in which they indulged. Was Jehovah prejudiced because He refused to recognise their imperfect service and insincere fasting, their hypocritical professions and sham loyalty?

The picture was not one of unrelieved gloom, however. Not all in Judah trod this path. There were still some who retained their allegiance to God and who remained faithful to Him in the midst of the prevailing disloyalty.

Jehovah's Treasure

"Then they who feared Jehovah spoke one to another: and Jehovah hearkened and heard, and a book of remembrance was written before him for them who feared Jehovah and who thought on his name. And they shall be mine, says Jehovah of hosts, in that day when I make up my special treasure: and I will spare them, as a man spares his own son who serves him" (3 : 16, 17).

God has always had a remnant of faithful ones in every day and there were those in Malachi's day who, despite the general apostasy of the nation, still feared Jehovah. They lived in reverential awe of Him and walked in godly fear. Their fellowship on earth was not with the mass of the people, but with others who were likeminded, and it became the characteristic of life for them to commune with one another. It was their habitual practice and not merely a casual conversation. The subject of their converse is not mentioned. It may have been the prevailing conditions and the need for a spiritual awakening in Judah, but it is more probable that their topic was Jehovah Himself, for it is said that they feared Him and thought on His name. With a realisation of the vacuity of life and the worthless character of their fellows, their thoughts rose to the heavens above and occupied themselves, not with the discouraging circumstances of earth, but with the perfection and holiness of the Eternal One.

Jehovah hearkened and heard, said the prophet. One rendering expresses aptly the significance of the words, when it says that He "pricked up His ears and listened." So intent was He to hear the conversation of those who were loyal to Him that the whole of His attention is depicted as focused upon them, as though He would not miss a word or an inflection. It is an amazing fact that the Eternal God is interested in His people to such an extent and that He still finds delight in their occupation with Him and His affairs. Their devotion and worship, their reverential awe, their undivided loyalty, are a joy to His heart.

In Solomon's day, Jehoshaphat, the son of Ahilud, was appointed as the king's recorder, or "remembrancer" (1 Kings 4 : 3), and this office was found in other courts as well as that of Israel. The remembrancer recorded events of particular significance and noted the names of those who had rendered special service to the king (Esth. 2 : 23; 6 : 1). God also has His records (Dan. 7 : 10; Rev. 20 : 12) and in His book of remembrance were inscribed the details of the faithfulness and conduct of the loyal remnant of Malachi's day. He never overlooks the fidelity of His people and will bestow His reward in respect of it in a coming day.

So great an estimation did God place upon this faithful remnant that He announced that they would be His —

jewels which were exclusively His own property — in the day wherein He made up His peculiar treasure. The future held a day when He would carry out His designs, when the warring nations of earth would become subject to Him, when the rebels would be destroyed, and sin be brought under restraint. In that day a special blessing would be the portion of those who had been loyal to Him. In a place of closest intimacy with Him, they would enjoy the blessings of His presence as the special treasure in which He delighted. "You shall also be a crown of glory in the hand of Jehovah and a royal diadem in the hand of your God" an earlier prophet had said (Isa. 62 : 3), and Malachi employed similar imagery.

Jewels (as in the A.V.) were always regarded as a special possession and that is the significance of the prophet's words. The word *segullah* (special treasure) has been defined as "that part of a man's possessions which he values most of all. For the building of the temple David prepared 3,000 talents of gold and 7,000 talents of silver, but over and above this gave of his own private treasure. To Israel, God promised that if they would obey His voice and keep His covenants, they should be His *segullah*."

In the day to which He referred, judgment would be poured out upon a guilty world, but He promised that this remnant, who had retained their allegiance to Him, should be spared, as a man spares his own son who serves him. The words presumably anticipated the day of tribulation which still lies ahead. Before the unmitigated wrath of the Almighty is felt upon earth in its fullest extent, the apocalyptic seer foretold the sealing for their security of 12,000 from each of the tribes of Israel (Rev. 7 : 2-8). God is never unmindful of His own and He will take special steps in that day to protect those who have been loyal to Him.

The third chapter concludes with a final reference to that day.

The Difference
"Then shall you return and discern between the righteous

and the wicked, between him who serves God and him who serves him not" (3 : 18).

In that day will be demonstrated clearly that it was profitable to serve God. Malachi declared that the people would turn and see clearly the difference between the lot of the righteous and that of the wicked, between those who served God faithfully and those who did not. The people had foolishly accused God of injustice and partiality. In that day, it will become abundantly clear that His dealings are completely just and fair.

Men reach conclusions on the basis of current circumstances. The final word is with God and His assessments and His decisions are not always disclosed in the present. We shall understand more fully, not now but in a coming day. Then it will be made clear, moreover, that it was worth while to serve Him.

CHAPTER 7

THE DAY OF THE LORD

THE reference to the day of reckoning naturally led on to a fuller revelation of the characteristics of the day of the Lord, of which so many of the Old Testament prophets had spoken. This was the final O.T. description of it, and Sir George Adam Smith claims that it is unequalled in Scripture. He writes (*ibid*, pp. 369, 370), "The apocalypse of this last judgment is one of the grandest in all Scripture. To the wicked it shall be a terrible fire, root and branch shall be burned out, but to the righteous a fair morning of God, as when dawn comes to those who have been sick and sleepless through the black night, and its beams bring healing, even as to the popular belief of Israel it was the rays of the morning sun which distilled the dew. They break into life and energy, like young calves leaping fom the dark pen into the early sunshine. To this morning landscape a grim figure is added. They shall tread down the wicked and the arrogant like ashes beneath their feet."

The Fire of Divine Wrath

"For, behold, the day comes, that shall burn as a furnace. And all the proud, yes, and all who do wickedly, shall be

stubble; and the day that comes shall burn them up, says Jehovah of hosts, that it shall leave them neither root nor branch" (4 : 1).

It has been claimed by some expositors that the opening verse of Malachi's last chapter (in Hebrew this chapter 4 is part of chapter 3) portrayed the trials and sufferings experienced by the Jews at the destruction of Jerusalem by the Romans in 70 A.D. but that is patently absurd. The terms used leave no room for doubt. The prophet was anticipating once more the terrible outpouring of wrath and the consequent tribulation of the people during the day of the Lord. There may be also a foreshadowing of the final day of judgment and the dissolution of the earth, but the primary reference is clearly to the period so often described by the Old Testament prophets. Wordsworth sees all the Divine judgments as reflections of the final one. He says, "All God's judgments are hours, marked on the dial-plates, and struck by the alarum of that great day."

The awful period of the day of Jehovah is pictured especially in Joel 1 : 15; 2 : 1, 2, 31; 3 : 16; Zaph. 1 : 15-18; Amos 5 : 18; Isa. 2 : 10-19; 34 : 1-8; Jer. 30 : 7, etc. It is consistently described as a period of darkness, and one in which the universe will be shaken, when Jehovah will "roar out of Zion and utter His voice from Jerusalem." It is a period so terrible that Isaiah urged the people of that day to "enter into the rock and hide in the dust, from before the terror of Jehovah and from the glory of His majesty . . . for the day of Jehovah of hosts shall be upon everyone who is proud and lofty, and upon everyone who is lifted up . . . and they shall go into the holes of the rocks and into the caves of the earth, for fear of Jehovah, and for the glory of His majesty, when He arises to shake terribly the earth" (Isa. 2 : 10-19). It is to be "the day of Jehovah's vengeance, and the year of recompences for the controversy of Zion." The stars of heaven will be dissolved and the heavens rolled up like a scroll (Isa. 34 : 1-8).

The day will burn as an oven, said Malachi (cf. Hos. 7 : 4). Barnes states that the word *tannur* was used of the ovens in which bread was made until relatively recently. "A large hole is made in the earth," he says, "the sides are plastered, a very fierce fire is made at the bottom with grass or thorns or twigs ('stubble'), and after the removal of the embers, flat cakes of bread are stuck against the plastered sides and very quickly cooked. The *oven* is a figure of fierce heat and swift destruction, the materials used in heating it being quickly consumed." It is, therefore, a most appropriate type of the judgment of that day. The Divine judgments are frequently represented by the figure of fire or burning (e.g. Isa. 4 : 4; 47 : 14).

The presumptuous and the wicked will be treated like the stubble used as fuel for the oven. They will be burned up and utterly destroyed (cf. John the Baptist's words in Matt. 3 : 12). Moore (*ibid*, p. 171) vividly describes the scene, "the prophet . . . exclaims, as if in breathless emotion, It comes! burning like a furnace! the wicked proud are chaff! the day burns them! There is something very forcible in these abrupt exclamations, as if the prophet was elevated on some mount of vision, and actually beheld this terrible power come rolling up the distant skies, on its reddening pathway of fire and blood. The finality of this day is distinctly declared in the utter ruin that it is predicted to bring."

The Lot of the Righteous

"But to you who fear my name will the sun of righteousness arise with healing in his wings; and you will go forth, and gambol as calves of the stall. And you will tread down the wicked, for they will be ashes under the soles of your feet in the day that I shall do this, says Jehovah of hosts" *(4 : 2, 3).*

In chapter 3 : 16 the righteous had been described as those who feared Jehovah and thought on His name. It was to such that He now spoke. To them would the sun of righteousness arise, with healing in his wings. The darkness of the day of the Lord was for the sinner and not for the faithful remnant who were true to Him. For them the night would be turned to day. The thick gloom of the night would be dispersed as the rays of the rising sun, like wings (cf. Psa. 139 : 9), touched every hill with glory and flooded every valley with light. As the warmth of the sun brings forth herb and flower from the earth, it is also depicted here as healing the wounds of the night or as bringing health and renewal to those who have been sick.

The early commentators consistently interpret the picture as one of the Messiah, who will bring light, life and health to His people. In relation to the church, the New Testament portrays Him as the morning star (Rev. 2 : 28; 22 : 16), but for Israel He becomes the sun of righteousness. The picture is an apt one. The morning star is seen prior to the dawn, when the night is reaching its end. When the sun rises, it is to flood the whole world with light. Before the outshining of His glory, Christ will remove His people of the present church era : He is their hope in the spiritual darkness of earth's night. But when He comes to Israel, His glory will shine out over all the earth.

Unprecedented joy will be the portion of God's people. The language used is very expressive. So great will be their excited ecstasy that they will gambol like calves skipping as they are released from the stalls to go out into the pastures in the early morning. As the liberated animal frolics in its delight at its freedom, so will the righteous find a similar pleasure in their liberation from the darkness and dreads of the night of suffering. The shadows and troubles of the great tribulation will be past: the day of Christ's presence will have dawned.

For the time being the ungodly seem to flourish and iniquity seems to go unpunished. But now the brief prosperity of the sinner will be reversed. The fires of Divine wrath will have reduced them to ashes, and the righteous will tread them underfoot like ashes in the street. Long before, Isaiah had prophesied, "he brings down them who dwell on high; the lofty city he lays low; he lays it low to the ground; he brings it to the dust. The foot shall tread it down, the feet of the poor and the steps of the needy" (Isa. 26 : 5, 6). Malachi employed the same phraseology: the wicked would be trodden down like ashes by the godly. There is an answer in the Divine plan and in God's time to all the circumstances of life. The wicked will not always prosper.

The Final Plea

"Remember the law of Moses my servant, which I commanded to him in Horeb for all Israel, even the statutes and judgments" (4 : 4).

The last three verses of Malachi form a colophon which, many expositors suggest, was contributed by another hand to enforce the teaching of the prophet and to reiterate his call to repentance. As Barnes (*in loc.*) points out, however, it is more probable that Malachi himself was the author because "(1) There is an abrupt vigour in the verses which is after the very manner of the prophet; (2) the language here, as elsewhere in the prophecy, shows the influence of the book of Deuteronomy." This is, in fact, the view taken today by most conservative scholars. Malachi had consistently exhorted the people to repentance and to a renewed observance of the law and this was the explicit purpose of the closing verses.

In chapter 3 : 7 the prophet deplored that the people had departed from God's ordinances and had not kept them. In ch. 4 : 4 he called upon Judah to remember the law of Moses, with its statutes and judgments, which had been given to God's servant at Horeb (Ex. 3 : 1; Deut. 1 : 5, 6; 4 : 10; 5 : 2). The plea was to a complete observance of the moral and ceremonial law (including, of course, the regulations governing tithes and sacrifices). The appeal was obviously made to the whole nation, thereby implying that it was still not too late to repent and to escape the threatened judgment.

The Septuagint places verse 4 at the end of the book, to avoid the prophecy closing with the word "curse," but the transposition is arbitrary and unsupported. The verses read more naturally in their present order.

The Coming of Elijah

"Behold, I will send you Elijah the prophet before the coming of the great and dreadful day of Jehovah. And he shall turn the heart of the fathers to the children, and the heart of the children to their fathers, lest I come and smite the land with a curse" (4 : 5, 6).

Before the judgment of the Flood had come upon the earth, God sent Noah as a preacher of righteousness to warn the people of impending wrath. Similarly He now indicated that, before the awful judgments of the day of the Lord are poured forth, He will send another to warn them and awaken a penitence of heart on the part of all, parents and children alike. The rabbis still teach that Elijah will come prior to the coming of Messiah and that his work will be to teach and enforce the law.

It is at first surprising that Elijah should be named in the context, but Keil's comment (*ibid*, p. 470) is pertinent, "by Elijah we are not to understand a lineal descendant of the Tishbite, but simply a prophet in whom the spirit and power of Elijah was revived. . . . But the reason why this prophet Elijah is named is to be sought for, not merely in the fact that Elijah was called to his work as a reformer in Israel at a period which was destitute of faith and of the true fear of Jehovah, and which immediately preceded a terrible judgment (Koehler), but also and more especially in the power and energy with which Elijah rose up to lead back the ungodly generation of his own time to the God of the fathers. . . . The greater the apostasy, the greater must be the power which is to stem it." It should be scarcely necessary to emphasise that no return of Elijah personally was envisaged, although this has been claimed by some writers.

Before the birth of John the Baptist, his father was told by the angel that his son would turn to God many in Israel, and that he would go before the Lord "in the spirit and power of Elijah, to turn the hearts of the fathers to the children, and the disobedient to the wisdom of the just, to make ready a people prepared for the Lord" (Luke 1 : 15-17) — in other words, that he was the one promised in Mal. 4 : 5. Strangely enough, however, when John was asked by the messengers from the priests and Levites (who were, of course, fully aware of Malachi's prophecy and who were clearly anticipating the coming of Elijah) whether he was Elijah, he emphatically replied in the negative (John 1 : 21). Yet, when His disciples asked our Lord why Elijah must first come, He confirmed that Elijah must first come and restore all things, and then stated plainly that "Elijah is come already, and they knew him not, but have done to him whatever they wished." The inspired record adds that "the disciples understood that He spoke to them of John the Baptist" (Matt. 17 : 10-13). Earlier He had referred to John as being the forerunner spoken of in Mal. 3 : 1 (Matt. 11 : 14). The implication of the Master's words is patently that John the Baptist was the one foretold in both passages.

If John was the forerunner of both the First Advent and the Second Advent of Christ, the two events were, *prima facie*, regarded as extremely close together. If this is correct, the day of the Lord could presumably have commenced at that time.

The work of Elijah (or of John) was to turn the hearts of all the people in repentance to God. Keil regards the fathers in verse 6 as the ancestors or patriarchs of Israel, and the children as the then living descendants of the fathers, i.e. the Jews of Malachi's day. The turning of fathers to the children he, therefore, interprets as the bestowal of their forefathers' disposition upon the descendants of that day. Hengstenberg,

85

preferring to take the words more literally, says, "The hearts of the godly fathers and the ungodly sons are estranged from one another. The fathers are ashamed of their children, and the children of their fathers." In the words of the angel to Zacharias regarding John the Baptist, however, the latter clause was rendered "the disobedient to the wisdom of the just" (Luke 1 : 17).

This work of Elijah was essential if the curse of God was not to fall upon the land of Israel (rather than upon the "earth," as in the A.V.). Although punishment will be meted out to the Gentiles (Isa. 34 : 5), it was particularly with His own land that Jehovah was concerned (Zech. 14 : 11). That curse could be averted by the repentance of the people. Just as the Canaanites had been extirpated for their sins, so would the hand of God fall upon the people of Israel if the impious did not turn penitently to the truth. The judgment which fell five centuries later is an indication that the opportunity for repentance was ignored.

Thus Malachi ended his prophecy. Wordsworth says, "Malachi, as successor to Zechariah, discharged a peculiar office. Zechariah is one of the most sublime and impassioned among 'the goodly fellowship' of the prophets. The light of the sunset of prophecy is as brilliant and glorious as its noon-day splendours. The prophecy of Zechariah is an impetuous torrent, sweeping along in a violent stream, dashing over rugged rocks, and hurling itself down, in headlong cataracts, and carrying everything with it in its foaming flood. In Malachi, it tempers its vehemence in the clear haven of a translucent pool; there it rested in peace for four hundred years, till it flowed forth again in the gospel."

APPENDIX

THE INTER-TESTAMENTAL PERIOD

THE Prophecy of Malachi closed the Old Testament and it was four centuries before the voice of God again broke into history. Once more the Divine message came to Israel, but conditions had changed considerably — both politically and religiously — in the course of four hundred years. The warnings of the last of the Old Testament prophets had had little effect upon the people and, if their conditions were different, their hearts were not. It is, however, important to appreciate the way in which circumstances had, in fact, altered in the period between the Old and the New Testaments.

Although numbers of Jews (not only of Judah but at least some of Israel) returned to their own land under Zerubbabel, Ezra and Nehemiah, the majority apparently remained dispersed throughout the Persian empire, enjoying in most cases the normal privileges of an ordinary Persian subject. The Medo-Persian rule continued for a century after the last message of Malachi, and had it not been for the continual warfare between Persia and Egypt, this period would have been one of prosperity and relative happiness for the little country of Judea. The people were allowed full religious liberty, and eventually the high priest was even made responsible for the immediate civil administration.

As had been foretold by the prophet Daniel, the Medo-Persian empire subsequently gave place to the Grecian and, in the course of Alexander's conquests, both Syria and Judea came into the Macedonian's hands. The Jews did not suffer unduly by the change. Indeed, as a result of a remarkable dream, in which Jaddua, the high priest, figured prominently, Alexander favoured them with the utmost respect and tolerance.

Following Alexander's early death, the great empire which he had built up was partitioned among his four principal generals. Judea was seized, first by Syria and then by Egypt, and after much warfare and passing from one hand to another, it was finally taken by Ptolemy Soter, king of Egypt. Ptolemy transported thousands of Jews to Egypt, where they settled, more or less as involuntary colonists. It was the descendants of these Egyptian Jews who, in the reign of Ptolemy II, Philadelphus, made the Septuagint translation of the Old Testament Scriptures. It is probable that the idea of the synagogue also first originated at this time.

After 130 years under the fairly beneficent rule of the Ptolemies, Judea was wrested from Egypt by Antiochus the Great and annexed to Syria. For some years, the Jews enjoyed a reasonable measure of peace and tranquility, but in 168 B.C., because of a minor insurrection, Antiochus Epiphanes entered Jerusalem, violated the sanctity of the temple, stole the temple treasures, and completed his profanation by sacrificing a sow upon the altar and sprinkling the broth all over the temple and its vessels. The temple worship was stopped and large numbers of the people were carried away captive. Details of the terrible persecutions and atrocities, which characterised this period, are furnished by the writings of Josephus and the apocryphal books of the Old Testament, particularly the books of the Maccabees. The sufferings of the Jews who refused to renounce the faith of their fathers or to eat swine's flesh were simply appalling, and the indignities and oppressions at last stung the people to revolt. Judas Maccabæus and his four brothers made a desperate resistance against their oppressors and eventually succeeded in gaining control of Jerusalem. Amidst the rejoicing of the nation, they cleansed the temple and rededicated it to the service of Jehovah.

A semblance of peace was secured after nearly twenty years of fighting, and the land settled down under the rule of the high priest.

With the rise of the Roman empire, however, Judea passed into the hands of the Romans and was governed by a procurator appointed by Caesar. After the murder of Julius Caesar, Herod, an Idumean and the son of this procurator, was appointed by Augustus as king of the Jews and was actually reigning as such when the New Testament history opened.

During the intervening period, certain sects came into existence among the Jews. Of these, the most important, as well as the most numerous, was that of the Pharisees. The members of this sect were held in veneration because of their extreme personal sanctity and their meticulous adherence to all the minutiae of the law. Their devotion extended, however, not only to the law of Moses, but to the traditions of the elders, and not infrequently they were guilty of placing the authority of the latter above that of the Scriptures. Their phylacteries were larger and the borders of their garments were wider than those of the average Jew; they prayed aloud at the street corners; and they were most ostentatious in their almsgiving and charity. They considered themselves separate from the ordinary Jew and, in fact, derived their name from the Hebrew word, *pharash*, to separate. The rigid observance of detail and general display of ultra-righteousness gradually deteriorated, in many cases, into sheer hypocrisy, and our Lord described them as play-actors.

The sect of the Sadducees, although not numerically strong, was extremely wealthy and influential. The name was derived from Sadoc, the founder, who lived about 250

B.C. The Sadducees did not bind themselves to a strict observance of the law, and were inclined to be careless about its requirements. At the same time, they inclined towards aestheticism and sought to serve God, as one writer says, "purely from love and gratitude towards Him, and not from an interested desire of reward or from a servile dread of punishment." Indeed, since they did not believe in a future existence or in the resurrection of the dead, they could have no fear of future judgment.

The Herodians were a political party of time-servers rather than a religious sect and, as their name indicates, they were supporters of the Idumean ruler, Herod, and, through him of Rome. As a general rule, they had no desire for spiritual things, but sought solely for worldly grandeur and position.

Certain institutions also came into being in the period between Malachi and Matthew. The most important of these was probably the Sanhedrim, the supreme council or governing body of the Jews, which had complete jurisdiction over religious matters and also over certain civil affairs. The Romans did not disturb this position, although they advisedly deprived the Sanhedrim of the power of inflicting capital punishment.

The council was composed of 72 members, the majority of whom were priests and elders. It had its own officers, who were empowered to make arrests. The *Nasi*, or President of the Sanhedrim, was normally the high priest, who thus combined in himself the offices of ecclesiastical and civil head.

Another feature of the period was in the religious realm. It was obviously impossible for the dispersed Jews to engage in the temple worship at Jerusalem, and it became the practice to gather together in appointed places for prayer and the reading of the Scriptures. To meet this need, synagogues sprang up in practically every town and city. As a rule, these buildings were nothing more than a simple room facing towards Jerusalem, and the chief article of furniture was an ark containing a copy of the Scriptures.

One of the inevitable results of the dispersion was that the Hebrew tongue gradually fell into disuse. Moreover, the conquests of Alexander ultimately led to Greek becoming the medium of conversation and communication throughout the civilised world. In order to make the Scriptures accessible to all Jews, a need, therefore, arose for a Greek translation of the Old Testament, and thus it was that the Septuagint version came into being.

Ptolemy Soter, king of Egypt, under whose sovereignty Palestine had fallen, was a patron of learning and the fine arts, and founded the famous museum and library of Alexandria. His son, Ptolemy Philadelphus, made constant additions to the library, and it was at the suggestion of his principal librarian, Demetrius Phalererus, that the translation of the Hebrew Scriptures was projected. An embassy was sent to Jerusalem to obtain from Eleazar, the high priest, a copy of the Scriptures, and also to request that 72 men (in theory, six from each tribe of Israel), who were learned in Hebrew and Greek, should be sent to Alexandria for the work of translation. The 72 men who were eventually sent were confined in the island of Pharos until the work was complete, and then the new version was deposited in the Alexandrian library. The version was later referred to as the Septuagint (seventy) from the number of men employed in the translation.

THE PROPHET OF
THE MYRTLE GROVE

An Exposition of the Prophecy of Zechariah

BY

FREDK. A. TATFORD, LITT. D.

Originally published by
Prophetic Witness Publishing House
Sussex, 1971

ISBN: 0-86524-135-X

Printed by Klock & Klock in the U.S.A.
1982 Reprint

Contents

Preface

The last three of the Minor Prophets seem to have a particular relevance to the present day. On the horizon they could see the indications that the Eternal was about to break into time. The details were not clear and the difference between the First Advent and the Second Advent was not plainly disclosed: but it was plain that climactic events were about to happen. That is also the position today. Life's uncertainties, economic instability, industrial unrest, political weakness, universal lack of leadership – all emphasize the necessity for a Divine intervention. We seem to be on the brink of some other climactic event. *We are!* The return of the Saviour for His Church is almost here. The signs accumulate: the only question is, When?

Zechariah has his message for days like ours. During the last few years the author has given quite a number of lectures and Bible readings on the Book, and has been urged repeatedly to put them into print. The lectures have now been expanded into book form in answer to such requests, and it is hoped that the following pages may prove of interest and help to some.

FREDK. A. TATFORD

CHAPTER 1

The Author and His Book

Relatively little is known of the three post-exilic prophets, of whom Zechariah was the second, but, unlike Haggai and Malachi, minimal details are at least given of his genealogy. The name he bore, which means 'God remembers', was that of more than twenty other persons in the Old Testament. He is personally described as the son of Berechiah (whose name meant 'God blesses') and the grandson of Iddo (the significance of whose name was 'the appointed time'). Ezra 5:1 and Neh. 12:16 refer to him as the son of Iddo, from which it may be deduced that his father Berechiah died while Zechariah was still young and prior to the death of Iddo and therefore before he could become the head of the family. The prophet was apparently born in Babylon during the exile and he evidently accompanied his grandfather on the return to Palestine of the first caravan under Zerubbabel in 536 B.C. (Neh. 12:4). Iddo was the head of one of the twelve priestly courses instituted by David and Solomon (1 Chron. 23:6; 2 Chron. 8:14), and Zechariah presumably succeeded him in this office some time after the return, although there is no specific indication of when this occurred in the book which bears his name. (There is possibly an implication of this in Neh. 12:16). He was, in any case, a priest as well as a prophet.

It is fairly clear that Zechariah was called to the prophetic office at a comparatively early age. As David Baron says in *The Visions and Prophecies of Zechariah* (p. 7), 'That he was scarcely a full-grown man may be inferred from the fact that in chapter 2:4 he is addressed as *naar* (i.e. boy, lad or youth)' – the same word as was used of David by Saul in 1 Sam. 17:38. He is said, however, to have still been active in the days of Nehemiah, somewhere about 455 to 433 B.C. and consequently to have lived to be over 100 years old.

He was not identical with the Zechariah to whom our Lord referred in Matt. 23:35, and who was there described as the son of Berechiah and as having been slain between the temple and the altar. An earlier Zechariah, who was the son of Jehoiada,

was stoned to death in the court of the temple in the reign of
Joash (2 Chron. 24:20, 21) and our Lord's allusion was almost
undoubtedly to that Zechariah and not to the author of the Old
Testament book. Since the corresponding record in Luke 11:51
omits any mention of Berechiah, it is possible that the Master
did not, in fact, quote any patronymic and that the name of
Berechiah was interpolated in error at a later date. It is reasonably clear that the Zechariah referred to in the gospel narra-
tives was the son of Jehoiada and not of Berechiah. Josephus
mentions the assassination in the temple of another Zechariah,
who was the son of Baruch, but this happened in A.D. 68 and
could not, therefore, have been the incident to which our Lord
referred. So far as is known, Iddo's grandson died peacefully and
naturally and did not suffer martyrdom for his faith in God.

Certain traditions regarding his life and ministry do exist but,
as one writer pertinently remarks, 'The patristic notices of the
prophet are worth nothing. According to these, he exercised his
prophetic office in Chaldea, and wrought many miracles there;
returned to Jerusalem at an advanced age, where he discharged
the duties of the priesthood, and where he died, and was buried
by the side of Haggai.' There is, however, no support for these
stories, either in secular history or in the Biblical records.
Certainly, on the Mount of Olives, there is a catacomb which
was used by early Christians as a burial place and which is also
venerated by the Jews as the tomb of the prophets Haggai,
Zechariah and Malachi, but confirmation of this traditional
site of Zechariah's grave is lacking. (To the west of this and
south of Absalom's Pillar along the valley of the Kidron is the
alleged tomb of the Zechariah of Matt. 23:35.)

According to Jewish tradition, Zechariah was a member of
the Great Synagogue, of which Ezra was the president, but if,
as is generally supposed this council (which had 120 members
and was succeeded by the Sanhedrin) was first organized by
Nehemiah between 400 and 410 B.C., it would have been wellnigh impossible chronologically for the prophet to have been a
member. It is alleged that he participated in the preparation of
the liturgical service for the restored temple, and that he also
took part in the compilation of the canon of the Old Testament:
these claims may very well have some substance in them, although
there is no definite confirmation available. The Septuagint

credits him furthermore with the authorship of Ps. 137 and 138 and, jointly with Haggai, of Ps. 145, 146, 147 and 148, although it must be acknowledged that Ps. 138 and 145 are commonly attributed to David.

The date of the Book of Zechariah is made clear in the opening verse – it was the eighth month in the second year of Darius Hystaspes, i.e. about 520 B.C. Not all of the book was penned at this time: in fact, there seems to have been a considerable lapse of time between the conclusion of chapter 8 and the commencement of chapter 9. The first eight chapters contain a number of references to the prophet by name and the chapters so cohere that no question has ever been raised regarding their Zecharian authorship. Chapters 9 to 14, which, it is generally concluded, were penned at a much later date than the first half of the book, make no mention of the prophet by name. The style of these later chapters is more lively and imaginative than the plain and prosaic record of the visions of the earlier chapters, and it has also been argued that there is even a different religious attitude: as one German writer puts it, 'One who denies salvation to the Samaritans as harshly as Zechariah did in chapters 5, 7, 8, certainly cannot, a few years later, include these Samaritans in his promises of salvation, chapters 9, 10', but this argument is somewhat fallacious – the alleged exclusion in the earlier passages is not so definite as implied and the argument also takes no account of the grace of God. The difference in style may be attributable partly to the different content and partly to the difference in age of the prophet. Some critics have maintained that the reference to the Ionian Greeks (Javan) in Zech. 9:13 necessitates a much later date for that section of the book than is normally allocated to it, but Greece was in existence well within Zechariah's day and Jewish captives had been sold as slaves by her (Joel 3:6; Obad. 20). Despite the case which is sometimes made out for a second author to chapters 9 to 14, there are many internal evidences to support the view that the whole of the book is by one author.

For over two thousand years the whole of the book was, in fact, recognized universally as the work of Zechariah, and it was included in its entirety in the Old Testament canon. It was not until 1644 that Hugo Grotius questioned the Zecharian authorship of chapters 9 to 14, and in 1653 Joseph Mede (*Works,*

pp. 786, 833) suggested that these chapters were the work of
Jeremiah. Mede used the arguments, *inter alia*, of the irreconcila-
bility of Matt. 27:9 with a Zecharian authorship of Zech. 11:12,
13, and also the differences in style employed. The arguments
for and against the unity of the book and the common authorship of the whole have been set out briefly by J. S. Wright in
The New Bible Dictionary (p. 1356) and more fully by W. A.
Wright in W. Smith's *Dictionary of the Bible* (pp. 1825–1833)
and by Sir George Adam Smith in *The Book of the Twelve Prophets* (pp. 450 – 455), and they have been repeated (in some cases
almost verbatim) in later works and there seems no point in
repeating them once more. It is perhaps pertinent to point out
that the canon of the Old Testament was completed in the
third century B.C. (Josephus indicates that the historical books
had been completed in the fifth century) and, as one writer
remarks, 'its compilers had abundant opportunity to satisfy
themselves as to the claims of the different classes of writings
upon which they adjudicated'. If tradition is correct in its assertion (which cannot be confirmed) that Zechariah played a
prominent part with Ezra in the compilation of the Old Testament canon, it is extremely unlikely that he would have con-
curred in the words of some anonymous prophet being added
to his writings or represented as an integral part of them. It is
also relevant that the references by the Master to 'all the
prophets' in Luke 24:25, 27 would have covered the Book of
Zechariah as a whole and, therefore, virtually constitute an
imprimatur upon it by our Lord. The testimony of the Jews
regarding the unity of the book is unanimous. As T. W. Chambers writes in Lange's *Commentary on the Minor Prophets* (p. 15),
'Not only the learned scribes in the days of Ezra and afterwards
who compiled the canon, but the schools of Hillel and Shammai
who flourished in Jerusalem just before and after the time of our
Lord, the great Jewish seminaries of Tiberias and Babylon, the
authors of the Targums, and the continuous series of learned
rabbis down to the Reformation, all with one consent, accept
the Book of Zechariah, just as it stands in the Old Testament, as
the product of one man, the contemporary of Haggai and Zerubbabel.'

The character and composition of the book reflect to some
extent the prophet's early upbringing. 'His birth and early

education in Babylon,' says T. T. Perowne (*Haggai and Zechariah,*
p. 48), 'account for his frequent use, in common with Ezekiel
and Daniel, of visions and allegories; the Divine Spirit adapting
Himself, as ever, to the capacity and training of the human
instrument, in imparting His revelations.' Perowne considers
that Zechariah's visions, in fact, are tinged with Persian imagery.
In *The Jewish Church* (vol. III, p. 102) Stanley remarks, 'He
saw the earth, as it now presented itself to the enlarged vision of
those who had listened to the wise men of Chaldea, its four
corners growing into the four horns that toss and gore the lesser
powers of the world (1:18, 19); the celestial messengers riding
on horses, red or dappled, hurrying through the myrtle groves
that then clothed the base of Olivet, or from the four quarters
of the heavens driving in chariots, each with its coloured horses, to
and fro, across the Persian empire (1:8-11; 6:1-8), as in the
vast machinery of the posts for which it was celebrated, and
bringing back the tidings of war and peace.' But the book has
always been regarded as difficult of interpretation. The Jewish
commentator, Solomon Ben Jarchi (usually referred to as Rashi)
for instance, says, 'The prophecy is very dark, for it contains
visions much like dreams, which want interpreting, and we will
never succeed in finding the true meaning until the Teacher
of righteousness arrives.' To the Christian, with the later revelation of the New Testament and particularly of its closing book,
there is perhaps greater light now than in an earlier day.

Zechariah's inspired utterances were concerned, in the first
instance, with the declension of his people and the need to
encourage them in the rebuilding of the temple, although, of
course, the implications of his statements were far deeper and
more far-reaching than the immediate circumstances. An
appreciation of the historical background is, however, essential
if the significance of the book is to be plain.

When Nebuchadnezzar captured Jerusalem in 598 B.C., he
spoiled the city and the temple and deported all but the poorest
of Judah (2 Kings 24:11–16). Nine years later, in consequence
of the rebellion of the puppet king Zedekiah, the Babylonians
destroyed Jerusalem and carried away captive the remainder of
the people (2 Kings 24:20 to 25:8–11). After Cyrus had added
Babylon to the Persian Empire, however, he issued a decree in
536 B.C., authorizing the exiled Jews to return to their own

country and to rebuild the temple (Ezra 1:1–4). A large company (estimated by Perowne to consist of 42,360 men and some 200,000 free persons – men, women and children – together with 7,327 male and female slaves – see Ezra 2) accordingly set out for their own land under the leadership of Joshua and Zerubbabel, and it was not long before they had laid the foundation of the sacred building. But the construction of the temple was hampered and frustrated by the opposition and intrigues of the surrounding nations, and eventually the discouraged Jews, forbidden by the Persian ruler to rebuild the city, gave up the temple work in despair (Ezra 4:21–24). For fifteen years it was left untouched, while the people devoted themselves to their own affairs and to the building of their own houses. At this stage, Haggai was called upon to prophesy to them. His words stirred the nation and shook the people out of their lethargy and despondency, converting them once more into zealous workers for God and His temple. The emperor's own approval was subsequently given and, in less than four years, the rebuilding of the temple was completed (Ezra 6:1–15).

Two months after Haggai's first message and only a few weeks after the Jews had recommenced the building of the temple, Zechariah was Divinely directed to confirm and supplement the message of the other prophet. He accordingly started to prophesy in November 520 B.C., between the second and the third messages of Haggai, but his utterances were by no means as simple and uncomplicated as those of the latter. To quote T. W. Chambers again (op. cit., p. 7), 'His utterances take in the whole character and condition of the remnant people, their present dangers and discouragements, their tendencies to formalism and self-deception, their relations to the surrounding heathen and their influence upon the future prospects of the world. His historical position in the second to fourth years of Darius merely furnishes the background of the delineations he presents of the present and coming fortunes of the kingdom of God.' He looked beyond the present, however, to the ultimate future and he glimpsed the glory of the Second Advent of the Messiah. We also stand in a day of sloth and lethargy, disillusionment and discouragement, with a realization – as Zechariah must have had – that a crisis is imminent and that some climactic event must inevitably burst upon us in the near future. The inspired messages of the prophet so long ago still have their significance for the present day and are perhaps more pertinent now than they have ever been in the past. Zechariah anticipated the first advent of Christ and also His ultimate return to earth. We look into the heavens as we await the first stage of His second advent – His descent to the air to call away His Church.

Zechariah's book may be analysed quite simply as shown below.

Part 1 (Chapters 1 to 8)

1. *Introduction* (1:1–6).
    (a) Date and authorship (1:1).
    (b) Call to repentance (1:2–6).
2. *Eight Visions* (1:7 to 6:6).
    (a) The horsemen in the myrtle grove (1:7–17).
    (b) The four horns and four artificers (1:18–21).
    (c) Measurement of Jerusalem's ground plan (2:1–13).
    (d) The cleansing of the high priest (3:1–10).
    (e) The lampstand and olive trees (4:1–14).
    (f) The flying roll (5:1–4).
    (g) The woman in the ephah (5:5–11).
    (h) The chariots of judgement (6:1–8).
3. *Crowning of Joshua* (6:9–15).
4. *Observance of Fasts* (7 and 8).

Part 2 (Chapters 9 to 14)

5. *First Burden* (9–11).
    (a) The coming of the King (9 and 10).
    (b) Rejection of the Shepherd (11).
6. *Second Burden* (12–14).
    (a) Gentile invasion of Israel (12 and 13).
    (b) The return in glory (14).

CHAPTER 2

A Call to Repentance

It was the common practice for the Jews to date all events by reference to the years of the reigns of their kings, e.g. Jeremiah declared that the Divine message came to him in the thirteenth year of the reign of Josiah, the king of Judah (Jer. 1:2). Unlike the pre-exilic prophets, Zechariah could not use this method of dating his prophecy, because the throne of Israel and Judah had now no rightful occupant. Instead, he related his ministry – as Haggai had done earlier – to the reign of the heathen Darius (i.e. Darius Hystaspes), thereby emphasizing the fact that the chosen people were without their own sovereign and were subject to the rule of a Gentile power. When God bestowed upon Nebuchadnezzar potential authority over the whole earth (Dan. 2:37, 38), He disclosed that Gentile supremacy would continue until the establishment of a theocratic kingdom on earth (Dan. 2:44, 45). Our Lord subsequently revealed that Israel's misfortunes would continue until the completion of the period of 'the times of the Gentiles' at the coming of the Son of Man (Luke 21:24–27). If the two parts of the Book of Zechariah are from the pen of the same author, the prophecy spans in its scope practically the entire period of 'the times of the Gentiles' and anticipates the succeeding one of the millennium. 'The times of the Gentiles,' writes Dr. H. Grattan Guinness in *Light for the Last Days*, 'are marked by Jewish loss of dominion and independence, by Jewish subjection to and suffering under Gentile conquerors, by the dispersion of the twelve tribes of Israel, and by the subjection of their land.' (See also pp. 30–32 of *God's Programme of the Ages*, by F. A. Tatford.)

Cyrus, the Persian ruler who had authorized the return of the exiles, was succeeded in 529 B.C. by Cambyses. On the latter's death, Darius Hystaspes became emperor of Persia in 521 B.C. and proved himself an outstanding administrator. It is this Darius by whose reign the prophets Haggai and Zechariah dated their messages. In his *Handbook of Biblical Chronology* (pp. 212–213), J. Finegan shows that the second regnal year of

Darius was 520–519 B.C. and that Zechariah's first address was given in October – November, 520 B.C.

The exordium to Zechariah's book was relatively brief but, as M. F. Unger remarks in his *Commentary on Zechariah* (p. 20), 'Its theme strikes the keynote of the entire book and forms an indispensable introduction to it. The truth that it enunciates is one which runs throughout the revealed ways of God with man; namely, the appropriation and enjoyment of God's promises of blessing must be perfected by genuine repentance. . . . Although the immutability of God's Word and the continuity of His plans for Israel assure the fulfilment of these purposes, nevertheless the people are not to divorce divine grace from human responsibility.' This is a lesson which should still be conned today. Communion with God is dependent upon spiritual condition and the deliberate eschewing of all that might dishonour Him.

The introduction to the book ran as follows:

'In the eighth month, in the second year of Darius, the word of Jehovah came to the prophet Zechariah, the son of Berechiah, the son of Iddo, saying, Jehovah was very angry with your fathers. Therefore, say to them, Thus says Jehovah of hosts, Return to me, says Jehovah of hosts, and I will return to you, says Jehovah of hosts. Be not like your fathers, to whom the former prophets cried, Thus says Jehovah of hosts, Return, I beseech you from your evil ways and from your evil deeds. But they did not hear or heed me, says Jehovah. Your fathers, where are they? And the prophets, do they live for ever? But my words and my statutes, which I commanded my servants the prophets. did they not overtake your fathers? So they turned and said, As Jehovah of hosts purposed to deal with us, according to our ways, and according to our deeds, so has He dealt with us ' (1:1 – 6).

Zechariah's opening words were arresting. As Wordsworth says, he 'comes forth like John the Baptist, and begins his preaching with a call to repentance, and warns the people by the history of their fathers, that no spiritual privileges will profit them without holiness, but rather will aggravate their guilt and increase their condemnation if they disobey God'. Verses 2 to 6 are possibly only a synopsis of a complete sermon on repentance delivered by the prophet, but their blunt statements and direct appeal certainly contain all the essentials required to touch the conscience of a people already aroused by the words of the contemporaneous prophet, Haggai.

A month earlier, Haggai had envisioned the filling of the millennial temple with the shekinah glory, and a month after Zechariah's first message, had emphasized the effect of the people's uncleanness (Hag. 2:1-14). Zechariah now pleaded for the repentance of the returned exiles. Pressel considers that verse 2 ('Jehovah was very angry with your fathers') was intended as an introductory word to the prophet himself and that it was indicative of the internal pressure under which he entered upon his prophetic ministry. 'A due sense of the power of God's wrath lies at the basis of all true earnestness on the part of the prophets,' he writes, 'imparts its own vehemence to the message, and produces corresponding conviction in them that hear.' Whether or not his restriction of the application of the verse is completely justified, his point is certainly pertinent. It is this vivid realization of the awfulness of the Divine wrath and the dreadfulness of alienation from God, that is so conspicuously missing from the emasculated preaching of the present day. The preachers of another age were far more conscious of its significance. In *Grace Abounding*, John Bunyan, for example, declares that, in his preaching, 'the terrors of the law and guilt for my transgressions lay heavy on my conscience; I preached what I felt, what I smartingly did feel, even that under which my poor soul did groan and tremble to astonishment. Indeed, I have been as one sent unto them from the dead! I went myself in chains, to preach to them in chains; and carried that fire in my own conscience that I persuaded them to be aware of.'

The prophet described God as 'Jehovah Sabaoth' or 'the Lord of hosts'. Jehovah was the name of the eternally existent God of Israel. The word Sabaoth disclosed His supreme authority in every realm, and the name was translated in the Septuagint as 'Ruler of all things'. W. E. Barnes (*Cambridge Bible*, p. xxiv) sees the title as portraying God's 'filling all the universe and possessing all the power and authority ascribed by the heathen to the heavenly bodies. . . . The chariots of Jehovah go through the whole earth, like the messengers of a king, and the Lord Himself decides the fate both of Jerusalem and of the nations which oppress her.' He is the supreme governor, not only over Israel, but over all the nations of the world and His armies stand waiting His behest.

Earlier prophets had repeatedly besought the previous generation of the people to desert their evil ways and deeds, and to turn in repentance to God (e.g. Isa. 55:6, 7; Jer. 3:12, 13; Hos. 7:10; Joel 2:12, 13; Amos 5:4–6), and had warned them of the consequences of their refusal to do so. But they had obdurately persisted in their course, blinded by their depravity to a sense of their sinfulness, and had declined to listen to God's words. Yet His statements were clear and explicit. 'Jehovah has sent to you all his servants the prophets, rising early and sending them; but you have not listened nor inclined your ear to hear,' said Jeremiah. The prophets said, 'Turn you again now, every one of you, from his evil way and from the evil of your doings . . . and go not after other gods to serve them. . . . Yet you have not listened to me, says Jehovah, that you might provoke me to anger with the works of your hands to your own harm' (Jer. 25:4–7; c.f. 35:14–17; 18:11, 12). The Divine pleas were reiterated through prophet after prophet in tones of compassion and warning (Isa. 31:6; Hos. 14:1), but the rebellious nation refused to listen. Ultimately, the long-threatened judgement (Exod. 20:5; Lev. 26:14 ff.; Deut. 28:15–68) fell upon the recusant people and they suffered the penalty of seven decades of captivity. It is insensate folly to imagine that the long-suffering of God implies a condonation of sin. His justice demands the punishment of offences.

Zechariah begged the returned exiles not to repeat the wilful folly of their predecessors. Where were their fathers now? T. V. Moore writes in his book on *Zechariah* (p. 42), 'Once they ruled and worshipped' as their descendants now did. 'The song of the Levite rang through the arches of the temple, the smoke of the victim ascended from its altars, their banner waved over these hills, and their armies struck terror into the hearts of their enemies. But where are they now? Some lie in slaughtered heaps, when the banner of Judah was trampled in the dust, and her bravest sons cut down like grass before the mower's scythe, by the fierce cohorts of the Assyrian. Some lie buried in the ruins of the holy city which they sought to defend from the spoiler. Some are sleeping by the flashing waters of the Euphrates, far from the graves of their fathers, after weeping out a weary life beneath the willows that bend in the land of the stranger.' Where are they now? They might have enjoyed Divine clemency had they turned to God when He appealed to them, but now, because of their deliberate intransigence, they were dead. They had turned a deaf ear to the remonstrances of the earlier prophets and, like the prairie wolf, which swiftly pursued and eventually overtook the fearful traveller, God's sore displeasure had relentlessly followed and overtaken them.

If their fathers had perished, did the prophets themselves live for ever? If the words were a rhetorical question of Zechariah's, the intention was presumably to stress the brevity of life and of the opportunity to repent. The sinners who had been warned, and the prophets who had been the vehicles of that warning, had alike passed off the scene, and the opportunity to respond in penitence had gone for ever for those who had died. Surely the present generation should realize the seriousness and the ominous character of the warning. C. F. Keil (*Commentary on the Minor Prophets*), however, suggests that, in reply to the prophet's question, 'Where are your fathers?' the people had impudently flung it back in the retort, 'And do the prophets live for ever?' In other words, they regarded the question as irrelevant. If God had judged their fathers and had punished them with death, might it not be logically assumed that the prophets had been deemed equally culpable, since they had met with the same fate? Although this is a possible interpretation, it is more probable that both questions were asked by Zechariah and that the implication of his words was that the impenitent, to whom the prophets had spoken, had perished, and that even the prophets, who had borne the message of monition, had also died, but that the Word of God still lived, and was only rendered more emphatic by the experience of those who had refused to hear it. In view of this, Zechariah pleaded, 'Do not be like your fathers'.

The words are even more pertinent today for, as Reinhold Niebuhr said in *Europe's Catastrophe and the Christian Faith* (p. 35), 'the New Testament invariably pictures human history as moving towards a climax in which evil becomes more naked and unashamed, pride more arrogant, and conflict more overt'. The lessons of the past seem to carry no weight. Yet, as D. E. Hart-Davis declared in *The Severity of God* (pp. 104 and 108), 'the judgements of God are continually in operation,' not only in a general sense, but in the particular. 'There is a law operating without cessation in our bodily constitution, and judgement proceeds according as we obey or disobey. The dipsomaniac, the drug addict, the inveterate sensualist, soon begin to manifest the operation of the law that the wages of sin is disease and premature decay. What is true in the realm of the body is equally true in the sphere of the soul. There is a moral order in the world, however dimly it is discerned. No man can continue to do wrong with impunity. There is a judgement ceaselessly dogging his footsteps as he proceeds on his evil way.' The warning has been given: refusal to heed the Divine admonition can only invoke the threatened consequences, as happened in Israel's history.

The punishment of the earlier generation had been decreed, but opportunity had been afforded for repentance, and Zechariah picturesquely portrayed this in the closing verse of his brief sermon. If a man accidentally killed another, he could flee to one of the cities of refuge and there find protection from the avenger of blood, but if the latter, in hot anger, pursued and overtook the manslayer before he reached the shelter of the city, he might very well take revenge – as he was perfectly entitled to do – and wound the other mortally (Deut. 9:6). The prophet implied that judgement could have been averted by repentance, but since that generation had remained impenitent, the words and decrees (cf. Ps. 2:7; Zeph. 2:2) of God had pursued them like the avenger of blood and had overtaken them. The same word is used in a similar setting in Deut. 28:15, 45. Escape for the unrepentant was impossible. As Horace has said, 'Rarely has punishment with limping tread parted with the forerunning miscreant'. God's punitive hand had fallen upon His people and they had suffered the penalty of the seventy years of captivity. They had been forced to acknowledge that what the prophets had foretold had come to pass; what Jehovah had threatened to do He had actually done. They had evidently admitted that what had happened was a just recompense for their character and conduct. There is possibly an implication in verse 6 that the earlier generation did, in fact, turn in repentance, not only to acknowledge the justice of the punishment which they suffered (cf. Lam. 1:18), but also contritely to change their attitude to

God. The word *shub*, translated 'turn or 'return', rather implies a change of heart or behaviour.

'Turn (or return) to Me,' was the essence of the Divine plea, 'that I may turn (or return) to you.' The One, who was entitled to command, presented Himself in the guise of a suppliant, pleading with His people for a change of attitude to Him. Wm. Kelly says in his *Lectures Introductory to the Minor Prophets* (p. 432), 'Every accomplishment of His chastening on Israel ought to be a call to their souls to hear the word of Jehovah now.' He waited to turn in blessing to them if only they would turn to Him. In our own day, He still waits for the repentance and confession of His people. The slightest indication of genuine contrition for the unspiritual and carnal course we follow, the smallest sign of penitence for our waywardness and sinful desires, would at once meet with a response from a Father Who loves His children. 'Turn to Me that I may turn to you.' Untold blessing is still available; all the riches of heaven's stores are still to be appropriated if we will only turn to Him. Obsession with the material and worldly can only divert the soul from Christ and rob the Christian of the enjoyment of all He proffers. The cry is still relevant, 'Turn to Me.' The Divine plea has long remained unheeded by Israel, but today there are some small signs of an inclination towards God, and it may well be that the events of recent years are heaven's reply to these indications of penitence and contrition. It could be so for the Christian also.

CHAPTER 3

The Myrtle Grove

On the twenty-fourth day of the month Shebat (the Assyrio –
Babylonian name of the eleventh month, cf. I.Macc. 16:14),
three months after Zechariah's introductory message, he was
given eight visions, apparently all in the course of one night. It is
evident that these were not dreams, since he seems to have been
in a fully conscious condition and to have been capable of hold-
ing converse with an angel, who acted as an interpreter of the
visions.

The people had responded to the exhortations of Haggai and
for five months had resumed with zeal and vigour the work of
rebuilding the temple. Zechariah's visions were timely since they
constituted an answer to some of the questions that were per-
plexing the Jews, but their message was very much more than
that and looked beyond the present into the eschatological future.
As Unger (op. cit., p. 25) says, the visions 'bridge the centuries
and extend to the period of the restoration of the kingdom to
Israel (Acts 1:6). They realize the ultimate in Jewish hopes and
Jewish eschatology. Although all of them had an immediate and
significant ministry of consolation and encouragement to the poor
and feeble remnant of that day lately returned from the Babylonian exile, and desperately struggling to establish themselves in a
ruined city under the heel of a foreign power, yet in no case, nor
in any sense, can any of these eight visions be said to be fulfilled
in the prophet's day.' Their complete fulfilment obviously lay in
the future – and, to a great extent, still does.

The account of the first vision was as follows:

'On the twenty-fourth day of the eleventh month, which is
the month Shebat, in the second year of Darius, the word of
Jehovah came to the prophet Zechariah, the son of Berechiah,
the son of Iddo, saying, I saw in the night, and behold, a man
riding upon a red horse, and he stood among the myrtle trees
that were in the glen: and behind him were red, sorrel and
white horses. Then I said, O my Lord, what are these? And the
angel who talked with me said to me, I will show you what these

are. And the man who was standing among the myrtle trees answered and said, These are they whom Jehovah has sent to walk to and fro through the earth. And they answered the angel of Jehovah who was standing among the myrtle trees, and said, We have walked to and fro through the earth, and behold, all the earth sits still and is at rest. Then the angel of Jehovah answered and said, O Jehovah of hosts, how long wilt thou not have mercy on Jerusalem and the cities of Judah, against which thou hast had indignation these seventy years? And Jehovah answered with good words and comforting words the angel who talked with me. So the angel who talked with me said to me, Cry out, saying, Thus says Jehovah of hosts, Jealous am I for Jerusalem and for Zion with a great jealousy. And I am very sore displeased with the nations that are at ease: for I was but a little displeased, but they aggravated the affliction. Therefore, thus says Jehovah, I have returned to Jerusalem with compassion; my house shall be built in it, says Jehovah of hosts, and the measuring line shall be stretched out over Jerusalem. Cry yet again, saying, Thus says Jehovah of hosts, My cities shall again overflow with prosperity, and Jehovah will again comfort Zion and will again choose Jerusalem' (1:7–17).

The seventy years of captivity to Babylon, predicted by Jeremiah (Jer. 25:11, 12; 29:10) were now reaching their end and the Jews not unnaturally anticipated the early restoration of their nation, since the prophet had foretold, not only that the Chaldeans would suffer for their iniquity, but that when the period was complete, God would cause His people to return to the place from whence He had driven them. Moreover, four months earlier, Haggai had declared that there would be an universal upheaval and that all nations would be shaken (Hag. 2:6, 7), but there seemed no indication that the fulfilment of this prediction was imminent. It was partly in response to the people's perplexity that Zechariah received his first vision.

In a shady, myrtle-covered glen, he saw a troop of horsemen, led by a rider on a chestnut-coloured horse, who was subsequently described as 'the angel of Jehovah' (v. 11). The angel of Jehovah was frequently mentioned in the Old Testament, and was evidently identifiable with the Second Person of the Holy Trinity prior to His incarnation. God identified this One with Himself (Gen. 16:7–11; Exod. 3:14; 23:20 ff.; Judg. 6:12; Isa.

42:8), and described Him as the angel of His presence (Isa. 63:9, literally 'of His face'). Hagar, Abraham and Jacob all described Him as God (Gen. 16:13; 22:11, 14; 48:15, 16), and He accepted sacrifices offered to God (Judg. 6:17–24; 13:3–23). Yet the angel of Jehovah was clearly depicted in the Old Testament as the messenger of God and it was in that capacity that He appeared in Zechariah's vision. (Others are termed 'sons of God' and 'angels' in the Scriptures, but the One who alone is the revealer of God, cf. John 1:18, is *par excellence the* Son and *the* Angel of Jehovah.)

The prophet referred to other horses, but patently these also bore riders. Their leader was described as an angel and these other horsemen were obviously angels or messengers of God too. These angelic horsemen rode chestnut, sorrel and white horses, and some expositors have attempted to identify the colours with particular judgements (war, famine, disease, conquest, etc.), but it is a little difficult to sustain this interpretation. It is by no means certain whether a specific colour or colours were implied by the term 'sorrel' (or 'bay' or 'speckled'), and this may have been left vague in order not to distract attention from the primary purpose of the vision.

To enable the prophet to understand the vision and its meaning, an angel stood by his side to answer his questions and to enlighten him regarding the significance of what had been said. The Divine message was normally imparted direct to the Old Testament prophets and not through an intermediary. This unusual feature of an interpreting angel is also found, however, in Daniel (Dan. 7:16; 8:16; 9. 21 ff.) and in Revelation (Rev. 17:1 ff; 21:9 ff.). The interpreting angel was not, of course, identical with the angel of Jehovah.

The myrtle was 'a beautiful shrub, with glossy, dark green leaves and white starlike clusters of fragrant flowers, whose leaves exhaled their richest odour only when bruised'. It is indigenous to Palestine and formerly grew in rich profusion there. Its fragrant blossom was worn by brides; and its dark berries were edible. Hadassah (myrtle) was a popular name for girls and was borne, of course, by Esther. Myrtle branches were among those used in the construction of the booths in which the people lived for a week at the harvest time at the feast of tabernacles (Neh. 8:15). The tree was regarded as the symbol of joy and happiness, and Isaiah declared that, in the future days of blessing, the thorn and brier would give place to the fir and myrtle (Isa. 55:13). Many commentators regard the myrtle as symbolic of Israel, and the shady myrtle grove of the vision as a picture of the nation's state of humiliation at that time. The Jewish Yalkut, for example, says that the angel 'was standing among the myrtles which were in the *metzullah* (depths). Now myrtles (*hadassim*) mean nothing else than saints, as it is said (Esther 2:7), and he was bringing up Hadassah (Esther), and the depths mean nothing else than Babylon.' But this can hardly be regarded as a satisfactory interpretation of the vision. The fact that the angel of Jehovah took his stance in the dark valley has been regarded as an indication of our Lord's deliberate association of Himself with His people in their troubled and down-trodden condition. Although this is not the primary significance of the vision, it is, nevertheless, true that the Lord has always made His presence felt (and still does) when His people are called upon to walk through the dark valleys of life. He never leaves them to walk alone in their troubles and tribulations. Indeed, it is in the dark hour of trial that we prove the reality of His presence. Many can echo the words of the psalmist, 'though I walk through the valley of the shadow of death, I will fear no evil: for Thou art with me' (Ps. 23:4).

Darius had organized couriers and posts throughout the Persian empire and his military bands and reconnoitring patrols continually traversed the countries, not only to maintain peace and order, but also to keep the court fully acquainted with the conditions in every part of the empire from the Hellespont to the Indus. The vision made clear that the Supreme Ruler of the universe was no less active. In reply to the prophet's inquiry, he was informed by the captain of the troop (the angel of Jehovah) that the horsemen had been sent forth by God to traverse the whole earth – evidently for the purpose of ascertaining the conditions prevailing, for they subsequently returned to their leader with reports of what they had found. Although God is both omniscient and omnipresent, it would seem that He employs His servants to report upon conditions throughout His dominions. (See also Job. 1 and 2, where it was disclosed that He required – and presumably still does periodically – an account of the stewardship of mighty spirit beings.) Having surveyed the whole of the world, the reconnaissance troop returned to report that the universal picture was one of quiet tranquillity. Historically this was true at the date of the vision – the second year of Darius' reign. To quote Barnes (op. cit., p. 24), 'The Persian King, after crushing Gaumata or Bardiya (Pseudo-Smerdis) in Media, passed the Tigris, defeated Nidintu-Bel, the claimant to the Babylonian throne, in two battles, and captured Babylon. . . . After this capture of the capital of western Asia, Zechariah might well say, "All the earth sitteth still and is at rest," for though Darius speaks in the Behistun Inscription of a series of revolts which followed, yet most of these occurred in lands remote from Judah, and great Babylon itself remained for a long time in the firm grasp of Darius. As we see from Ezra 6:1, 2, communication between Judah and Babylon and Ecbatana was maintained, and this could hardly have been the case, if the confusions of the Persian empire at this period were as great as they are sometimes said to have been.'

'All the world sits still and is at rest,' was the unanimous report of the angelic members of the troop. There was no sign of the predicted upheaval which was to result in Judah's blessing (Hag. 2:6, 7). It was this fact that was disturbing the returned exiles and causing them to ask when God intended to fulfil His word, and this first vision was given in order to bring their queries to the surface and to provide an answer to them. Identifying Himself with His people, the angel of Jehovah referred to the seventy years during which God had been vehemently and justifiably angry against the nation of Judah, and asked how long His mercy was to be withdrawn from Jerusalem and the cities of Judah. (Laetsch suggests that the seventy years may not refer to the period of the exile, 605–536 B.C. see, Dan. 1:1 ff., but to that from the destruction of Jerusalem and the depopulation and devastation of the country, i.e. from 586 B.C., see 2 Chron. 36:17–21, but it seems more appropriate to relate it to the exile: that had been the specific punishment for the nation's sins). In 520 B.C. the appointed period of judgement had expired: was the Divine indignation still to continue? The angel of Jehovah became the nation's intercessor with God, just as He is still the advocate of His people today (1 John 2:1).

Heaven's reply came in terms of comfort and sympathy (not to the angel of Jehovah, who knew the answer, but to the interpreting angel), and the interpreting angel was instructed to transmit the message to the prophet and he, in turn, was to convey it, with a loud voice of proclamation, to the people. God had used the nations as His instrument for the castigation of His people, but the nations had grossly exceeded their commission. They had cruelly maltreated the Jews, had dispossessed them of their property, and had dispersed them far and wide. At this aggravation, God's wrath against Judah for her sins had melted into pity, and He declared that He was exceedingly jealous or, perhaps, extremely zealous on behalf of Jerusalem and Zion. As another says, 'He will make His people the object of His deepest concern.' On the other hand, His anger had been aroused against the nations who were living in undisturbed peace and in the enjoyment of Judah's possessions. The clear implication was that, if Judah had suffered so grievously for her sins, her oppressors would pay dearly for all they had done to increase her burden of suffering. If the words had their significance two and a half millennia ago, how much greater force there is in them in view of the terrible experiences of Jewry over the centuries and particularly during the twentieth century. That the period of travail is not yet ended is plain from the prophetic word, but Matt. 25 makes it clear that there will be a day of reckoning, and it seems evident that God will soon rise up to take vengeance on His people's oppressors. It is a Divine principle, not only that the wicked must be punished, but that those who oppose or afflict God's people must pay the penalty for their crime (Matt. 25:31–46).

Jehovah then declared that He had returned to Jerusalem with compassion (or 'mercies'). He had promised that, if they would return to Him, He would return to them (Zech. 1:3). The intercession of the angel of Jehovah had been an indication of a change of heart on the part of the remnant who had returned to the land – real, even if scarcely perceptible – and a faithful God honoured His word. His return, as A. C. Gabelein has pointed out in his *Studies in Zechariah* (p. 20), 'does not mean a spiritual return or a return of God's mercies to Jerusalem only, but it means likewise the literal return when He appears the second time; and connected with this same appearing of the great Jehovah in Jesus Christ will be seen the shekinah cloud as Israel had it in the wilderness and their first temple. . . . The

Lord had withdrawn from His people. . . . The Lord being absent in His person from His people, Israel is forsaken, the land desolate. There can be no true restoration of Israel till He has come whose right it is.' That the words had a direct application to those to whom they were addressed at the time, there can be no question, but they clearly have an eschatological significance as well. The past historical perfect can surely be construed in this case (as in many others) as a prophetic perfect, implying with certainty that an event still future is regarded as having already taken place. The restoration of the shekinah glory and the realization of Jehovah's presence in the midst of His people may not yet have occurred but, in the Divine purposes, the programme is deemed to be already complete.

The consequences of God's turning to Judah were then detailed. First of all the temple would be rebuilt. If the Divine presence was again to be known among the chosen people in the shekinah cloud of glory, there must be a dwelling-place. The temple was already in course of construction and the work was actually completed four years later (Ezra 6:15). But the promise obviously looked beyond the immediate fulfilment in Zerubbabel's temple and anticipated the establishment of the millennial temple described by Ezekiel, into which the shekinah glory could again take up residence (Ezek. 40–42; Isa. 2:2, 3).

At an earlier date, Jerusalem had been measured for destruction (2 Kings 21:13), but it was now to be measured for the purpose of planning its rebuilding, which was accomplished seventy years later by Nehemiah (Neh. 6:15). Again, however, the prophecy obviously looked on beyond Nehemiah's day to a rebuilding of the metropolis in a future day, when God will 'create Jerusalem a rejoicing and her people a joy' (Isa. 65:18).

Furthermore, the material blessings accruing to the other cities of Judah were to be so great that prosperity would cause them to expand far beyond their prescribed boundaries. Some expositors have suggested that the meaning is that other cities owned and blessed of God would be scattered through the land, but it is more probable that the term 'My cities' refers primarily, if not entirely, to cities already existent. This third promise was partially fulfilled in the times of the Hasmonean princes of the Maccabean period, but it also patently anticipated another day in which the Holy Land will experience untold millennial blessing.

Finally God declared that He would show tenderness to Zion and would set His choice upon Jerusalem. By inference, the city would become His dwelling-place amidst His people. Here again, the complete fulfilment of the promise has not yet been experienced. As Wm. Kelly (op. cit., p. 442) remarks 'these words were uttered after the return from captivity. Consequently this return could not furnish the complete fulfilment of the divine assurance, though it was no doubt a pledge of it. Therefore the object of these words was not to make them contented with the measure of mercy already shown them, but to use the present as a ground to look for greater blessing which grace has in store. . . . As far as the return from Babylon is concerned, it was already accomplished; and there has never been a return since, but another and worse scattering. It is plain and certain, therefore, that God intimates a fresh return. 'He shall yet comfort Zion and shall yet choose Jerusalem.' The establishment of a Jewish state in 1948 and the return of so many Jews, which has taken place during the present century, may be a preparation for the day which is still to come.

Behind all the changing scenes of life, the Divine purpose remained immutable and sure. What God had pledged through Jeremiah and Haggai, He would perform. Today the wicked may seem to flourish, and the rebellious world to continue its course unchecked, but God's will must ultimately triumph, and blessing will then be the portion of His people.

CHAPTER 4

The Gentile Powers

Zechariah's first vision had concluded with a promise of blessing and prosperity, but before this could become effective, it was obviously necessary for the power of Judah's oppressors to be broken. Only a remnant of Judah had returned to the land: a large number still remained in Babylonia. A relatively small number of Israel may possibly have accompanied the exiles in their return, but the great majority of the people of the northern kingdom were still exiled in the land formerly occupied by Assyria. The fulfilment of the Divine pledge of blessing must have seemed wellnigh impossible, even if it was restricted to Judah, but even more so if it was regarded as applicable also to Israel (as might perhaps be deduced from the second vision). There were enemies without and within, there were obstacles and hindrances, and there was also the people's own sinful and guilty condition, all of which must first be dealt with. Priority was evidently to be given to the external forces which affected the people, and the second vision disclosed that every antagonistic power and nation was to be destroyed, and the way prepared for the implementation of the Divine purpose. As in the first vision, however, it seems evident that, while the prophecy clearly had its primary relevance to the time in which it was uttered and to the immediate benefit of the people of that date, its full significance extended far beyond that comparatively small remnant and stretched over the centuries to the end of the age, its complete fulfilment being patently linked with the Second Advent of Christ.

The account of the vision is brief.

'Then I lifted up my eyes and saw, and behold four horns! And I said to the angel who talked with me, What are these? And he answered me, These are the horns which have scattered Judah, Israel and Jerusalem. And Jehovah showed me four artificers. Then I said, What are these coming to do? And he spoke saying, These are the horns which scattered Judah, so that no man lifted up his head; but these are come to terrify them, to cast down the horns of the nations, who lifted up their horn against the land of Judah to scatter it' (1:18–21).

In the vision of the myrtle glen, God had declared His sore displeasure with the nations whom He had employed as instruments of punishment for His people. Their brutal treatment of Judah, which far exceeded the terms of the commission which He had given them (without, of course, their realizing the true reason for their subjugation of the people and their devastation of the land), was, by implication, to invoke Divine chastisement of themselves, but no indication was given of the specific means by which their punishment would be inflicted. The second vision supplied this information, although in barest outline, making it plain that oppression does not go unobserved and that the Almighty always reserves a commensurate retribution for the malignance of the persecutor.

Zechariah was doubtless bowed in meditation at the scene of the myrtle glen and the revelation it gave that the Supreme Ruler takes cognizance of every happening in His universe. But when he lifted up his eyes, it was to see four horns, which the angel interpreted as the powers which had scattered Judah, Israel and Jerusalem. No fuller description was given of the horns, either as regards their nature and composition, or as to whether they were attached to beasts or to some other object, or were merely floating loosely in the air. The intention was obviously to focus attention on the horns and not to divert it to any other particular feature. The introduction of animals, for example, would inevitably have resulted – as has happened with so many other details in prophecy – in speculation and argument regarding their significance or identity, and this was plainly not pertinent to the message of the vision.

A horn is a familiar Biblical symbol of honour (1 Sam. 2:1; Job 16:5) or of power – regal, political, religious or military (Pss. 75:4, 5; 92:10; Jer. 48:25; Dan. 7: 24; 8:3, 4; Amos 6:13; Rev. 17:12). In this instance, the angel's explanation made it clear that the horns were figurative of the great nations or empires which had not only oppressed Israel and Judah, but had driven them out of their lands or had forcibly deported them.

It is probably useless to speculate on the identity of the powers represented by the four horns. It seems evident that they were human agencies and not angelic ministers as has sometimes been suggested. Some expositors have identified those powers with Pul, Shalmaneser, Sennacherib and Nebuchadnezzar. Others have seen in them a reference to the Persians, Alexander of Macedon, Antiochus of Syria, and Ptolemy of Egypt. Others again have suggested that the horns depicted Assyria, Chaldea, Egypt and Persia. More recent writers have queried whether it is possible to relegate the application to ancient history and to ignore the sufferings inflicted upon the Jewish race in medieval times and, in our own twentieth century, by Germany, Russia, China, etc. Some of the interpretations are clearly fallacious: the Persians and Macedonians, for example, could hardly be described strictly as enemies of the Jews, while others of the nations and leaders could not properly be said to have dispersed, or 'scattered' God's people. The powers represented by the horns are specifically stated to have been those who 'scattered Judah, Israel and Jerusalem'. The more common interpretation is that Zechariah's vision referred to the same four powers as those portrayed in Daniel's prophecy (Dan. 2 and 7). viz. Babylonia, Medo-Persia, Greece and Rome. Certainly, if the view is taken that the vision covers the whole period of 'the times of the Gentiles', i.e. from the days of Nebuchadnezzar to the return of the Lord Jesus Christ to earth, it is difficult to find a more satisfactory explanation, although it may be questioned whether the description given in the vision is completely applicable to the second and third of these world empires. The fact that only four horns are mentioned has sometimes been assumed to have reference to the four cardinal points of the compass and, therefore, to be indicative of the universality of the hostility to Israel and Judah. On the north, for instance, they were faced by the active opposition of Assyria, Chaldea and Samaria; on the south by Egypt; on the west by Philistia; and on the east by Moab and Ammon. But this seems to conflict with the clear implication that only four powers were concerned.

The horns were stated to have scattered God's people. The relentless rage of the nations was, in fact, poured out upon the Jews, and the Gentile powers tossed and gored and dispersed them as dust is driven by the wind (cf. Exod. 32:20; Isa. 30:22). Barnes says (op. cit., p. 32), 'No doubt the Chaldeans carried away thousands of the Jews into captivity in Babylonia, but the allusion here is rather to the neighbours of Judah, who forwarded the work of depopulation begun by Nebuchadnezzar (cf. verse 15). Thus the Tyrians sold many of the Jews beyond the sea (Joel 3:3–6), and the Edomites carried off captives under cover of the Chaldeans (Obad. 11). There were exiles in Syria, Egypt, and the Mediterranean lands, as well as in Chaldea (2:6).' The implication is more than a mere dispersing of the people. It is rather the thorough 'winnowing' of them as grain was winnowed, indicating a severe and intensive action. Israel was said to have suffered as well as Judah. It has been suggested that the inclusion of the name of Israel was due to a subsequent interpolation of a scribe, but there is no reason to assume that Israel was excluded in the angel's explanation. It is clear from later sections of the book that the ultimate blessing of the whole nation was envisaged. The ten tribes of Israel were not lost, so far as God was concerned: they have merely been dispersed among the heathen, and one day will be restored to their own land as predicted by many of the prophets.

'God has for every hostile power which has sinned and sins against His people a correspondingly greater power to overcome it, break it in pieces, and cast it down,' says Gaebelein (op. cit., p. 23), and this was confirmed by the remaining details of the vision. As the prophet realized the strength and power of his people's foes and their ruthless determination to drive them out of their land, he might well have been depressed. What possible hope could there be? The Jews had been captive in a land whose rulers suffered no intractability and tolerated no intransigence. Their position seemed utterly hopeless. How could God possibly fulfil His pledges? Similar doubts may arise in the minds of believers today, when they realize the tremendous weight of opposition that exists and their general inability to meet it. But God's purposes can never be frustrated.

Zechariah was accordingly shown four artificers or technicians (the word used is applicable to skilled workers in wood, metal or stone – see Exod. 35:35; Deut. 27:15; Isa. 44:12, 13; 2 Sam 5:11), who had come upon the scene to terrify or to throw into a state of panic the powers represented by the horns (cf. Jer. 7:33), and vehemently to cast them down. The instruments used by these four 'carpenters', as they are decribed in the A.V., were not mentioned, and no clue was afforded regarding the identity of the workmen who were to enfeeble the great world powers. It has sometimes been suggested that they represented the four sore judgements of Ezek. 14:21 – the sword, famine, wild beast and pestilence – or, alternatively, that the reference was to mighty spiritual forces. But as the oppressors were human, it seems more logical to conclude that the counter-active agencies were human also. Each empire which has appeared upon the world's stage has been swept away in due course and replaced by another. Those, which have been the cause of trouble and tribulation to Israel and Judah, have suffered at the hands of their successors, and the prophetic word indicates that the powers which attack God's earthly people will ultimately meet with a retributive fate at the hands of the Son of God. Isa. 2:10–22 and Rev. 6 to 16 reveal something of the horrors of the future as well as of the terror of those upon whom the Divine judgements fall.

The 'nations who lifted up their horn against the land of Judah to scatter it' were to be thrown down by the four workmen. Like ferocious beasts they had charged their victims in an attempt to gore and maim. Their assault had been so fierce and unrestrained that the Jew had not even the strength to lift up his head: their inhumanity and terrible maltreatment (and often sadistic torture) of the sufferers had destroyed the latter's hopes and eventually even the will to resist. This accords with the picture painted by history.

But retribution was inevitable. None could attack God's people with impunity. The arrogant persecutors would be terrified by the instruments of God's punitive hand. The vision does not refer only to the past: it undoubtedly anticipates a day which is still future, when all Israel's foes will suffer at the hands of Messiah for their insolent cruelty and malice, and Israel and Judah (eventually one nation again) will finally enter into blessing. 'Jews take comfort in the ancient prophecies of the Hebrew seers,' says a writer of their own race, 'but history also points to the fact that though the Jews have lived by "the bread of tears", yet from the time of the triumphant proclamation on the Egyptian stele of the Pharaoh Menremptah, in the thirteenth century B.C., recording that the rebellious Israelites in Palestine had been utterly defeated – "Israel is desolated, its seed is not" – destiny appears to have ordained that this people shall not perish from the earth.'

There must be an answer to Israel's sufferings. The pogroms of Europe, the untold savagery and bestiality, bitter hatred and consistent hostility, must meet with a reply. Referring to the conditions after the First World War, the writer just quoted describes the chauvinism that arose in the new states 'that came to be regarded as essential to the assertion of a national individuality from which the Jews, as an ethnical and religious minority, were to be excluded. . . . The liberal professions were gradually closed to the Jews by the adoption of a numerous clausus at the universities. . . . The economic boycott of Jewish traders was made more effective by the increasing nationalization of commerce and industry, and ultimately they suffered the unleashing of the unbridled fury of Nazi Germany, when it was said, "Their temples have been destroyed by dynamite or deliberately devastated, and the scrolls of the law defiled; the State has confiscated their property and deprived them of the means of livelihood; they have suddenly been driven from their homes like dumb cattle and confined to the meanest streets; they have, as pariahs, been banned from the society of their non-Jewish neighbours",' and finally their lives were taken from them. A holy and righteous God must repay their persecutors and this is what the vision implied.

The lesson is not only for the Jews. When evil is in the ascendancy and the floods of trouble burst upon God's people today, we may always rest confidently in the assurance that nothing will frustrate the Divine purpose for the believer. Opposition may mass against us in terrifying volume, but eventually the forces of darkness will be overthrown and the glory of the Eternal will shine out in delivering power. God *will* redeem His pledges.

CHAPTER 5

The Measurement of the City

In the first vision God declared His jealousy for Jerusalem and His anger at the nations which had oppressed her, and announced that He would again choose Jerusalem. The second vision anticipated the ultimate defeat of the nations in question and the consequent removal of all obstacles to Judah's blessing, and referred to words of comfort being given by Jehovah. The third vision then logically provided a picture of Jerusalem's future prosperity and blessing and, as one writer says, it was virtually 'an amplification and realistic unfolding of the "comfortable words" in the second vision.' The vision fell into two parts, the first dealing with the city (2:1–5) and the second with the nation (2:6–13). The first part was relatively brief.

'I lifted up my eyes again and looked, and behold a man with a measuring line in his hand. Then I said, Where are you going? And he said to me, To measure Jerusalem, to see what is its breadth and what is its length. And behold, the angel who talked with me went forth, and another angel went forth to meet him, and he said to him, Run, speak to the young man yonder, saying, Jerusalem shall be inhabited as towns without walls because of the multitudes of men and cattle in it. For I will be to her a wall of fire round about, says Jehovah, and will be for glory in the midst of her' (2:1–5).

In the same pattern as the first two visions, the third cannot be limited to the immediate circumstances of the prophet's own day, but evidently related to the whole of the period up to the return of Christ to the earth. As Zech. 14:2, 4 indicates, at the time of the second advent, Jerusalem will have suffered the ravages of war, its walls will have been battered, its treasures looted, and half of its people carried away. Then the Mount of Olives will split in two and the whole city will naturally be affected physically by the upheaval. It will obviously be necessary for the metropolis to be entirely rebuilt, and this was principally what the third vision envisaged.

Zechariah saw a man going forth with a measuring line and

was told, in response to his inquiry, that the man's object was to
measure the length and breadth of the city – presumably to
determine the ground plan and to mark the proposed location
of the walls and buildings, with the evident intention of rebuilding the strong walls of a mountain fortress. As the prophet
watched, the interpreting angel stepped forward, but another
angel intervened with an urgent message to the interpreting
angel. It is not clear whether the message was to be conveyed to
Zechariah or to the man with a measuring line: it was addressed
to 'this young man' or 'the young man yonder', who may very
well have been the prophet himself, but the point is of little
consequence, for the message was plain. The man with a
measuring line was a new character in the *dramatis personae*.
It is not apparent whether the angel who halted the interpreting
angel was also a new character or whether he was identical with
the angel of Jehovah. The term 'young man' (*naar*) was probably more appropriate to Zechariah himself. In other words, the
message was for him and not for the man who was about to
survey the city.

In the past Jerusalem had been measured before its destruction, as an indication that the whole city was to be brought
under the judicial hand of the Almighty (2 Kings 21:13; Lam.
2:8), but in the first vision God had declared that the temple
would be rebuilt and the measuring line stretched forth upon
the city – obviously to measure it for the purpose of planning its
reconstruction as in the third vision. There are other interesting
prophecies regarding the use of the measuring line, e.g. in Ezek.
40–42 in regard to the measurement of the millennial temple
and in Rev. 11 in connection with the measurement of the
heavenly temple. It is not obvious whether the measurement
actually proceeded in Zechariah's vision or whether the purpose
of the angelic intervention was to arrest the action on the
ground that it was inappropriate or virtually pointless.

It was disclosed by the intervening angel that Jerusalem was
to be no more a citadel, dependent for its strength and defence
upon massive walls and fortifications. Its population and
material prosperity were to be so great that walls would be
impracticable. An earlier prophet had already said, 'your waste
and desolate places and devastated land shall even now be too
narrow because of the inhabitants. . . . The children of your

bereavement shall yet say in your ears, The place is too narrow
for me: give me room to dwell in' (Isa. 49:19, 20). Zechariah's
prophecy now declared that so great would be the influx of men
and cattle into Jerusalem that the city would overflow into
open villages on the mountainside and its extent would be
beyond measurement. The A.V. refers to 'towns without walls'
and the R.S.V. to 'villages without walls' but as David Baron
points out (op. cit., p. 58), 'the word strictly describes "plains",
or an open country in which there is nothing to circumscribe the
inhabitants, or to prevent them from spreading themselves
abroad: thus in Ezek. 38:11 it is used of the land where people
dwell in peace and prosperity, "without walls, bolts or gates",
in contrast to those in walled cities'. Older commentators, as an
indication of its possible future extent, have quoted the particulars of the city in the time of Alexander the Great, when Jerusalem was fifty stadia in circumference and was inhabited by
120,000 men. But what is envisioned in Zechariah is something
very much vaster, with people living in complete peace and
freedom and expanding at will.

The prophecy referred to the multitude of cattle in the city
(v. 4) and the appropriateness of this has been questioned
but, as Barnes (op. cit., p. 35) points out, 'ancient cities contained space for cattle' (see Jer. 33:10, 13; Jonah 4:11), and it
would appear strange to a pastoral people if no provision was
made for the accommodation of flocks and herds in the area of
the city.

There would be no need for walls, since Jehovah promised
Himself as their defence. He would be a protective wall of fire
around the city. As the caravan camping in the wilderness sets
fires around the encampment to keep off marauders and wild
animals, so the Almighty would become a continuous ring of
fire around His people. No other defence would be required if
He was their protection. Their security was assured. None
could assail or overthrow that city. Although the promise was
made to Judah and is yet to be fully implemented in a coming
day, it is still applicable to God's people today. The one
who has sheltered in Christ is absolutely safe and secure. He is
surrounded by a wall of fire and no foe can touch or destroy
Him.

Moreover, Jehovah declared that He would be for glory in the midst of Jerusalem. In other words, the shekinah glory, which once filled the holy of holies of the tabernacle and the temple, would return to the city – not to be restricted as formerly to a hidden shrine, but to fill the whole of the city with glory (cf. Ps. 3:3). Ezekiel foretold the return of this shekinah to the future millennial temple (Ezek. 43:1–5), but Zechariah's vision is of an even greater and fuller revelation of God. In the past there had been a mysterious cloud of light, seen dimly through the cloud of incense by the high priest once a year. But, by implication, Jehovah now promised the display of the unveiled glory of God for the constant and continual occupation of every citizen of Jerusalem. During Israel's exodus and journeyings, the angel of Jehovah associated Himself with the pillar of cloud and fire, by which the nation was guided and protected, and inferentially it will be the same One (now accepted as Messiah) who will dwell in the midst of the city in a future day. The description given is evidently of the New Jerusalem, of which the seer of the Apocalypse said centuries later, 'the city had no need of the sun, neither of the moon, to shine in it: for the glory of God did lighten it, and the Lamb is its light' (Rev. 21:23). Zechariah's description plainly anticipated the millennial age, although it has its application already to the Christian, who gazes upon the unveiled glory of God in the face of Jesus Christ (2 Cor. 4:6).

It has been said that the second part of this third vision was a lyric appended to it but having no vital relation to the first part. Sir George Adam Smith (op. cit. pp. 290, 291) maintains that it is of an earlier date than the remainder of the book. 'Israel is addressed,' he says, 'as still scattered to the four winds of heaven, and still inhabiting Babylon. While in Zechariah's own oracles and visions, Jehovah has returned to Jerusalem, His return according to this piece is still future. There is nothing about the temple; God's holy dwelling position from which He has roused Himself is heaven.' But there is good reason for the view that it refers to the exiles who remained in Babylon and that it also anticipates the future. The terms of this second part of the vision were as follows.

'Ho! ho! Flee from the land of the north, says Jehovah: for I have spread you abroad as the four winds of the heaven, says Jehovah. Deliver yourself, O Zion, that dwells with the daughter of Babylon. For thus says Jehovah of hosts, After glory has he sent me to the nations which spoiled you: for he who touches you touches the apple of his eye. For, behold, I will shake my hand over them, and they shall be a spoil to their servants: and you shall know that Jehovah of hosts has sent me. Sing and rejoice, O daughter of Zion: for lo, I come, and I will dwell in the midst of you, says Jehovah. And many nations shall join themselves to Jehovah in that day, and shall be my people: and I will dwell in the midst of you, and you shall know that Jehovah of hosts has sent me to you. And Jehovah will inherit Judah his portion in the holy land, and will again choose Jerusalem. Be silent, O all flesh, before Jehovah: for he is raised up out of his holy habitation' (2:6–13).

Over two centuries earlier, the people of Israel had been deported by the Assyrians. More than a century afterwards, the people of Judah had been carried away by the Babylonians and subsequently dispersed throughout the 127 provinces of the Persian empire from India to Ethiopia. Both Assyria and Babylonia were commonly referred to as the land of the north (Jer. 1:4; 3:18; 6:22; Zeph. 2:13) since their invasions of Israel and Judah came from that direction, and Zech. 2:7 specifically linked it with Babylon.

Jeremiah foretold that the Lord would bring His people ou of the north country and gather them from the coasts of the earth (Jer. 31:8) and from all countries whither He had driven them (Jer. 23:8). Zechariah now heard the voice of God calling upon His people to flee from the north. Barnes (op. cit., p. 35) says, 'Many captives were deposited in north Syria (Hamath, 9:2; Isa. 11:11), while others were carried further to the north-east into Assyria (Mesopotamia), (10:10; Isa. 11:11) and Media (2 Kings 17:6). . . . northern Syria remained a typical land of captivity, for thither in the first instance all these captives were taken.' Jehovah declared that He had dispersed them 'as the four winds of heaven' – a phrase which may mean either their dispersal to every part of the earth or the manner in which He had 'spread them abroad' – but now they were to flee. The immediate objects of the injunction were clearly the many exiles who had remained behind when others had returned to the land under Joshua and Zerubbabel. The injunction patently presaged the impending judgement on Babylon and was directed at securing the evacuation of the exiles before the judgement fell. Isa. 48:14, 20; Jer. 50:8, 10; 51:6, 45 specifically connect the judgement of Babylon with the escape of Judah.

Baron (op. cit., pp. 70, 71) argues that this part of the prophecy had 'only a partial reference to the times in which the prophet wrote his visions. Though a remnant had returned, by far the greater number were still in the land to which they had been exiled. Some of them had grown rich and prosperous in the strange land. Their love for Jerusalem and all that it stood for had cooled down, and they were content to become dwellers "with the daughter of Babylon". They were reluctant to leave their comfortable homes and vineyards (which they had indeed been encouraged to build and to plant, but only as temporary possessions during the seventy years of the captivity, Jer. 29) for the rough journey and hard life in the desolated land. And so they are exhorted to flee out of Babylon, not only because of the goodness of the Lord which is to be shown to His people in their own land, but because of the evil which was about to overtake the country of their sojourn, and the calamities which would come on its people, occasioned probably by the two great rebellions in Babylon, and the two captures of the city of Babylon – one by Darius in person, and the other by one of his generals – which had just taken place when the prophet wrote his visions. At the same time, this call to come out of the Babylon of that time, which met with only a very partial response, was also a foreshadowing of the future, when Jehovah shall lift up His hand again a second time to recover the remnant of His people which shall be left from Assyria and from Egypt, and from Pathros and from Cush, and from Elam, and from Shinar, and from Hamath and from the islands of the sea.' The call now made, however, was, in the first instance, to the exiles in Babylon to come out and to return to their own country.

'After glory' had God sent His agent to Judah's oppressors. There is a wide variety of interpretations of this term. It can scarcely refer, as some have suggested, to the bestowal of glory in verse 5, or to the Divine acquisition of glory or a desire to acquire additional glory. The more probable significance is that the action taken was a demonstration of God's glory or a vindication of it. To quote Baron again (op. cit., p. 73), it 'means to vindicate and to display the glory of God, first in the judgements which He is to inflict on the nations who have oppressed

Israel, and then in the exhibition of His grace in the deliverance and salvation of His own people, and also in the blessing which is to come to the Gentile nations after Israel is restored, and Mount Zion becomes not only the seat of Messiah's governmental rule over the nations, but the centre of the true worship of God on the earth'. The context tends to imply that what is in view is the Second Advent of Christ in power and glory to smite the nations with the rod of His anger and to bring salvation to His people. As another has said, God's 'glory is inseparably linked with the fortunes of His people. He cannot be glorified as long as His people are disgraced and persecuted by their enemies.' That will be ended when the Son of God returns to Olivet to execute judgement upon a guilty world. The Masoretic text marks a pause after the word 'glory', so that the text might very well read, 'After glory! He has sent me. . . .'

God declared that He had sent His agent in judgement to the nations which had oppressed His people. They had afflicted His elect, who were as dear to Him as the apple of His eye. In daring anthropomorphic picture, the prophecy declared that whoever touched God's people touched God at the most tender point. The pupil of the eye is the most sensitive part of the human body (cf. Deut. 32:10; Ps. 17:8), feeling acutely the most minute injury. The maltreatment of Judah affected the Divine feelings as a sudden jab would affect the contractile opening of the visual organ. When Saul of Tarsus was suddenly arrested by the Christ of the glory on the Damascus road, the Master's words of remonstrance for his persecution of His followers were significant. 'Why do you persecute *Me*?' (Acts 9:4), He asked Saul. Every attack today upon the Christian, who is a member of the body of Christ, is inevitably felt by the Head of the body. This has always been true. The Eternal so closely associates Himself with His people that their sorrows and sufferings are His.

In a menacing gesture, Jehovah declared that He would shake (or brandish) His hand (Isa. 11:15; 19:16) over those who had spoiled Judah and that they should themselves become a spoil to the people whom they had held in servitude (cf. Isa. 14:1, 2). The tables were to be turned. Laetsch says (op. cit., p. 420), 'When He shakes His hand, which formed the earth (Ps. 95:5 and makes the mountains smoke (Ps. 104:32), the proud masters will become servants, the presumptuous rulers, abject slaves. So will the glory of the Lord . . . become manifest and be gratefully praised by all His people, and acknowledged, with bitter resentment and horrified fear, by His enemies.' At an earlier date the prophet Isaiah had declared that their former oppressors would be possessed by Israel as slaves (Isa. 14:2). When this complete reversal of their fortunes occurred, it would be convincing evidence that Jehovah had sent His servant – a statement which is repeated in verse 11.

In anticipation of their salvation and of the blessings yet to be experienced, the people (portrayed as a young woman, the 'daughter of Zion') were called upon to burst forth in jubilant psalm, because Jehovah was coming and would dwell in their midst (cf. Isa. 12:6; Zeph. 3:14, 15). Perowne says (op. cit., pp. 77, 78) that 'this prophecy had a fulfilment, when the temple was rebuilt and the worship of God was resumed on Mount Zion. But it had a higher fulfilment when 'the Word was made flesh and dwelt among us" (John 1:14; Mal. 3:1), and the promise of the Gentiles being joined to the Lord (v. 11) was also accomplished. It awaits its highest fulfilment in both particulars in the times that are yet future (Rev. 7:15; 21:3, 22–26).' The coming referred to was not merely our Lord's first advent. In view of the context and the statements immediately following it seems clear that it is the second advent that is primarily envisioned. The Almighty, in the person of the Messiah, is to break into time once more and His coming will bring joy and gladness to His people and, in all His wonder and glory, He will then actually dwell in their midst. God will again take up residence on earth, not this time in humiliation and lowliness, but in all His power and majesty.

In that day (a term which tends to confirm the millennial setting of the scene), the prophecy declared that many nations would join themselves to Jehovah. Through the preaching of the gospel of the coming King by Jewish missionaries and ultimately by the revelation of the Eternal, multitudes of Gentiles will be converted and will, of their own volition, join themselves to Him, precisely as the prophet Jeremiah had previously predicted (Jer. 50:4, 5). Even during the period of the great tribulation, it is clear that many Gentiles will be saved (Rev. 7:9, 10; 14:1–4), and when the revelation of the Messiah comes at His appearing, others will be attracted to Him (Isa. 56:3, 6). Again the promise was repeated that Jehovah would dwell in the midst of His people, and once more God's messenger declared that, by the fulfilment of what had been predicted, Judah would know that God had sent him.

The conversion of Gentiles in such large numbers might possibly give rise to doubt whether the Divine pledges to Israel had been annulled or abrogated in some way. The original election of Israel was an irrevocable one, and nothing will alter it. (See *Will there be a Millennium?* by F. A Tatford). The character and conduct of the people were irrelevant: the choice was not conditioned by their behaviour. They are the portion and inheritance of Jehovah (cf. Deut. 9:24; 32:9), His portion in the holy land (the only occurrence in Scripture of the term 'the holy land'). The apostle Paul indicates that, during the present era, 'the riches of His glorious inheritance in the saints' has reference to the church (Eph. 1:18), but in the millennial age, Israel will be Jehovah's inheritance (Isa. 19:25).

Once more the Almighty stated that He would again choose Jerusalem: in other words, He would demonstrate the immutability of His original choice. Feinberg says in *God Remembers* (p. 51), the statement 'does not imply that God must choose Israel afresh, but that now, at long last, He will be able to manifest to the world the immutable character of His original choice and its practical outworking in renewed, restored and resettled Israel.' The fact will be established beyond all possible doubt. This is God's chosen city, the place where He will set His name.

The whole scene is obviously of the commencement of the millennial period of bliss and happiness, peace and prosperity. The nations will have been dealt with, the sinner trampled under foot, and the glory of Jehovah will cover the earth as the waters cover the sea. 'Be silent, all flesh, before Jehovah,' came the imperative (cf. Hab. 2:20). The judicial glory of God was about to be manifested and all might well fear for He was coming to judge the earth. He had awakened or roused Himself up from the habitation of His holiness. All mankind might well be hushed in awe at His presence. He does not, of course, actually sleep. 'He who keeps Israel will neither slumber nor sleep' (Ps. 121:3, 4). When the earth was at rest and evil continued unchecked, it must have seemed as though God was asleep. But now there was no doubt regarding His activity. He had risen up out of the habitation of His holiness (Deut. 26:15; Jer. 25:30), and was about to issue forth to succour His people and to discomfit their foes.

CHAPTER 6

The Cleansing of the Priesthood

The preceding visions had disclosed the retribution to be meted
out to the Gentile powers and the ultimate blessing of the nation
of Israel. But before the people could be restored to communion
with God, it was essential for their defilement to be removed,
and it was with this matter that the third chapter of the book
was concerned.

Seraiah, the grandfather of Joshua, the high priest, was
among those taken captive by Nebuchadnezzar after the sacking
of Jerusalem and he was subsequently slain by his captor at
Riblah (2 Kings 25:18–21). His son, Josedech, was also among
the deportees (1 Chron. 6:15) and Joshua was evidently born in
Babylon. During the lifetime of Josedech, while the temple was
in ruins and the people in captivity, the high priesthood had
virtually been in abeyance, since the exercise of the sacerdotal
functions was clearly impossible. With the return of the exiles
and, Josedech having apparently died prior to that return, Joshua
had become his legitimate successor as high priest. Now, after
fifty-two years, the office had again been filled, and Joshua stood
as the representative of his people before God, and the question
arose of his suitability to fill the sacred office. The high priest,
as Leupold says in his *Exposition of Zechariah* (p. 64), 'represents
and practically impersonates Israel in his holy office. For the
nation he prays; for it he enters the holy place; he bears the
nation's guilt. We must not, therefore, refer the issues and implications of this chapter to Joshua as an individual, nor merely
to Joshua, the high priest. We must conclude that *his* condition
is *Israel's* condition, *his* acquittal a typical way of expressing
theirs; the words of comfort and assurance given *him* apply with
equal validity to *them*.' God referred to His choice of *Jerusalem*
and not of *Joshua* (vv. 2 and 4) and verse 9 states that the
iniquity of the *land* has been removed. Zechariah's next vision
was thus concerned with the cleansing of the priesthood as
representative of the cleansing of the people.

'And he showed me Joshua the high priest standing before the angel of Jehovah, and Satan standing at his right hand to accuse him. And Jehovah said to Satan, Jehovah rebuke you, O Satan; even Jehovah who has chosen Jerusalem rebuke you. Is not this a brand plucked out of the fire? Now Joshua was clothed with filthy garments, and was standing before the angel. And he answered and spoke to those who were standing before him, saying, Take away the filthy garments from him. And to him he said, Behold, I have caused your iniquity to pass from you, and I will clothe you with change of raiment. And I said, Let them put a clean mitre upon his head. So they put a clean mitre upon his head and clothed him with garments. And the angel of Jehovah was standing by. And the angel of Jehovah solemnly affirmed to Joshua, saying, Thus says Jehovah of hosts, If you will walk in my ways, and if you will keep my charge, then shall you also judge my house, and you shall also keep my courts, and I will give you a place of access among these who stand by. Hear now, O Joshua, the high priest, you, and your fellows who sit before you: for they are men of portent. For behold, I will bring forth my servant, the Branch. For behold the stone, that I have laid before Joshua; upon one stone are seven eyes; behold, I will engrave the graving of it, says Jehovah of hosts, and I will remove the iniquity of this land in one day. In that day, says Jehovah of hosts, shall you invite every man his neighbour under the vine and under the fig tree' (3:1–10).

One of the most amazing features of the Christian era is that, through the work of Calvary, the believer has the right of access at all times into the immediate presence of God – the *sanctum sanctorum* of the celestial heights (Heb. 10:19). Under the Mosaic economy, by contrast, the individual's approach to God was solely through the medium of the priesthood, and even the high priest could enter the Divine presence only once a year (Lev. 16:2, 29–34). Since the priesthood thus represented the nation, it was essential that no taint of sin or defilement should attach to those who officiated in the temple service, and it was, therefore, required that the priest should offer first for his own sins before he made any sacrifices on behalf of the people (Heb. 7:27). Zechariah must consequently have been gravely disturbed at the vision to which his attention was drawn by the interpreting angel, for the high priest stood in the presence of God attired in filthy robes.

Joshua was standing before the angel of Jehovah and it has been suggested that the term employed was that commonly used of an assembly at the royal court, when nobles and officials stood in attendance upon their sovereign, to learn his will and to carry out his behests. But the expression, 'to stand before Jehovah', was consistently used in the Old Testament in a technical sense to denote the ordinary service of the priests in the sanctuary (Deut. 10:8; 2 Chron. 29:11; Judg. 20:28; Ps. 134:1; Ezek. 44:15). The implication was clearly that Joshua stood in the Divine presence in his official capacity to intercede on behalf of his people.

The description of the high priest's garments in verse 1 is amplified in verse 3, where it is specifically stated that Joshua was standing, clothed in filthy garments. The presumption that, in the description given, there is an allusion to the Roman practice of compelling an accused person to wear sordid attire unless and until his fate was determined, is obviously fallacious since the high priest was not arraigned for trial. It is clear also that there is no ground for the fantastic idea that 'an accusation had been lodged against Joshua in the Persian court', says Stanley (*Jewish Church*, vol. III, p. 103) and that 'the splendid attire of the high priest, studded with jewels, had been detained at Babylon or, at least, could not be worn without the special permission of the king; and until the accusation had been cleared away, this became still more impossible'. The clothes worn by Joshua were covered with excrement or vomit (Jer. 28:8) and were evil-smelling as well as filthy. The clothes (symbolizing the uncleanness of the priesthood and the people) were similar to those which would be worn by a foul criminal and, *prima facie*, were the irrefutable evidence that he was disqualified for his high office. How could a holy God countenance such an unclean person? The garments worn by Joshua disclosed his uncleanness. As habits or clothes are to the body, so are actions to the real man. What was visualised, of course, was not merely the defilement of the high priest, but that of the nation as a whole – their constant sins, their apostasy and their infidelity.

Also standing before the angel of Jehovah was the adversary to accuse the people's representative. In a paronomasia the inspired writer declares that Satan was there to *satanize* him –

the accuser, to accuse. The reference was clearly to a person. 'It is a favourite notion,' says Chambers (op. cit., p. 39) 'that Zechariah imported his conception of Satan from the Zoroastrian doctrine of Ahriman, the original source of all moral and physical evil, the chief of malignant spirits, the king of darkness and of death, and consequently the eternal enemy of Ormuzd, and of his kingdom of light,' but long before the Babylonian captivity, the Scriptures had clearly indicated the existence of a mighty spirit being, bitterly opposed to the Almighty. (See *The Prince of Darkness*, by F. A. Tatford).

Satan was ready to challenge Joshua's title to represent his people because of his defilement (and, by implication, his sinnership). Before the adversary could utter a word, however, the angel of Jehovah intervened and rebuked him for his presumption. The God, who had in sovereignty chosen Jerusalem, was under no compulsion to explain His ways or defend his actions (Exod. 33:19). He had brought His people out of captivity, snatching them out of the furnace of Babylon. Was it likely that He would cast back into the fire a brand which He had so recently snatched therefrom and surrender His servant (i.e. the nation and not merely Joshua) to destruction? The words probably have a prophetic significance as well as an immediate application, and the fire may refer to Israel's sufferings, in the future as well as in the past. The devil is still the accuser of God's people (Rev. 12:10), and the Christian who commits sin is particularly susceptible to his attack and is open to his accusation (1 Cor. 5:5; 1 John 5:10). What an assurance there is in the knowledge that, whatever our failure and wrongdoing, the One who died to redeem us will never allow His people to come into condemnation (John 5:24). The evil one may attack and may seek to accuse us in the presence of God, but the blood of Christ shelters us from all his assaults.

Joshua uttered no word in his own defence, and some have suggested that this was the palpable evidence of his guilt. But the Almighty had intervened before the accuser could speak and had silenced the devil before any case could be submitted. Twice the presentation of the accusation was forestalled, and there was neither opportunity nor reason for any plea to be made by the accused. His defilement was obvious, but Jehovah declared that He had caused his iniquity to pass away. His

disqualification was to be removed and he was to be rendered
fit to undertake his sacerdotal ministry again.

The filthy garments with which he was clad made him unfit
to stand in the Divine presence, but his absolution was confirmed when the angel of Jehovah instructed the angels who
stood in attendance upon him to remove the vomit-covered
and excrement-bespattered clothes from Joshua. The defiled
clothing was replaced by festal robes – a reference to the high
priest's garments of glory and beauty (Exod. 29:4, 5; Lev. 8:7–9)
thereby confirming that he was to be retained in office. As
another says, 'the God of absolute holiness, justice and righteousness is, at the same time, the God of unalterable and everlasting
grace, forgiving iniquity, trespasses and sin, without relinquish-
ing the least iota of His holiness'. There may be a subtle reference in the priest's defiled clothing to the earlier description of
the people as unclean and their good deeds as filthy rags (Isa.
64:6). The purification of the nation's representative may also
prefigure the cleansing of the nation described in a later part of
the prophecy. Whatever other message was conveyed, it was
clear that none can stand in the Divine presence in his own
merit: his title is dependent upon the grace of God and virtually
lies in the merits of Another.

At Zechariah's cry, the mitre of the high priest (a turban of
byssus or white linen) was then placed upon Joshua's head. To
the mitre, of course, would be attached the golden plate with
its inscription, 'Holy to Jehovah' (Exod. 28:36). Grace had
adorned the high priest with clothes suitable for his ministry
and functions and he now received the Divine commission
to minister before God on behalf of his nation. It was always the
purpose of God that Israel should act as priests on behalf of the
nations of the world, but in general the people ignored the
spiritual needs of others and attempted to focus the Divine
blessings solely upon themselves. They failed the purpose of God.
But in a future day, the nation will be universally known as
'priests of Jehovah' and 'ministers of our God' (Isa. 61:6), and
the original purpose will be completely achieved.

The angel of Jehovah then solemnly affirmed to Joshua that,
if he walked in God's ways and kept His ordinances, the responsibility for the administration and direction of all temple
affairs would be vested in him. Furthermore he would preserve

the temple courts from defilement. The inestimable privilege
would also be bestowed upon him of free entry among the angels
who stood in the presence of God, i.e. admission to the immediate presence of God. Unimpeded ingress would be allowed to
him. So far as Israel and her representative are concerned, the
complete fulfilment of the prophecy plainly relates to a period
still future. The access promised to the earthly people of God is,
however, already the privilege and experience of the heavenly
people of today and they do not await a future day for the
appropriation of this blessing.

The vision so far had been concerned with the high priest,
but in verse 8 the remainder of the priests were called upon to
listen to the angel of Jehovah. They were described as those who
sat before Joshua – not, of course, at that particular moment, but
in their official capacity. David Baron (op. cit., p. 106) says that
they were 'the ordinary priests who, in meetings of the order for
the purpose of discussing or deciding matters connected with
their office, "sat before" the high priest, who was the president of
the assembly'. The angel referred to them as 'men of portent'
or 'men of sign' (the A.V. renders 'men wondered at'). C. H. H.
Wright remarks, 'The vision had pictured to the eye of the
priest-prophet the manner in which the priesthood of Israel,
represented by Joshua, though defiled with iniquity, had been
cleansed by Divine grace, and rendered acceptable to God. By
that grace, priest and people had been snatched like half-burnt
brands from the fire of a well-deserved punishment. That deliverance was, however, typical of a greater salvation, which the
angel was now about to reveal. Hence Joshua and his fellows
were typical men.' They were also symbolic of another priesthood (the New Testament holy and royal priesthood of which
every true Christian is a member). They were servants of
Jehovah in the temple and typical of another Servant, whom
God was about to bring forth in the guise of a Branch or
Sprout.

The title 'the Servant of Jehovah' was used of the nation of
Israel in Jer. 30:10; 46:27 and possibly in Ezek. 28:25; 37:25
(although the Ezekiel passages may refer to Jacob personally).
It is developed more fully in the prophecy of Isaiah (see e.g.
Isa. 41:8; 42:19, 43:10; 44:1, 21; 45:4; 48:20) and particu-
larly in what are usually described as the 'Servant songs', i.e.

Isa. 42:1-6; 49:1-6; 50:4-9; 52:13 to 53:12. There is a considerable difference of opinion regarding the interpretation of these passages and the Servant is variously identified as (*a*) the nation of Israel, (*b*) spiritual Israel, (*c*) ideal Israel, (*d*) a historical person (probably a religious teacher) and (*e*) an ideal individual whose appearance was still future (i.e. the Messiah). Whilst there are arguments for the theory that the references must be to a collective body, it is more logical to treat them as having a personal application. J. Skinner, in *The Book of the Prophet Isaiah* (volume II, p. xxxiii) says, 'The Servant is one who endures persecution and opposition from his own countrymen (Isa. 50:6-9) and dies the death of a martyr at their hands (53: 1-9). His sufferings and death constitute an atonement for the sins of his people, so that with his stripes they are healed (53:4-6, 8). He is one also who is in conscious and perfect sympathy with Jehovah's purpose in raising him up; he is neither blind nor deaf, but alert and sensitive and responsive to the divine voice (50:4, 5).' Many of the expressions, which are used in Isaiah can scarcely apply to any other than our Lord Jesus Christ and Zech. 3:8 seems a clear prediction of the Messiah. In *The Suffering Servant in Deutero – Isaiah*, C. R. North maintains that the Servant is a soteriological messianic figure and this conclusion is really inescapable.

The second expression used by God was the Branch or Sprout. Here again, there can be little doubt that the reference was to the Messiah, of whom the title is frequently used in the Old Testament. It is significant that He was not described as a tall, stately tree, but as a shoot from the roots. With the removal of Israel and Judah from their own land, the royal house of David gradually sank into obscurity, and Calvin aptly remarks that 'so much was the dignity of that family diminished that it seemed to be a rustic, ignoble family rather than a royal one.' In such a reduced condition, the prospect of a fulfilment of the Davidic covenant of 2 Sam. 7 seemed very remote. When the royal tree was thus cut down to the ground, however, a shoot (the Messiah) sprouted out from its roots (Isa. 11:1; Job. 14:7 –9), presenting a picture, as Luther says, 'of the whole of theology and the works of God; that Christ did not come till the trunk had died and was altogether in a hopeless condition'. This Branch is later described as Jehovah's servant and is represented as a mighty ruler. So closely is the name associated with the Messiah that Zechariah later spoke of Him as 'the Man whose name is the Branch' (Zech. 6:12). It is interesting to note, on the other hand, that the same One is described in Rev. 5:5 and 22:16 as 'the root of David'.

In the prophecies concerning the Branch, two Hebrew words are used. The first of these, *netser*, which means 'a shoot', is used only four times in the Old Testament (Isa. 11:1; 14:19; 60:21; Dan. 11:27). It is allied to the name of Nazareth, and the statement of Matt. 2:23 may possibly have a reference to the prophecies containing the word. The other word employed, *tsemach*, means 'a sprout' or 'a budding plant' (Isa. 4:2; 23:5; 33:15; Zech. 3:8; 6:12). The related verb, *tsamach*, is also used in Ps. 132:17 and Ezek. 24:21, which both appear relevant to the subject.

Of the occurrences of the word *netser*, the only one which has an undoubted Messianic connection is that in Isa. 11:1 which the R.V. renders, 'There shall come forth a shoot out of the stock of Jesse, and a branch out of his roots shall bear fruit.' In Isa. 10 the prophet likens the Assyrian to the mighty forests of Lebanon being hewn down under the hand of God in final destruction for, as Kay points out, 'when a cedar is cut down, it sends out no fresh suckers. Therefore, when Asshur fell, it perished.' Long before this the house of David had undergone judgement, and in Isa. 11 it is described as a stump of a tree. Out of this stump, however, there was to come forth a shoot which, although insignificant and unassuming at first, would develop into a glorious tree. As Hengstenberg writes, 'a shoot proceeding from his roots (i.e. the cut-off stem of Jesse) shall grow up into a stately fruitful tree. As a tree cut down throws out from its roots a young shoot which, at first, inconsiderable, grows up into a stately fruitbearing tree, so from the family buried in contempt and lowliness, a King shall arise who, at first humble and unheeded, shall afterwards attain to great glory.' In this prophecy there is an unmistakable picture of the two advents of the Lord Jesus Christ. Born in Bethlehem's manger, living in the comparative obscurity of despised Nazareth, in the bosom of a humble family, our Lord – to human eyes – was insignificant and unimportant. Indeed, Isa. 53:2 states that He grew up 'as a tender plant and as a root out of a dry ground', giving offence as Michaelis says, in 'that He does not rise or stand out like the cedar, but He grows up gradually'. He 'sprang from a decayed family', says Lange. 'The Davidic trunk had fallen and this was a mere sucker growing out of one of the upturned roots.' In a coming day, however, He will be accorded the place of glory and exaltation.

The many references in which the word *tsemach* is used indicate that the Branch will have not only a human but also a divine nature, for Isa. 4:2 describes Him as 'the Branch (or Sprout) of Jehovah' and 'the fruit of the land'. Hengstenberg aptly writes, 'As the words "Sprout of the Lord" denote the heavenly origin of the Redeemer, so do the words "fruit of the land" the earthly one, the soil from which the Lord causes the Saviour to sprout up.' The phrase, 'fruit of the land', has undoubtedly a reference to Num. 13:26 and Deut. 1:25, the only two other passages in which the phrase occurs, the natural fruit being regarded as a type of Christ Himself.

In Jer. 23:5 and 33:15 (300 years before Christ this was recognized by the Jews as referring to Messiah) God specifically promised to fulfil the Davidic covenant by the raising up to David of a righteous Branch (see also Ps. 132:17), who would introduce millennial blessings and sit as king and priest upon the throne of David (Zech. 3:8; 6:12). The One who commenced as a tiny shoot will eventually become a flourishing tree and the source of blessing to the whole earth.

After the reference to God's Servant, the Branch, the attention of the priests was directed to a mysterious stone, which Jehovah had laid before Joshua. Chambers sees the stone as a symbol of the covenant people, but this can hardly be regarded as tenable. It could scarcely have been the foundation stone of the temple, which had been laid years before, although Baron evidently concludes that it was, for he says (op. cit., p. 117), 'According to the Talmud, the *Eben Shetiyah* – the foundation stone of the second temple, which was some inches higher than the level of the holy of holies – had the sacred Tetragrammaton (the four Hebrew letters making up the ineffable name, "Jehovah") graven upon it.' It seems more likely that the reference was rather to the headstone (cf. Zech. 4:7, 9), which would be the final stone to complete the temple. The stone is frequently used as a type of Messiah and He is often described as the chief

corner stone (Ps. 118:22; Matt. 21:42; Eph. 2:20) and Daniel
featured His kingdom as a stone which would crush the Gentile
colossus (Dan. 2:45).

Seven eyes were directed upon the stone and it was beautified
by engravings. Some have thought that the eyes were actually
engraved upon the stone, but this does not seem implicit in the
description given. The seven eyes seem rather to be indicative
of the perfect intelligence and omniscience of the Almighty. His
infinite watchfulness and care were to be fixed upon the stone,
not only to make certain that no harm came to it, but also to
ensure that His purpose concerning it was effected. The seven
eyes are stated in Zech. 4:10 to be the eyes of Jehovah, and it
is pertinent that the Lamb in Rev. 5:6 also had seven eyes.
Ewald considers that 'the conception of the seven eyes of Jehovah
was derived from the Persian notion of the seven Amahaspands,
who surround the throne of the Supreme Being', while Barnes
(op. cit., p. xxiv) maintains that Zechariah was 'explicitly
claiming for the one true God the sevenfold power ascribed by the
Babylonians to the Pleiades (cf. Job. 38:31) and also to the
"planets" as known to them (i.e. the sun, the moon, Mercury,
Venus, Mars, Jupiter and Saturn)'.

The interest of God in the stone was also indicated by the fact
that He personally undertook the engraving of the stone. On the
assumption that the seven eyes were not engraved on the stone,
no information is given as to what was, in fact, engraved upon it.

In one day, God declared that the iniquity of the land would
be removed. Under the Levitical economy, the transgressions
of the nation of Israel were brought under review each year on
the day of atonement and were figuratively borne away by the
scapegoat into the wilderness (Lev. 16). What was envisioned
in the Divine promise, however, was not the ceremonial of the
annual day of atonement, but presumably the complete cleansing from defilement predicted in Zech. 13:1. The fountain to be
opened for sin and uncleanness would remove all the people's
guilt. The term used in verse 10 ('in that day') has an eschatological significance in Zechariah and anticipates the Second
Advent of Christ to establish His kingdom upon earth.

In that day the picture would be completely transformed, and
the land would enjoy peace, joy and prosperity. Neighbours
would engage in social intercourse under the vine and fig tree,

and gladness would prevail on every side. The conditions described have never been seen in history and it is evident that the prophecy anticipates the bliss and happiness of the millennial age. Mic. 4:4, in fact, does invest the vine and the fig tree with a millennial significance. The joy described by Zechariah follows upon the cleansing of the land and C. H. H. Wright in his *Bampton Lectures* (pp. 77, 78) pertinently points out that 'when, on the great Day of Atonement, the high priest had performed the various duties of that solemn day, he was escorted home in a festive manner, and was accustomed to give a festal entertainment to his friends. The maidens and youths of the people went forth to the gardens and vineyards with songs and dances; social entertainments took place on all sides, and universal gladness closed the festival of that solemn day.' His remarks are obviously based on the Talmud, Yoma 7:4, which is also quoted by David Baron – op. cit., p. 122. If that was true after the temporary work of that earlier age, how great will be the joy when God removes His people's defilement and reconciles them to Himself.

CHAPTER 7

The Golden Lampstand

Zechariah had seen four visions and the strain of observation and of seeking to understand the explanations provided had evidently exhausted him, so that he almost appeared to be asleep. But the revelations of the night had not yet ended, and the interpreting angel aroused him to full consciousness again. It had been disclosed that the Gentile oppressors of God's people were to be punished, that restoration of the nation to blessing was to be effected, that a cleansed priesthood was to ensure the renewal of communion with God, and that the Messiah was yet to come. The prophet may well have questioned how all this was to be accomplished, and the next vision made it clear that human ability and effort were insufficient and that Divine power alone could achieve the fulfilment of God's purpose. The lesson was again cast in illustrative form.

'Then the angel who talked with me returned and aroused me as a man aroused out of his sleep, and said to me, What do you see? And I said, I have seen and behold a lampstand all of gold, with its bowl upon the top of it, and its seven lamps on it, and seven pipes to each of the seven lamps which are on its top: and two olive trees by it, one on the right side of the bowl and the other on the left of it. So I answered and spoke to the angel who talked to me saying, What are these, my lord? Then the angel who talked with me answered and said to me, Do you not know what these are? And I said, No, my lord. Then he answered and spoke to me, saying, This is the word of Jehovah to Zerubbabel, saying, Not by might nor by power, but by my Spirit, says Jehovah of hosts. Who are you, O great mountain before Zerubbabel? Be a plain! And he shall bring forth the head-stone with shoutings, Grace, grace to it. Moreover the word of Jehovah came to me saying, The hands of Zerubbabel have laid the foundation of the house; his hands shall also complete it: and you shall know that Jehovah of hosts has sent me to you. For who has despised the day of small things? For they shall rejoice, and shall see the plummet in the hand of Zerubbabel, even these seven; they are the eyes of Jehovah, which run to and fro through the whole earth. Then answered I and said to him, What are these two olive trees on the right of the lampstand and on its left? And I answered again and said to him, What are these two olive branches which through the two golden pipes empty the golden oil out of themselves? And he answered me and said, Do you not know what these are? And I said, No, my lord. Then said he, These are the two anointed ones, who stand by the Lord of the whole earth' (4:1–14).

On the left of the altar of incense in the tabernacle stood a golden candelabrum or lampstand, which was beaten out of a talent of pure gold. It consisted of a main shaft, out of which proceeded seven branches, one upright and three on either side. On the extremities of these branches were placed seven lamps containing pure olive oil. The branches were ornamented with almond-shaped bowls, knops, and flowers, bowl or calyx, knop and flower alternately. The golden lampstand furnished the only light in the holy place and was kept burning continually. Adolph Saphir regards the vessel as an expressive symbol of our Lord Jesus Christ. 'Here', he says, 'we behold Jesus Christ, the Son of God incarnate, the light of the world; the Lord, upon whom was the Spirit of the Lord, anointing Him, to declare salvation unto the broken-hearted; the Messiah, Who came in the sevenfold plenitude of the Holy Ghost, and Who was continually revealing the Father. . . . It is as Immanuel that He is the candlestick. He came to be a mediator, to reveal God, and to bring the light of God in our hearts. He is the light of the world in such a way that sinful men, becoming one with Him, are also the light of the world. He is able to say unto His disciples, "Let your light so shine before men!"' Another writer also suggests that the lampstand symbolized the glory and the work of Christ. 'The pure gold reflects His divinity, the beaten work His sufferings, the olive oil the indwelling Holy Spirit.' In Solomon's temple, the place of the golden lampstand of the tabernacle was taken by ten golden lampstands, five standing on each side of the holy place (1 Kings 7:49). Their construction was similar to that of the one in the tabernacle, and seventy lamps, therefore, provided light for the holy place of the temple. The writer previously quoted suggests that 'the oil used for the lighting can refer only to the Holy Spirit, and the lampstands

c

suggest the realized presence and power of the Holy Spirit in testimony'.

In Zerubbabel's temple, there was only one lampstand (1 Macc. 1:23; 4:49; see also the sculpture on the Arch of Titus), and significantly the prophet, when aroused, saw a single golden lampstand, but one which was entirely different in construction from that used in the tabernacle and the temple. The vessel he saw in vision had seven lamps and these were provided with oil from a receptacle on the top of the lampstand, this bowl or receptacle being replenished with oil from two olive trees, which stood on either side.

The purpose of the lampstands in the tabernacle and the temple was, of course, to shed light in the darkness, but the light was dependent upon the maintenance of the supply of oil for the lamps. Without the oil there could be no light. Olive oil is frequently used in the Old Testament as a type of the Holy Spirit, and it could be said of the Christian today, as much as for Israel or Judah in their day, that there can be no light or inspired witness to God, except by the power of the Holy Spirit. The greater the measure of the Spirit personally realized and experienced, the brighter will be the light of testimony. It had always been God's intention that Israel should be a light to the nations, and the lampstand in the tabernacle and those later in the temple were the constant reminder of her vocation. She failed, but the Divine purpose remains unaltered and one day she will become a light to the Gentiles (Isa. 49:6; 60:3). During His earthly life, our Lord was personally the light of the world (John 8:12; 1:9). Now, His followers are those from whom the light shines (Matt. 5:14). but they also may fail and our Lord warned the church of Ephesus of the possibility of the removal of her lampstand (Rev. 2:5) as an indication of His possible rejection of her testimony.

Zechariah's lampstand, as already indicated, was entirely different from those of the tabernacle and the temple. The lamps of those vessels were daily trimmed and supplied with fresh oil (Exod. 27:20, 21), but there was no need for this in the case of the one seen by the prophet. It had a container above it, from which the oil flowed by gravity to the seven lamps by forty-nine pipes (seven to each of the seven lamps). The container received its supplies of oil from two olive trees with fruitful branches. In the normal course, the olive oil was extracted by crushing the olive berries, but in this case the bowl was supplied direct from the trees through two additional golden pipes, which ran from the trees to the bowl. There was no intermediate extraction of the oil from the fruit: no human agency was required.

Zechariah frankly acknowledged that he did not understand the symbols, and the interpreting angel accordingly explained that God's work was not accomplished by human might or power (cf. Hos. 1:7), but by the Holy Spirit, of whom the olive oil was such an apt type. It was also tacitly implied that even the gift of the Holy Spirit and the outpouring of His power are not dependent upon the efforts of the individual: human endeavour is superfluous and inappropriate. The Spirit is given without measure to those who are prepared to receive Him unhinderedly and to abandon themselves to His control. Nothing is accomplished in the service of God merely by human ability: we are dependent entirely upon the Holy Spirit. 'Not by might, nor by power, but by my Spirit,' said God. David Baron (op. cit., p. 137) says that the word 'might' is one which also 'means a host or army and may mean "the strength of many"'. The word 'power', however, 'stands for that of one man. The two might be taken to express human strength and power of every description – physical, mental and moral – individual or the combined strength of the multitude'. The work of God is not accomplished in human strength. 'Not many wise men after the flesh, not many mighty, not many noble, are called,' wrote the apostle Paul, 'but God has chosen the foolish things of the world to confound the wise; and God has chosen the weak things of the world to confound the things which are mighty; and base things of the world, and things which are despised, has God chosen, and things which are not, to bring to nought things that are: that no flesh should glory in His presence' (Cor. 1:26 –29). This is the constant lesson which God's servant is to learn: he is completely insufficient and inadequate: his sufficiency is of God.

It mattered not if difficulties seemed to be mountains high and completely insuperable, if defence against political attacks and intrigues seemed impossible, and if the machinations of the surrounding nations seemed destined to hamper the work still

further. The power of the Holy Spirit would level the mountain to a plain before Zerubbabel, the builder of God's temple.
Schemes and intrigues counted for nothing with Jehovah. When
He blew upon the enemy's plans, they disintegrated and disappeared. The same power is available to the Christian today.
God is his sufficiency. Mountains disappear and difficulties
vanish at the breath of the Divine Spirit. Chambers (op. cit., p.
43) says, 'In the sixteenth century one man entered the lists
against the Antichristian corruptions of the time . . . in the
issue one half of Europe was emancipated from the papal yoke.'
One man indwelt and empowered by the Holy Spirit is greater
than an army.

In the previous vision, the Servant of Jehovah had been
referred to, *inter alia*, as a stone – evidently the headstone and the
crowning stone which completed the building. The angel now
declared that, in due time, Zerubbabel would bring forth the
headstone to crown the reconstruction of the temple. Then the
shoutings of builders and people would be heard, 'Grace, grace
to it!' or, as another renders it, 'What gracefulness it has!' or
'How perfectly graceful it is!' When Solomon's temple was being
built, every stone was prepared in the quarry below and shaped
for its appointed place in the building, so that no sound of
hammer or chisel was heard on the site above (1 Kings 6:7).
The stones were brought out to harden in the sun and the workmen took from the piles as they built the temple. Tradition says
that, among the stones one day the builders came across one of
different size and shape, for which there seemed no place in the
building. It was consequently cast aside, rejected by the builders.
When the darkness suddenly fell at night, they would sometimes
stumble over the rejected stone and it was often referred to as
the stumbling-stone. In due course, however, the work reached
its final stages and the appropriate stone was sought to fill the
place of the head of the corner. No other stone filled the vacant
place, but the workmen presently brought forth the stone they
had rejected and over which they had stumbled, with glad
shoutings of 'Grace, grace to it', for the rejected stone exactly
fitted the vacant place for the topstone – the place of glory and
honour. Whether or not there is any substance in the tradition,
our Lord certainly referred the figure to Himself (Matt. 21:42
–44; Luke 20:17, 18). He was the One whom the nation rejected

and over whom they had stumbled, but one day He will be acknowledged as the worthy One and the crown and headship will be His.

The rebuilding of the temple was nearing completion and God declared that Zerubbabel, who had laid the foundation, would see the last stone – the headstone – fitted into its place. He would complete the building. Since it was to be completed in the lifetime of the one who had laid the foundation, it was evident that God was not going to allow the work to drag on interminably. The promise not only guaranteed the completion, but virtually declared its imminence. When the work was finished in such difficult and adverse circumstances, incontrovertible proof would have been furnished that the message which the people had received through Zechariah had originated with Jehovah – that He had sent His messenger (either the interpreting angel or the prophet).

Some of those who had watched the rebuilding of the temple had evidently poured scorn and ridicule on the work. It was not an elaborate or ornate building that was being erected and was certainly not comparable for splendour with its predecessor. The critics evidently declared that if it was not deserving of respect. It was an age, they declared, when relatively little was accomplished: it was a day of small things. But Jehovah interposed again with the question, 'Who has despised the day of small things?' It was not for others to estimate the value or importance of the work. God alone assesses the work at its true value and the final judgement rests with Him. How often today the Lord's servant is discouraged by the depreciation of his service by those who establish themselves as critics. God has called His servants to undertake a work for Him. Others may deem it of little value or importance and the work may seem small even to those engaged upon it. But who are we to judge? He that is faithful in little is also faithful in much. Even if it seems a day in which little is accomplished. God's question is still pertinent, 'Who has despised the day of small things?' The trivial task upon which we are employed may be the key to the whole of a great project. Who dare despise what God has entrusted to us?

Some had despised the day of small things, but the Divine message declared that there would be rejoicing (whether by the

critics or by the seven eyes of Jehovah is not clearly indicated)
when the plummet was seen in the hand of Zerubbabel. Perowne
(op. cit., p. 87) renders verse 10, 'For who has despised the day
of small things? For (seeing that) these seven eyes of Jehovah,
which run to and fro throughout all the earth, shall rejoice to
see the plummet in the hand of Zerubbabel,' and pertinently
remarks, 'Since then God beholds the progress of the work with
joy and favour, who will venture to despise it?' Those eyes which
ranged through the whole earth and detected every happening,
and which were focused upon the stone symbol of Jehovah's
Servant in chapter 3, now found joy in the completed
temple and the provision again of an earthly dwelling place
for the Eternal, where His people could have communion with
Him.

The plummet was a string from which was suspended a heavy
weight and it was used as a plumbline to ensure that the stones
and walls of the temple were in perfect alignment. The fact that
it was in the hand of Zerubbabel was an indication that he was
actively engaged in ensuring the completion of the temple and
its perfect precision.

The prophet was, however, still without an explanation of the
lampstand and the trees and he asked for enlightenment. The
angel then explained that the two olive trees symbolized the
two anointed ones (or 'sons of oil'), who stood by the Lord of
the whole earth. Only kings and priests were anointed, and it
is usually suggested that the reference was to Zerubbabel and
Joshua, the civil and religious leaders, who were the medium of
Divine contact with the people. It was their responsibility to ensure that the Divine will in civil and religious matters was implemented by the nation and, in the purpose of God, they were set
apart for this purpose. In Rev. 11:4 the two witnesses of a
future day are described as 'the two olive trees and the two
lampstands standing before the God of the earth', clearly a
reference to Zech. 4. They may also be symbolic of spiritual
powers. The antitype of Zerubbabel and Joshua is, of course,
to be found in the Messiah, who combines both offices in Himself (see Zech. 6:13), and is the source of all sufficiency for His
people.

The branches poured a copious supply of oil (symbolized as
liquid gold in verse 12) into the bowl through two pipes. The

angel's interpretation in the closing verse of the chapter did not
distinguish between the pipes and the trees, but virtually implied
that both were symbolic of the 'two anointed ones'. Certainly
Messiah is to be the source and means of supply to Israel – as,
of course, He is today to the Christian.

CHAPTER 8

A Holy People

Zech. 3 described the cleansing of the priesthood and provided
the nation with an assurance of access to and communion with
Jehovah. Zech. 4 showed the means by which sanctification and
spiritual enduement were obtained and emphasized the complete inadequacy of all human effort. Zech. 5 is concerned with
the cleansing and sanctification of the nation and the land and,
by inference, stresses the Divine intolerance of sin in the individual or the nation. Sin must be judged and iniquity must be
removed. God is infinitely holy, and His people must be holy
too. Those, who harboured their sin and refused to put it
away, must suffer under the hand of God. There is no place for
the impenitent and the recalcitrant. It has been suggested, with
some justification, that the inexorable judgement of sin and
sinners portrayed in the sixth vision, while applying in the
first instance to the returned exiles, has an even greater pertinence to the period of Christ's theocratic kingdom, when He
will rule the nations with a rod of iron and dash the wicked to
pieces like the smashing of a potter's vessel (Ps. 2:9). The
immediate application, however, was to those who had now
returned to the land under Joshua and Zerubbabel.

The description of the sixth vision was brief.

'Then I lifted up my eyes again and saw and behold, a flying
roll. And he said to me, What do you see? And I answered, I
see a flying roll: the length of it is twenty cubits, and the breadth
of it ten cubits. Then he said to me, This is the curse that is
going forth over the face of the whole land: for every one who
steals shall be cut off as on this side according to it; and every
one who swears shall be cut off as on that side according to it.
I will cause it to issue forth, says Jehovah of hosts, and it shall
enter into the house of the thief and into the house of him who
swears falsely by my name: and it shall abide in the midst of his
house, and shall consume it with its timber and its stones' (5:1
−4).

The vision that now crossed the prophet's eyes was a remarkable one. He saw an enormous roll, like an expanded banner, flying swiftly through the air, and evidently bearing writing on both sides. 'Books were written,' to quote one expositor, 'on long sheets or rolls made of papyrus, a sort of paper made of the pith of the papyrus plant, the paper reed. The pith was cut into strips, layers of which were laid crosswise and pressed or glued together to form the writing paper. Sometimes both sides were used (cf. Rev. 5:1).' Sir George Adam Smith (op cit., p. 301) however, considers that the roll was not of papyrus since Zechariah used 'the ordinary Hebrew name for the rolls of skin or parchment,' but the material used matters little. A scroll was normally wound around a rod (sometimes one was used for each end), but the one seen by Zechariah was obviously unrolled so that all might read its contents. It seems clear that a table of the law was written on each side.

The roll was of an extraordinary size – twenty cubits by ten cubits, or roughly ten yards by five yards, the same size as the tabernacle in the wilderness (Exod. 26:15–25) and also the same size as the porch of Solomon's temple (1 Kings 6:3), where the law was normally read. There is possibly the implication that judgement would be meted out in accordance with God's holiness and in accordance with the measure of the sanctuary.

The angel described the roll as the curse that was going forth over the whole land, since it conveyed a curse upon the transgressor of the law inscribed upon it. Smend regards as relevant the practice in ancient times for curses to be written on pieces of paper and for these to be sent down the wind into the houses of those against whom they were directed, but Smith sees a picture of birds of prey as more appropriate. The central commandment from each of the two tables of the decalogue was selected as illustrative of the whole, plainly implying that the breach of one commandment constituted a breaking of the whole law and rendered the individual a transgressor (see also Jas. 2:10). From the first table, stealing was selected as 'representing all violations of the rights of one's fellow men'. From the second table, swearing or perjury was chosen as 'representing all sins directed specifically against God and His holy name.'

The one who transgressed the law thereby brought himself under its curse (Deut. 27:26; Gal. 3:10), and the flying roll, therefore, became the vehicle of the curse to be judicially laid upon the guilty. Every infraction of the law was to be relentlessly punished and there was no suggestion of mercy or leniency. The time for repentance had passed and the sinner was to be 'cut off' – or possibly 'purged out' of the land. The nation and the land must be cleansed of every contamination, and the sinner must be dealt with in unmitigated justice. The minatory character of the vision was in startling and salutary contrast to the consolatory terms of the preceding visions, but God's holiness was at stake.

The roll would enter the house of the guilty one, declared Jehovah, and, by inference, ferret out his wrongdoing and reveal his sin. It would convict him of the evil of his ways, thoughts and speech, and it would abide in his house to effect the complete and unrelieved destruction of every stone and timber. Nothing would be preserved. Such was the unquenchable fire of God's holiness. He would by no means clear the guilty. The curse would abide upon the house. Perowne (op. cit., pp. 89, 90) refers, 'in illustration of the curse abiding till it has accomplished its mission, the story of Glaucus (Herodotus vi 86), who consulted the oracle as to whether he was at liberty to perjure himself, and retain for his own use a sum of money which had been committed to his trust. The response was that though such a course would be for his present gain, "yet an oath hath a nameless son, headless and footless, yet swift in pursuit till he seize and destroy the whole race and house". And accordingly, though Glaucus restored the money and asked for forgiveness for the thought of his heart, it was observed that, since to design evil was to incur the guilt of executing it, his family became extinct.'

The message of the vision is not without its significance for the present day. The standard of holiness which God required from His people has not been lowered, and even the Christian needs the constant reminder of the apostle John that the one who claims to belong to Christ should conduct himself as the Master did and that the one who commits sin is of the devil (1 John 2:6; 3:8). Our Lord's own prayer was that His people might be sanctified through the truth (John 17:17). The disregard of business morality, the laxity in general conduct and morals, the association with the questionable things of the world, the frequent impurity of thought and word are completely irreconcilable with the unblemished purity of Christ. In view of the price paid at Calvary for the removal of the believer's defilement, how can he possibly give rein to desires and actions which so obviously contaminate mind and life? God cannot tolerate sin and impurity and, if there is a deliberate refusal to put away the unclean thing, the flying roll may still enter the house and wreak complete destruction of all that has been treasured. We ignore the implicit warning of the vision at our peril. T. V. Moore (*Zechariah*, p. 80) says, 'There is something most vivid and appalling in this image of the hovering curse. It flies viewless and resistless, poising like a falcon over her prey, breathing a ruin most dire and desolating, and when the blind and hardened offender opens his door to his ill-gotten gains, this mysterious roll, with its fire-tracery of wrath, enters into his habitation, and fastening upon his cherished idols, begins its dread work of retribution, and ceases not until the fabric of his guilty life has been totally and irremediably consumed.'

If the sixth vision was concerned with the sin of the individual, the seventh was directed to the cleansing of the nation from what has been termed the 'ungodly secularism and intense commercial preoccupation' which had gripped them. The message was presented in a picturesque form.

'Then the angel who talked with me came forth, and said to me, Lift up now your eyes and see what it is that is going forth. And I said, What is it? And he said, This is the ephah that is going forth. He said, moreover, This is their appearance through all the land. And behold, a circle of lead was lifted up: and this is a woman sitting in the middle of the ephah. And he said, This is wickedness. And he thrust her down into the middle of the ephah; and he cast the weight of lead upon its mouth. Then I raised my eyes and saw, and behold, there came forth two women, and the wind was in their wings; for they had wings like the wings of a stork; and they lifted up the ephah between earth and heaven. Then said I to the angel who talked with me, Whither do these bear the ephah? And he said to me, To build a house for it in the land of Shinar, and when it is established, it shall be caused to rest there on its own base' (5:5–11).

As part of the Divine plan for the removal of sin and uncleanness from the land, God was about to take further action.
Zechariah saw an ephah, a large container, adequate to hold a
bushel of corn or ten omers (Exod. 16:36). It would not be large
enough to hold a human being of average size, but, as indicated
later, one was held therein. The angel explained that the ephah
was a representation of the sinful state of the people throughout
the land of Judah.

The ephah was an appropriate symbol of trade or commerce.
As a pastoral people the Jews had little experience of the soul-
less self-centredness of commercialism until they had been
exiled in Babylon, but there it had gripped them to such an
extent that it became an outstanding characteristic of them on
their return to their own land. Unger (op. cit., p. 93) says, 'It
was the new principle with which the Jews had become imbued
in Babylon, and which had exercised such a potent formative
influence over them throughout the centuries and will continue
to do so until it is removed from them at the advent of their
Messiah.' Commerce is not, of course, wrong in itself, but the
temptations to which Judah had been exposed had led to an
inordinate obsession with material prosperity and an insatiable
greed for gain. Laetsch (op. cit., p. 433) points out that 'the
Lord demands a just ephah, full measure, integrity and honesty
in selling and buying in all business and judicial transactions
(Lev. 19:35 f.; Deut, 25:4 f.; Ezek. 45:9 ff.; Mic. 6:10–15)'.
Commercial morality was disappearing and the mercenary spirit
was affecting every business transaction. In the words of another
prophet, they were 'making the ephah small and the shekel
great and falsifying the balances by deceit' (Amos 8:5). The
amoral and incurable cupidity and unlawful practices of the
market-place were spreading throughout the country and were
even affecting judicial decisions in their courts.

The prevalent condition was due not only to the unfortunate
commercial practices with which Judah had become acquainted
in Babylon, but at least partially to the low state of morality
generally in Babylonia. Of the city itself, a Roman historian
declared that 'nothing could be more corrupt than its morals,
nothing more fitted to excite and allure to immoderate pleas-
ures. The rites of hospitality were polluted by the grossest and
most shameless lusts. Money dissolved every tie, whether of

kindred, respect or esteem. Drunkenness and the grossest immoralities were practised in public.' 'This is their appearance (or possibly "their iniquity") throughout all the land', declared the angel. The whole of the country was affected. There was a need for the cleansing of the returned exiles and their land.

The conditions of the present day are not very dissimilar. Even Christians seem to be completely obsessed by an inordinate and unhealthy desire for gain, and to be prepared to sacrifice any principles for personal benefit. The same grasping spirit, the same ruthless endeavour to improve or to increase wealth, the same insensate desire for the material rather than the spiritual, all indicate the extent to which Babylonian 'commercialism' has affected those who belong to Christ. If there was a need for a purging from wrong desires and motives in Zechariah's day, there is a comparable need today.

As the ephah drew nearer, the prophet saw that a lid (described as a talent or circle of lead), which had apparently closed it, was being pushed up from within and that a woman contained within was evidently trying to escape. This, the angel informed him, was wickedness, i.e. the personification of unrighteous actions and intentions; sin was naturally unwilling to accept restriction and was endeavouring to secure liberty to roam at will. But the angel pushed the woman back into the confined space of the ephah and slammed the leaden lid upon the mouth of the container. A talent was the largest measure of weight used by the Jews and was equivalent to just over 66 lb. or 30 kg. Baron (op. cit., p. 164) says that 'the talent, with which she carries on her unrighteous trade, becomes the heavy weight by which she is held down till she is landed safely in her own place!'

The point of the vision, however, was not the governmental repression of the woman or the restraint of wickedness in the land, nor even its punishment or destruction, but rather its complete removal from the land. Two women, with huge wings like those of a stork (an unclean bird – see Lev. 11:19; Deut. 14:18) outstretched for flight as if their pinions already felt the power of the wind, seized the ephah and its evil occupant and flew away with it between earth and heaven. The wind was not merely to increase their velocity; carrying away by the wind is consistently regarded in the Scriptures as indicative of judgement (e.g. Job. 27:20, 22; 30:22; Isa. 41:16; 7:13; 64:6).

The two women have been interpreted in a variety of ways. Many deem them to be instruments of God's justice and their removal of the ephah as an action taken at Divine direction, although there is no indication of this in the record. Others, *per contra*, regard the two women as evil agents who acted to deliver the imprisoned woman from the impending vengeance which seemed imminent. David Baron, who is followed by M. F. Unger in this, inclines to the second view. He says (op. cit., p. 166) that the two women 'may be apostate Christianity united in the last days to apostate Judaism, and both given over to the worship of Mammon, on which the power of the ephah is based' or that symbolic reference may be to 'the civil and ecclesiastic powers. . . . The two women here may, perhaps, be meant to signify civil government broken loose, even outwardly, from every acknowledgement of God (and, therefore, an instrument in the hand of lawlessness), and a corrupt antichristian and antitheistic priesthood – both Jewish and Gentile – ready to unite as spouses and protectors to a system which, though as yet not so regarded, even by the elect, is characterized by God as "the wickedness").' This seems somewhat fanciful. T. V. Moore (op. cit., p. 84) argues that 'they symbolized the messengers of God's wrath that should desolate Judea and banish the people. They were to carry it into Shinar, which is here the symbol for an enemy's country, and not the exact country to which they were to be exiled . . .weighed down like lead with judicial blindness, stupidity, darkness, and hardness of heart.' In other words, he sees the long *diaspora* of nineteen centuries symbolized in the carrying away, but this is hardly tenable since the context is the cleansing of the land from that which defiled it. Commercial inequity and amorality had seized hold of the people: the vision showed that this kind of unrighteousness or wickedness must be removed from the land before the ultimate blessing of God was experienced. It was not the people but their iniquity that was to be removed. Whether the instruments used were themselves evil characters or not, is not of great importance. Ungodly nations and evil men have been frequently used by the Almighty to achieve His purposes.

The perplexed prophet asked where the ephah was being borne and was informed that the women were carrying it away to build an abode for it in the land of Shinar and when it was settled there, it would rest on its own base. Keil takes the view that Shinar was not intended here to denote a particular geographical location, but rather as an ideal designation of the sphere of ungodliness. Smith says, 'Shinar, from its earliest days, was a land of open rebellion against God. Throughout Scripture it is symbolic of wickedness and opposition to God. Shinar is the symbol of Satan's kingdom of wickedness.' Kelly (op. cit., p. 457) remarks, 'From Shinar religious corruption came, and thither it must go, forcibly and swiftly carried off: such is the measure meted by Jehovah . . . it is the idolatrous evil of the Jews derived from and sent back to Babylon.' Certainly Shinar was the origin of paganism as well as of the first attempt to establish a world empire (see pp. 91, 92 of *God's Programme of the Ages*, by F. A. Tatford). The wickedness described in the vision originated in Babylon: it has infected the Jewish race for centuries as with a virus. But the day is coming when they will be purged of this spirit and the evil be removed. It is only appropriate that symbolically it should be returned to the place of its origin.

An abode was to be built for the ephah in its own land of Shinar. An anonymous writer's comments are pertinent. He says, 'While iniquity is away from its base, it is iniquity in mystery. But once returned, its house is built: it is settled, no more to be moved till judgement crush it: it is expanded, and its manifestation is to meet and receive the full wrath of God.' Zechariah's vision merely foretells the removal of the evil from the land of Israel, but the apocalyptic writer discloses the ultimate doom which befalls the whole of this evil system in the day of Divine judgement (Rev. 18).

There is obviously a lesson for the believer of the present age. One writer expresses it succinctly, 'Whilst even the justified and sanctified believer needs daily cleansing and forgiveness, wickedness and manifest rebellion against God could not be tolerated. It must be removed by removing the wicked man or men' (cf. 1 Cor. 5:5; 11:30).

CHAPTER 9

The Four Chariots

Zechariah's long night was nearly over and the last vision now broke upon his gaze. 'The first vision and the eighth,' says Barnes (op. cit., p. 51), 'form together the framework in which the whole section (1:7–6:8) is set. The one appropriately begins, the other appropriately closes the series of visions. Neither is a theophany (a revelation of God) but each stands instead of a theophany. . . . In the first the angel of Jehovah appears and converses through the veil with Jehovah Himself. In the last the gate between heaven and earth is opened and the "four spirits of heaven" in the guise of chariots come forth.' The account of the vision was as follows.

'And once more I lifted up my eyes and saw and, behold, there came out four chariots from between the two mountains; and the mountains were mountains of brass. In the first chariot were red horses; and in the second chariot black horses; and in the third chariot white horses; and in the fourth chariot grisled and bay horses. Then I answered and said to the angel who talked to me, What are these, my lord? And the angel answered and said to me, These are the four spirits of the heavens, which go forth from standing before the Lord of all the earth. The chariot in which are the black horses is going forth into the land of the north, and the white went forth to the land which was behind them; and the grisled went forth toward the land of the south. And the bay went forth, and sought to go that they might walk to and fro through the earth. And he said, Get you hence, walk to and fro through the earth. So they walked to and fro through the earth. Then cried he upon me and spoke to me, saying, Behold, these that go toward the north country have caused my spirit to have rest in the north country' (6:1–8).

Judgement always begins with the house of God, but it then reaches out to those around. Having dealt with the sin in Judah and having removed wickedness from the land, Jehovah proceeded with the execution of judgement in a wider field. 'The **wrath** of God,' says one writer, 'is not a caprice or an impulse, but the steady, uniform, eternal element of His being. He is necessarily "of purer eyes than to behold evil".' His abhorrence of sin must consequently demonstrate itself in the judgement of the guilty. In the first vision, the reconnaissance troop reported that the whole earth was at rest and tranquil, and Jehovah intimated that His anger would break out upon the nations which had oppressed His people and were themselves enjoying peace and quiet. In the eighth vision the threat was symbolically fulfilled and judgement was poured out – at least, in figure. The eight visions, therefore, virtually formed a circle.

Zechariah saw four chariots issue forth from between two mountains of brass or copper. The use of the definite article indicates that the mountains were well known, and expositors have suggested that they were either Zion and Moriah, or Zion and Olivet, and that the chariots would rush through the valley of Jehoshaphat on their appointed mission. Joel 3:2 reveals that this valley will be the site of the future judgement of the nations and presumably has reference to the period described in Zechariah. Some writers, however, have taken the view that the two indestructible mountains form the gate towers guarding the entrance to the palace of the Supreme Ruler of the universe, from which the messengers of judgement would issue at the Divine command. Others have argued that the mountains refer to the great spiritual powers or agencies, which overthrow empires and shake the destiny of nations, but this view can hardly be sustained because the judgement came by the medium of the chariots and not by the mountains. Brass or copper (or military bronze) is usually regarded as figurative of judgement (e.g. the brazen serpent of Num. 21:9 and the brazen altar of Exod. 27:2), but it would be unwise to regard the mountains as anything more than the gates through which judgement came.

The interpreting angel explained that the four chariots represented the four spirits of the heavens, which issued forth from the immediate presence of the Almighty. Baron (op. cit., p. 175) considers that they should be interpreted 'either as ideal appearances, personifying the forces and providential acts which God often uses in carrying out His judgements on the earth, or . . . angelic beings, or heavenly powers – those invisible messengers of His'. The number four may perhaps indicate the universality of the Divine judgements. The identification of the chariots with the four great empires of Dan. 2 and 7 or with the four sore judgements of Ezek. 14:21 can scarcely be accepted. As one writer remarks, the picture is not of the great Gentile world powers, but rather 'the overthrow and judgement of these by means of invisible heavenly powers appointed of God as a necessary precursor to the establishment of Messiah's kingdom, and the blessing of Israel, which is symbolically set forth to the prophet in this last vision'. God had declared in the second vision that the four artificers whom He sent would terrify the Gentile nations and destroy their power because of what they had done to Judah.

The chariots were drawn by horses of various colours. The first had red horses, the symbol of war and bloodshed (cf. Rev. 6:4); the second had black horses, the figure of famine and death (cf. Rev. 6:5, 6); the third had white horses, which some have identified with the peaceful conquest of Rev. 6:2; the fourth chariot had grisled and bay horses (or possibly 'dappled and strong'), perhaps symbolic of plague and pestilence (Rev. 6:8). The Eternal uses His own intruments for the destruction of His foes.

The second chariot, with its black horses, was about to drive forth on its punitive expedition against the north country. The north was the direction from which the most serious invasions of Israel and Judah always came; Assyria, Babylonia and Medo-Persia were all located to the north of the land. Jehovah's spirit had been unquiet, because the nations which had afflicted His people were enjoying the fruits of their ravages with impunity and it is specifically recorded that the avengers who swept against the north thereby quieted His spirit. It was in the north that apostasy first broke out in human history and it was there that the foundations of the first world empire were laid by rebels against the Almighty. It was under the yoke of the northern power that many of God's people were at that moment groaning. His anger, therefore, rested first and most fully upon the north and, not until the objects of His wrath had suffered the determined chastisement, was His mind at peace again. The use by the prophetic word of anthropomorphic expressions in relation to God was, of course, only to convey to human minds an understanding, however faint, of the Divine actions. The judgement of the north was not restricted to what is now past history: it patently anticipated the events of the future to which Daniel referred in Dan. 11:36–45, and confirmed the complete destruction to be meted out upon the northern foe.

The chariot in which were the white horses, according to the A.V., followed the black horses to the north, but a more probable rendering is that they 'went forth to the land which was behind them', i.e. to the west. As Barnes says (in loc.), 'An Eastern in reckoning the points of the compass faces the rising sun; consequently behind him is the west.' In the day of Israel's future extremity, it seems evident that the land will suffer invasions from every point of the compass. If, as seems implied by Dan. 9:27, there is to be a treaty between Israel and a western group of nations, with a guarantee, *inter alia*, of protection from invasion by the northern power, the events described in the closing verses of Dan. 11 would obviously invoke an intervention by the western powers. But their character will be as godless as that of the northern power (see Rev. 13:1–8) and the judgement of God will inevitably fall upon them also (Rev. 19: 20). It is thought by some students of prophecy that the rider on the white horse of Rev. 6:2 is to be identified with the first beast of Rev. 13, i.e. the ultimate dictator of the ten western countries: this would certainly provide a link with Zech. 6:6.

The grisled or dappled horses drove southwards. To ..e south of Judah lay the ancient land of Egypt, which, for centuries, was the foe of Israel and Judah. It is evident from Dan. 11 that the antagonism of Egypt will yet burst into active opposition, and Ezek. 35 and Ps. 83 indicate that the permanent hatred of the Edomites (or of the Arab nations which have succeeded them and the Ishmaelites) will flare up, presumably at the same time. For the trouble inflicted upon God's people in the past and for all that is still presaged, the punitive hand of the Almighty will rest upon the land of the south.

The bay or strong horses may be identical with the red horses of the first chariot, since these are not otherwise referred to when the action commences. The Peshitta or Syrian version of the first or second century A.D. and also the Greek translation made by the Jewish proselyte Aquila in the second century A.D. both translate the word as 'red' instead of 'bay'. On the other hand, the word 'bay' (or 'strong') is used in verse 3 as one of the two appellatives for the horses of the fourth chariot. Baron argues that the omission of any reference to the red horses after verse 2 is due to the fact that Babylonia had already been destroyed by Medo-Persia and that further punitive action was, therefore, unnecessary, but this explanation seems rather weak. These bay (or strong) or red horses petitioned (i.e. their riders did) to be allowed to traverse the earth – obviously to deal with any other hostile forces. Barnes (op. cit., p. 53) writes, 'The strong horses are those which are assigned the task of patrolling; their function is to keep Judah safe.' In answer to their request, the Divine commission was given to go and walk to and fro through the earth (or possibly 'the land').

It was essential (and still is) that judgement should be unleashed upon the Gentile nations preparatory to the setting up of the theocratic kingdom at the coming of the Messiah. So the messengers of Divine vengeance issue forth. 'A voice says, "Go", and they at once start out on their punitive expedition. As they rush by, Zechariah hears a voice above the rattling of the chariots. It is the voice of Jehovah, speaking of Himself. The chariots going towards the north will satisfy Him by allotting His enemies the full measure of their well-deserved punishment.' He had been sore displeased, but now He was at rest. In pursuing their own course, the nations leave God out of their deliberations, and act as if the Almighty did not exist. But the Supreme Ruler of the universe has not abdicated. He still fills the eternal throne in the celestial heights and takes account of every act, thought and word – not only of the individual, but of the nations of earth. One day He will once more intervene in human affairs and display His absolute righteousness in the chastisement of the guilty – both nations and men.

Moore's comment is worth quoting in extenso. He says (op. cit., pp. 90–92), 'how striking the fulfilment of this threatening when we remember the circumstances under which it was made. Could the haughty nobles of Babylon, in the gorgeousness of its magnificence and the pride of its power, have heard the threatening of this obscure Jew, amidst the ruins of Jerusalem, with what derision and contempt would they have treated the threat! The anathema that was so feebly uttered against the mightiest and richest city of the world, to the eye of sense seemed like the ravings of lunacy. Yet that feeble whisper was the uttered voice of Jehovah, and the elements of ruin in their remotest lurking-place heard the summons and began to come forth. Slowly and silently did they come up to this dread work, and yet surely and resistlessly, until the glory of these high palaces was dimmed, and the magnificence of these gardens and temples was covered, and now the winds whistle through the reeds of the Euphrates, where Babylon then sat in her pride: and loveliness; desolation and death are stationed there; the sentinel witnesses of the truth that His word returns not to Him void, that His spirit is quieted in the land of the north. Egypt also was yet proud and powerful. Memphis still sat in her queenly pride by the old and solemn Nile, and Thebes still retained the glory of that wonderful architecture that yet amazed the world. They had stood thus from the hoariest antiquity, and how should it be thought that, at the bidding of the descendant of an Egyptian slave, this ancient magnificence would depart. Yet this bidding was obeyed, and wave after wave of desolation swept over this haughty land, until now the pyramids, the sphinxes and the temples of the mighty past but mock the degenerate baseness of the mournful present. Thus was it later in history with Greece and Rome, thus shall it be with guilty and godless Europe, thus shall it be with every enemy of the Church, who attempts to thwart the designs of God in the world. But as the final development of this vision of judgement was to be subsequent to the completion of the threatened punishment of the Jews, we know that it has not yet received its last and mightiest fulfilment. That shall take place only when the Lord . . . shall be revealed from heaven in flaming fire, taking vengeance on all His enemies. Then, and not until then, shall this vision receive its last, its most terrible and complete fulfilment.'

Thus the night of the eight visions concluded.

CHAPTER 10

Joshua's Coronation

The visions of the long night were over and were succeeded (not necessarily immediately) by a symbolic action obviously taken in full view of a number of spectators. It is desirable to understand the circumstances of the people in Judea at the time in order to appreciate the full significance of the incident. We can do little better than quote Barnes again on this point. He says (op. cit., p. 54) that the people 'were sharply divided into two sections: those who had had experience of captivity and those who had not. The latter, the remnant left in Judea by the Chaldeans, being deprived of their best leaders, were very weak in religious and national feeling; they had begun, in fact, to be absorbed by their heathen neighbours. In Babylonia, on the contrary, exile from Jerusalem tended to increase the devotion of the exiles to their city. So it was that many responded to the edict by which Cyrus invited them to rebuild the temple; they proved their zeal for their religion and country by breaking up their homes in Babylonia and returning to a half-ruined province which was little ready to receive them. In Judea these men and their descendants were known as *Bene-golah*, 'children of captivity' or (more briefly) as the *Golah*, "captivity"'. They regarded themselves as distinct from and superior to those who had never experienced exile. The incident now described by Zechariah concerned the visit to Jerusalem of a Jewish family ('the household of Josiah the son of Zephaniah') with gifts for the work of the temple.

'And the word of Jehovah came to me saying, Take men of the *golah*, even their leaders, of the families of Tobijah and Jedaiah, and enter in the same day and go in unto the household of Josiah the son of Zephaniah, who have come from Babylon. Then take of them silver and gold and make crowns, and set them on the head of Joshua, the son of Josedech, the high priest. And speak to him, saying, Thus speaks Jehovah of hosts, saying, Behold a man whose name is the Branch; and he shall shoot forth from under him, and he shall build the temple of Jehovah. Even he shall build the temple of Jehovah, and he shall bear the glory, and shall sit and rule on his throne; and he shall be a priest on his throne, and the counsel of peace shall be between them both. And the crown shall be for health to Tobijah and Jedaiah and for favour to the son of Zephaniah, for a memorial in the temple of Jehovah. And they that are far off shall come and build in the temple of Jehovah, and you shall know that Jehovah of hosts has sent me to you. And it shall come to pass if you will diligently obey the voice of Jehovah your God' (6:9–15).

In the translation of verse 2 we have followed Dr. W. E. Barnes, who takes the view that the household of Josiah, the son of Zephaniah, had returned as pilgrims from Babylon and that, on the day of their arrival, the prophet was instructed to take certain leaders (the word 'Heldai' is used by the Septuagint, for example, as a common noun with the meaning of 'rulers') of the *golah*, men of the families of Tobijah and Jedaiah, to welcome them. The A.V. regards 'Heldai' as a proper name and it also (as does the R.S.V.) incorrectly places the clause, 'who are come from Babylon', after Jedaiah instead of after 'Zephaniah', where it correctly belongs (and is so placed by the R.V.). Moore, on the other hand, correctly places the clause at the end, but renders the verse, 'Take of (them of) the captivity, of Heldai of Tobijah, of Jedaiah, and go thou in that day, and go to the house of Josiah the son of Zephaniah, who (all) have come from Babylon.' The matter is not of great importance, but it seems more probable that Barnes' rendering is the most correct and also the most appropriate. 'Helem' in verse 14 is usually regarded as another name for 'Heldai', but it could more correctly be translated as 'recovery' or 'health'. In the same verse, 'Hen' is regarded as an alternative for 'Josiah', but there is no justification for rendering it in any other way than 'favour' or 'kindness'.

The exiles in Babylon had heard of the resumption of the work of rebuilding the temple and doubtless a number of pilgrims came to Jerusalem from time to time. At any rate, the family of Josiah came with their gifts for the temple. With some of the leaders of the *golah*, Zechariah went immediately to visit the family. Acting under the direction of God, he took silver and gold from the gifts the exiles had brought and, with these materials, constructed crowns or, more probably, a crown composed of circlets of gold and silver. This he placed upon the

brow of Joshua, the high priest. Joshua of course, had no claim
to regal dignity and never, in fact, became the civil or political
ruler of Judah. He was not a scion of the royal tribe, as Zerubbabel was, but was a member of the priestly tribe. It was clear,
therefore, that his coronation was symbolic and not personal
and this is confirmed by the following verses. It might have been
expected that Zerubbabel, as the civil leader, would have
received the honour rather than Joshua, but as Unger points
out (op. cit., p. 112), the crowning of Zerubbabel as 'an heir
of the Davidic dynasty would have been misleading, pointing to
a re-establishment of the Davidic kingdom, which was not the
divine purpose at that moment'.

Joshua was not acknowledged as king of Judah or of Israel,
but he was told, in effect, that he was figurative of 'a man whose
name is the Branch'. As already indicated in chapter 6, this was
used particularly of the Messiah, and Joshua's coronation
was obviously prefigurative of that of God's chosen King in a
coming day. It was predicted that that One would 'shoot forth
from under Him', or 'grow up out of His place' (A.V.). In other
words, He would be of lowly and humble origin (cf. Isa. 53:2).
Certainly this was true of the Messiah at His first advent. He
lived in humble circumstances and probably worked as a
village carpenter; His disciples were relative nonentities; during
His public ministry He was dependent upon the charity and
hospitality of others; He had nowhere to lay His head; on the
cross the seamless robe of the Palestinian peasant – His last
garment – was taken from Him; His body ultimately lay in a
borrowed tomb. The words uttered to Zechariah were clearly
true of the One who came.

The temple was being rebuilt now, but God declared that
this One would build the temple of Jehovah. The temple of
Zerubbabel was, therefore, regarded as only a temporary building. The building of the true temple was reserved for the
Messiah himself. This cannot refer, as some expositors have
argued, to our Lord's statement that, if the temple (of His body)
was destroyed, He would raise it up in three days (John 2:19–
21), nor to the spiritual temple which is the Divine habitation
today (Eph. 2:21, 22). Nor is it possible to regard the prophecy
as relating to Zerubbabel and the completion of the temple
which was then under construction, since the Branch was not a

title pertinent to Zerubbabel. The words clearly anticipated the building of a literal temple and presumably relate to the millennial temple described by Ezekiel (Ezek. 40–42; Isa. 2:2, 3).

Jehovah declared that the One who was to build the temple would also 'bear the glory'. Haggai had averred that the temple would be filled with glory and that the latter glory (rather than the 'glory of this latter house') would be greater than the former glory (Hag. 2:7, 9). Since Christ, who is the effulgence of God's glory, will enter the millennial temple to dwell among His people (Ezek. 43:2; cf. 1:26–28; Rev. 21:23), it is obvious that the future glory will be incomparably greater than the shekinah of old. But the expression used signifies 'royal majesty' rather than 'glory'. Unger says that the Hebrew word *hodh*, which is here translated 'glory', 'is used almost exclusively of the divine splendour' (Ps. 8:1; 45:3; 148:13; Hab. 2:3). This is confirmed by the following statement that He 'shall sit and rule on His throne'. Joshua's coronation was symbolic of that of a worthier One, when the despised Nazarene will be universally acclaimed as King of the kings and Lord of the lords. His rule will not be limited to the tiny state of Israel; Phil. 2:10 indicates that His sovereignty will be acknowledged in the celestial heights, the terrestrial scene and the infernal regions, and Eph. 1:10 reveals that He will be the Divinely-appointed head over the whole creation. Regal glory and the honour and dignity of majesty are to be supremely His.

It was also predicted that He would 'be a priest on His throne'. Barnes maintains that, in view of the next clause, a more appropriate rendering would be, 'there shall be a priest beside His throne', and he identifies the priest as Joshua as the chief counsellor of Zerubbabel, to whom pertained the civil authority. The prophecy looks beyond Joshua and Zerubbabel, however, and we see no reason for departing from the normally accepted view that the reference is to the occupant of the throne, so that Messiah is envisioned as filling the offices of both king and priest. This, of course, was forecast in Ps. 110:4, where Messiah's priesthood was said to be 'after the order of Melchizedek', the priest–king of Gen. 14:18 (see also Heb. 6:20–7:17). Since He would fill both offices, it was added that 'the counsel of peace shall be between them both'. In the past there had not always been complete accord between the priesthood and the monarchy, but all possibility of discord or disagreement was removed if the functions of both were vested in one Person. Messiah would be the securer and dispenser of peace. Moore (op. cit., p. 98) interprets 'the counsel of peace' as 'the counsel that precedes peace, and this is done by Christ in the exercise of these two offices, by one of which He purchases redemption, and by the other applies it; by the one expiates sin, and by the other extirpates it; and thus reconciling man and God, causes peace on earth, and good will to men'.

Perowne's comments are worth quoting. He says (in loc.), 'This has been explained to mean that the two offices, the sacerdotal and the regal, being merged in the one person of Him, who "shall be a priest upon the throne" shall be exercised in perfect harmony, as though a treaty of peace were ratified between them. "The counsel of peace," however, would seem to mean more than this, and to denote a counsel, or measure, devised by "them both", of which the fruit would be peace to those whom it contemplated. This counsel, by which peace is procured and bestowed (Eph. 2:14; John 14:27) is for its execution "between them both", i.e. between the two offices, or rather between the Holder of them both regarded now as King and now as Priest. The view that "them both" refers to the Eternal Father and Messiah, Jehovah and the Branch, though it has been ably advocated, is scarcely warranted by the context, in which the mention of Jehovah is not sufficiently direct and prominent to sustain such a reference.'

The crowns which had been placed upon the head of Joshua were then to be taken and hung in the temple as a memorial – possibly as a reminder of the link between those who had returned from Babylon and those who were still exiled from home. On the basis of Barnes' rendering the crown (or crowns) were for health (or recovery) to Tobijah and Jedaiah and for favour (or beauty) to the son of Zephaniah. The more normal interpretation makes the crown suspended in the temple 'a lasting memorial, not only of the zeal and piety of these offerers of gifts from a far-off land, but also of the kindness shown them by Josiah the son of Zephaniah, who had received them into his house' (cf. Matt. 10:41). If the latter view is taken, the honour paid to the three delegates was surely in their character of representatives of the exiles; the honour paid to their host presumably had reference to more than the hospitality displayed to them, but no other details are given. Some writers find a significance in the materials of which the crown was made, gold being regarded as a type of the deity of Christ, and silver of His redemptive work, but it would be unwise to press the typological significance too far.

The presence of the suspended crown in the temple was also to become a visual intimation, not merely that gifts and offerings would be transmitted by the exiles, but that other contingents would one day return and participate in building the temple of Jehovah – doubtless anticipating the millennial temple. 'The Jews in Judah,' writes Barnes (op. cit., p. 58), 'formed a small, poor and depressed community needing badly the encouragement which could be given by the arrival of co-religionists from afar supplied with means and zealous for the welfare of Jerusalem. Zechariah points to the arrival of the household of Josiah the son of Zephaniah as foreshadowing such reinforcements.' Another *golah*, or new return from Babylon, would assuredly eventuate.

The people's participation in the future blessing was stated to be dependent upon their faithfully rendered obedience to God. The events foretold were in the Divine purpose and would inevitably occur precisely as foretold, but the part they took depended upon themselves. What had occurred, however, was a clear indication that Zechariah (or possibly the angel) had been divinely sent.

CHAPTER 11

Problems of Fasting

There had been a lapse of nearly two years since the events of the first six chapters, without any recorded message through the prophet. Then a deputation arrived at Jerusalem to inquire of the priests and prophets their opinion regarding the necessity for the continuance of a national fast which had been instituted some seven decades before, and the reply to their questions came through the mouth of Zechariah. The circumstances and the problem were detailed in the first three verses of Zech. 7, and the reply was given in four sections, each commencing with the words, 'And the word of Jehovah of hosts came to me, saying . . .' (7:4, 8; 8:1, 18).

'And it came to pass in the fourth year of king Darius that the word of Jehovah came to Zechariah, in the fourth day of the ninth month, Chisleu, when they of Bethel had sent Sherezer and Regem-melech and his men, to entreat the favour of Jehovah and to speak to the priests who were in the house of Jehovah of hosts, and to the prophets, saying, Should I weep in the fifth month, separating myself, as I have done these so many years?' (7:1–3).

The reconstruction of the temple was progressing extremely favourably and in another two years the work would be complete. Although the restoration was not yet finished at the time of this particular incident, the building had reached such a stage that it was evident that the reinstitution of the full services and worship could now be envisaged. It was in these circumstances that a deputation of two men was sent to Jerusalem. The two men concerned were named Sherezer and Regem-melech, and David Baron (op. cit., p. 212) draws attention to the fact that they bore 'foreign names which originally were associated with the false worship of their oppressors. Sharetser was the name of one of the parricide sons of Sennacherib (Isa. 37:38), and also of one of the princes of Babylon who desolated Jerusalem and destroyed the temple (Jer. 39:3–13). The full Assyrian name was Nergal-Sarusur or Nergal-Shar-Ezer, which, according to Schrader, means "May Nergal protect the king". Here

Nergal, the name of the Assyrian false god, is dropped, but the prayer, originally idolatrous, is retained. Regem is found as a proper name in 1 Chron. 2:47. Gesenius explains Regem-melech as signifying "friend of the king". It may originally also have been an Assyrian name.' The two men may have held office in the court of Assyria or Babylonia and to have derived their names from their occupation. Their names may provide a clue to the true reason for their question of the priests and prophets at the city. It is, at any rate, impossible not to be impressed by the contrast between their names and those of the bearers of the gifts referred to in the previous chapter.

According to the A.V., the deputation was sent to the house of God or Bethel (which is literally 'house of God'). But the temple was never described in this fashion and there seems little doubt that the wording should read, 'when they of Bethel had sent'. Bethel was one of the cities to which some of the exiles had returned (Ezra. 2:28; Neh. 11:31). It lay to the north of Jerusalem and had been a religious centre in the kingdom of Israel until the latter's fall. It was here that Jeroboam set up the golden calves and it had been a centre for idolatrous worship (1 Kings 12:28; 13:1; Amos 7:13). The fact that the people of Bethel now sent to Jerusalem was a clear indication that they did not anticipate the revival of the ten-tribed kingdom of Israel and that they recognized the kingdom of Judah as the only national hope. As another says, 'Notwithstanding the many sacred memories connected with their city, and the fact that it had been the seat of a temple in the days of the Israelitish kingdom, to which the tribes of Israel had resorted in numbers, no attempt was now made on their part to dispute the legitimate right of Jerusalem being regarded as the only place where the sacrifices and services enjoined by the precepts of the Mosaic law could be offered.'

The Bethel representatives came to Jerusalem to entreat the Divine favour and to consult the priests in the temple and also the prophets (presumably Zechariah and Haggai). Seventy years earlier Nebuchadnezzar had destroyed the temple of Solomon and most of the buildings of Jerusalem by fire. This had occurred in the fifth month (August) of the year, and from the seventh to the tenth day of the month, the flames had raged through the doomed city (2 Kings 25:8, 9; Jer. 52:13). The

Jews had instituted a special fast in commemoration of the event, and they had observed it as a period of mourning for seventy years. They had fasted and wept, had worn sackcloth and had rent their clothes in memory of the national calamity. It was not a divinely ordained fast and had not been required of God. At the same time, if it was a season of true humiliation and penitence, the observance would have had a spiritual significance and value. Fasting *per se* was not meritorious, but it could have the effect of teaching the mourner his utter dependence upon God. But it was clear that this particular fast had become symptomatic of the mechanical formalism and religious externalism of a people who were weary of what had become a meaningless ritualism. In any case, now that the temple was being rebuilt, this fast seemed completely pointless and superfluous. Surely it was a work of supererogation, significant while the temple lay waste, but meaningless now that it was being restored. It was in this spirit that the messengers came to Jerusalem.

They posed their question to priests and prophets. Was it necessary in present circumstances, to abstain from normal practices and to devote themselves to lamenting the destruction of a temple which was now being rebuilt? There is an indication that they were, in fact, weary of the practice and all that it entailed, for the messengers referred to the people having abstained from meat and drink (or 'separating' themselves) 'these so many years'. The fast had become a legalistic ritual in which they had no heart. Chambers (in loc.) says that fasting 'is an expression of sorrow and humiliation proper to be used on the occasions which call for great feelings; then it is fitted to help the discipline of the soul and to lead to benefits quite beyond itself. . . . But whenever the exercise is made to recur statedly at regular intervals without regard to circumstances, its inevitable tendency is to degenerate into a barren form and a mischievous self-deception.' This is what had happened to them. The fast, instituted by their fathers (doubtless well-intended and commendable, even though not divinely appointed) had become devoid of spiritual import or value. It irked them and they wanted to put an end to it. Their current conditions might have been construed as a call to what one writer terms 'continued fasting and humiliation', but they were oblivious to their spiritual need.

The Divine reply to the question which so agitated them was, as already indicated, given in four sections, viz. 7:4–7; 7:8–14; 8:1–17; and 8:18–23. The parenthesis in 8:1–17 is not, of course, irrelevant to the reply, but did not, in itself, really constitute part of the direct answer. The first section of the reply was couched in the form of a reproof.

'Then came the word of Jehovah of hosts to me, saying, Speak to all the people of the land, and to the priests, saying, When you fasted and mourned in the fifth and seventh month, even those seventy years, did you at all fast to me, even to me? And when you eat and drink, is it not you who eat and drink? Should you not hear the words which Jehovah cried by the former prophets, when Jerusalem was inhabited and in prosperity, and the cities thereof round about her, when men inhabited the south and the plain?' (7:4–7).

God's answer was not given directly to the two delegates from Bethel. Zechariah was commanded to address his words to all the people of the land, including the priests. (No mention is made of the prophets, from which it may presumably be deduced that the prophets referred to in verse 3 were merely Zechariah and Haggai). The question had been propounded to the priests, but they had evidently been incapable of providing the counsel sought, and since God's message was addressed *inter alia* to them, the inference is that they were as culpable as the rest of the nation of substituting external formalism for inward reality. It is a salutary thought that even the leaders of God's people can lose sight of spiritual realities and see nothing more than forms and ceremonies – a lifeless ritual bringing no honour to God or blessing to man.

The reply referred not only to the fast in the fifth month, which had been the subject of the inquiry, but also to the fast in the seventh month. It was in that month that Gedaliah, the governor appointed by Nebuchadnezzar, had been murdered by Ishmael and his supporters and that the rest of the people left in the land of Judah fled to Egypt for fear of the murder being avenged upon them by the Chaldeans (2 Kings 25:25, 26). This completed the calamities of Judah and was virtually the end of the little state for the time being and, in memory of this further trouble they had instituted another day of mourning and fasting. Neh. 9:1 refers to another fast (probably a special

one and not an annual event) on the twenty-fourth day of the
seventh month on which the people confessed their sins in sackcloth and ashes. The day of atonement was also celebrated on
the tenth day of the same month (Lev. 16:29). It is reasonably
clear however, that the reply related only to the two fasts which
the Jews had instituted and made no reference to Nehemiah's
fast or to the day of atonement (Lev. 23:26–32).

The seventy years' servitude to Babylon (Jer. 25:11) would
expire at the next fast, and the people were challenged by the
One who realized that the question they had posed was symptomatic of their real attitude to Him. When they had fasted
during those seventy years, He asked, had they sincerely fasted
to Him? Were they not more concerned with their loss of home
and material possessions, with the indignity they had suffered
of exile from their own land, and with the humiliation of servitude to a pagan country? Their abstinence from food, their
mourning and lamentation had not been an expression of contrition for their transgressions, or a recognition of the justice
of the Divine hand which had inflicted chastisement upon them.
Their legalistic asceticism and their punctilious observance of
their self-appointed fasts were little more than an indication of
their grief for their own distress and personal loss. It was concerned with self and not with God, and He virtually exposed
their insincerity and self-centredness. He was more interested
in truth than in sackcloth.

If their fasting sprang from selfish motives, their feasting was
no more commendable. It was equally as egoistic and, by
implication, just as God-dishonouring. Their concern was only
to satisfy their natural appetite, and they paid no regard to the
One by whom even the material benefits of life are bestowed,
and they clearly gave no thought to the needs of others who
were less fortunate than themselves. Their actions were a
barometer, revealing their spiritual attitude and condition. The
reference was not merely, of course, to the appointed feasts
(Lev. 23), but to the basic practice in connection with the
Levitical offerings, where, except in the case of burnt offerings
(which were devoted entirely to God), the worshipper and his
family feasted upon part of the offering after the appointed
portion had been presented to God and the priest's portion
had been given to him (cf. Deut. 12:5–7) There seemed no

appreciation of the relationship of the eating and drinking to the sacrifice which had just previously been offered, and no understanding of the spiritual significance of the actions.

Zechariah reminded the people of the messages proclaimed by earlier prophets in the days of peace and tranquillity, when Jerusalem and the other cities were safe and prosperous, fully populated centres, when the southern Negev was fertile and inhabited, and the Shephelah, or lowland country, experienced the blessings of nature. Judah was divided into (1) the Negev or south, (2) the Shephelah, the stretch of low hills running from north to south, and (3) the hill country (i.e. Jerusalem and the cities referred to). The remonstrances made by God in those earlier days went unheeded, but they were still relevant: ought not Judah to listen to them now? Their fathers had refused to respond to the prophets' pleas for repentance and had ignored their warnings of consequent judgement. There was a danger that the returned exiles might be just as obtuse and would lapse into the same ways. By inference, the blessings enjoyed in pre-exile days could be restored if the people turned in sincerity of heart to Jehovah; the prophet's words were still pertinent, and neglect of God's claims could only result once again in Divine discipline. This was, in fact, what actually occurred. Even today, we avoid the message at our own peril.

The second section of the reply dealt with the cause of the chastisement inflicted upon people and land.

'And the word of Jehovah came to Zechariah, saying, Thus speaks Jehovah of hosts, saying, Render a judicial decision based on truth, and show kindness and compassion every man to his brother, and oppress not the widow, nor the fatherless, the sojourner nor the poor; and let none of you devise evil against his brother in your heart. But they refused to hear, and gave a rebellious shoulder, and made heavy their ears, that they might not hear. Yes, they made their hearts as an adamant stone, lest they should hear the law, and the words which Jehovah of hosts has sent by his Spirit by the former prophets. Therefore came great wrath from Jehovah of hosts. Therefore it is come to pass that, just as He cried and they would not hear: so they shall cry and I will not hear, says Jehovah of hosts: but I will scatter them with a whirlwind among all the nations whom they have not known. Thus the land was desolate after them, so that no

D

man passed through nor returned: for they laid the pleasant land desolate' (7:8–14).

In the second section of the reply to the Bethel delegates, the prophecy emphasized by implication the conduct which had eventuated in the judgement experienced by the earlier generation. Barnes says (op. cit., pp. 61, 62), 'The prophet never forgets the awful chastisement inflicted on his people for their past sins of oppression, and by reminding them of it, he warns them against persisting in similar sins in the present. The Jewish nobles were themselves in a depressed condition, and yet they in turn became oppressors of their weaker brethren.' Zechariah accordingly again explained the necessity for moral and spiritual reformation in substitution for the external observances which had been the subject of the Bethelites' inquiry. The reality of their attitude to God was evidenced by their attitude to their fellow-men and the prophet reiterated the age-long principles which should govern the relationship of man with man. Those principles were to be seen in God's dealings with His creatures, and He expected His people to follow the pattern thus set.

To others, to whom fasting was proving irksome in their day, a message had been given through Isaiah at an earlier date, 'Is not this the fast that I have chosen? to loose the bands of wickedness, to undo the heavy burdens, and to let the oppressed go free, and that you break every yoke? Is it not to deal your bread to the hungry, and that you bring the poor who are afflicted to your house? When you see the naked to cover him; and that you hide not yourself from your own flesh?' (Isa. 58:6, 7). There should be true judgement or perfect justice, and mercy and kindness should be practised to others. In pity and compassion, they should refrain from oppressing the widow and orphan, the stranger and the poor. These were specific injunctions under the Mosaic law (Exod. 22:21, 22; see also Isa. 1:17). Fraud and violence were the evidence of a heart turned away from God. The devising of evil against others was not to be allowed in their thoughts.

Yet it was just in these respects that their fathers had failed (Isa. 10:1, 2; Jer. 5:28). They had refused to listen to the Divine injunctions and, like an ox intractably refusing to be yoked, they had obdurately resisted the imposition of any control or restraint by God. In their recusance they had closed their ears to the Divine admonitions and pleas, and had resolutely hardened their hearts. They were adamant in their refusal to listen to the commands of the *Torah*, reiterated as they had been in the messages sent by the prophets of an earlier day.

Since that earlier generation would listen to neither the law nor the prophets, Divine wrath fell upon them. So serious was their refractory disobedience that the judgement meted out to them was a punitive and unmitigated infliction. They had suffered under the hand of the Chaldeans, but the latter were simply the instrument of God. Moore says (op. cit., p. 109), 'As they refused to wear the yoke of obedience, God laid upon them the yoke of oppression; and as they hardened their hearts like the diamond against God's words, God broke these hard hearts by His judgements.' But their descendants continued blindly and impenitently, refusing to conceive that the same judgement might fall upon them.

Jeremiah had warned their fathers that Jehovah would bring evil upon them which they would be unable to escape and God had declared, 'though they shall cry to Me, I will not hearken to them' (Jer. 11:11). What he had foretold had come to pass. When God had cried to the people, they had refused to listen. When later they realized their jeopardy, they cried to Him in their extremity, but then He refused to listen. The experience of the past should have been a warning to the present generation.

Because of the impenitence of their fathers, judgement had fallen, and God had whirled them away like a mighty hurricane (cf. Job. 27:21; Amos 1:14), scattering them among nations who were strangers to them. Their land was laid waste and no one passed through or returned. It had been a pleasant or desirable land, but the nations had made it desolate. The experience was so recent in history that it should have needed no emphasis, but should have been effective in winning back to God the descendants of those who had suffered the Divine discipline, but it seemed to have made little more than a temporary impression. Man never seems to learn the lessons of history and what was true of Judah is equally true of God's people today.

CHAPTER 12

Restoration to Blessing

'Jerusalem in the prophet's day was still for the most part in ruins and grievously depopulated,' wrote Barnes (op. cit., p. 64). 'Nothing except the "zeal of Jehovah" could restore it to any measure of its former prosperity. But Zechariah is assured that if his people repent, Jehovah will indeed be zealous in their behalf. So he promises that exiles shall return from east and west to replenish Jerusalem, and the city shall be at peace and in security again and filled with rejoicing.' The next section of the reply to the Bethel delegation, therefore, anticipated the future blessing and prosperity in the millennial age, and regarded the partial restoration of Zechariah's day as the symbol and precursor of what was yet to happen. The eighth chapter was divided into ten subsections, each marked by the introductory phrase, 'Thus says Jehovah' (vv. 2, 3, 4, 6, 7, 9, 14, 19, 20, 23).

'Again the word of Jehovah of hosts came, saying, Thus says Jehovah of hosts, I am jealous for Zion with great jealousy, and I am jealous for her with great wrath. Thus says Jehovah, I am returned to Zion, and will dwell in the midst of Jerusalem: and Jerusalem shall be called the city of truth; and the mountain of Jehovah of hosts, the holy mountain. Thus says Jehovah of hosts, There shall yet old men and old women dwell in the streets of Jerusalem, and every man with his staff in his hands for very age. And the streets of the city shall be full of boys and girls playing in the streets. Thus says Jehovah of hosts. If it be marvellous in the eyes of the remnant of this people in those days, should it also be marvellous in my eyes? says Jehovah of hosts. Thus says Jehovah of hosts, Behold, I will bring them and they shall dwell in the midst of Jerusalem: and they shall be my people and I will be their God in truth and righteousness. Thus says Jehovah of hosts, Let your hands be strong, you that hear in these days these words from the mouth of the prophets, which were spoken concerning the day that the foundation of the house of Jehovah of hosts was laid, even the temple, that it might be built.

For before those days there was no return for his labour for man
nor any for beast; neither was there any peace to him that went
out or come in because of the adversary: for I set all men every one
against his neighbour. But now I will not be to the remnant of this
people as in the former days, says Jehovah of hosts. For the seed
of peace, the vine, shall give its fruits, and the ground shall give
its increase, and the heavens shall give their dew; and I will
cause the remnant of this people to inherit all these things.
And it shall come to pass that, as you were a curse among the
heathen, O house of Judah and house of Israel, so will I now
save you and you shall be a blessing. Fear not, but let your
hands be strong. For thus says Jehovah of hosts, As I thought to
punish you, when your fathers provoked me to wrath, says
Jehovah of hosts, and I repented not; so again have I thought
in these days to do good to Jerusalem and to the house of Judah.
Fear you not. These are the things that you shall do. Speak
every man the truth to his neighbour; execute the judgement
of truth and peace in your gates; and let none of you devise evil
in your hearts against his neighbour; and love no false oath:
for all these are things that I hate, says Jehovah' (8:1–17).

Zech. 8 was still part of the reply to the Bethelite inquiry
regarding fasting, although the answer was virtually not given
until the second section of the chapter. The first section (vv. 1–
17) was composed of a series of promises to Judah of future
blessing, each introduced – as already mentioned – by the
phrase, 'Thus says Jehovah'. This first section portrayed the
restoration of peace, happiness and prosperity to Jerusalem and
the people of Judah, and indicated the intense interest still
displayed by Jehovah in this wayward nation. Despite all their
failures His affection was still set upon them and He declared
that He was jealous for Zion with great jealousy and great fury.

Because of the nation's sin, unrelieved judgement fell upon
them. God left them to their foes and allowed them to be carried
away captive and their country to be depopulated and devastated.
The vehemence of His anger and the severity of their punishment had been justified in view of their disloyalty and idolatry.
But now God had resumed His relationship with His people and
had returned to Zion. (This statement was not completely
applicable in Zechariah's day and was patently predictive of a
day which is yet to come.) His people's former distress was,

however, to be banished by the realization of His presence in the midst of them, for He would actually dwell in Jerusalem. By implication, the temple would be completed and He would take up His residence as in the days of old. It seems evident that the promise extends beyond Zerubbabel's temple and the immediate circumstances of Judah to a period still future, when the glory of God will again be seen in a millennial temple and His presence will be realized in blessing in Jerusalem (Ezek. 43:2–7; 44:4).

By His sanctifying presence, the city of Jerusalem, which had proved so unfaithful and disloyal to Him, would become the city of truth and holiness. Isaiah had described the city as a harlot and the abode of murderers, but even he had foreseen the day when Jerusalem would be renamed 'the city of righteousness, the faithful city' (Isa 1:21, 26). Although this may have been partially fulfilled in the days of Zerubbabel, Zech. 14:20, 21 makes it evident that the prophecy was looking on to the still future period of millennial blessing. Even the mountain of Jehovah, 'which had been a heap of ruins, shall again be the holy mountain, where the Holy One will sit in the majesty of His unchanging justice and mercy' (Smith).

Jerusalem had suffered the ravages of war; her buildings had been torn down; her inhabitants had been either massacred or deported; disease had swept over the tragic metropolis. The old people had been killed, and any young ones who survived had been carried away as captives. All that was now to end. The city was to be restored to its former condition, and death should no longer stalk its streets. Once the parks and thoroughfares had been filled with soldiers' camps: now they were to be filled with old and young, enjoying the city's newfound peace and tranquillity. The aged, supported by their sticks, would walk without fear in the streets, and the city would resound with the mirth and merry laughter of the happy carefree children playing in the streets (cf. Matt. 11:16). In the times of the Maccabees, we are told that 'the ancient men sat all in the streets, communing together of good things' (1 Macc. 14:19) and, in a coming day, the conditions will, of course, be seen once again. This might now seem marvellous to the remnant of the people. The transformation predicted must have appeared almost incredible, but God declared that it would not be marvellous in His eyes.

The things that are impossible with man are possible with God.

In 721 B.C. the ten tribes of Israel had been deported to Assyria, and in 598 and 589 B.C. the majority of Judah had been removed as captives to Babylon and, although some returned to their own land under Joshua and Zerubbabel, the majority presumably did not. With the destruction of Jerusalem by the Romans in A.D. 70 and the quashing of the rebellion of Bar Cochba in A.D. 134 the Jews were not normally allowed access to Jerusalem. They were dispersed all over the world, but principally in countries to the west of their own country. God now declared that He would regather His people from the east and the west and bring them home to dwell in Jerusalem. (Jerusalem doubtless was a metonymy for the country as a whole.) This, of course, has never yet been completely fulfilled, but Isaiah declares that, in the day of Messiah's presence, 'Jehovah shall set his hand again the second time to recover the remnant of His people, who shall be left . . . and gather together the dispersed of Judah from the four corners of the earth' (Isa. 11:11, 12, and reiterates the Divine promise, 'I will bring your seed from the east, and gather you from the west; I will say to the north, Give up; and to the south, Keep not back: bring my sons from far, and my daughters from the ends of the earth' (Isa. 43:5, 6). Although Jews have returned to their own land, the universal regathering predicted by the prophet has patently not yet taken place, and the national acknowledgement of God which he foresaw has certainly not yet occurred.

Jehovah declared that He would bring the exiles to dwell in the midst of Jerusalem. In that day they will be His people and He will be their God in truth and righteousness. There has hitherto been no spiritual regeneration of the nation of the character implied by the prophet, and it is, therefore, clear that the restoration referred to is that which is to occur after our Lord's return to earth. It is then that Jehovah will become their God in truth and righteousness, i.e. to quote another, 'Jehovah will be true to His people and perhaps perform acts of righteousness for them, and conversely His people will be true to Him, and will act righteously one to another.'

Although these promises will not find their consummation until the millennial age, they would, of course, have come into effect immediately had the Jews of our Lord's day accepted Him.

Their rejection of Him has postponed the fulfilment of these prophecies of future blessing. The people were, however, exhorted to strengthen their hands, in view of the words uttered by the prophets when the foundation of the temple was laid seventeen years before. Although the reference is primarily to exhortations of Haggai and Zechariah (see Ezra 5:1, 2) at that time, there is doubtless also the inference that the promises just uttered should be a further incentive to unflagging effort in the rebuilding of the temple.

Haggai tells the story of the trials experienced by the people. They had been forbidden to continue the work (Ezra 4:21) and they had supinely accepted the royal prohibition. But their failure had met with Divine chastisement. Crops had failed and trade had dwindled to negligible proportions. A severe economic depression had led to unemployment and to poor recompense even when there was work (Hag. 1:6). Men and animals were both affected. Internecine strife and dissension had resulted and the spirit of true neighbourliness had evaporated. The nation's sufferings had been the discipline of God for their neglect of His work and their virtual apostasy from Him. But His attitude to the remnant of His people was about to change.

The vine (frequently used as a type of Israel), described as the seed of peace because it can flourish only when conditions are peaceful and the land is not suffering the ravages of war, would now prove fruitful. (Most commentators interpret verse 12 as 'There shall be a sowing of seed in peace' and take the reference to the vine as a separate clause.) The ground would no longer be sterile, but would yield her crops. The heavens had given no dew (Hag. 1:10), but they would now supply the constant need of moisture. And all these would be the heritage of the remnant in the land.

Addressing both Israel and Judah, not only in anticipation of the future, but also because there had been representatives of both among the exiles who had returned from Babylon, God declared that they had been an object of cursing, scattered among the nations (Jer. 24:9). Unger (op. cit., p. 143) says that the 'curse was predicted as the result of apostasy and sin (Deut. 28:15–62) and was to eventuate in the punishment of a worldwide dispersion (Deut. 28:63–68). The full reach of Zechariah's words extends to the sufferings and persecutions of this final diaspora, sweeping the entire span of the *loammi* period when their national election has been set aside (Rom. 11:1–12).' Just as they had been a curse, however, Jehovah would now save them and they would be an object of blessing. Therefore, they should strengthen their hands and busy themselves in the building of the temple. When their fathers had provoked God to wrath by their transgressions, it had been His mind to punish the nation and he did not relent in pouring out His anger. So it was now His purpose to do well to Jerusalem and Judah. They were not to fear.

God then set out the principles which should guide His people's lives. Jerusalem was to become the city of truth and holiness (v. 3). Consequently truth should characterize personal intercourse between its inhabitants (cf. Zeph. 3:13), and truth and peace the administration of justice in the city. (The 'gates' of verse 16 were the place at which cases were judged and the administration of the city took place). He had previously told the Bethelite deputation not to devise evil in their hearts against their brother (7:10), and the same injunction was reiterated that none in Judah should devise evil in their hearts against their neighbours. Perjury was a common sin of the period: the people were now commanded to love no false oath – a stronger expression than to swear none – since untruth was detestable to God. He sought sincerity and reality.

The same principles are, of course, applicable to the Christian today. The one who follows Christ will be characterized by righteousness and practical holiness, by truth and fairness and his relations with his fellow-men will display his honesty of purpose and freedom from evil intent.

The last six verses of the chapter formed the fourth and final section of the reply to the Bethelites and showed the complete transformation which was to take place in a future day.

'And the word of Jehovah of hosts came to me, saying, Thus says Jehovah of hosts, The fast of the fourth month, and the fast of the fifth and the fast of the seventh, and the fast of the tenth, shall be to the house of Judah joy and gladness, and cheerful feasts; therefore love truth and peace. Thus says Jehovah of hosts, It shall yet come to pass that there will come peoples and the inhabitants of many cities. And the inhabitants of one city will go to another, saying, Let us go speedily to entreat the favour of Jehovah and to seek Jehovah of hosts. I will go also. Yes, many peoples and strong nations will come to seek Jehovah of hosts in Jerusalem, and to entreat the favour of Jehovah. Thus says Jehovah of hosts, In those days it shall come to pass that ten men out of all languages of the nations will take hold, will even take hold of the skirt of him that is a Jew, saying, We will go with you, for we have heard that God is 'with you' (8:18–23).

In the concluding section of this part of the book, the question posed by the deputation from Bethel was answered in a manner that must have been totally unexpected. They had inquired about the necessity for the continued observance of the fast in the fifth month which their predecessors had instituted (7:3). The reply referred to four fasts: the first, in the fourth month, instituted as a reminder of the capture of Jerusalem by Nebuchadnezzar (Jer. 39:2); the second, in the fifth month, which commemorated the burning to the ground of the city of Jerusalem and of the temple (2 Kings 25:8); the third, in the seventh month, which commemorated Gedaliah's murder (Jer. 41:2); and the fourth, in the tenth month, which related to the commencement of the siege of Jerusalem (2 Kings 25:1). All of these fasts had been instituted by the people themselves and without any Divine direction to do so. The divinely appointed fast of the Day of Atonement on the tenth day of the seventh month (Lev. 16) was evidently not under review. The exiles had consistently observed the four fasts mentioned with sorrowful hearts, albeit, as God had previously indicated, with no real grief for their sins nor contrition towards Him. But now these periods of mourning were going to be transformed into seasons of joy and gladness (cf. Isa. 61:2, 3). They were to become no longer fasts but cheerful feasts. It is clear that this has not yet become true in Israel's history and that one must look on to the millennium for the complete fulfilment of the Divine promises. In view of the coming substitution of joy for sorrow and happiness for mourning, the command was repeated that the people were to love truth and peace.

From the cities of Israel and Judah (the former must presumably have been implied if the message was to be of any comfort to the Bethelites) the people (i.e. the tribes of Israel, as in Deut. 33:3, 19, and not the foreign nations referred to in verse 22) will come in that day, joining together to seek God's face at Jerusalem, and persuading others to join them. So complete will be the turning to God that some straggler, realizing the urge, will say, 'I will go also'. (The implication may possibly, however, be that, when the inhabitants of one city eagerly run to beseech other cities to go, the instant reply is an indication of readiness to go too.) 'Thus they start, not by ones and twos, but in crowds to hasten to Jerusalem, that they may secure the favour of God.'

The enthusiasm will spread to other nations and Gentile peoples will also make their way up to the city (Mic. 4:2) to seek the favour of Jehovah. As they draw near to the holy city, the Gentiles surround any Jew in sight, ten (i.e. metaphorically, a large number) of them seizing the edge of his shawl or outer garment to identify themselves with him, will declare their intention of going with him, because they have heard that God (Elohim) is with him. 'When this prediction was uttered,' writes Moore (op. cit., p. 123), 'nothing seemed more hopelessly improbable than its fulfilment. The Jews were a poor, despised, obscure tribe in the heart of Syria, whose existence was only known to the mighty world by their furnishing a trophy to the victorious arms of Babylon. Greece was just rising in the firmament of human history, and as she ascended to her brilliant zenith, her track was marked by the sweeping of the phalanxes of Alexander and the legions of Antiochus over the hills and valleys of Judea. And yet this prophecy remained unfulfilled. Rome was then in the rugged feebleness of her wolf-nursed infancy, and slowly continued to grow until she reached that gigantic stature in which she ruled the earth, and her conquering legions under Pompey again swept over the fated land.' The centuries have passed and other empires have filled the world's stage and have disappeared from view. But one day, what seems so improbable now will be a realized fact, and Jerusalem, the city of the great King, will be the centre of the earth.

CHAPTER 13

The Conquests of Alexander

Chapters 9 to 14 form the second part of the book of Zechariah and it is probable that several years had elapsed since the first part had been uttered. The building of the temple had been completed and the levitical forms of worship had been reinstated. The six chapters look on to the first and second advents of the Messiah and are divided into two sections (Chapters 9 to 11, and 12 to 14), each described as a 'burden of the word of Jehovah'. The 'burden' may mean the utterance of God or the pronounced judgement of God, and it has been interpreted as a burdensome message. 'It is an oracle that is heavy; freighted with war or judgement' says one writer.

The fact that the prophet's name is not mentioned in the whole of these chapters and that the style is so different from that of the first eight chapters of the book has led to doubts regarding the Zecharian authorship, although the canonicity of the chapters does not seem ever to have been questioned. The primary reason adduced for the doubt is not, however, the absence of the prophet's name or the difference in style, but the New Testament ascription (in Matt. 27:9, 10) of the authorship of Zech. 11:12, 13 to Jeremiah and not to Zechariah. Fuller reference is made to this later and it may suffice, for the time being, to point out that the passage in question was ascribed to Zechariah in the days of our Lord and the New Testament writers for it occupied the same place in the Septuagint, which was completed three centuries earlier, and which was used by our Lord and the apostles. One writer pertinently remarks, 'It does not seem probable that the Evangelist would make a correction of the Jewish canon in this indirect manner, without giving some intimation to that effect'. Taking all the facts into consideration, there seems no substantial reason for questioning the date or authority of these chapters.

Through the centuries, both Israel and Judah had suffered from the active opposition of their neighbours, but now these were to be dealt with for their oppression and enmity, and

Zechariah disclosed the manner in which their retribution would come. Even if the date of this second part of the book was towards the end of the prophet's life, the events foretold still lay in the future, and the empire which God purposed to use as His instrument for the castigation of His people's foes had not yet come into existence. With meticulous accuracy, however, Zechariah described the military activities and conquests of the Macedonian empire, particularly as they related to God's people and to their land. The details recorded are, in fact, so remarkably accurate that they constitute one of the strongest evidences of the reliability and inspiration of the book.

The first 'burden' concerned Syria, Phoenicia, and Philistia.

'The burden of the word of Jehovah upon the land of Hadrach, and Damascus shall be its resting-place: for the eyes of man, as of all the tribes of Israel, shall be toward Jehovah. And Hamath also which borders thereon; Tyre and Zidon, because she is very wise. And Tyre did build herself a stronghold, and heaped up silver as the dust, and fine gold as the mire of the streets. Behold, the Lord will dispossess her and he will smite her power in the sea; and she shall be consumed by fire. Ashkelon shall see it and fear; Gaza also shall see it and tremble exceedingly; and Ekron for her expectation shall be put to shame. And the king shall perish from Gaza, and Ashkelon shall not be inhabited. And a mongrel race shall dwell in Ashdod, and I will cut off the pride of the Philistines, and I will remove his blood out of his mouth, and his abominations from between his teeth: but he also shall remain as a remnant for our God, and he shall be as a chieftian in Judah, and Ekron as a Jebusite. And I will encamp about my house against the army, that none pass through or return: and no oppressor shall pass through them any more: for now have I seen with my eyes' (9:1–8).

'The eyes of all look unto thee,' declared the psalmist (Ps. 145:12). 'Our eyes are upon thee,' said Jehoshaphat in the day of Judah's extremity (2 Chron. 20:12). Zechariah declared that the burden was pronounced because the eyes of man, as of all the tribe of Israel, were towards the Lord, but the significance may possibly be that Jehovah's eyes were upon man and upon all the tribes of Israel. C. H. H. Wright, however, considers that the import is that, 'When the fulfilment of the oracles takes place upon Hadrach and Damascus, and the wrath of God descends upon those cities and districts, the eyes of the nations as well as those of the people of Israel will look towards Jehovah, and marvel at the wonders of judgement which will then be performed in their sight in accordance with the solemn warnings of the prophet.' This is perhaps the most logical interpretation. The prophecy indicated that judgement was to fall upon Hadrach, Damascus and Hamath of Syria, Tyre and Sidon of Phoenicia, and Ashkelon, Gaza, Ebron and Ashdod of Philistia.

Some doubt exists regarding the identity of Hadrach, but Sir H. Rawlinson said some years ago, 'It is now certain that there was a city called Hadrach in the neighbourhood of Damascus and Hamath, although the exact site is unknown.' But Laetsch (op. cit., p. 450) says, 'Hadrach, for centuries a puzzling historical problem, has now been definitely identified with Hatarika mentioned in the annals of Assyrian kings as an Aramaean country near Damascus and Hamath, against which Assyria campaigned in 772, 755 and 733 B.C.' The three cities of Hadrach, Damascus and Hamath together represented Syria and they shared the same fate at the hands of the conqueror.

While the judgement was to fall upon Syria, as represented by three of its principal cities it was to remain upon Damascus (cf. Zech. 6:8). The punitive hand of Jehovah was to fall upon the city, not to destroy it or to put an end to its existence, for it still continues to the present day. Judgement was to light upon Damascus and settle there: retribution would justly fall upon the oppressor and particularly upon the city, primarily responsible. For centuries Damascus had been the formidable and bitter foe of God's people, but she was now to suffer herself. Hamath, bordering on Damascus, would also share similarly the punishment to be meted out by God.

The period described by the prophecy is undoubtedly that of Alexander the Great in the fourth century B.C. Alexander was one of the most remarkable administrators and military leaders in history. Succeeding his father Philip, as King of Macedon at the youthful age of 20 in 336 B.C., he brought a great part of the world under his control. H. A. L. Fisher, in *A History of Europe* (p. 42), says that in his short reign of thirteen years, he 'reasserted the Macedonian authority in Hellas and Thrace, levelled

Thebes to the ground, conquered with his small, mobile and most effective army, Asia Minor, Syria, Egypt, and Persia, and marched his Macedonian veterans over the Khyber Pass into the plains of India'. When Alexander invaded Asia Minor he first defeated the Persian army at the passage of the river Granicus and then took most of Asia Minor before routing the forces of Darius near the city of Issus in 333 B.C. He swept on to subdue Syria and Phoenicia, the city of Tyre being finally subjugated in 332 B.C., before an expedition was made against Egypt and Libya and then against Babylon. The young king was undoubtedly the instrument of God and his conquests fulfilled several of the Old Testament prophecies.

Zechariah disclosed how the punishment of the oppressors of Judah and Israel would occur. Following the battle of Issus, Alexander set out to conquer Syria. He sent Parmenio to capture Damascus, at which Darius had deposited a large amount of treasure, and to take possession of the Persian's wealth. One after another, practically all of the Syrian cities capitulated without offering any resistance. According to the prophet, Tyre and Sidon were to be the next to fall a prey to the conqueror. Sidon did, in fact, quickly surrender, but Tyre considered herself completely impregnable and she refused entry to the Macedonian. Tyre was commonly termed the queen of the sea and she claimed to have invented and taught the principles of navigation. Her position seemed secure, but she had invoked judgement. M. Rollin says in *Ancient History* (volume II p. 87). 'She was not satisfied with having reduced the Jews to a state of captivity, notwithstanding the alliance between them; with selling them to the Gentiles, and delivering them up to their most cruel enemies (Joel 3:4-8; Amos 1:9, 10): she likewise had seized upon the inheritance of the Lord, and carried away from His temple the most precious things to enrich therewith the temples of her idols.' Their actions attracted God's vengeance (Ezek. 26:3-12, 19; 27:27, 34), but it was not until Alexander's day that the predicted punishment really fell (Isa. 23:1-9). Tyre boasted of her wisdom, but it was ineffective to deliver her.

Zechariah declared that she had built herself a stronghold and had heaped up silver as dust and gold as mire in the streets. Although she was one of the richest and most prosperous

commercial cities in the world, the reference to the city's wealth
was presumably intended as a contemptuous assessment of it as
worthless in practice. In dry weather the dust was a nuisance
to the citizens, but the inspired word describes Tyre's silver as
a heap of dust, which would, of course, be scattered in the wind.
In the wet weather the mud or mire would be an equal nuisance
in the unpaved streets, but this was the simile used for the
Tyrians' store of gold. Ezek. 28, which, like Zech. 9, referred to
the wisdom of Tyre, also referred to her opulence and deliberate
amassing of gold and silver and implied that this was one of the
causes of her downfall. She was the emporium of the world's
most varied and rare products: gold and precious stones from
Ethiopia and Arabia, silver from Spain, emeralds from Damascus, wheat, honey and oil from Palestine, linen from Egypt,
ivory from the East. She carried most of the world's trade by
ship.

Zechariah's statement that she had built herself a stronghold
is a paronomasia in Hebrew – *Tsur* (Tyre) and *Matsor* (stronghold). Old Tyre on the mainland was destroyed by Nebuchadnezzar, 240 years before Alexander. At the time to which the
prophecy related, the city was no longer situated, even partly,
on the mainland, but on an island about half a mile from the
shore. It was nearly twenty miles in circumference and was
surrounded by massive walls 150 feet high. 'Proudly confident
in the strength of their island fortress,' says C. H. H. Wright,
'the Tyrians mocked the attempts of Alexander to reduce their
city. Every engine of war suited for defence had been stored up
in their bulwarks, and every device which their skilful engineers
could suggest was had recourse to and for a time with marked
success.' It was obvious that the only way in which the city
could be attacked was by building a causeway from the mainland
to the island, and Alexander stripped Old Tyre of stones and
rubbish for this purpose, thus fulfilling Ezek. 26:4–12. His
mole was demolished by the defenders and ravaged by storm,
but he patiently went on building and ultimately it was completed. The mole, in fact, was so well built and so great in size
that it has permanently converted Tyre from an island into a
promontory. With Cyprian and Phoenician fleets blockading
the harbour, the Macedonian forces attacked and captured the
fortified city, massacred 10,000 of its defenders and sold the rest

into slavery. Tyre had withstood a five years' siege by the Assyrians and a thirteen years' siege by the Chaldeans, but Alexander took it after a siege of seven months. God had foretold that it would become a bare rock and a place for the spreading of nets (Ezek. 26:14). Keith says that on his visit there, he 'came suddenly on five or six fishermen sitting on some prostrate columns, with their nets spread on the sand upon the site of the mole "in the midst of the sea." '.

Tyre was (a) to be dispossessed, (b) to have her power smitten in the sea, and (c) to be consumed by fire. Patently she was literally ejected and dispossessed by the victorious Macedonians. Regarding the second point Pusey says, 'The scene of her pride was to be that of her overthrow; the waves which girt her round should bury her ruins and wash over her site. Even in the sea the hand of God should find her and smite her in it and into it, and so that she should abide in it.' Thirdly, the city was actually consumed by fire when all of its inhabitants had been put to death. God's threatened judgements have been executed. As one writer says, 'Over 200 years before Nebuchadnezzar's siege Joel foretold her judgement; then Isaiah in 712 B.C., Ezekiel in 590, and Zechariah in 457. Yet still judgement lingered. Again and again Tyre was overthrown, but not obliterated. In the days of Jerome, in the fifth century, it was an opulent city. In the time of the Crusades it was still a city. But in 1291 the Mohammedan approached. In terror the Tyrians took to their ships in mass, never to return. The Sultan of Egypt overthrew the city, choked her matchless harbour with her ruins, cast into the sea statues and columns, and the huge stones of warehouses and the palaces of the merchant-princes, and scraped the very rock. Tyre is dead; whatever inhabited ruins or temporary revivals may survive – and such are assumed by the predicted "spreading of nets" – the proud, imperial mistress of the seas had, like Capernaum, gone down to the pit (Ezek. 26:20), the dark underworld of the dead.'

After the subjugation of Syria and Phoenicia, Alexander turned to Philistia, precisely as foretold by Zechariah. Four of the principal cities of Philistia were mentioned (Ashkelon, Gaza, Ekron and Ashdod – see also Zeph. 2:4). Gath was not mentioned and may have been destroyed already. The fact that the mighty city of Tyre had fallen struck fear into them. It has been said that 'Philistine arrogance in their independence, their nationality and their prowess was proverbial,' but the cities of Philistia were now to be humbled and brought low. Their rulers were slain since Alexander's policy was to destroy tributary monarchies and to maintain a consolidated empire: fallen kings were, therefore, replaced by his own appointed governors. Ashkelon was to be left without inhabitant, Gaza was to lose its ruler, Ekron was to experience grief and the dashing of her hopes, and Ashdod was to be occupied by a mongrel race. The predictions were completely fulfilled. Ashkelon was depopulated, Gaza was destroyed after five months' siege and its ruler was killed by being dragged through the streets, Ekron certainly had her hopes dashed to the ground: Tyre was not, as she had hoped, an obstacle to the imperial forces, yet the prophet foretold that one day Ekron would be like a Jebusite. Amos had also declared, 'I will send a fire on the wall of Gaza, which shall devour its palaces: and I will cut off the inhabitant from Ashdod, and him that holds the sceptre from Ashkelon, and I will turn my hand against Ekron: and the remnant of the Philistines shall perish, says the Lord God' (Amos 1:8; see Zeph. 2:4). Ashdod was to be occupied by aliens and the whole region fell a prey to the Macedonians.

The pride and arrogance of Philistia was brought down to the dust but, at the same time, God indicated that He had purposes of blessing for the Philistines. He declared that He would remove the blood out of his mouth and his abominations from between his teeth. 'The Philistines were considered by the Jews as an unclean people,' writes Barnes (op. cit., p. 73), 'partly because they were uncircumcized (Jud. 14:3), partly because they ate food forbidden by the law, particularly the blood of sacrificial victims (cf. Ps. 16:4; Ezek. 33:25). Here the promise is that some of the Philistines (the inhabitants of Ekron) shall be purified and united as proselytes to Israel.' Calvin takes the view that verse 6 visualizes Philistia as a wild beast from whose jaws the prey which he is devouring is torn, but this is not really tenable. The word 'abominations' is consistently used as a symbol of idols or idolatry, and this seems to be the significance here. Jehovah intended to cleanse the Philistines of their idolatry and to fit them for incorporation into Israel. A remnant would be saved and would become part of Judah. Because of its geographical situation, close to the borders of Israel, Ekron was chosen as an illustration: she would be like the Jebusites whom David incorporated when he captured their stronghold of Zion (2 Sam. 5:6). Philistia, in general, would become a chieftain (or chiliarch, the head of a thousand) in Judah. This prediction has not, of course, yet been fulfilled and it presumably awaits the coming of Messiah.

Judah might well have been fearful at the approach of the great conqueror, but Jehovah declared that He would protect His temple (and inferentially the city) against any attack by the Macedonian army. He would encamp around them to be their shield from the armies passing to and fro and to ensure that no oppressor passed through the land any more. It is remarkable that, although the Macedonian armies passed and repassed the city of Jerusalem, they left the temple and God's people unharmed. According to Josephus (*Antiquities* XI, 8:3), after taking Gaza and razing it to the ground, Alexander advanced quickly towards Jerusalem. He demanded the payment of tribute which the Jews had customarily paid to the Persians. Jaddua, the high priest, refused to break his agreement of loyalty to Darius. In a dream given to the high priest, God encouraged him to faith and confidence, and instructed him to fling open the gates and to go forth, clad in his priestly robes, with all the priests in his train, and all the people clad in white garments. Jaddua obeyed and the gates were opened, and the Macedonians gazed upon the remarkable spectacle. When Alexander saw the procession and the high priest in his gold-embroidered robes and his mitre with its golden plate of holiness, he fell upon his face and worshipped. Parmenio asked him the reason for his obeisance. The youthful ruler replied that he had seen the high priest in a dream at Dios, clad in purple and scarlet, and attended by priests in white. Alexander entered the city with Jaddua, and the latter acquainted him with the prophecies of Daniel which appeared to be relevant to himself and his empire. The Macedonian was so impressed that he accepted the message as Divinely given and spared the Jews. There is an implication in verse 8, of course, of a Divine protection extending beyond the period of the Macedonian invasion and realized more fully in a day still to come. God will yet protect His own land from all who threaten to invade and overrun it.

'Now have I seen with My eyes', said God. Not only did He observe every act, but He could read the motives and could, in addition, peer into the future. The most pertinent significance is perhaps that He took notice in order to intervene if He considered it necessary.

CHAPTER 14

The Coming of the King

At the close of the preceding sub-section, Jehovah had declared that He had seen with His eyes, tacitly implying that He was aware of the afflictions and trials of His people and that He would interpose on their behalf when the time came, as He did when Israel suffered at the hands of their taskmasters in Egypt (Exod. 3:7). He provided protection for them in the days of Alexander the Great, but will yet prove Himself to be their deliverer in the fullest possible sense. The next sub-section accordingly announced the event through which complete deliverance might have come (and was only delayed because of the Jews' rejection of the Deliverer). 'Sion is called upon,' says Perowne (op. cit., p. 113), 'to welcome with exultation her just and lowly King, who comes to her in humble state (v. 9), whose kingdom of peace shall cover all the land and embrace all nations (v. 10), and who, mindful of His covenant with her, shall give deliverance to the captives of Israel (vv. 11, 12). Using them, now once more an united nation, as the instruments of His warfare (v. 13), Himself fighting for them and manifesting Himself as their Protector (v. 14), He will make them victorious over all their enemies (v. 15), and will promote them to safety and honour (v. 16), magnifying His "goodness" and his "beauty" in the prosperity with which He crowns them (v. 17).' We have quoted *in extenso* because Perowne's summary is so concise and yet complete.

There can be no dubiety about the identity of the One described in verses 9 to 11. Even Rashi, the well-known Jewish commentator, said, 'It is impossible to interpret it of any other than King Messiah', and the Christian, with the pages of the New Testament open to him, unhesitatingly identifies the 'king' with the Lord Jesus Christ.

'Rejoice greatly, O daughter of Zion. Shout, O daughter of Jerusalem. Behold, your king comes to you. He is just and showing himself a Saviour, lowly and riding on an ass and on a colt, the foal of an ass. And I will cut off the chariot from Ephraim and the horse from Jerusalem, and the battle bow shall be cut off. And he shall speak peace to the nations. And his dominion shall be from sea to sea, and from the river to the ends of the earth. As for you also, because of the blood of your covenant, I have sent forth your prisoners out of the pit wherein is no water. Turn you to the stronghold, you prisoners of the hope. Even today do I declare that I will render double to you; when I have bent Judah for me, filled the bow with Ephraim, and raised up your sons, O Zion, against your sons, O Greece, and made you as the sword of a mighty man. And Jehovah shall be seen over them. And his arrow shall go forth as the lightning: and the Lord Jehovah shall blow the trumpet, and shall go with the whirlwinds of the south. Jehovah of hosts shall defend them. And they shall devour, and subdue with sling-stones. And they shall drink, and make a noise as from wine; and they shall be filled like bowls, as the corners of the altar. And Jehovah their God shall save them in that day as the flock of his people: for they shall be as the stones of a crown, lifted on high over his land. For how great is his goodness and how great is his beauty: Corn shall make the young men thrive, and new wine the maids. Ask of Jehovah rain in the time of the latter rain; so Jehovah shall make lightnings, and give them showers of rain, to every one grass in the field' (9:9–10:1).

Having implied that He would constantly watch over His people, God now called upon Zion and Jerusalem to exult and shout for joy. Their King was coming to Jerusalem. But the Jews had no king at that time and were subject to a Gentile power; no Jew had borne the title of king after the exile. Here was One who had been designated God's King centuries earlier (Ps. 2:6), the One of whom the earlier prophets had spoken (Isa. 9:6, 7), and for whom the nation waited in anticipation. This King was just or righteous, completely unlike the capricious and unjust rulers of history, and He was the dispenser of salvation. If deliverance had virtually been assured in the earlier half of the chapter, here was the One by whom it would come.

It might have been anticipated that the King would come in glory and splendour, with regal pomp and dignity, but He was described as lowly or humble, in complete contrast with the proud and arrogant rulers of this world (cf. Phil. 2:5–7). Illustrative of His character was the beast that carried him. From the days of Solomon onwards, the poor might ride upon an ass, but kings and nobles were always borne by a horse. Yet this King was to come, riding on an ass and on a foal of she-asses. This was precisely how He came, for the prophecy was literally fulfilled at the first advent of our Lord (Matt. 21:1–9; Mark 11:1–10; Luke 19:28–38; John 12:12–15). His entry into Jerusalem on that first Palm Sunday was on a beast of burden – not even a full-grown animal, but an untrained and unbroken colt – to be hailed with Hosannas by the crowds which, the same week, were to yell for His blood. Lange says that the prophecy 'presents a person in whom the greatest grandeur, magnificence, power and influence are associated, without confusion or contradiction, with the greatest humility, gentleness, poverty, suffering and weakness. No judge, king, or ruler of any sort in all Jewish history ever united in his character or experience these two extremes. None was so lowly, none so exalted. None without arms spoke peace even to his own people, much less to the heathen, and least of all to the entire known world. It is true of only one being in all human history that he had not where to lay his head and rode upon an ass, and yet acquired a limitless dominion over land and sea.' The Deliverer came, but His own people were so blind that they rejected Him.

Chambers (op. cit., p. 71) says that the Jews had a 'fable that the ass created at the end of the six days of creation was the same which Abraham saddled when he went off to offer Isaac, and which Moses set his wife and sons upon when he came out of Egypt; and that this distinguished animal was to bear the Messiah. . . . It is supposed that the prophecy in some way gave rise to the foolish statement of Tacitus, that the Jews consecrated the image of an ass in the inmost shrine of their temple, and hence probably arose the calumny upon the early Christians, who were often confounded with the Jews, that they worshipped an ass's head – a fable which Tertullian takes the trouble to repeat.'

As happened so often in the prophetic Scriptures, Zechariah apparently ignored the whole of the period between the two advents of our Lord and turned immediately to what would occur at and immediately prior to the second advent. Since the king was also the generalissimo of the forces, the announcement of the coming of the King would at once have conjured up, in the minds of those who heard (or subsequently read) the prophecy, the picture of war and the advent of a captain to lead his people into battle and victory. They were disabused of this potential misunderstanding, however, for Jehovah declared that He would cut off the chariot from Ephraim (i.e. Israel) and the horse from Jerusalem (metonymically Judah), the battle bow would be cut off and the King would speak peace to the nations. Israel and Judah had been separate kingdoms from the rebellion of Jeroboam in the tenth century B.C. (1 Kings 12:16, 17). Often at war with one another, horse, chariot and battle bow were the apt symbols of their means of offence and defence. But these were to be cut off and, by inference, the two kingdoms to be reunited (cf. Ezek. 37:16–22). Messiah would bring salvation, but not by military weapons. His victory would be won by the word of His mouth, and He would proclaim peace, not only to Israel, but to the Gentiles as well. Patently this has not yet been fulfilled and the prophecy obviously anticipated the Second Advent.

Moreover, the dominion of God's King, the Messiah, was not to be restricted to Israel and Judah. He would reign in peace over the whole world. In the picturesque language of the prophecy, his dominion would be from sea to sea (an idiom for the whole earth) and from the river (i.e. the Euphrates, the future boundary of the promised land – see Gen. 15:18) to the ends of the earth (Ps. 72:8). Jerusalem would be the focal point of His rule, but all nations would be subject to Him and own His sovereignty. This is the day for which creation had waited. This is the day so long foretold by prophet and seer, when the unhewn stone will pulverize the Gentile colossus and then expand to fill the whole earth (Dan. 2:34, 35).

Still addressing Zion and Jerusalem, Jehovah promised the return of the exiles to their own country. His covenant with His people had been ratified by blood. It is not clear whether the reference was to the Sinaitic covenant (Exod. 24:8), the Palestinian covenant (Deut. 30:1–10), or the Davidic covenant (2 Sam. 7:14–17), or even possibly to the Abrahamic covenant (Gen. 15:1–21) which preceded the nation as such. Ratification by blood was essential if any covenant was to be binding upon the parties to it. Because of the blood of the covenant God promised to deliver Zion's prisoners from the waterless pit. It was often the custom to confine prisoners or criminals in a cistern or dry well (Gen. 37:24; Jer. 38:6), and the prophecy visualized the exiles as symbolically imprisoned in similar fashion. Some commentators see an allusion to the Maccabean period in the description, while others claim that it is a reference to the great tribulation of a future day. Like many other Biblical prophecies, it is probably susceptible to more than one fulfilment, but its final fruition doubtless still lies in the future.

The sufferers were exhorted to turn to the stronghold, or, as Barnes renders it, 'Return to Him who is a stronghold', i.e. to God himself (Joel 3:16). These exiles hoped for early release and were, therefore, appropriately described as 'prisoners of the hope' (i.e. the hope of freedom or the Messiah Himself as the hope of the ages). David Baron (op. cit., p. 323) points out that 'Zech. 9:12 is the only place in the Hebrew Bible where the word for hope has the article. It is, therefore . . . not any hope, or general hope, that the prophet speaks about, but the special hope of Israel, the hope which sustained him through all the years of patient expectation. The centre and essence of it is the Messiah, and the great promised material and spiritual redemption which He was to accomplish.'

That very day, Jehovah declared, He would recompense to them double. The law stipulated that the firstborn son should receive a double portion of his father's property, but the term is also sometimes employed of the punishment meted out (Exod. 4:22; Deut. 21:15–17; Isa. 40:2; Jer. 16:18). In the context the implication is that double blessing would be the lot of God's people.

The concluding verses of the chapter are usually interpreted as a description of the struggle for independence in the times of the Maccabees (175 to 43 B.C.), which commenced in a determined resistance to the attempts of Antiochus Epiphanes to impose the idolatrous Greek worship upon the Jews. The verses may also be regarded, however, as anticipative of the coming of Messiah in glory and power to deliver His people. Certainly God portrayed Himself as a mighty warrior directing His power against Javan. He took Judah as His bow, treading upon it as He bent it, and He used Ephraim as the arrow to fill the bow. He raised up Zion's sons like a spear to attack the sons of Javan (or Greece), and wielded Zion as the sword of a mighty man. 'The mighty man,' as another remarks, 'did not use His sword until the enemy had been put to flight by the bow; the sword was used in the pursuit; it was, therefore a symbol of victory.' The figurative language, therefore, portrayed various stages in the conflict, but throughout it was clear that God was fighting on behalf of His people, albeit using them as His weapons.

In a number of Assyrian and Persian pictures of reliefs of a battle, the patron god or goddess is shown in the air above the human combatants, affording them supernatural help and protection in the fray. Jehovah declared that He similarly would be seen above His people and that His arrow would go forth as lightnings. The picture was that of a storm, the thunder-blasts serving as the sound of His trumpet, and the lightning as the swift flight of the arrow. God would sweep on with His people and with the whirlwind of the south: the Negev and Teman were regarded as the home of the whirlwind (Isa. 21:1; Hab. 3:3); it was from that direction that the fearful storms came and they were frequently pictured as the instrument of the Divine wrath (Ps. 83:15; Jer. 23:19). His fury would be irresistible in that day: nothing could withstand the vehemence of His anger.

The prophecy declared that Jehovah would protect His people as with a shield. They would be completely enveloped by His guard, and the enemy's attacks would consequently be ineffective and unavailing. Like a wild beast Judah would devour or consume their assailants and would tread them down like sling-stones. Sir George Adam Smith suggests that they will subdue the foe with sling-stones, and Barnes argues that the reference is to hailstones by which God crushes the attackers, but the purport seems rather that they will trample their foes under foot as fallen sling-stones are trampled in the mud and mire. They would treat the enemy as mere pebbles from the brook.

The victors (although Barnes suggests that it is the Lord's arrows) would metaphorically drink the blood of the defeated as a wild beast does the blood of its victim as it devours its flesh.

Victory would be complete and in their exuberance they would hilariously celebrate their triumph with boisterous shouting, like those who were intoxicated with wine. In the temple service, the blood of the sacrifices was caught in the sacrificial bowls and then sprinkled upon the corners of the brazen altar (Lev. 4:7, 18, 30). The prophet pictured the victors in the guise of the sacrificial bowls, filled with the blood of the slain: bespattered with the blood of the gory battle, they were like bowls filled with the blood of the sacrifice. Most commentators treat the imagery as pertinent to the Maccabean victories, but the experiences of that period can scarcely exhaust the significance completely, and there is a great deal to be said for the view that the complete fulfilment of the passage will not occur until the coming of Messiah as the great warrior to deliver His chosen people.

This is possibly confirmed by the statement that God would save His people 'in that day' (a phrase with an eschatological significance). This implied more than deliverance from their foes, for the promise was that He would save them as 'the flock of His people'. Isaiah declares that in a coming day, 'He shall feed his flock like a shepherd: he shall gather the lambs with his arm, and carry them in his bosom, and shall gently lead those that give suck' (Isa. 40:11). The implication of both prophets is that regeneration must have been effected and that there had been a restoration of communion with God. They could hardly otherwise be referred to as His flock. Like the sparkling jewels of a crown, honoured and glorified, would they be lifted up as an ensign over the land (cf. Mal. 3:17). Barnes argues that Zion is the crown and its inhabitants the glittering jewels. An 'ensign' was the indication of the presence of the king. The victorious Jews were to shine as precious gems and themselves to serve as Messiah's ensign as evidence of His return. Clearly, therefore, the prophecy looked beyond the times of the Maccabees to the Second Advent of our Lord.

Contemplating the wonder of the Divine purpose and the extent of His interest in His people, the prophet burst out with an expression of praise of God. (The words obviously cannot apply to Israel, as is sometimes suggested.) 'How great is His goodness! How great is His beauty!' Pusey quotes Osirius as commenting, 'The prophet, borne out of himself by the consideration of the Divine goodness, stands amazed while he contemplates the beauty and Deity of Christ: he burst out with unwonted admiration! How great is His goodness, who to guard His flock shall come down on earth to lay down His life for the salvation of His sheep! How great His beauty, who is the brightness of the glory and the image of the Father, and comprises in His Godhead the measure of all order and beauty.' Goodness is repeatedly ascribed to God (e.g. Ps. 31:19; 145:7) and beauty is ascribed to the Messiah (Isa. 33:17; Ps. 45:2, 3).

Corn would make the young men flourish, and wine would have a similar effect upon the young women. The prophecy was patently anticipating the material prosperity of the millennium and not merely that which ensued after the Maccabean victories. The blessings of the golden age would cause youth to flourish spiritually and materially. Barnes (op. cit., p. 78) says, 'Resolving the poetic parallelism we may paraphrase as follows, "corn and new wine shall bring forth fruit, even young men and maidens". Renewed fertility of the soil will result in a growth of the population, both of young men and of maidens.' Corn was necessary to provide the staff of life, and wine symbolized the joy and happiness of the people. All needs would be met and happiness would be Judah's portion.

One of the greatest needs in the Middle East is of water, and rain is regarded as a tremendous blessing. The early rain falls in the autumn and is 'essential for the sprouting of the newly-sown grain'. 'The latter rain falls in March and serves to swell the grain then coming to maturity' (Perowne). God promised Israel that the result of obedience to His commands would be the bestowal of the first rain and the latter rain (Deut. 11:14; see also Joel 2:23). One of the punishments inflicted upon Israel and Judah for their sinfulness was the withholding of rain (e.g. 1 Kings 17:1): when they repented the rain was restored (1 Kings 18:45). Now He bid them to seek the gift of rain, the latter rain. If they did, He would cause lightning to induce the clouds to yield up their moisture and the abundant rains to fall. He would give them showers of rain to produce 'grass in the field' (Gen. 1:29). The copious downpour would supply their need in full. All they had to do was to ask. The same circumstances apply today and if the blessing of the outpouring of the Divine Spirit is to be experienced, we must ask. The outpouring of the rain was, of course, typical of the outpouring of the Spirit which is yet to be experienced by Israel (Joel 2:28), and the same blessing is the need of the believer today. But the infilling of the Spirit is available to the one who desires it and will yield to God for it.

CHAPTER 15

The Only Answer

Zech. 10 is closely connected with the previous chapter and it is impossible to detach verse 1 from chapter 9. The prophet had clearly indicated that all blessings and temporal benefits were derived from God and that His people's hearts should, therefore, be turned to Him. But they had sought help from other sources and it was with this that the prophecy went on to deal.

'For the idols have spoken vanity, and the diviners have seen a lie and have told false dreams. They comfort in vain. Therefore they went their way as a flock; they were troubled because there was no shepherd. My anger is kindled against the shepherds and I will punish the goats; for Jehovah of hosts has visited his flock the house of Judah, and will make them as his goodly house in the battle. From him shall come forth the corner, from him the nail, from him the battle bow, from him every oppressor together. And they shall be as mighty men, who tread down their enemies in the mire of the streets in the battle. And they shall fight, because Jehovah is with them, and the riders on horses shall be confounded' (10:2–5).

Judah had resorted to the idols or *teraphim*, i.e. the household gods (Ezek. 21:21; Jud. 17:5; Hos. 3:4). The *teraphim* were actually small images of the divinities of the home, and were apparently consulted for guidance regarding proposed actions (Ezek. 21:21). They figured largely in the idolatry of the northern kingdom of Israel, but were also found in Judah, although their use was Divinely condemned (1 Sam. 15:23; 2 Kings 23:24). But they were in use in Babylonia at quite an early date, and Rachel stole those of her father Laban (Gen. 31:34), since possession of them was linked with leadership of the family and they also ensured her husband's ultimate entitlement to her father's property. When Jacob reached Shechem, he commanded that all *teraphim* and other idols held by the members of his company should be surrendered (Gen. 35:2–4). If Judah had consulted the *teraphim*, it was to no purpose, for they only uttered falsehoods (or wickedness). Their guidance was worthless.

The people had, therefore, consulted soothsayers or diviners, but this was equally ineffective. Their divination, to quote J. D. Davis, was an 'attempt to read the future and utter soothsaying either by a kind of inspiration or afflatus (Acts. 16:16), or else by means of signs. In the latter sense, it includes augury or foretelling the future by means of natural signs, such as the flight of birds, the disposition of the liver (Ezek. 21:21); hydromancy or foretelling from the appearance of water poured into a vessel or of objects dropped into the water (Gen. 44:5); foretelling by casting lots (Ezek. 21:21); and astrology or the determination of the supposed influence of the stars or the destiny of a person or a nation (cf. Isa. 17:13). The Hebrews also included in divination necromancy or foretelling the future by calling up the spirits of the dead and conversing with them (1 Sam. 28:8). The Babylonians were famous for their liver divination (hepatoscopy).' A scrutiny of an animal's liver was supposed to reveal the god's will through the manner in which that organ was fashioned. But Zechariah declared that what the diviners had seen was untrue. They had simply uttered vain or empty dreams and their comfort was as empty as the air (or, to use a modern idiom, only 'hot air').

In consequence, the people went their way like sheep. Because the grass was quickly consumed by the sheep or burnt up by the sun, it was necessary for sheep to be continually led to fresh pastures by the shepherd. Judah resembled the sheep in their wandering but, unlike the usual flock, they were without a shepherd and, therefore, strayed to their own hurt. Chambers (op. cit., p. 78) remarks, 'Israel having lost its native rulers, fell under the power of the heathen governors, here styled shepherds and he-goats.' Jehovah declared that His anger was burning against these brutal and self-appointed shepherds – the nations which had oppressed His people – and He would punish the he-goats, i.e. the rulers of the heathen nations (Isa. 14:9). Those who afflicted His people would eventually suffer at His hand. The complete fulfilment of the prophecy must, of course, await our Lord's return in judgement, although a partial fulfilment may have been seen in the past. It was appropriate, therefore that the prophecy should announce that Jehovah of hosts had visited His flock, the house of Judah. The great Shepherd would come to His shepherdless people. And, in that day, He would make them 'as his goodly horse in the battle'. As Moore puts it (op. cit., p. 160), 'God will visit His flock in mercy and make each one, instead of a timid sheep, to be a war-horse, decked for battle.' The final conflict was coming and the oppressors would be routed by the mighty warrior, but He would employ Judah as the strong and powerful steed to carry Him to victory.

If the clash of arms seemed already to be sounding, the prophet now painted the most reassuring picture of the suffic-iency of the Messiah for all Judah's needs and in all her circum-stances. Zech. 10:4 is perhaps one of the most remarkable portrayals of the Messiah. The fourfold picture of corner-stone, tent peg, battle bow and exactor was graphic and its signifi-cance far-reaching. That One was to come 'from him', i.e. out of the people of Judah as, in fact, actually occurred.

Out of Judah, Messiah came forth as the corner, or corner-stone. The corner-stone was the principal stone of the founda-tion, and the security of the whole superstructure virtually depended upon the stability and sureness of the foundation-stone. It was laid at the corner of the building, at the point at which two walls would be constructed. If it was unstable or badly laid, the whole of the building was jeopardized. Its stability was of fundamental importance. An earlier prophet said, 'Behold I lay in Zion for a foundation a stone, a tried stone, a precious corner-stone, a sure foundation' (Isa. 28:16). The apostle Paul declared that the Church as a whole and the believer personally were 'built upon the foundation of the apostles and prophets, Jesus Christ himself being the chief corner-stone' (Eph. 2:20). With that One as the foundation, none need fear or be in doubt. There was absolute security. Messiah was the corner-stone.

The corner-stone, however, was not only the foundation-stone, but also the headstone. As already mentioned in chapter 7, that headstone had been literally rejected by the builders of the temple of Zerubbabel's day and it had become a stumbling stone or 'rock of offence'. But when the builders sought a stone to fill the vacant place at the top of the corner, the only one that would exactly fit the gap was the stone which they had rejected and over which they had stumbled, and with songs of triumph they brought out the rejected stone and placed it in its appointed place as head of the corner. There is no dubiety about the interpretation, for our Lord specifically applied the type to Himself (Matt. 21: 42), as did also the apostle Paul (Rom. 9:32, 33; 1 Cor. 1:23). He is both foundation-stone and top-stone. The whole building is held together by and in Him. This is just as much the case today as for Judah centuries ago.

Out of Judah also was to come the nail or tent peg. The reference was not to the stake driven into the ground, to which the ropes were fastened, but to the large wooden peg inside the tent or, in later days, fastened to the wall of the house. Upon that 'nail' would be hung all the domestic utensils of the tent. It bore the load. In Oriental houses subsequently, the nail became a number of ornamental pegs around the walls, the treasures of gold and silver and objects of beauty being suspended therefrom. The nail not only carried the burdens of the household, but also its beauties and glories. The Messiah was to become the great burden-bearer for His people, but additionally, all the glory should hang upon Him. When Hezekiah's steward, Shebna was deposed from his position, Eliakim, the son of Hilkiah, succeeded him, and God declared that He would 'fasten him as a nail in a sure place' and that they would 'hang upon him all the glory of his father's house, the offspring and the issue, every small vessel, from the cups to all the flagons'. The prophet saw figuratively every tent door flung open and from the surface of every burnished vessel, hanging from the nail, the reflection of the morning sun. All the glory of the tent was hung from the nail (Isa. 22:20–25). Messiah was to be not only the bearer of all the burden of life, but the One on whom the glory hung. As a result of the practical significance attached to the nail, it became used metaphorically of the head of the household, because all other members of the family were dependent upon him.

Thirdly One was to come forth as the battle bow. A strip of elastic wood or metal with a cord stretched between its two ends, the bow was used for both hunting and war (Gen. 27:3; 48:22). It was in general use among the nations at an earlier date, but was still regarded as the symbol of armed might. The little country of Judah had no military strength and would be quite unable to face the attack of a hostile power. So Messiah was presented as the Divine archer, who would uncover His bow (Hab. 3:9) and direct His arrows into the hearts of His enemies (Ps. 45:4). Zechariah evidently anticipated the moment of Divine interposition in the affairs of men of which the Apocalypse later gave so much more detail (Rev. 19:11). Judah was incapable of confronting the foe, but she was not called upon to fight the battle. Another would stand beween her and the forces of the enemy, and the battle would be fought and the victory won by a Captain from above. How true for the Christian also that he fights not his own battles: the mighty Warrior stands beween him and the foe and the victory is won, not by the arm of flesh but by the power of God.

From Judah also was to issue forth 'every oppressor (R.S.V. "ruler") together'. The oppressor was the exactor of tribute and Unger argues that *noges* invariably has an evil connotation and the reference must, therefore, be to oppressive rulers and tyrants. Feinburg also, in *God Remembers*, p. 188, maintains that 'the reference cannot possibly be to the Messiah because *yahdaw* ("together") proves definitely that more than one oppressor will go forth'. On this basis, the implication would be that, through the presence and power of Messiah, all oppressors would unitedly depart from Israel. Barnes (op. cit., p. 80) puts a different complexion on it in his comment, 'The *noges* is one who exacts from the people (1) taxes (cf. 2 Kings 23:35); (2) forced labour (cf. Exod. 3:7); (3) military service, as in the present passage. Here the "exactors" correspond to the "scribes" of 1 Macc. 5:42, who had to see that none of the army of Judas Maccabaeus shirked the fighting. The prophet says that all the army of Judah, commander, subordinate officers, rank and file, and provost marshal, come from Jehovah. All authority is from Him.' The text is certainly as susceptible to this interpretation as to that of Unger and Feinberg.

David Baron, who frankly admits that the constructon of the sentence in the original is unusual and peculiar, gives the following possible renderings of the verse, 'Out of him (Judah) shall come (or go) forth every exactor (in the sense of absolute ruler) together,' while he quotes Prof. Aaron Pick as rendering the text in his *Literal Translation of the Twelve Minor Prophets* as, 'From him the corner, from him the nail, from him the battle bow, yea, from him shall come forth He that conquereth all together.' But then Baron says (op. cit., pp. 355, 356), 'In rendering the words *khol noges yachdaw* "every ruler together" or "he that will exercise all rule", I am guided more by the context and obvious sense than by strict principles of Hebrew grammar. It seems to me that, as the first terms in this verse undoubtedly refer to the Messiah in allusion to utterances about His person and mission by the former prophets, so must this last clause also. Certain it is that the Messiah at His Second Coming shall gather up in Himself all authority and rule.' This seems the most logical interpretation. The One to whom all tribute is due (and who should receive it from willing hearts and not by compelled exaction) shall come forth from Judah. In that day, the rejected Christ will be acknowledged as the supreme ruler in every sphere – celestial, terrestrial and infernal – and every knee shall bow to Him and every tongue acknowledge His lordship (Phil. 2:10, 11; Eph. 1:10, 20–23).

Judah was totally unprepared for the military conflict which faced her. But Jehovah was to raise up a leader in the person of the Messiah, who would be all-sufficient for the nation's need. With the realization of His presence and the inspiration of His leadership, the weakling became strong, and the army of Judah became valiant heroes, trampling underfoot their enemies in the mire of the streets. The description given can scarcely be restricted to the period of the Maccabees, although it was presumably partially fulfilled then, but essentially it seems to relate to the end time when God's people are confronted with the greatest opposition and danger of their history. But in that day, they will fight in confidence because Jehovah is with them. No doubt as to the ultimate result enters their mind. Victory is assured. The cavalry of the mighty Gentile forces are overthrown. The proud cavalry of Antiochus was, in fact, trampled down by the irresistible force of the Maccabean army. 'As soldiers trample through mud and mire,' writes Smith, 'as their bespattered uniforms, as well as their bloodstained clothes, proclaim their valiant bravery, so the soldiers of the Lord go on. They fight, not in their own strength, but in the power of the Lord who is with them, so that even the riders on horses, the most feared and most powerful of their foes, shall be confounded and put to shame.'

The prophetic Word indicates that, at the end time, the land of Israel will suffer invasion from the south and from the north and possibly also from the east, and that an attempt to deliver may well come from the west. The picture painted, even in Zechariah's last chapter, is of a nation in her extremity and only delivered by the Second Advent of Christ. It is difficult to pinpoint precisely when this particular prophecy may be fulfilled, but one fact that emerges is that God has not utterly forsaken His people and that one day He will once more intervene on their behalf.

CHAPTER 16

The Nation's Restoration

If the interpretation of the earlier verses of Zech. 10 is restricted to the period of the Maccabees, there is obviously a considerable gap between them and the fulfilment of the verses that follow. If, however, the first five verses are regarded as applicable to the period of the Second Advent, the remainder of the chapter follows logically, since it clearly describes the repatriation of the whole nation at the coming of Christ.

'And I will strengthen the house of Judah, and I will save the house of Joseph. And I will bring them back to place them, for I have mercy on them, and they shall be as though I had not cast them off: for I am Jehovah their God and I will hear them. And they of Ephraim shall be like a mighty man, and their heart shall rejoice as with wine. Yea, their children shall see and be glad; their heart shall rejoice in Jehovah. I will hiss for them and gather them; for I have redeemed them: and they shall increase as they have increased. And I will sow them among the peoples: and they shall remember me in far countries. And they shall live with their children and shall return. I will bring them again also out of the land of Egypt, and gather them out of Assyria; and I will bring them into the land of Gilead and Lebanon, and place shall not be found for them. And he will pass through the sea of affliction and will smite the waves in the sea. And all the depths of the Nile shall dry up: and the pride of Assyria shall be brought down, and the sceptre of Egypt shall depart. And I will strengthen them in Jehovah; and they shall walk up and down in his name, says Jehovah' (10:6-12).

Visualizing the possibility of the whole of the nation as being once more reunited, God announced that He would make the house of Judah strong and would save the house of Joseph, i.e. Ephraim or Israel. Nearly three centuries earlier, Israel had been deported by the Assyrians (2 Kings 17:6) and just over a century later, Judah had been deported by the Babylonians (2 Kings 24:14-16; 25:11). God had given Israel a bill of

divorce (Isa. 50:1): He treated her as no longer His. But now
His mercy reached out once more to His people and He purposed
to treat them as though He had never rejected them. He would
not only save Israel, but repatriate them. He would bring them
back to cause them to dwell (inferentially in their own land).
It is usually argued that, since the partial restoration from
Babylon, Israel and Judah have been regarded as one nation
with one hope and destiny. Chambers (op. cit., p. 80), for
example, says, 'The prediction of the return of Ephraim in this
chapter has been sometimes cited as evidence that the ten tribes
are' still somewhere existing as a separate community, and as
such are yet to be restored to their own land. But this is an
error. The words of the prophet were fulfilled in the period to
which he refers. Many of the transplanted Ephraimites fell
away from the faith and became absorbed in the heathen by
whom they were surrounded, but many who remained true to
Jehovah, joined their fortunes with those of their brethren of
Judah. Their common calamities softened and, at last, obliterated the old feelings of enmity towards each other. Jerusalem
became again the central point of the whole nation, and while
not a few actually shared in the restoration, others who remained
in exile, yet adhered to the second temple, aided it by their gifts,
and often attended the yearly festivals. Hence all the latter
were comprehended under the term, the *Diaspora* (Jas. 1:1).
In the New Testament there are repeated allusions to the twelve
tribes, conveying the distinct impression that the inhabitants of
Palestine in our Lord's day represented both parts of the nation.'
    Certainly it seems probable that some members of the north-
ern kingdom of Israel returned to the land with the exiles of
Judah. It is also clear that the ten tribes of Israel do not exist as
a distinct and recognizable community today, although again,
members of the ten tribes may well be among those who are
commonly described as Jews. Many theories have been propounded regarding the 'lost ten tribes' and they have been identified with the Nestorians, Afghans, Red Indians, etc. and
British-Israelism claims to have found links with Britain and the
U.S.A., but a positive identification of Israel as a separate body,
distinct from Judah, has not proved possible. Yet there are not
lacking Scriptures which clearly indicate that Israel is to be
restored to her own land and reunited with Judah (e.g. Isa.

27:12; 43:5–7; Ezek. 28:25, 26; 37:16–23; Amos 9:14, 15).
Zechariah plainly envisions the repatriation of the whole of the
twelve tribes, reunited as one rejoicing people. Jehovah's
compassion will reach out to His own and He will hear their
cries. He is 'Jehovah their God and will hear them'.

Lest there should be any doubt, the prophecy stated plainly
that Ephraim or Israel, although still in dispersion, would be
like a mighty man and would exult in jubilant joy. Judah's
future might seem assured, but Ephraim's was equally definite.
Exhilarated as though by wine, they will then rejoice in Jehovah.
The apparently impossible will have become an achieved fact
– and solely through the hand of God. No evanescent joy is theirs,
for another generation, their own children, will see the wonder-
working of Jehovah and will be so stirred by the amazing
happenings that they will share in the general rejoicing.

It is usually maintained that Zech. 10:8–12 forms an explanation of the manner in which the ten tribes will be restored to the
land, but this is open to question and it seems probable that the
verses relate to the whole of the twelve tribes, or 'the house of
Judah' and 'the house of Joseph', visualized now as one company. Obviously there are many of Judah to be regathered as
well as those of Israel. Jehovah announced that He would
personally summon His people from their world-wide dispersion. In Matt. 24:31, however, our Lord disclosed that, at His
coming, His angels would be sent to 'gather together His elect
from the four winds, from one end of heaven to the other'.
The regathering, therefore, will not take place until the return
of Christ to earth.

The summons, described by our Lord as with a trumpet, is
described by Zechariah as the shrill whistle or the piping used
by the apiarist to summon his bees and unite his swarm. Previously God had gathered hostile nations against His people by
'hissing' or whistling for them, and like the countless numbers of
the insect world the messengers of His vengeance had assembled
(Isa. 7:18, 19; 5:26, 27). Then the shrill call was one denoting
impending judgement. Now he would summon His people in
similar fashion, but for their blessing. Since the same word was
used in both cases, there may be a tacit implication that the first
call having achieved its purpose, the second call would be
equally unfailing. Indeed, God explicitly stated that He would

gather them for He had redeemed them. They were to be ransomed, not only from banishment and exile, but from their sins and iniquities. They were His. Moreover, despite all their experiences, they would increase phenomenally, just as they did in Egypt before the exodus.

The people had been scattered, but their disciplinary dispersion had not been for the ultimate loss. Seed was sown by scattering it over the land, not that it might be lost but, on the contrary, that it might produce a far more abundant harvest. Similarly, God's people had been sown among the nations in order that they too might prosper and multiply (see also Hos. 2:23). The time would come when, in their dispersion in far countries, their minds would return to former things and they would remember Jehovah. Their revival and turning to God at His call would be permanent and complete, for their children would be associated with them. The spiritual regeneration barely hinted at in Zechariah is, of course, plainly described in Ezek. 37:14.

Isa. 11:11 declared that Jehovah would recover the remnant of His people a second time from Assyria, Egypt, etc. Zechariah made the same statement – that He would bring them again out of Egypt and gather them out of Assyria (see also Hos. 11:11). Gesenius opines that 'Egypt and Assyria are mentioned here in place of the different countries into which the Jews were scattered.' Moore (op. cit., p. 166) also considers that 'Egypt and Assyria are taken as types of all the lands of their dispersion, the one being the first great oppressor of the chosen people and the other among the last, and the one lying on the north whilst the other lay on the south. Hence they are here taken merely as types of the universal dispersion.' Although, in the past, captives have been carried to both the south and to the lands in the north, they have since been scattered to almost every part of the world, and Moore's suggestion is possibly the only satisfactory explanation. The typical use of the names of Egypt and Assyria would, as Chambers remarks (op. cit., p. 79), be 'neither unnatural nor unusual. Egypt was the first oppressor of the convenant people, and Assyria was the final instrument of overthrowing the ten tribes, and the two terms might well be combined as a general statement of the lands of the dispersion' (cf. Isa. 27:13; 10:24; 11:11, 16; 19:23; 52:4; Hos. 11:11).

On their return to the land, however, they would be allotted

Gilead and Lebanon, i.e. the northern part of Palestine on both sides of the Jordan, previously occupied by the ten tribes. Gilead on the west of the Jordan, was originally occupied by Reuben, Gad and Manasseh: the area from Gilead to the Lebanon range in the north is not very extensive, but was the extent of the territory promised under the various covenants with Israel (Gen. 15:18; Deut. 30:3-5; etc.). But so numerous will the people be that the space will be inadequate to accommodate them (cf. Isa. 49:20, 21).

When Israel made their exodus from Egypt, they were faced with the obstacle of the sea, but the Almighty made a passage for them through the sea (Exod. 14:27-31). Nothing was to prevent their future restoration to the land. God declared that He would pass through the sea of affliction and smite the waves in the sea. The reference is not, of course, to a literal sea; the term is used metaphorically of any obstacle which might confront them. Just as God had opened a passage through the waters in the earlier history of His people, so He would now quash all opposition and remove all obstacles. In their journey into the promised land, Israel passed over the river Jordan dry-shod (Josh. 3:14-17). Similarly (but again only in a metaphorical sense presumably) the river Nile would dry up so that nothing might hinder the course of God's people. The overweening pride of the northern oppressor would be brought down, and the sceptre (or rod) of Egypt, the symbol of Egyptian authority and restraint, would no longer be able to oppress (cf. Isa. 9:4) or to obstruct the people of Israel. Everything would be swept away in that day to give them a clear passage on their return home.

Nor was this the end. As Unger (op. cit., p. 186) pertinently remarks, 'the phenomenal regathering of His people out of their world-wide dispersion and settling them in their own land, at the same time removing every obstacle in the way of their return, is only part of the Divine undertaking for them. In their own land they shall experience a copious outpouring of the Spirit that will enable them to do marvels in God's name.' God declared that He would strengthen them and that they should walk up and down in His name. Barnes sees this as signifying that their whole life and conduct will be in accord with the name of their God, but Baron undoubtedly is more to the point in his assumption that the allusion is rather to their acting as the messengers and representatives of Jehovah dispensing the blessings of Messiah's gospel among the nations. This was God's original purpose for His people, but in a future day, it will be fully realized and Israel will be a missionary nation among the peoples of the earth.

It is patently possible to allegorize the specific promises made to Israel and Judah. The attempt to evacuate these predictions of their literal meaning and to apply them spiritually to the church is poor exegesis and poorer interpretation. Indeed, the concluding words of the chapter, 'says Jehovah', seem to set the Divine seal upon the explicit statements made and to assure their fulfilment.

CHAPTER 17

The Northern Scourge

In view of the spiritual insight he shows and the structural comparisons he makes, David Baron's introductory remarks to Zech. 11 are well worth quoting *in extenso*. He says (op. cit., pp. 375, 376), 'The 11th chapter stands in the same relation to the verbal prophecies which make up the second part of Zechariah, as the 5th does in relation to the first part of the visions. . . . In the first part we have first a series of five visions which in various symbols set forth "the good and comfortable words" of promise concerning restoration, enlargement, and temporal and spiritual blessing which God has yet in store for the land and the people of Israel. But to complete the prophetic forecast of the future, . . . the obverse side of the picture, which sets forth a yet future apostasy and judgement, had to be presented. This is done in the visions of the flying roll and the ephah, in the first of which we hear God's great curse pronounced against sin; and in the second we see its banishment from His own land and presence "to the land of Shinar" – the original place of rebellion and apostasy against God – where it shall meet with its final doom. In the 6th chapter, however, we emerge again from the dark valley of sin and apostasy, and we are shown in the symbolical transaction there set forth how, in spite of it all, Israel's Messiah will yet be crowned, and sit and rule upon His throne, and be a priest upon His throne; and how, not only Israel, but "they that are far off", shall find a place in the glorious temple which He shall build.

'And thus it is also with the second part. First, we have a series of verbal prophecies, which are full of promise of future restoration and blessedness; and then, in order to prevent a carnal misuse of the promises of salvation on the part of the godless majority in the nation, and also as a hint that the full realization of the promises was, from the prophet's point of view, in the yet distant future, we are suddenly in the 10th chapter brought to the precipice of a tremendous gulf of national apostasy and consequent judgement. But even from this deep abyss we shall emerge again in the last three chapters, where Israel's national repentance and mourning over Him whom they have sold for thirty pieces of silver, and "pierced", are depicted for us in inspired language, which reads almost like history instead of prophecy. And the end and blessed issue of Israel's national conversion and reunion with their Messiah will be that "Jehovah will be King over all the earth".'

The comparison is significant. At the same time, it seems almost incredible that apostasy should take place when the promises of God shine so brightly before the gaze of His people.

Zech. 11 is the second section of the first 'burden of the word of Jehovah', and it is concerned primarily with the rejection of the Shepherd, whose coming had been foretold in Zech. 9. The first sub-section of three verses, painting the impending devastation of the land in the imagery of a tremendous storm, form a prelude to what follows. The verses portray in symbolic language the story of the invasion of the land from the north – in the view of some by the Chaldeans, when they captured Jerusalem, destroyed the people and carried away captives to Babylon. But it is more probable that the prophecy looked on to the future rather than back to the past. The Assyrian and Babylonian invasions of an earlier day were past history. It is more likely that what is pictured is the ruthless savagery of Antiochus Epiphanes and the Syrian forces in a later day – and possibly even an invasion which still lies in the future.

'Open your doors, O Lebanon, that the fire may devour your cedars. Wail, fir tree; for the cedar is fallen; because the mighty goodly ones are spoiled. Wail, O you oaks of Bashan; for the impenetrable forest is come down. There is a voice of the wailing of the shepherds; for their glory is spoiled: a voice of the roaring of young lions; for the pride of Jordan is spoiled' (11:1-3).

The 100 miles long Lebanon range of mountains runs parallel to the coast and its western flanks sweep down to the sea, leaving a narrow coastal plain for the cities of Tyre, Sidon, Beirut, etc. The height of its peaks varies from 6,000 to 10,000 feet. Its white limestone and the snow that caps its peaks for much of the year have given it its name (white). Its slopes were covered with forests of gigantic cedars and lower down with an abundance of fir or cypress trees, the lowest being covered with vines. Lions, leopards and other wild beasts found a shelter in its woods. An invasion from the north might well come along the Phoeni- cian littoral on its west.

Apostrophizing the mountain range as though it was a mighty fortress, the prophet called upon Lebanon to throw open its doors to admit the devastation that was threatened. Resistance was pointless, because the doom was inevitable. Then, in startling imagery, he presented the picture of a tempest of unprecedented fury. It tore down the steep mountain paths of Lebanon – open to its tornado-like force – setting the massive cedars on fire with its lightnings and utterly consuming the proud monarchs of the forest. As the conflagration rapidly spread, the prophet dramati- cally declared that the cypresses wailed as they saw the fate of the cedars and realized what would be their own. If the im- penetrable forest of Lebanon had been consumed, the oaks of Bashan howled in fear and despair at their own impending doom.

The Chaldean forces had swept down in such a fashion (Isa. 14:8), Sennacherib of Assyria had threatened to do the same (Isa. 37:24). The enemy had literally felled the cedars of Leb- anon in earlier days and his reckless torch had set fire to the forests of fir and cypress. The picture painted may not relate only to the past: there may be an allusion also to the horrors of a future invasion – evidently far more destructive and far-reach- ing than any which has preceded it – when the hordes of the northern confederation of powers sweep down through Pales- tine to plunder and destroy (Dan. 11:40–45). History has a habit of repeating itself and Biblical prophecies often have more than one fulfilment.

Bashan was located on the east of the river Jordan and ran to the border of the Arabian desert. Davis says, 'It is a broad fertile plateau, of volcanic formation, and well adapted for pasture. It was celebrated for its cattle (Ps. 22:12; Ezek. 39:18; Amos 4:1), and for its breed of sheep (Deut. 32:14). It was known also for its oak trees (Isa. 2:13; Ezek. 27:6; Zech. 11:2). Forests of evergreen oak still survive.' Bashan's forests had been deemed strong and inaccessible, but the fire swept over the oaks of Bashan and consumed them.

The desolating tempest which had wrought such havoc on the highlands now travelled down to the lowlands and from the plateau to the plain. Here there was fresh tragedy and as the fire reached the rich pasture lands, the shepherds were called upon to wail for the loss of their very livelihood. The fields in which they had their sheep and cattle were now scorched and useless. They howled lugubriously as they saw the spoiling of their 'glory' (the pasture lands).

Another howling came from the Jordan valley, for 'the pride of Jordan' (Jer. 12:5; 49:19; 50:44) was also desolated. The banks of the river were fringed with close thickets, a luxuriant jungle of willows, tamarisks, and cane, in which lions made their covert. As the fire swept over the banks of the river and devoured the thick growth, the roaring of fierce young lions was heard, furious at the destruction of both their lairs and their food. The whole of the country was in flames: everything had been destroyed. History apparently records no literal fire or storm so completely devastating as having occurred in the part.

It would be difficult to find a more terrible picture of utter desolation. Whether it is intended to be taken literally or figuratively, the description is of an appalling devastation. Many expositors have attempted to see typology in the mountains and plains, the various trees and the animals but, as Leupold (*Exposition of Zechariah*, p. 206) pertinently remarks, 'A literal interpretation . . . carries us far enough. For surely, if the land is so completely devastated as is here described, all greatness and great men will also have been involved in the universal ruin.' Smith, on the other hand, sees no doubt regarding the interpretation. He says, 'A ruthless army, who knows no pity, who delights in destruction, murder and oppression, is advancing against Judah and Jerusalem. As the vultures gather from afar around the carcass, so the enemy forces are seen gathering about Jerusalem. Since the context refers to the days of Messiah (v. 12), the reference is to the siege and destruction of Jerusalem and the devastation of the entire land by the armies of Rome, A.D. 70 and 71. The Jewish nation will be rejected by the Lord because of its rejection of Him and His Shepherd.'

That no mere natural happening is portrayed is evident from the opening words, 'Open your doors, O Lebanon'. They constitute a command by God to prepare no resistance, but to make way for the destruction that is impending. Plainly what is envisaged is a judgement directed by the Almighty Himself. Human or natural instruments may be employed but the ultimate cause is the will of God – patently in judgement upon a guilty and rebellious people. 'Our God is a consuming fire.' Another writer aptly remarks, 'The agency of God is still exerted as really in the continued existence of the universe, as in its original creation.' He has not abdicated His sovereignty of the universe and none sins against Him with impunity.

Moore is convinced that the reference is to the judgement which fell after the rejection of the Lord Jesus Christ, and consequently applies the scene to the Roman invasion of the first century. He writes (op. cit., p. 171), 'The metaphor describes the storm of invasion, bloodshed and oppression that should roll over Palestine after the glorious Maccabean era, and before the coming of the Messiah. The designation of Lebanon and Bashan belong to the metaphor, and not to the fulfilment, being designed to set forth by the usual course of such storms the track of this tempest, and hence it is not necessary for us to show that any invasions actually came by the way of the Lebanon. The reference is to that desolating storm of civil war that caused the calling in of the Romans, whose legions swept like a whirlwind of steel over the land, and finally prostrated every vestige of independent authority, from the cedar of Lebanon to the lowliest cypress, from the peaceful shepherd to the lionlike spirit that refused to be subdued, and humbled the whole land beneath the mighty power of Rome. It was this state of deep prostration that constituted the dark hour before the dawn, the fulness of time on the arrival of which the great shepherd was to come.'

If this interpretation is accepted, the next section of Zech. 11 furnishes an explanation of the cause of the fearful judgement described in this first section. The crime committed by the people was so heinous and of such a character that the judgement had to fit the crime. Even if the primary fulfilment occurred nineteen centuries ago, however, the description given seems extremely appropriate to the dark period of trouble for the land which still lies ahead. The significance is not entirely exhausted by what has already occurred in the past.

CHAPTER 18

Rejection of the Shepherd

The remainder of Zech. 11 is devoted to the rejection of the Good Shepherd but, for convenience, may perhaps be divided into three sub-sections: (1) the flock of slaughter (vv. 4–7a); (2) the two staves (vv. 7b–14) and (3) the foolish shepherd (vv. 15–17).

'Thus says Jehovah my God, Feed the flock of slaughter; whose buyers slay them and hold themselves not guilty: and they that sell them say, Blessed be Jehovah, for I am rich: and their own shepherds pity them not. For I will no more pity the inhabitants of the land, says Jehovah: but, lo, I will deliver each man into the hand of his neighbour, and into the hand of his king. And they shall smite the land, and out of their hand I will not deliver them. So I fed the flock of slaughter, verily the poor of the flock' (11:4–7a).

As happened not infrequently in the ministry of the prophets (e.g. Ezek. 4:1–17; 5:1–4), Zechariah was called upon by Jehovah to enact a parable in order that the Divine message might be conveyed to the people. He was directed to act in the capacity of the shepherd of a flock. Dressed in the appropriate garb and carrying the two staves which a shepherd would normally carry, he assumed the charge of the flock. In his capacity of a shepherd, he was, of course, representing the line of true shepherds which culminated in the Good Shepherd our Lord Jesus Chtist. It is occasionally suggested that the parable was merely an inward vision and not an actual occurrence, but there is no sound reason for treating it as anything else than a genuine commission intended to be acted out before his contemporaries.

He was to 'feed' or 'shepherd' the flock. The word used implies far more than mere feeding and it includes the concept of the full range of the shepherd's duties – feeding, leading, guiding, nursing, protecting, healing (cf. Ps. 23:1–6). The sheep he was to care for were termed 'the flock of slaughter' (cf. Ps. 44:22; Jer. 50:6, 7, 17), i.e. those destined to be butchered. The reference was, of course, to the prophet's own people, and it is usually suggested that the description appropriately delineated, by inference, the conditions at the time of the Roman siege and capture of Jerusalem. It seemed then as if nothing could save the Jews from their fate and, in fact, over 1,100,000 Jews perished at the fall of Jerusalem and another half a million during the war and the siege. They certainly seemed to be a flock for slaughter. It is questionable, however, whether the Romans alone can be regarded as the slaughterers in view of the following verse, since it was the buyers or possessors who slew the sheep.

The flock had been treated as mere chattels, to be bought or sold without compunction and without any consideration for the animals themselves. Those who bought or possessed them slew the sheep without any sense of wrongdoing, or guilt. Barnes (op. cit., p. 85) considers that 'the allusion is to abuse of justice; the "buyers" are the oppressors who give bribes; "they that sell them" are the judges who accept the bribes'. Moore (op. cit., p. 173) maintains that 'by the buyers and sellers are meant the Romans, who used the Jews, as they did all their conquests, as mere merchandise, making from them the greatest possible gain for themselves'. As already suggested, this does not seem completely tenable, however, in view of the words attributed to the sellers in the same verse. E. Henderson (*The Book of the Minor Prophets*, p. 420) suggests more consistently that 'by the buyers and sellers of the Jewish people, we are not to understand the Romans, but their own unprincipled teachers and rulers'.

Those who sold the sheep turned complacently to Jehovah and blessed Him for the profit made on the sale and for the fact that they were becoming rich. They had the barefaced hypocrisy to thank God for the ill-gotten wealth derived from unmercifully fleecing the sheep and then selling it. The fact that they attributed their wealth to Jehovah appears a clear indication that those alluded to were themselves Jews rather that Romans, since the latter would never have given even a nominal recognition to Jehovah.

Pathetically the prophecy stated that 'their own shepherds pity them not'. The shepherds are deemed by most expositors to be 'the civil and ecclesiastical rulers of the Jews', and it is claimed that what is depicted is the 'extortion and treachery in which the Pharisee and Sadducee wrung from the unhappy people what the Roman had failed to extort, and both combined thus in spite of their mutual hate in this work of shameless robbery'. If the period referred to prophetically was the first century A.D., the avaricious exploitation of Jew by fellow-Jew implied in Zechariah was demonstrated to the full. The tragedy was that this ruthless exploitation was Divinely permitted as a means of punishment. As Moore remarks (op. cit., p. 173), 'although once they who oppressed the covenant people would be guilty and so treated by God, now the sins of the people were such that these oppressions were righteous punishments, and their agents, therefore, not guilty for the execution itself, however they might be for the mode and motives with which they performed it'.

Even more tragic was that God Himself had no more pity for the inhabitants of the land. Their experiences were no more than they deserved. When they rejected the Messiah and cast Him out, they exposed themselves to the pitiless wrath of the God against whom they had sinned (cf. Ezek. 8:18). Their wickedness was of such a character as to be completely intolerable to Him, and their misery was the direct result of their conduct. They were delivered, every man into the hand of his neighbour and into the hand of his king. They chose a thief and a murderer in preference to Christ, and God surrendered them to their fate. Civil war and internal discord raised the hand of Jew against Jew. Factions bitterly opposed one another in bloody strife. In their rejection of Christ, they had cried, 'We have no king but Caesar' (John 19:15). God delivered them into the hand of the one whom they acknowledged, and the Romans destroyed their city and temple. As the prophecy foretold, the land itself suffered. In the words of Zechariah it was to be beaten to pieces: in fact, it was laid completely waste. There was no help and no hope, for the God of Israel had declared that He would not deliver His people. Accordingly, they paid the price of their crimes in bloodshed and death. Their protection had been withdrawn and they were exposed to the merciless assaults of the heathen.

Nevertheless, even in that dark hour of Israel's extremity, there were still some who retained their loyalty to Jehovah. They had been left untended and uncared for by the shepherds who should have cared for them, and had been cruelly treated and oppressed by those who had assumed authority. God aptly termed them the poor of the flock, although one translator renders the phrase, 'the most miserable of sheep'. But that faithful remnant were not lost to the eyes of the Great Shepherd, and on His behalf, Zechariah declares that he shepherded the poor of the flock, who also seemed destined for slaughter. He deemed it his duty to fulfil the terms of his appointment and to afford them his special care.

A shepherd normally carried a strong stick or club, with which to beat off any wild beasts who sought to attack the flock, and also a crooked staff to facilitate the retrieving of sheep which had fallen into difficult places and could not recover themselves. The psalmist referred to these as the Lord's rod and staff (Ps. 23:4). It is with these and with the rejection of the shepherd that the next sub-section is primarily occupied.

'And I took unto me two staves; the one I called Beauty, and the other I called Bands. And I fed the flock. Three shepherds also I cut off in one month, for my soul was weary of them, and their soul also loathed me. Then said I, I will not feed you: that that is dying, let it die; and that which is being cut off, let it be cut off; and let the rest eat every one the flesh of his fellow. And I took my staff, Beauty, and cut it asunder, that I might break my covenant which I had made with all the peoples. And it was broken in that day. And so the poor of the flock that gave heed to me certainly knew that it was the word of Jehovah. And I said to them, If it be good in your eyes, give me my wages; and if not, forbear. So they weighed for my wages thirty pieces of silver. And Jehovah said to me, Throw it to the potter: the goodly price at which I was valued by them. And I took the thirty pieces of silver and threw them into the house of Jehovah to the potter. Then I cut asunder my other staff, Bands, that I might break the brotherhood between Judah and Israel' (11: 7b–14).

Zechariah took the usual two staves of the shepherd and named one Beauty (or grace) and the other Bands (or union). They were indicative of the Divine purposes for Israel and Judah in the Good Shepherd. He came to establish peace and to display grace and to reunite completely the peoples of the twelve tribes. So equipped the prophet cared for the flock.

Then Jehovah suddenly announced that He would cut off three shepherds in one month. He had become impatient with them and a mutual antipathy had developed, for they, on their part, loathed or abhorred Him. There has been a great variety of interpretations of the three shepherds. Ewald suggested that the reference was to the last three kings of Israel, viz. Zechariah, Shallum and Menahem (2 Kings 15:8–17). Marti and others saw in them the high priests, Lysimachus, Jason and Menelaus; Sellin substituted for these the names of Simon, Menelaus and Lysimachus. Perowne put the alternative of Antiochus Epiphanes, Antiochus Eupator, and Demetrius I, in the times of the Maccabees. The consensus of opinion, however, is that it was none of the many persons whose names have been suggested, but the three offices of king, priest and prophet. As one writer points out, 'These three classes are mentioned together in Jer. 2:8, 18 as perverters of the nation and causers of its destruction.' These consequently were to suffer.

They were to be cut off (i.e. disavowed rather than destroyed) 'in one month'. It is not possible to identify a literal period of thirty days in which what was prophesied occurred, and the import seems rather to be a short period than a specific time. Unger considers that it was 'the period of culminating unbelief just before the national leaders crucified our Lord and thus sealed the fate of the Jewish state'.

The prediction of Zechariah that the leaders would be disavowed by God because He had lost patience with them is extremely pertinent to the events subsequent to the crucifixion of Christ. He had grown weary of their perverse impenitence which culminated in their rejection of His Son, but it was equally true that they had no real desire for Him. As Smith says, 'Their soul abhorred Him. They thought Christ their political liberator. When He taught them the true nature of His kingdom, they abhorred Him and turned away in disgust and hate. . . . They rejected Christ as Messiah. Finally they were rejected as a nation by God and never again as a nation had their own divinely appointed kings, priests and prophets.'

In the light of what had happened, the shepherd declared that he would no longer feed the flock. His care of them would be withdrawn and he would abandon them to their fate. He would not intervene to save them. Those who were dying would be left to die without help or sympathy. The scattered or straying would be left to follow their wayward desires and, in all probability fall into pits or crevices or be lost on the hillside: no one would seek them. The rest would be left to devour one another. The three forms of calamity mentioned, as Chambers points out, are death by natural causes, plague or famine; violence at the hand of foreign foe; and intestine discord. The words were evidently applicable particularly to the remnant who escaped from the destruction of Jerusalem (cf. Jer. 44:27). Many would be destroyed by the Romans, but the country would be torn by dissension and domestic strife, various opposing factions bitterly quarrelling and attacking one another and thereby weakening the strength of their own country. Instead of pacifying his sheep and healing their wounds and supplying their needs, the shepherd surrendered them to the cruelty and oppression of their foes. This was certainly evidenced after the fall of the city and the temple.

Then the shepherd took his staff, Beauty, and deliberately broke it in pieces before the eyes of the people and declared that God had broken the covenant which He had made with the nations (cf. Hos. 2:18). The latter possibly referred to the restraint laid upon the nations that Israel might be safeguarded. Now, that restraint was to be removed and the grace shown to God's people was to be ended. 'This staff,' says Barnes (op. cit., p. 86), 'stands for all the institutions which Jehovah gave to Judah for advantage – the kingdom, the priesthood, the temple with its services, etc. All were broken.' The covenant with the peoples is sometimes said to relate to the twelve tribes and not to other nations. (The word used is *ammim*, peoples, and not *goyim*, nations or Gentiles. The word *ammim* is used for the tribes of Israel in Deut. 33:3; Hos. 10:14, etc.) Whatever interpretation is placed upon the details, the broad significance is clear. For their rejection of His Son, God will give up His people to a righteous retribution and will no longer be known as their defender and protector. When the staff was broken, the 'poor of the flock', who had retained their trust in God through difficult circumstances would acknowledge that all these events were the fulfilment of God's word.

Completely abandoning his office of shepherd, Zechariah (clearly under Divine direction) asked for the wages due to him but, at the same time, indicated his indifference to the reaction of the owners of the flock. 'If it be good . . . and if not forbear.' Chambers (op. cit., p. 85) saw in the words an implied final appeal to all of the people, 'the form of the inquiry, which arises simply to ascertain whether they are willing to acknowledge and appreciate his pastoral care, shows that it must be addressed to the whole flock'. On the other hand, the words emphasize the mutual aversion which now existed between the shepherd and the flock.

In reply to the shepherd's request, the people meticulously weighed out thirty pieces of silver as a suitable measure of reward. Their action could scarcely have been more insulting. Thirty pieces of silver was the amount stipulated by the law as the payment to be made in respect of a slave gored by an ox (Exod. 21:32). Such was their estimation of the value of the faithful service of the shepherd. In the New Testament counterpart of Zechariah's prophetic allegory, the people paid the same amount of thirty pieces of silver to the traitor Judas for his betrayal of his Master. So contemptuous were they in their evaluation of His worth.

Jehovah viewed the insult paid to His servant as an insult paid to Him personally. Thirty shekels was the wage of one of the lower grades of workers and, in Eccles. 38:29 ff. potters were included in manual workers who were not 'sought for in the council of the people'. A magnificent price, God ironically termed it, and directed the prophet to throw it to the potter. 'Throw it to the potter' was a proverbial phrase, contemptuous of the worth of the article concerned, and comparable with our own phrase, 'Throw it to the dogs.' Zechariah obeyed the Divine instruction and threw the silver to the potter in Jehovah's house. Köhler says, 'The sum is just large enough to pay a potter for the pitchers and pots which he furnishes, and which are thought of so little value that men are easily comforted for the breaking of any by the thought that others can be readily obtained in their stead.' This does not explain, however, the contemptuous spurning of the sum expressed in the command to cast or throw it to the potter.

Hengstenberg argues from Jer. 18:2; 19:2 that a potter was employed in the temple, whose workshop was in the valley of Hinnom, because the most suitable clay was found there. The valley was deemed an unclean place because of the idolatrous worship of Moloch formerly carried out there, and because of the defilement of it by Josiah with carrion, bones, etc. (2 Kings 23:10). He claims that the throwing of the thirty pieces of silver to the potter (whose workshop and himself were unclean because of their location) was simply a renewal of the symbol of the smashing of the potter's vessel in Jer. 19:10, 11 and a fresh pledge of God's purpose to punish. Ingenious although his theory is, there is no evidence of a special potter associated with the temple nor of a potter's workshop in Hinnom.

When Judas Iscariot repented of his treachery, he flung down in the temple the thirty pieces of silver which he had received as the blood money. Since dishonourable money could not remain in the temple (Deut. 23:18, 19), and could not be put into the treasury, the priests used it to purchase 'the potter's field, to bury strangers in' (Matt. 27:3-7). Commenting on the events, the Evangelist added, 'Then was fulfilled that which was spoken by Jeremiah the prophet, saying, And they took the thirty pieces of silver, the price of him that was valued, whom they of the children of Israel did value, and gave them for the potter's field, as the Lord appointed me' (Matt. 27:9, 10). There is no Biblical record of Jeremiah having said this and the story seems to find its closest parallel in Zech. 11:12, 13. In a note in *The Harvester*, Prof. F. F. Bruce suggests, as a possible explanation 'that in the source from which the Evangelist drew the quotation, Zech. 11:13 was combined with a quotation or quotations from Jeremiah (whether Jer. 18:2, 3 along with 32:6-15, or Jer. 19:1-13, or some other passage), and that the earlier of the two prophets alone was mentioned by name. You have something similar in Mark 1:2, 3 (R.V., etc.), where the words "As it is written in Isaiah the prophet", introduce two quotations, the former of which is from Malachi and only the latter from Isaiah. Some have emphasized that the prophecy quoted in Matt. 27:9 is there said to have been *spoken*, not *written*, by Jeremiah; but "that which was spoken" is Matthew's regular wording in introducing his "formula-quotations", without any distinction between speaking and writing (see e.g. Matt. 2:17; 4:14; 8:17; 12:17).'

Zechariah says nothing about the purchase of a field, but Jeremiah, who says nothing about the betrayal, states that

Jehovah appointed him to buy a field (Jer. 32:6–8) as a solemn
guarantee by God that fields and vineyards would again be
bought and sold in the land. Jeremiah had regarded that as
impossible, but God assured him that nothing was too hard for
Him. The potter's field would not have been purchased by the
priests if the threefold divine assurance had not been fulfilled
(Jer. 32:15, 43 f.). This potter's field was one of the fields God
had in mind when He spoke to Jeremiah. On the other
hand, Jeremiah says nothing of another circumstance closely
connected with the purchase of the potter's field, viz. that it was
to be bought for the thirty pieces of silver, the price of Him that
was valued, nor that this money would be cast into the temple.
These details were added by Zechariah. Matthew combines
both prophecies and names Jeremiah because he was the major
prophet and had foretold what Matthew particularly intended
to stress, the purchase of the field (see also A. Edersheim's
Life and Times of Jesus the Messiah, pp. 573–6).

Then Zechariah broke in pieces his other staff, Bands, to
signify the breaking of the brotherhood between Judah and
Israel. The rupture between the shepherd and the flock inevitably involved the end of fraternal unity as well. Unger (op. cit.,
pp. 201, 202) writes, 'The prediction made here involves the
utter breaking up of those social and religious ties that had
always united the people of Israel into a solidly knit-together
people. This fearful dissolution of their own national solidarity
was occasioned largely by the internal dissensions brought about
by the conflicting parties which prevailed among them, which
at the last pitilessly pitted brother against brother, and was
more cruel and destructive than the suffering occasioned by the
besieging Romans. . . . God would no longer interpose to check
disunifying factors.'

The good shepherd having been rejected, the worthless shepherd was now presented in his place.

'And Jehovah said to me, Take to you yet the equipment of a
foolish shepherd. For, lo, I will raise up a shepherd in the land,
who will not visit those that are cut off, neither will seek the
scattered, nor heal that which is wounded, nor feed that which
stands firm. But he will eat the flesh of the fat sheep, and tear
their hoofs in pieces. Woe to the worthless shepherd who forsakes
the flock! The sword shall be upon his arm, and upon his right

eye: his arm shall be utterly withered and his right eye shall be utterly blinded' (11:15-17).

Zechariah was called upon to enact another parable before the people. Once again he took the shepherd's equipment – presumably rod, crook, bag, pipe and knife – and now acted the part of an unfaithful shepherd. As such, he was typical of another shepherd who was to be raised up in the land, who would callously ignore the needs of the flock and his responsibilities to them, and would instead show an insatiate rapacity and gluttonous desire for gain. Commentators have seen in this foolish shepherd a picture of Pekah, Hosea, Menahem, Zedekiah, Herod, the Romans, etc., but Chambers is possibly more to the point when he interprets him as 'the ruling power in whomsoever vested'. It was the duty of the ruler to care for his subjects; he was their shepherd. A good ruler was concerned about the welfare of his people. A bad ruler offered no care or protection and was absorbed only by his own interests. The foolish shepherd, of whom Zechariah was symbolical, would not visit or search for the wandering sheep who had strayed from the flock and who might well be in danger. He would not solicitously seek the young who might need special care. He would be indifferent to the needs of the wounded and enfeebled. He would not provide food for the robust, who stood firmly when the weakling fell (cf. Ezek. 34:4-6). In blatant unconcern, he would pay no regard for their need, but instead would display insensate and diabolical greed and aggressive gluttony. Like a voracious beast, he would feast upon the plump animals instead of nourishing and feeding them, and would even tear their hoofs to pieces to extract any goodness for himself.

Chambers sees in the imagery a representation of the suffering of Judea at the hands of the Roman Empire at and after the siege of Jerusalem. He writes (op. cit., p. 88), 'The ruin of the place and the people was overwhelming. Scarce any siege in the history of the world was attended with such cruelties and horrors as preceded and followed the fall of Jerusalem. There was a deliberate and energetic effort to exterminate the race. The whole power of the Roman Empire was brought to bear upon this one province. . . . And the subsequent history of the Jews for many centuries illustrated in the same manner the symbol of Zechariah. Their rulers were evil shepherds, mock shepherds. Giving nothing, they exacted everything. They taxed, they pillaged, they oppressed, they insulted, habitually and on principle. The Jew was an outcast without any right, and when tolerated it was only as a sponge to be squeezed when it was full.' Our Lord declared that He was the good shepherd, but that the hireling would flee from danger and leave the sheep to their fate (John 10:11–14). The good shepherd was rejected, but 'another shall come in his own name', He said, 'him you will receive' (John 5:43). When His people yielded Him up, they cried, 'His blood be on us and on our children' (Matt. 27:25). They suffered for their self-appointed malediction four decades later but they have continued to suffer through the centuries. Although there have been many precursors, the false shepherd, who will come in his own name, has not yet appeared, but when this Antichrist appears, the Jews will receive him to their suffering and loss.

'Woe to the worthless shepherd,' said Jehovah. It is said that the words were a proverbial taunt by shepherds against an incompetent or unworthy fellow-shepherd, but in this case it was the pronouncement of judgement too. The one who had so shamefully neglected his charge and abused the flock was to be punished. The sword would smite his arm and his right eye: his arm would wither and his eye would be blinded. His eye should have watched over the sheep, and his arm should have protected them. His fate was, therefore, a fitting one. Chambers comments (op. cit., p. 88), 'The worthless shepherds, who battened like vultures on the wretched flock of Judea, the haughty Romans who inflicted the divine judgements upon the apostate and incorrigible nation, were themselves in turn exposed to a righteous retribution.' The threatened judgement did, of course, actually occur in history. 'Rome,' says Moore (op. cit., p. 185), 'like some old lion who had ravaged for many years, when his eye grew dim and his arm grew weak, lay down to die. And it was precisely then that, in addition to the internal feebleness, there came upon them, from the forests of the north, the sword, and thus were literally fulfilled the terms of this passage.' Rev. 19: 20 reveals that another, the worthless shepherd, of whom the others were all typical, will one day also meet with his fate at the hand of Christ. Zech. 11:17 is to have more than one fulfilment.

CHAPTER 19

Deliverance and Repentance

The first 'burden of the word of Jehovah' (chapters 9 to 11) is concerned primarily with the first advent of the Messiah, culminating in His rejection as the good shepherd and the nation's acceptance of Antichrist, the worthless shepherd. The long parenthesis between these two events, during which God has been calling out the church, is not indicated in Zechariah. A hint that a hiatus would take place was given in Dan. 9:26, but again no clear statement was given respecting it (see *The Climax of the Ages*, by F. A. Tatford).

The second 'burden of the word of Jehovah' (chapters 12 to 14) is concerned principally with the second advent of the Messiah and the effect of His return upon the people and the land. Like the first burden, it is divided into two parts, chapters 12 and 13, dealing with the deliverance and conversion of Israel, and the second part, chapter 14, dealing with Messiah's advent in glory and power. Sixteen times in the three chapters the phrase 'in that day' occurs (12:3, 4, 6, 8, 9, 11; 13:1, 2, 4; 14:4, 6, 8, 9, 13, 20, 21). It seems clear that the reference is to 'the day of Jehovah', in which the judgements of God will be poured out and the unparalleled troubles of the great tribulation will be experienced until the climax is reached in the return of the Lord Jesus Christ to earth. A comparison of the occurrences of the phrase show that it has an eschatological significance.

The first sub-section (12:1-9) describes the future siege of Jerusalem in the most graphic manner.

'The burden of the word of Jehovah concerning Israel. Says Jehovah, who stretches forth the heavens, and lays the foundation of the earth, and forms the spirit of man within him, I will make Jerusalem a bowl of reeling to all the peoples round about. And upon Judah also shall there be affliction in the siege against Jerusalem. And in that day will I make Jerusalem a burdensome stone for all the peoples: all that burden themselves with it shall tear themselves to pieces, though all the nations of the earth be gathered together against it. In that day, says Jehovah, I will smite every horse with terror, and his rider with madness. And I will open my eyes upon the house of Judah, and will smite every horse of the peoples with blindness. And the chieftains of Judah shall say in their breast, The inhabitants of Jerusalem are my strength in Jehovah of hosts their God. In that day will I make the chieftains of Judah like a pot of fire among the wood, and like a torch of fire among sheaves; and they shall devour all the peoples round about, on the right hand and on the left. And Jerusalem shall be inhabited again in her own place, even in Jerusalem. Jehovah shall also save the tents of Judah first, that the glory of the house of David and the glory of the inhabitants of Jerusalem might not be magnified above Judah. In that day shall Jehovah defend the inhabitants of Jerusalem. And he that is feeble among them at that day shall be as David; and the house of David shall be as God, as the angel of Jehovah before them. And it shall come to pass in that day, that I will seek to destroy all the nations that come against Jerusalem' (12:1–9).

The second burden is stated to be concerning Israel, although the details which follow relate to Judah, Jersusalem and the royal house. The view is usually taken that the name is used here in a religious, and not in a political, sense and that it relates to Judah, Jerusalem and such members of the northern kingdom as had associated themselves with Judah.

God declared that He who spoke stretches forth the heavens, lays the foundation of the earth, and forms the spirit of man within him. The heavens are sometimes described in the Old Testament as though they were a curtain (Ps. 104:2) and at other times as though they were a metal plate or firmament (Gen. 1:6). In this case, the analogy of the curtain was employed. It is significant that the verbs used imply a continued action and not a completed event. As Moore (op. cit., p. 189) says, 'The Bible is ignorant of that philosophy which teaches that God has created the universe and wound up its machinery like a clock and then left it to run on by its own inherent energies. From moment to moment He is exerting His power in maintaining the movements of visible things.' 'Every day,' says Hengstenberg, 'He spreads out the heavens, every day He lays the foundation of the earth, which, if it were not upheld by His power, would wander from its orbit and fall into ruin.' Again, the reference to the forming or fashioning of man's spirit does not as Keil remarks, refer merely 'to the creation of the spirits or souls of men once for all, but denotes the continuous creative formation and guidance of the human spirit by the Spirit of God'. It is the mighty omnipotent and omniscient God who utters the burden.

Immediately prior to Christ's return to earth, it is evident that there will be an invasion of the land of Israel, and Zech. 12 pictures all nations gathering against Jerusalem. The prophet gives no clue to the identity of the nations concerned, but Dan. 11 indicates that attacks upon the land will come from both the south and the north. The treaty mentioned in Dan. 9:27 will presumably cause an intervention from the west. In addition, Rev. 16 implies that there will also be an invasion from the east. The circumstances and period seem to be identical with those in chapter 14:2, except that in the latter case, God states that He has gathered the nations against Jerusalem, whereas the earlier reference implies that they will gather of their own volition.

The gathered nations will reach out to seize the city and to take possession of all its treasures. Zechariah portrays the city as a bowl of wine which they eagerly quaff. But Jehovah has converted the contents into an intoxicating draught, which causes them to reel and stagger like a drunken man, confused and discomfited (cf. Isa. 51:22, 23; Ps. 75:8). The word cup or bowl, which is used, was also employed of the bowl in which the blood of the paschal lamb was caught (Exod. 12:22), but it has been argued that the word *saph* means 'threshold' and not 'cup' and that what was envisaged was the quaking threshold of the city, its tremors being due to an earthquake which disturbed the whole area. This, of course, would be in agreement with Zech. 14:4.

The grammatical construction of the latter part of verse 2 is difficult and it has been deduced from the literal rendering, 'and also upon Judah shall be in the siege against Jerusalem', that Judah will ally herself with the hostile forces attacking the metropolis. But, as Keil observes, 'There is no indication whatever of Judah's having made common cause with the enemy against Jerusalem; on the contrary, Judah and Jerusalem stand together in opposition to the nations, and the princes of Judah have strength in the inhabitants of Jerusalem (v. 5), and destroy the enemy to save Jerusalem (v. 6).' The rendering we have given, 'and upon Judah also shall there be affliction in the siege against Jerusalem', seems more appropriate than the A.V. and others.

It was the custom for athletes to develop their strength by lifting and throwing heavy stones. God declared that He would make Jerusalem a burdensome stone, which the nations would essay to lift, only to find it too heavy to handle. In consequence, the stone would slip and grievously injure those who thought it was an easy burden to hold. They would be badly wounded. Some expositors have seen in the illustration a reference to the heavy mortality of labourers engaged in the transport of huge stones for the building or embellishing of cities, and the implication that those who attempted to move Jerusalem would also suffer a heavy toll. The phrase 'tear themselves to pieces' (A.V. 'be cut in pieces') is used in Lev. 21:5 in regard to cuttings being made in the flesh in token of mourning. The metaphorical lacerations of Zech. 12:3 would cause mourning and grievous disappointment.

Furthermore, Jehovah declared that He would smite the horses of the attackers with terror and blindness and afflict the riders with insanity. One writer dramatically depicts the scene. 'The terrified horses of the cavalry of the assembled hosts, being thus suddenly smitten with bewilderment or terror, are represented as unable any longer to be guided by bit and bridle. The riders in their madness are described as unable to manage their steeds, while the steeds themselves are portrayed as struck with blindness, and therefore unable to escape from the dangers around them. And while the enemies of God's people will find themselves in such straits at the very moment when they imagined that they had gained the victory and, instead of chasing the vanquished Jews in headlong flight, they themselves are described as rushing upon destruction.' All the power of the enemy will be nullified by the Divine action, and a complete state of panic will be created. Centuries earlier, Deut. 28:28 detailed such an affliction as the judgement of God, and it would perhaps be unwise to discount the picture as entirely metaphorical rather than literal.

At the critical time, Jehovah would 'open His eyes' upon the house of Judah, i.e. He would show favour to Judah (cf. Gen.

44:21). What had happened was for their deliverance. The chieftains (or chiliarchs, i.e. rulers over a thousand) of Judah, with deep conviction, would acknowledge Jerusalem as their bulwark. The city was their stronghold, but the strength of the city was in God.

In startling similes, Jehovah then declared that He would make the chieftains (or chiliarchs) of Judah like a pot of fire among wood and a torch of fire among sheaves, destroying everything on every side. The pot of fire was a chafing pan full of burning coals set among faggots (1 Sam. 2:14) and the torch of fire was literally a flaming torch which would soon set fire to the sheaves of corn and completely devastate everything in sight. In such fashion would Judah's chieftains (and inferentially Judah as a whole) completely destroy the Gentile nations gathered against them.

In consequence of the Divine interposition and the exploits inspired by God, Jerusalem would be inhabited again in its own place. The implication is that the city had been affected by the attacks made upon it and possibly even partially destroyed (see Zech. 14:2). In such a case, the city might be rebuilt on a different site or upon the foundations of the old city, in which case all traces of the damage done would be concealed. It was the latter that was envisaged. Jerusalem would rise again on the same site ('in her own place, even in Jerusalem') and the metropolis would again be fully populated – in part, by some who may have fled before the oncoming forces.

Deliverance would come first to the country-dwellers before it came to Jerusalem, however, since they were relatively defence-less as compared with the occupants of the fortified city. The latter would have no cause for boasting above the people of Judah. Each would have his due share of honour. Perowne (op. cit., p. 131) says that 'the meaning seems to be that the besiegers shall reel back like drunken men from the walls of Jerusalem (v. 2), smitten with panic by God (v. 4); the first to fall upon them and put them to the sword shall be, not the inhabitants of the besieged city by sallying forth from its walls, though they by their gallant and successful defence had rightly been regarded as the bulwark of the whole land (v. 5), but the inhabitants of the open country, who shall have the honour of consuming their adversaries (v. 6), and so of saving themselves and then the capital, which as the result of their prowess shall be completely delivered'. This was, of course, a complete reversal of what would normally happen. In ordinary warfare, the dwellers in the villages and open country suffer first, but in this instance, the city will be besieged and it is the villagers and countrymen who will come to the aid of the beleaguered garrison.

On the other hand, God declared that the inhabitants of Jerusalem in that day, would be under His protection. He would be their shield and no one could, therefore, destroy the city or the population. The feeble weakling (the same word as in 1 Sam. 2:4) would be as valiant as David, the great hero of Jewish history. The house of David in turn would be as God, as the angel of Jehovah. The significance of the angel of Jehovah has already been discussed, and the plain indication is that 'the royal family shall lead the nation no less worthily than the angel of Jehovah did in old time'.

Again, in that day, Jehovah declared that He would seek to destroy all the nations that came against Jerusalem. Rashi renders this last clause of the sub-section, 'I will make research as to destroying them and I will make minute inquiry into their guilt.' There is no suggestion of Divine inability or even of possible change of mind. There was to be a full investigation and the appropriate punishment would be meted out and it would be in proportion to the transgressions committed.

The second sub-section of Zech. 12 relates the effect of the vision of Messiah upon the people.

'And I will pour upon the house of David, and upon the inhabitants of Jerusalem, the spirit of grace and of supplication. And they shall look to me whom they have pierced, and they shall mourn for him, as one mourns for his only son, and shall be in bitterness for him, as one who is in bitterness for his firstborn. In that day shall there be a great mourning in Jerusalem, as the mourning of Hadadrimmon in the valley of Megiddon. And the land shall mourn, every family apart; the family of the house of David apart, and their wives apart; the family of the house of Nathan apart, and their wives apart; the family of the house of Shimei apart, and their wives apart; all the families that remain, every family apart, and their wives apart' (12:10–14).

The miraculous deliverance of Judah and Jerusalem, described in the first nine verses of the chapter, cannot be separated from the repentance and conversion of the people, detailed in the closing verses. Whenever there is a turning to God, however slight the inclination of heart towards Him, God turns in response to the soul's desire. It may perhaps be assumed that the Divine interposition on behalf of the beleaguered city and the invaded country is not unconnected with the spiritual attitude of the people. But their awakening and spiritual revival in the truest and fullest sense can only spring out of their contrition and heartfelt penitence for their sin and particularly for the blackest crime of deicide of which the nation was culpable. The chapter indicates that that will happen coincidentally with a copious spiritual effusion and a revelation of the Messiah who had been pierced.

The 'spirit of grace and of supplication' will be poured out upon the house of David and the inhabitants of Jerusalem, i.e. not merely the effusion of the Holy Spirit promised in Joel 2:28, but the creation by His power of a spiritual attitude in which grace is able to operate and the soul bows down before its Maker. The outpouring occurs first upon the house of David, clearly implying that descendants of the royal line occupy the place of rule and leadership of the nation, but the inhabitants of the city are also the recipients.

The consequence of this work of the Holy Spirit in the individuals is that a revelation is made of the Messiah – 'they shall look to me whom they have pierced'. It has been thought that, in view of the next clause, the word 'me' in the Massoretic text is a scribal error for 'him', but almost all the mss. and versions support the word 'me'. To the Christian, there can be no question as to the identity of the Person thus described: it is obviously the Lord Jesus Christ. Rabbi Solomon Bar Isaac, or Rashi, the Jewish commentator, rendered the clause, 'And they (i.e. the house of David and the inhabitants of Jerusalem) shall look up to Me because of Him whom they (i.e. the nations which come against Jerusalem) have pierced.' Aben Ezra, however, translated it, 'All the heathen shall look to me to see what I shall do to those who pierced Messiah, the son of Joseph.' Abarband says, 'It is more correct to interpret the passage of Messiah, the son of Joseph . . . for he shall be a mighty man of valour of the

tribe of Joseph, and shall at first be captain of the Lord's host in
that war (namely against Gog and Magog), but in that war
shall die.' The rabbis fairly generally apply the passage to
Messiah ben Joseph, who was to suffer and die, and not Messiah
ben David, who was to reign in power and glory – a distinction
invented by themselves. When the revelation of the crucified
Messiah is made and the people realize that He is the One whom
their forefathers pierced – or delivered up to be crucified – the
whole nation will mourn for Him. Then will the language of
Isa. 53 become pertinent to those for whom it was primarily
intended. The rejection of Christ was a crowning act of con-
tumacy and now they will deem it such for themselves.

As they realize the enormity of their guilt, they will give
themselves to mourning unparalleled in the nation's history.
The bitterness of remorse and regret will sweep over them as
their eyes are opened to a realization of the Person who was
crucified at Calvary, and their bitterness will be comparable to
that felt by the mourner for an only son. They will lament for
Him as for a first-born son. Unger says (op. cit., pp. 215–16),
'Mourning for an only son is represented in the Old Testament
as the acme of sorrow that may invade a home (Amos 8:10), and
the death-wail over the first-born became proverbial in Israel
from the time of the tenth plague in Egypt and the Exodus
(Exod. 11:6).'

The mourning in Jerusalem is compared with that of Hadadrimmon in the valley of Megiddo. Hadadrimmon was a city
near Jezreel and was the spot at which Josiah was slain by
Pharaoh-Necho in 609 B.C. (1 Kings 23:9; 2 Chron. 35:22).
'He was the first king of Judah,' says Smith, 'to fall in battle and
leave his country at the mercy of foreign conquerors. His death
was a catastrophic loss for Judah, for with him passed away the
last bulwark against the flood of wickedness which now swept
through the land and carried it to its destruction.' The king was
only thirty-nine and the nation's grief was deep and universal.
An official decree appointed an annual day of mourning in
memory of the event, and the elegies composed on him by
Jeremiah were still sung many years after. If the lamentations
then were widespread, they were but typical of those in which
the nation is yet to indulge.

Every family was to mourn separately and those of David,

Nathan, Levi and Shimei were specifically named, the first two
being representative of the royal house and the other two of the
priestly tribe. Pusey writes, 'The sorrow shall be universal but also
individual, the whole land, and that family by family; the royal
family in the direct line of its kings, and in a branch from Nathan,
a son of David and whole brother of Solomon (1 Chron 3:5),
which was continued on in private life, yet was still to be an
ancestral line of Jesus (Luke 3:31); in like way the main priestly
family from Levi, and a subordinate line from a grandson of
Levi, the family of Shimei (Num. 3:21); and all the remaining
families, each with their separate sorrow.' Husbands and wives
would mourn separately from each other – an indication of the
serious and solemn character of the occasion, sexual intercourse being refrained from at such times (see e.g. Exod. 19:15).
Such will be the effect of the revelation of the Messiah as the
One whom the nation had pierced.

CHAPTER 20

Israel's Cleansing

The penitential sorrow when Israel sets eyes on the One Who was crucified on their behalf – wounded for their transgressions and bruised for their iniquities (Isa. 53:5) – with the sense of guilt entailed in their awakening, will naturally demand some means of cleansing from sin and defilement. This is the subject of the next section of the prophecy.

'In that day there shall be a fountain opened to the house of David and to the inhabitants of Jerusalem for sin and for uncleanness. And it shall come to pass in that day, says Jehovah of hosts, that I will cut off the names of the idols out of the land, and they shall no more be remembered. And also I will cause the prophets and the unclean spirit to pass out of the land' (13:1, 2).

The opening words of this sub-section at once indicate that the events described all fall within the period already referred to in the previous chapter, i.e. the day of Jehovah. The many references to that period portray it as one of clouds and thick darkness, when the indignation of Jehovah will result in the meting out of punishment upon a guilty world, and Israel will experience the unparalleled suffering and trial of the great tribulation (Joel 1:15; 2:1, 2; 3:16; Isa. 2:10–18; 34:1–8; Jer. 30:7, etc). That period will, of course conclude with the Second Advent of Christ. But if Israel is to enter into the blessings of His kingdom, her people will need cleansing to render them suitable to be subjects of it. So the prophet declared that a fountain for sin and uncleanness would be opened. The word 'fountain' is never used of a stagnant pool and it implies a spring of fresh water. It was to wash away the defilement of the people, as the red heifer was provided for their purification in an earlier day (Num. 19). That fountain could, of course, be nothing else than Calvary and the cleansing which became available through the blood out-poured then.

It was provided for the house of David and for the inhabitants of Jerusalem. The royal family were the shepherds or rulers of Israel and it was imperative that the defilement which hindered their communion with God should be removed, in order that they might be fit to shepherd His people. 'Sin and uncleanness' were terms used for idolatry (1 Kings 17:30; Ezek. 7:19, 20), but they doubtless covered the actual condition of the nation as well as the spiritual state.

The besetting sin of Israel in earlier days (but apparently not in the post-exilic period) was that of idolatry and for this they were Divinely chastised on a number of occasions. But now God declared that He would cut off the name of the idols and that they would be remembered no more. 'The name of the idol', says Barnes (op. cit., p. 96) 'represents the idol as a power which exercises influence over its worshippers and induces them to pay it reverence and ascribe supernatural works to it. To "cut off the names of the idols" is to take away all their authority and all men's acknowledgement of them. Men will cease to invoke them.' The idols would no more be remembered. In other words there was to be a complete extinction of idolatry. There are indications in the New Testament that idolatry will affect the nation again in a future day (Rev. 9:20; 13:4, 15). It is clear, therefore, that the pledge in Zech. 13:2 has not yet been implemented. Idolatry and false prophecy were obviously intended as typical of all forms of spiritual impurity or unfaithfulness: restoration to communion with God was patently dependent upon their extirpation. It has been maintained by some that the references to idolatry indicate that this part of the prophecy was uttered in pre-exilic days, because idolatry was not in evidence in the post-exilic period. But this ignores the Biblical practice of using the occurrences of the past as the basis of warnings for the future.

The prophets and the unclean spirit were also to be dismissed from the land. The association of the two indicates that the prophets in question were false ones. Chambers (op. cit., p. 100) argues that the spirit of uncleanness is 'not merely a pervading principle, but an active, conscious agency, standing in direct contrast with the Spirit of grace (12:10), which works in its human instruments and leads them to their lying utterances. The false prophet, as well as the true, were subject to an influence from without (cf. 1 Kings 22:21–23; Rev. 16:14; 2

Thess. 2:9; 10; 1 Tim. 4:2).' Both land and people were to be cleansed.

The subject of the false prophet was still pursued in the next few verses.

'And it shall come to pass, that when any shall yet prophesy, then his father and his mother who begot him shall say to him, You shall not live; for you speak lies in the name of Jehovah. And his father and his mother who begot him shall thrust him through when he prophesies. And it shall come to pass in that day, that the prophets shall be ashamed every one of his vision, when he prophesies: neither shall they wear a hairy mantle to deceive. But he shall say, I am no prophet, I am a husbandman; for a churl possessed me as a serf from my youth. And one shall say to him, What are these wounds between your hands? Then he shall answer, Those with which I was wounded in the house of my friends' (13:3-6).

Despite the banishment from the land of false prophecy and uncleanness, there will apparently be individuals who will still have the impudence to prophesy without a divine commission or authority. Centuries earlier, specific instructions had been given for such a case – 'the prophet, who shall presume to speak a word in my name, which I have not commanded him to speak, or that shall speak in the name of other gods, even that prophet shall die' (Deut. 18:20; 13:6). Accordingly, Jehovah required his parents to be responsible to inflict on him the pre-scribed penalty of death. Obedience to God took priority even over parental affection. Because their apostate son had told lies in the name of Jehovah, he was not to be allowed to live. His own parents were obliged to pronounce his sentence and to stab the renegade to death. The words are not irrelevant to the present day. Our Lord foretold that, prior to His second advent, false prophets would arise (Matt. 24:24). There can be no toleration of such. God's honour is at stake.

The jeopardy in which the false prophet stands and the con-viction of his own conscience will evidently cause him to disavow entirely all claims to the possession of the prophetic gift. Shame and fear will compel him to dissemble. He will discard the hairy mantle which he formerly wore and will deny all connection with the prophetic office. 'The hairy mantle worn by the proph-ets (2 Kings 1:8) was not a form of ascetic discipline, but a

symbol of the prophet's grief for the sins which he was com-
missioned to reprove. It was an acted parable of repentance.'
It originated with Elijah, but in time became the badge of the
prophet. Even in New Testament days, it was worn by John the
Baptist (Mk. 1:6). But, in the day of which Zechariah spoke,
it will be dangerous for a deceiver to wear the prophetic garb
without the authority to utter God's message to the people.

Such a man will furthermore vehemently disclaim even having
occupied the prophetic office, using the untrue argument that
he had been sold as a slave in his youth, whose time belonged
entirely to his master. He will declare that he had been only a
tiller of the ground and one who was obviously so tied to his
owner and his work that it would have been impossible for him
to engage in a ministry which would necessitate complete freedom to travel wherever he was directed by the Spirit of God.
There may also be a hint that, in such a lowly state of serfdom,
he was unlikely to acquire the knowledge or ability required
by a prophet.

His dissimulation will not deceive everyone, however. Working in the fields and stripped to the waist, he will be unable to
hide the scars on his breast, and those who are dissatisfied with
his explanations will demand to know the meaning of these
wounds. *Prima facie*, they seem the self-inflicted wounds of a
worshipper of the false gods, and caused by a sense of guilt and
the impression that the punishment of the body would propitiate
the gods (1 Kings 18:28). The injuries could not have been
caused by his owner: the scars borne by a slave would be in the
back and not in the front. What explanation can he give?
Kimchi writes, 'He shall say these wounds are not on account
of prophecy, but my friends wounded and chastised me because
I was abandoned, and was not industrious in cultivating the
land in my youth: and they beat me that I should cease from the
profligacy of young men, and should set to my work. And the
reason for the wounds being in the hands is that they used to
bind his hands and feet that he should not go out.' While this is
a possible interpretation of his words, it is more likely that he
alleges that the injuries were received in a drunken brawl in the
house of some of his dissolute friends. This would add emphasis
to his claim of unsuitability to be a prophet. Verse 6 is sometimes interpreted as applying to Messiah, but it is more logical

to regard it as part of the preceding sub-section and not of the following one. The question was clearly asked of the one who is the subject of the earlier verses and not of another to whom reference is not made until the following verse. For no obvious reason, except the committee's apparent preference and mistaken impression of relevance, the N.E.B. transposes these verses to follow Zech. 11:17..There seems no textual justification for this. In fact, as Cowles points out (*The Minor Prophets*, p. 367), 'The close analogy between the false prophet, whose hands had been gashed and pierced "in the house of his friends", and the Messiah, whose hands were pierced in a deathly crucifixion among those who ought to have been His friends' shows how appropriate the verses are to this particular chapter.

The last three verses of Zech. 13 are plainly concerned with the Messiah as the shepherd and the nation as His sheep.

'Awake, O sword, against my shepherd, and against the man that is my fellow, says Jehovah of hosts. Smite the shepherd, and the sheep shall be scattered: and I will turn my hand upon the little ones. And it shall come to pass that in all the land, says Jehovah, two parts therein shall be cut off and die; but the third shall be left therein. And I will bring the third part through the fire, and will refine them as silver is refined, and will try them as gold is tried. They shall call on my name, and I will answer them. I will say, He is my people: and he shall say, Jehovah is my God (13:7–9).

In Zech. 11 the foolish shepherd had been contrasted with the good shepherd. In the closing verses of Zech. 13 the true prophet is contrasted with the false prophet and the manner of his wounding with the self-inflicted scars of the latter. Once again too he is introduced in the character of the shepherd. The change of subject is not so abrupt and dramatic as, superficially, it might appear. Expositors have varied in their identification of this One, and it has been suggested that Judas Maccabeus, Pekah, Jehoiakim, and others were the one here represented. But there can be no dubiety on this matter, for our Lord quoted Zech. 13:7 just prior to His betrayal and applied the words to Himself and His disciples (Matt. 26:31; Mark 14:27). His quotation was from the Septuagint except that He used the future tense.

Jehovah Himself called upon the sword to awake as though the weapon was a living thing (cf. Jer. 47:6). The sword was the expressive symbol of judicial power. The highest order of governor in the Roman provinces was the one in whom the 'right of the sword', *jus gladii*, or the power of life and death was vested (Rom. 13:4). The One who apostrophized the sword was the One with the supreme authority, and He summoned the sword into activity. The implication, of course, was that death was about to be judicially inflicted (cf. Ps. 17:13). But the One who was to be executed was described as God's shepherd (John 10: 14) and 'the man that is my fellow'. Our Lord's citation of the verse leaves no room for doubt that the One thus described was Himself and that it was His death that was in view. That death was, in fact, essential if the fountain for sin and uncleanness, of which verse 1 spoke, was to be opened. Cleansing could only be effected because of the blood shed at Calvary. His death was a judicial one. He bore the penalty of the law. But His was a vicarious death, merited by the sheep and borne by the shepherd.

Not only was He God's shepherd, but His fellow. The N.E.B. renders this (quite unjustifiably) as 'him who works with me' and thereby, of course, eliminates the evidence of our Lord's equality with God. The word *anith* is used eleven times in the Book of Leviticus and its significance is the nearest kin. Hengstenberg renders the phrase 'A man, my nearest relation' and rationalistic De Wette as 'the man my equal'. One writer puts it succinctly when he says that the idea of the nearest one involves 'community of physical or spiritual descent, according to which he whom God calls His neighbour cannot be a mere man, but can only be one who participates in the Divine nature, or is essentially Divine. The Shepherd of Jehovah, whom the sword is to smite, is therefore, no other than the Messiah, who is also identified with Jehovah in Zech. 12:10; or the Good Shepherd, who says of Himself, "I and My Father are one" (John 10:30)'. The N.E.B. rendering could well be viewed in the light of Moore's comment (op. cit., p. 213) that the word *anith* is never used to indicate similarity of office, as Socinians assert on this passage, but always nearness of relation or kindred. Hence it here must refer to a human relation to Jehovah, which, of course, must be a divine nature. Hence we have here clearly

a twofold nature in the suffering Messiah, human and divine.'
It was this One who was to be smitten with the sword.

· The result of the smiting of the Shepherd was that the sheep
would be scattered, and the New Testament record shows how
literally and quickly the words were fulfilled in the case of our
Lord's disciples (Matt. 26:31, 56). The prophecy extended
beyond the immediate desertion of the disciples, however, and
patently predicted the worldwide dispersion of the Jewish race,
a flock without a shepherd. The past nineteen centuries of
Israel's *diaspora* have carried prophecy into history. Not only
would the sheep in general be scattered, but God would also
turn His 'hand upon the little ones'. The expression is consistently used in a punitive and uncomforting sense and does not,
as is suggested by some, imply mercy to the faithful ones. Indeed
our Lord plainly warned His disciples that persecution, suffering and death would be their portion (Matt. 24:9; John 15:20,
etc). A comparison with Zech. 11:7, 11 might have saved the
N.E.B. from the absurd translation of 'little ones' as 'shepherd
boys'.

Jehovah then declared that, in all the land, two-thirds would
be cut off and die, and one-third be left. Hengstenberg has an
interesting comment on this verse. He says, 'The whole of the
Jewish nation is introduced here as an inheritance left by the
Shepherd who has been put to death, which inheritance is
divided into three parts: death claiming the privilege of the
first-born, and so receiving two portions, and life one – a div-
ision similar to that which David made in the case of the Moabites (2 Sam. 8 :2).' Most commentators apply this verse to the
Jewish war of A.D. 67 – 70, when a million and a half Jews
perished by sword, famine and pestilence, and thousands were
sold as slaves. But as Perowne points out, those who survived
were not a refined and regenerated people, but unbelievers. It
seems more probable, therefore, that the prophecy looks on to the
sufferings of the great tribulation and to the preservation of a
faithful remnant in that day (Rev. 7:1–8; 14:1–5).

This is confirmed by the concluding verse of the chapter,
where it is stated that the third who remain will be brought into
the fire and refined as silver is refined and tried as gold is tried.
The intense heat of the furnace of the tribulation through which
the future saints pass will purge all the dross and remove all the

impurities and they will finally emerge freed from all that might hinder their suitability to enter into the millennial kingdom. In the midst of the fire, the suffering remnant will call on the name of Jehovah – a prayer born out of adversity but patently leading to repentance and regeneration, for He will not only hear but answer their cry. The reply from heaven regards the whole of the remnant as one person, 'He is my people,' and the people gladly respond, 'Jehovah is my God' (cf. Jer. 32:28; Ezek. 37:23). The centuries of suffering and the fires of tribulation past, they will be established in blessing in their own land under the beneficent rule of their Messiah.

CHAPTER 21

The Second Advent

Zech. 14 arises naturally out of the last three verses of the previous chapter and in some respects it may be regarded as an expansion and extension of the subject of those verses, 'attention being concentrated, however', as Perowne remarks (op. cit., p. 141), 'on the city rather than on the land (13:8), and on the final act rather than on the long previous process of purifying discipline'. The chapter is wholly prophetic and none of the events described therein has yet been fulfilled. It is interpreted by many works as a description of the current and future experience of the Church, but this interpretation is clearly inappropriate. The only satisfactory interpretation is that which regards the prophecy as literal. As Feinberg (*God Remembers*, pp. 248–249) says, if this passage 'is interpreted in the literal sense, it harmonizes with all that Zechariah has revealed thus far and with the prophecies concerning the consummation for Israel found throughout the Scripture.'

The chapter opens with a description of Jerusalem's suffering in the day of trouble looming ahead.

'Behold a day comes to Jehovah, when your spoil shall be divided in the midst of you. For I will gather all nations against Jerusalem to battle; and the city shall be taken, and the houses rifled and the women raped. And half of the city shall go forth into captivity, but the residue of people shall not be cut off from the city' (14:1, 2).

The period described is obviously the day of Jehovah, so frequently referred to in the Old Testament prophets, although the expression used in verse 1 is not the usual one in this connection. The phrase is literally, 'A day is coming – Jehovah's'. The events detailed in the chapter are those which are to occur during the period of judgement of the day of Jehovah and leave no doubt as to the significance of the phrase. The dire straits to which Jerusalem has been reduced are evident from the first verse. The city has been so completely subjugated by the armies which attacked her that the soldiers are able unhinderedly to apportion between themselves the booty they have taken as they have rampaged through the streets. Houses rifled and shops presumably looted, everything of value has been pillaged.

According to Zechariah, all nations will be gathered against Jerusalem (cf. Ezek. 38 and 39). From all directions, forces will pour into the land. Invaders from Egypt clashing with hordes from the north (Dan. 11:40), western armies intervening to implement their pledge of protection (Dan. 9:27), eastern multitudes pouring in from another direction (Rev. 16:12), all acting in pursuance of their own aims and objects, will be unaware that another hand controls their activities and directs their course that they might be prepared for their own destruction. But judgement is first to fall upon God's own people and the nations are employed as His instrument for the purpose.

The statement of Zech. 1 : 15 seems applicable in this instance also – the nations exceeded their commission and added to the sufferings of Israel. Following the investiture of the city, every house will apparently be invaded by the rude soldiery and all the horrors of war enacted in rape, cruelty and murder. Half of the population will be carried away captive, doubtless to fill the labour camps of the enemy or to satisfy the lust of the troops. Only a small number will be left in the city, a remnant who are not cut off. The sufferings and tribulations of the centuries will seem to have no end. Yet, at the moment of the people's greatest extremity, salvation comes.

'Then shall Jehovah go forth and fight against those nations as when He fought in the day of battle. And His feet shall stand in that day on the mount of Olives, which is before Jerusalem on the east, and the mount of Olives shall cleave in its middle toward the east and toward the west, and there shall be a very great valley. And half of the mountain shall recede toward the north, and half of it toward the south. And you shall flee by the valley of my mountains; for the valley of the mountains shall reach unto Azal: yes, you shall flee, like as you fled from before the earthquake in the days of Uzziah king of Judah: and Jehovah my God shall come and all the holy ones with you' (14:3–5).

The small remnant left in the city might well despair: despite all the promises of the past, their future could only be total extinction. It is at this point that Jehovah will suddenly intervene, breaking into man's world in all His power as a mighty warrior (Judg. 4:14; Ps. 108:11) and accompanied by all the 'holy ones', i.e. both the angels and the redeemed (Jude 14). In the past He has on more than one occasion fought for His people (e.g. Josh. 10:14) and now He will do so again. The tremendous forces of the nations will evidently smash the army of Israel and, in a virulent and venomous display of antisemitism, use the utmost brutality and sadism in their treatment of the chosen race, but God's purposes can never be thwarted and when He comes, it will be in incomparable might to crush and destroy His foes and to deliver His people.

Olivet, which saw the ascent of our Lord Jesus Christ, is to be the scene of His return (for Jehovah's revelation of Himself must surely be in the person of the Messiah). It was from this mountain that the shekinah glory departed prior to the Babylonian captivity (Ezek. 11:23) and it will be from this direction that it will reappear in a future day (Ezek. 43:2). 'The mount of Olives,' says Pusey, 'is the central eminence of a line of hills, of rather more than a mile in length, overhanging the city, from which it is separated only by the narrow bed of the valley of the brook of Kidron. It rises 187 ft above mount Zion, 295 ft above mount Moriah, 443 ft. above Gethsemane, and lies between the city and the wilderness toward the Dead Sea.' At its highest point, it is 2,680 ft above sea-level. When the Lord's feet stand on Olivet, the prophet predicted that the mountain will split apart, one part moving northward and the other part southward, so that a great valley will be formed. There was an earthquake on July 11th, 1927, which shook Palestine from the Sea of Galilee to the border of Egypt and, after the tremors, geologists discovered a fault in Olivet, running from east to west. Prof. Bailey Willis, of Stanford University, said that the land could expect to suffer from seismological disturbances and that the area around Jerusalem was a region of potential danger, a fault line, along which earth slippage might occur, passing directly under the Mount of Olives. It is evident, therefore, that what Zechariah described is precisely what geologists would expect to occur. The alteration in the physical contour of the country will leave Jerusalem standing on a mountain in the centre of a very large valley (cf. Ps. 48:1–3).

Mabie says, 'This earthquake will not only change the whole topography of Palestine, but it will cut in two the mountain backbone of that land, right through the Mount of Olives. By it at one stroke, east and west, the land will divide, and a great ship canal be formed from the Mediterranean Sea to the Jordan valley and the Dead Sea. The waters of the great sea, rushing down through that earthquake chasm, with a fall about eight times the height of Niagara – or an average of about 22 ft. to the mile – would fill the Jordan valley to the sea of Galilee and above. To the southward the waters would sweep down to the Gulf of Aqaba and the Red Sea. So, if the Jordan valley should remain at about its present level, it would form the bed of a great and deep inland sea, approaching to the very suburbs of Jerusalem. So the city of the great king would become the seaport of the world – the business emporium of the nations.' The commercial potentialities are patent.

The cataclysmic earthquake will provide the solution to the problem of the beleaguered remnant in Jerusalem. The newly-formed valley will extend from Azal (the location of which is uncertain) across the Kidron valley to the wall of the city, providing a way of escape from Jerusalem, which the refugees will gladly take. It is said that the people will flee as they fled from before the earthquake in the days of Uzziah. No details are given in the Biblical record of that earlier earthquake, but two centuries before Zechariah, Amos stated that he began to prophesy in the days of Uzziah, 'two years before the earthquake' (Amos 1:1). The earlier prophet also predicted that Jehovah would 'roar out of Zion and utter His voice from Jerusalem' (Amos 1:2). Subsequently (presumably after the earthquake had taken place), he declared that 'the lion has roared' and 'the Lord God has spoken' (Amos 3:8). His prophecy gave no indication of the date of the earthquake nor any further details concerning it (except possibly those in Amos 8:8; 9:5), although C. T. Francisco, in *Introducing the Old Testament,* argues that Amos 4:13 associates the earthquake with a total eclipse of the sun, which is known to have occurred during Uzziah's reign.

It is evident from the words of Amos that the earthquake was regarded as a Divine judgement and that it was apparently accompanied by thunder and lightning, the roll of thunder and the rumble of the trembling earth being identified with the roar of Jehovah and the sound of His voice. It is equally clear from Zechariah that this seismic disturbance was of such a character, either in its context or its effects, as to live permanently in the memory of the people, and to be a fitting comparison for the terrible upheaval and topographical changes occurring at the Second Advent. But when did it take place and what were the circumstances in which it happened?

The historical record discloses that when Uzziah 'was strong, his heart was lifted up to his destruction' and that he entered the temple to burn incense on the golden altar. The king resisted the priests who attempted to prevent his sacrilegious act, but God intervened and, as leprosy rose in Uzziah's forehead, the priests thrust him out of the temple (2 Chron. 26:16–21). Josephus states that, at the time of Uzziah's impious attempt, the earth quaked and the voice of God was heard (*Ant.* ix 10:4) and, according to tradition, the inhabitants of the city fled in terror from the place. If this is correct the earthquake, which caused such consternation at the time and which was still remembered so long afterwards, was due to the interposition of God, and marked His judgement of the guilty king. The fear caused by the enemy and by the earthquake and its serious effects in Zechariah's day will drive the inhabitants of Jerusalem once again to flee in terror and this time along the new valley.

Other phenomena of this period of judgement are described in the succeeding verses.

'And it shall come to pass in that day that there shall not be light, the bright ones shall be contracted: but it shall be an unique day, which is known to Jehovah, not day nor night: but it shall come to pass that, at evening time, there shall be light. And it shall come to pass in that day, that living waters shall go out from Jerusalem; half of them toward the eastern sea, and half of them toward the western sea; in summer and in winter shall it be. And Jehovah shall be king over all the earth; in that day Jehovah shall be one and his name one. All the land shall be transformed like the Arabah from Geba to Rimmon south of Jerusalem: and she shall be lifted up and shall dwell in her place, from Benjamin's gate to the place of the first gate, to the corner gate, and from the tower of Hananeel to the king's wine-presses. And men shall dwell in it, and there shall be no more curse; but Jerusalem shall dwell safely' (14:6–11).

Unger renders verse 6, 'And it shall be in that day that there shall not be the light of the luminaries but thick murkiness.' In

His Olivet discourse, our Lord predicted signs in the heavens at the time of the Second Advent (Matt. 24:29, 30). According to Zechariah, at the time of the Lord's return to earth, not only will there be seismological disturbances, but the heavenly bodies will fail to give their light, and the earth will be in a state of mingled light and darkness. Barnes (op. cit., p. 102) puts it aptly 'for a small space chaos is to return and light, the first-born of the cosmos will fail. Darkness, partial or complete, is sometimes the accompaniment of earthquakes.' It will be an unique day, known or understood only by Jehovah. It will be neither day nor night, but at evening time light will be restored.

The upheaval caused by the earthquake will leave Jerusalem as a kind of watershed and perennial streams will flow from the city to the east and to the west to irrigate the thirsty land which has needed water for all the centuries. Joel 3:18 foretells a similar transformation at the same time. Unger considers that the convulsion of the earth at the Lord's coming will open up vast subterranean springs and that the new rivers will flow to the Dead Sea on the one side and to the Mediterranean on the other. Most rivers and streams in Palestine today are seasonal and dry up in the summer. But these springs are to be permanent and they will flow in summer as well as in winter, bringing blessing to land and people. Water is one of the greatest needs of this region, and the provision of an abundant supply will be deemed a boon that must have originated in some supernatural action. It will, of course, be through the presence of Christ alone that this and every other blessing comes – in that day as in this.

In that day Jehovah is to be acknowledged as king by the whole earth. Naturally, His reign will not be restricted to earth for the whole of God's creation is going to be placed under the headship of Christ, and every being in the heights above or in the depths beneath will be compelled to acknowledge His sovereignty. Many of the heathen gods were worshipped under more than one name, their character being revealed by their names. In that day, however, Jehovah alone will be worshipped. He will be one and His name one. The full revelation of Himself is unambiguously made in that one name.

The whole land is to be transformed in topography and become like a plain, stretching from Geba to Rimmon, and Jerusalem alone will be left in a position of pre-eminence. According to the prophet, the plain is to be like Arabah. Chambers (op. cit., p. 111) says, 'The article is emphatic in "the plain", which in Hebrew always denotes the Arabah or Ghor, the largest and most celebrated of all the plains of Judea, the great valley extending from Lebanon to the farther side of the Dead Sea. Geba was on the northern frontier of Judah (cf. 2 Kings 23:8). Rimmon, distinguished from two other Rimmons on the north (Josh. 19: 13; Judg. 20:45), by the added clause, 'south of Jerusalem,' was a city on the border of Edom, given up by Judah to the Simeonites (Josh. 15:32; 19:7). In consequence of this depression of all the surrounding country, Jerusalem becomes high. The capital, seated on her hills, shines conspicuous as the only elevation in a very wide region.'

The exalted metropolis was to be peacefully inhabited, the occupied area being delineated as from Benjamin's gate (or the gate of Ephraim – 2 Kings 14:13) to the centre of the north wall, through which the road ran to Benjamin and Ephraim; it was to reach from there to the first gate to its east in the north-east corner of the city (possibly identical with the 'old gate'); from thence it extended to the corner gate in the north-western extremity of the city (2 Kings 14:13; Jer. 31:38); then from the tower of Hananeel in the north-west corner of the temple area, it stretched southwards to the king's winepresses near the valley of Hinnom. It was to be fully populated and people would live there in security and no more danger would threaten.

Verses 12 to 15 really supplement verses 1 to 3 and disclose how the foes of the Jerusalem remnant are destroyed.

'And this shall be the plague with which Jehovah will smite all the peoples who have fought against Jerusalem. Their flesh shall consume away while they stand on their feet, and their eyes shall consume away in their sockets, and their tongue shall consume away in their mouth. And it shall come to pass in that day that a great tumult from Jehovah shall be among them, and they shall lay hold every one on the hand of his neighbour, and his hand shall rise up against the hand of his neighbour. And Judah also shall fight at Jerusalem: and the wealth of all the nations round about shall be gathered together, gold and silver and apparel in great abundance. And so shall be the plague of the horse, of the mule, of the camel, and of the ass, and of all the beasts that shall be in these camps, as this plague' (14:12–15).

The three means by which comes destruction of the enemies of God's people are stated in these verses to be a terrible plague which Jehovah inflicts upon them, a panic with which He confuses them, and the intrepid valour of the people of Judah. Behind all three media is clearly the person of Jehovah Himself, and the victory belongs not to man but to Him.

An unparalleled plague was to smite the great armies which were arrayed against Jerusalem and which so brutally and ruthlessly maltreated its inhabitants. They had engaged in military combat, not against Judah but, by implication, against God, and their flesh would inexplicably fester where they stood. They had looked covetously on Jerusalem's possessions, and their eyes would rot away in their sockets. They had impudently spoken against God and His people, and their tongues would become putrid in their mouths. The imagery is appalling: these wretches are doomed to a living death. The plague will come upon them in the moment of their victory. In his book, *In the Days to Come*, W. A. Peterson writes, 'In Hiroshima on August 6th 1945, 60,000 people were killed and 100,000 wounded by one atomic bomb. The flesh literally roasted and fell off the bones of the people who were walking in the streets. In every case the eyes just disappeared, dissolving out on to the cheeks. Apparently the eyes are very sensitive to radiation, and in many cases the tongue as well was loosened and affected.' What manmade weapons are capable of doing is not comparable with what may result from the hand of God, and it is unwise to regard the language used as anything but literal. Verse 15 indicates that the plague will not be confined to human beings but, as would be expected, will affect every beast in the camps of the nations who have gathered against Jerusalem. This is in full accord with Scriptural precedent and the Divine methods.(Josh. 6:21).

In addition, a great tumult or consternation, inspired by God, will cause a frightening confusion among the mighty forces. Its nature is not stated, but its result will be a panic-stricken commotion, which causes every man to attack his neighbour and effect a complete mutual annihilation. If the terrifying plague is caused by the emission of rays resulting from some form of thermonuclear explosion, the latter would presumably be accompanied by a tremendous noise which would itself have disastrous effects. Uncontrolled noise can cause emotional instability, disorganized behaviour and violence, and it is not inconceivable that this may be the cause of the mutual antagonism and destruction.

Thirdly it is stated that Judah will fight at Jerusalem. The old rivalry between Judah and Jerusalem now banished, the people's only desire will be to deliver the city. Amid the disarray and confusion resulting from the miraculous interposition of Jehovah, Judah will gallantly rally to the attack. The immense booty captured from the invaders will fall to Judah. Gold, silver, garments, evidently in tremendous quantities, will be taken from the defeated armies, together presumably with all of which they had robbed the population of Jerusalem. The defeat will be conclusive.

CHAPTER 22

Worship and Holiness

Every foe defeated, the Messiah will be supreme and His long-promised reign will ensue. In the Annunciation, Gabriel declared that Mary's Babe would receive 'the throne of his father David' and would 'reign over the house of Jacob for ever' (Luke 1:32, 33). The pledge of the centuries will now be redeemed and our Lord Jesus Christ will reign over the earth. His rule, beneficent although it will be, is to be with a rod of iron, and the nations will be compelled to render obedience to him. Annually they will pay their worship to Him at Jerusalem.

'And it shall come to pass that every one that is left of all the nations which came against Jerusalem shall go up from year to year to worship the King, Jehovah of hosts, and to keep the feast of tabernacles. And it shall be that whoso of all the families of the earth will not come up to Jerusalem to worship the King, Jehovah of hosts, upon them there shall be no rain. And if the family of Egypt go not up and come not, neither shall it be upon them. There shall be the plague, wherewith Jehovah will smite the nations that come not up to keep the feast of tabernacles. This shall be the sin of Egypt and the sin of all the nations that come not up to keep the feast of tabernacles' (14:16–19).

The survivors from the nations who attacked Jerusalem, in many cases, will apparently have turned in repentance to God to learn His righteousness and ways (Isa. 26:9), but all the nations will be required annually to go up to Jerusalem to worship Jehovah the King. Presumably this will be by delegates or representatives, since it is impossible to imagine millions of people making their way to the holy City simultaneously. The occasion of the gathering is the feast of tabernacles. This was held in the seventh month and the rainy season commenced soon afterwards. Perowne suggests that there are three reasons for the choice of this particular festival from the Jewish calendar, viz., (1) the feast of tabernacles was held in the autumn, when travelling would be most convenient and possibly least arduous; (2) it was a festival of thanksgiving for the fruits of the earth, in

which all could readily take part; (3) it was the last and greatest festival of the Jewish year, gathering up in itself the year's
worship and, at the same time, typifying the ingathering of the
nation.

Tabernacles was a seven-day feast of joy and gladness. The
people lived for that week in rudely constructed booths, made
of tree branches. Unger (op. cit., pp. 265–6) suggests that the
reason for the continued observance of this feast during the
millennium is that 'it is the only one of the seven feasts of the
Lord which at that time will be unfulfilled typically and the
only one which will be in process of fulfilment by the kingdom
itself. The passover (Lev. 23:4, 5) was fulfilled in the death of
Christ the Redeemer (1 Cor. 5:7; 1 Pet. 1:19). The feast of
unleavened bread (Lev. 23:6–8) is being fulfilled in the holy,
separate walk of the believer in fellowship with his Saviour (1
Cor. 5:6–8; 2 Cor. 7:1; Gal. 5:7–9). The feast of first-fruits
(Lev. 23:9–14) was fulfilled in the resurrection of Christ (1 Cor.
15:23. The feast of Pentecost (Lev. 23:15–22) was fulfilled in
the formation of the Church at Pentecost fifty days subsequent
to the resurrection of Christ (1 Cor. 10:16; 12:12, 13). The
feast of trumpets (Lev. 23:23–25) will be fulfilled in the future
regathering of Israel at the beginning of the kingdom (Isa. 18:
3, 7; 27:12, 13; Ezek. 37:1–14). The day of atonement (Lev.
23:26–32) in its prophetic feature will be fulfilled in the conversion of Israel at the second advent (Zech. 12:10–13; 13:1)
and preparatory to the millennium. Only the feast of tabernacles
at that time will be unfulfilled in its prophetic aspect as typical
of the kingdom rest of Israel after her regathering, and the blessedness typified by that festival will be in process of fulfilment
throughout the kingdom age.'

Those who fail to fulfil their obligation of visiting Jerusalem
for this feast are to suffer the penalty for their failure – there
will be no rainfall in their area. Rain is essential for the land
and for the well-being of man. Without it, particularly in hot
countries, there would be no harvest, and famine would ensue.
It is the sign of God's blessing, and its lack is a serious one. With
the Son of God upon the throne of the universe, there can, of
course, be no difficulty about the deprivation of one country
and the blessing of an adjoining country in this respect.

Egypt, the ancient foe of Israel, is singled out for special mention. Egypt enjoys no rainfall, except in negligible quantities at the coast, and it might be argued that such a penalty would be irrelevant to her. But the ultimate penalty was not merely the withholding of rain, but the famines which inevitably resulted from drought. The fertility of Egypt depends on the annual inundation of the Nile and this is caused by the torrential rains in the region of the Upper Nile. If the rain is withheld in the upper regions of the river, the delta and the river area of Egypt must inevitably suffer. The punishment is, therefore, equally pertinent to Egypt.

The One who sits on the throne will exercise an iron rule. His administration will be just and equitable, but wrongdoing will be punished immediately. His holiness is to characterize not only His actions in general, but even the city of the great King.

'In that day, shall there be on the bells of the horses "Holy to Jehovah", and the pots in Jehovah's house shall be like the bowls before the altar. Yes, every pot in Jerusalem and in Judah shall be holy to Jehovah of hosts; and all who sacrifice shall come and take of them and boil in them. And in that day there shall be no more a Canaanite in the house of Jehovah of hosts' (14:20, 12).

The character of the great Ruler will be reflected in everything about Him. The unclean is to be banished! sin is to be crushed and the evildoer removed. The whole land is to be sanctified to God, but the city of Jerusalem is to be demonstrably set apart to Him. Even the most ordinary things of everyday life are to be holy. On the mitre of Israel's high priest was a golden plate bearing the words, 'Holy to Jehovah'. Even the bells of the horses in that future day will bear the same inscription.

The very domestic utensils in the home are to be sanctified: everything is to be holy to God. The cauldrons used in the temple to boil the flesh of the sacrificial victims before it was eaten were now to become as holy as the sacred bowls in which the blood of the sacrifice was caught to be sprinkled upon the corners of the altar. Where the Messiah ruled, everything became sacred.

There is a practical import for the believer still. The one who belongs to Christ is set apart to Him and that sanctification or separation applies to his whole being and to every sphere of life. The Christian cannot speak of his time, his possessions, his abilities, his wealth. All he has is sanctified to his Lord.

The concluding statement of the book is in harmony with the preceding verses. In a holy city and a holy temple, there is no place for the unholy, and the prophecy declared that in that day, there shall be no Canaanite in the temple. The gross immorality of the Canaanites and the degrading and licentious character of their religion are fairly clearly indicated in the Old Testament record. It was because of their degeneracy, and the danger of Israel's corruption through contact with them, that they were to be extirpated when the land of Canaan was conquered. The term Canaanite was proverbial for a morally unclean person. It also became a metaphor for the trafficker (Hos. 11:7, where 'merchant' should read 'Canaan'). It seems incredible that one of such a character should be found in the temple, but now they were to be permanently excluded. Let the Christian also jealously guard his life that no unclean or undesirable thought or action may find a place in it.

So the prophecy concludes with the glorious picture of millennial bliss and holiness. Zechariah does not see beyond the age to come and no glimpse was given to him of the eternal state. Nevertheless, he confirms the statements and predictions of the earlier prophets that an age is to come when evil shall be under rigid restraint and God shall reign supreme in His creation.

1982-83 TITLES

0203	Dolman, Dirk H.	The Tabernacle	19.75
0603	Lang, John M.	Studies in the Book of Judges	17.75
0701	Cox, S. & Fuller, T.	The Book of Ruth	14.75
0902	Deane, W. J. & Kirk, T.	Studies in the First Book of Samuel	19.00
1301	Kirk, T. & Rawlinson, G.	Studies in the Books of Kings	20.75
2102	Wardlaw, Ralph	Exposition of Ecclesiastes	16.25
4603	Jones, John Daniel	Exposition of First Corinthians 13	9.50
4902	Pattison, R. & Moule, H.	Exposition of Ephesians: Lessons in Grace and Godliness	14.75
5104	Daille, Jean	Exposition of Colossians	24.95
5803	Edwards, Thomas C.	The Epistle to the Hebrews	13.00
5903	Stier, Rudolf E.	Commentary on the Epistle of James	10.25
6202	Morgan, J. & Cox, S.	The Epistles of John	22.95
7000	Tatford, Frederick Albert	The Minor Prophets(3 vol.)	44.95
7107	Cox, S. & Drysdale, A. H.	The Epistle to Philemon	9.25
8403	Jones, John Daniel	The Apostles of Christ	10.00
8404	Krummacher, Frederick W.	David, King of Israel	20.50
8405	MacDuff, John Ross	Elijah, the Prophet of Fire	13.75
8406	MacDuff, John Ross	The Footsteps of St. Peter	24.25
8801	Lidgett, John Scott	The Biblical Doctrine of the Atonement	19.50
8802	Laidlaw, John	The Biblical Doctrine of Man	14.00
9513	Innes, A. T. & Powell, F. J.	The Trial of Christ	10.75
9514	Gloag, P. J. & Delitzsch, F.	The Messiahship of Christ	23.50
9515	Blaikie, W. G. & Law, R.	The Inner Life of Christ	17.25
9806	Ironside, H. A. & Ottman, F.	Studies in Biblical Eschatology	16.00

TITLES CURRENTLY AVAILABLE

0101	Delitzsch, Franz	A New Commentary on Genesis (2 vol.)	30.50
0102	Blaikie, W. G.	Heroes of Israel	19.50
0103	Bush, George	Genesis (2 vol.)	29.95
0201	Murphy, James G.	Commentary on the Book of Exodus	12.75
0202	Bush, George	Exodus	22.50
0301	Kellogg, Samuel H.	The Book of Leviticus	21.00
0302	Bush, George	Leviticus	10.50
0401	Bush, George	Numbers	17.75
0501	Cumming, John	The Book of Deuteronomy	16.00
0602	Bush, George	Joshua & Judges (2 vol. in 1)	17.95
1101	Farrar, F. W.	The First Book of Kings	19.00
1201	Farrar, F. W.	The Second Book of Kings	19.00
1701	Raleigh, Alexander	The Book of Esther	9.75
1802	Green, William H.	The Argument of the Book of Job Unfolded	13.50
1901	Dickson, David	A Commentary on the Psalms (2 vol.)	32.50
1902	MacLaren, Alexander	The Psalms (3 vol.)	45.00
2001	Wardlaw, Ralph	Book of Proverbs (3 vol.)	45.00
2101	MacDonald, James M.	The Book of Ecclesiastes	15.50
2201	Durham, James	An Exposition on the Song of Solomon	17.25
2301	Kelly, William	An Exposition of the Book of Isaiah	15.25
2302	Alexander, Joseph	Isaiah (2 vol.)	29.95
2401	Orelli, Hans C. von	The Prophecies of Jeremiah	15.25
2601	Fairbairn, Patrick	An Exposition of Ezekiel	18.50
2701	Pusey, Edward B.	Daniel the Prophet	19.50
2702	Tatford, Frederick Albert	Daniel and His Prophecy	9.25
3001	Cripps, Richard S.	A Commentary on the Book of Amos	13.50
3201	Burn, Samuel C.	The Prophet Jonah	11.25
3801	Wright, Charles H. H.	Zechariah and His Prophecies	24.95
4001	Morison, James	The Gospel According to Matthew	24.95
4101	Alexander, Joseph	Commentary on the Gospel of Mark	16.75

TITLES CURRENTLY AVAILABLE

4102	Morison, James	The Gospel According to Mark	21.00
4201	Kelly, William	The Gospel of Luke	18.50
4301	Brown, John	The Intercessory Prayer of Our Lord Jesus Christ	11.50
4302	Hengstenberg, E. W.	Commentary on the Gospel of John (2 vol.)	34.95
4401	Alexander, Joseph	Commentary on the Acts of the Apostles (2 vol. in 1)	27.50
4402	Gloag, Paton J.	A Critical and Exegetical Commentary on Acts (2 vol.)	29.95
4403	Stier, Rudolf E.	Words of the Apostles	18.75
4501	Shedd, W. G. T.	Critical and Doctrinal Commentary on Romans	17.00
4502	Moule, H. C. G.	The Epistle to the Romans	16.25
4601	Brown, John	The Resurrection of Life	15.50
4602	Edwards, Thomas C.	A Commentary on the First Epistle to the Corinthians	18.00
4801	Ramsay, William	Historical Commentary on the Epistle to the Galatians	17.75
4802	Brown, John	An Exposition of the Epistle of Paul to the Galatians	16.00
5001	Johnstone, Robert	Lectures on the Book of Philippians	18.25
5102	Westcott, F. B.	The Epistle to the Colossians	7.50
5103	Eadie, John	Colossians	10.50
5401	Liddon, H. P.	The First Epistle to Timothy	6.00
5601	Taylor, Thomas	An Exposition of Titus	20.75
5801	Delitzsch, Franz	Commentary on the Epistle to the Hebrews (2 vol.)	31.50
5802	Bruce, A. B.	The Epistle to the Hebrews	17.25
5901	Johnstone, Robert	Lectures on the Epistle of James	16.50
5902	Mayor, Joseph B.	The Epistle of St. James	20.25
6201	Lias, John J.	The First Epistle of John	15.75
6601	Trench, Richard C.	Commentary on the Epistles to the Seven Churches	8.50
7001	Orelli, Hans C. von	The Twelve Minor Prophets	15.50
7002	Alford, Dean Henry	The Book of Genesis and Part of the Book of Exodus	12.50
7003	Marbury, Edward	Obadiah and Habakkuk	23.95
7004	Adeney, Walter	The Books of Ezra and Nehemiah	13.00
7101	Mayor, Joseph B.	The Epistle of St. Jude and The Second Epistle of Peter	16.50
7102	Lillie, John	Lectures on the First and Second Epistles of Peter	19.75
7103	Hort, F. J. A. & Hort, A. F.	Expository and Exegetical Studies	29.50
7104	Milligan, George	St. Paul's Epistles to the Thessalonians	12.00
7105	Stanley, Arthur P.	Epistles of Paul to the Corinthians	20.95
7106	Moule, H. C. G.	Colossian and Philemon Studies	12.00
7107	Fairbairn, Patrick	The Pastoral Epistles	17.25
8001	Fairweather, William	Background of the Gospels	17.00
8002	Fairweather, William	Background of the Epistles	16.50
8003	Zahn, Theodor	Introduction to the New Testament (3 vol.)	48.00
8004	Bernard, Thomas	The Progress of Doctrine in the New Testament	9.00
8401	Blaikie, William G.	David, King of Israel	17.50
8402	Farrar, F. W.	The Life and Work of St. Paul (2 vol.)	43.95
8601	Shedd, W. G. T.	Dogmatic Theology (4 vol.)	52.50
8602	Shedd, W. G. T.	Theological Essays (2 vol. in 1)	26.00
8603	McIntosh, Hugh	Is Christ Infallible and the Bible True?	27.00
8701	Shedd, W. G. T.	History of Christian Doctrine (2 vol.)	31.50
8703	Kurtz, John Henry	Sacrificial Worship of the Old Testament	16.50
8901	Fawcett, John	Christ Precious to those that Believe	10.00
9401	Neal, Daniel	History of the Puritans (3 vol.)	54.95
9402	Warns, Johannes	Baptism	13.25
9501	Schilder, Klass	The Trilogy (3 vol.)	48.00
9502	Liddon, H. P. & Orr, J.	The Birth of Christ	15.25
9503	Bruce, A. B.	The Parables of Christ	15.50
9504	Bruce, A. B.	The Miracles of Christ	20.00
9505	Milligan, William	The Ascension of Christ	15.00
9506	Moule, H. C. & Orr, J.	The Resurrection of Christ	20.00
9507	Denney, James	The Death of Christ	12.50
9508	Farrar, F. W.	The Life of Christ	24.95
9509	Dalman, Gustaf H.	The Words of Christ	13.50
9510	Andrews, S. & Gifford, E. H.	Man and the Incarnation & The Incarnation (2 vol. in 1)	15.00
9511	Baron, David	Types, Psalms and Prophecies	14.00
9512	Stier, Rudolf E.	Words of the Risen Christ	8.25
9801	Liddon, H. P.	The Divinity of Our Lord	20.50
9802	Pink, Arthur W.	The Antichrist	12.00
9803	Shedd, W. G. T.	The Doctrine of Endless Punishment	8.25
9804	Andrews, S. J.	Christianity and Anti-Christianity in Their Final Conflict	15.00
9805	Gilpin, Richard	Biblical Demonology: A Treatise on Satan's Temptations	20.00